...usin.
It's great to
know you!
Keep up your
brave approach.
Your friend,
Jan

Songs of Petroleum

The autobiography of Jan Lundberg

Independent oil industry analyst and eco-activist

Culture Change Press

Songs of Petroleum / Jan C. Lundberg

Published by Culture Change Press
www.CultureChange.org
P.O. Box 4347, Arcata, California 95518 USA

ISBN (ten digit) 0-615-34373-2
ISBN (thirteen digit) 978-0-615-34373-0

1. Oil 2. Elder abuse 3. Medical fraud 4. Activism
2. Environment 5. Autobiography 6. Music I Title

Printed in the United States of America in March 2011

Jan Lundberg

I dedicate this book and all my work and songs to my daughters, the memory of my parents, and our Earth.

Contents

From Youthful Rebellion to a Conceptual Contribution

The U.S. Energy Awakening

Family of Organic Sailors

Song: Peace Now, my reaction to 9-11

Dan Lundberg — in a devoted, rebellious son's perspective

Mesa Vernell Dobson Lundberg, farm girl making it in Los Angeles

The Dan Lundberg Show, Channel 13

Hollywood activists

Jimmy Fields, child-prodigy pianist

Sail off to circumnavigate the world

Memorable co-workers and strange characters at Lundberg Survey

A making of enemies

From Whiskey-A-Go-Go to the mansion to the skateboard commute to Pacific Palisades

Lundberg Survey at its height

Leaving the Fold

My Career Change

The personal life is affected too

Discovering what kind of environmentalist I was

Single dad

Soaking up breakthroughs and creating my own world

Preface

We activists are incorrigible optimists. We sometimes feel like giving up, but we're rejuvenated by a new crisis. Just when I thought I might hang up my activist boots after 22 years, in a not so hopeful mood for Earth's biosphere, the catastrophe in the Gulf of Mexico at BP's Macondo oil well hit. I wasn't surprised at this inevitable "accident," although the negligence, secrecy and corruption proved shocking. But as the unchecked disaster went on for months, I was appalled at the absence of a meaningful response by those calling themselves leaders.

The corporate news media and U.S. politicians were even weaker than one would have predicted, given the extreme circumstances of the toxic gusher. Underneath their mild outrage it became clear they were whitewashing, especially considering the full story that was kept from the public through suppressed coverage and restricted access that served BP. But it was the absence of an ecological and ethical response to the catastrophic emergency by anyone visible that motivated me to start something that honest people could get behind.

Why should I have to? Well, the major environmental groups' reaction to the gusher was a let down. Of course these groups called for the oil clean-up and better federal regulation, but their prime message was to call for a cleaner energy future. The problem was that this approach omitted any push for immediate curtailment of petroleum use by the consumer. This is the same dangerous omission they make regarding fossil fuels — and that governments make — for the climate crisis and for the intensifying effects of peak oil (petrocollapse).

So I began blogging about targeted curtailment of oil use for the sake of the ailing Gulf of Mexico and the greater global ecosystem. The idea needed much more attention, so I wrote and circulated a Resolution for local governments to adopt the concept. This was the basis of a new coalition that a few activists and I formed: World Oil Reduction for the Gulf (worldoilreduction.org). The simple idea was to cut oil consumption at the local level to compensate for BP's pollution spewed into the Gulf. Grassroots bottom-up organizing for immediate curtailment of petroleum use at the local level was key. Unfortunately, the whole disaster mostly disappeared from the news a few weeks after the well was capped — even though the disaster will take years to "go away" both ecologically and economically. What typically happens when a crisis grabs attention, people must resume as soon as possible their normal daily concerns, coping with the usual bombardment of infotainment, Madison Avenue ads, terror alerts, etc.

The World Oil Reduction for the Gulf group deactivated soon after our campaign took shape, just as we started to attract interest. Our lost chance brought us to weighing, as optimistic activists do, the good effort with the iffy results. Maybe greater awareness would sprout from seeds we planted. We did not want to face that the public was still not ready to deal directly with the clearly worsening environmental crisis. Nor were people willing to question our petroleum-addicted, self-destructive economic system and the cultural values feeding the system. Ample oil supply remains one of the highest priorities of modern living, as short-term considerations trump wise, long-term planning.

In the same fashion, the Fukushima nuclear disaster appeared to me at first, through the horror and sorrow, as a rallying point that seemed obvious as a "final straw" for public outrage to deal with perhaps the worst form of assault on Mother Nature. But as we go to press, I'm dismayed to admit that momentum seems to be surprisingly slow. We shall just have to see, and go on to implement our hopes to the extent we can. I don't foresee how I can retire from activism when nukes are very much on the loose, while the corporate state seems determined to enable yet more Chernobyl-scale "mishaps."

We desperately must see a positive tipping point and achieve a critical mass of awareness. As the generation on the spot, we have very little time left to save the Earth as we know it. We of the environmentally aware population don't have much to show for ourselves after over four decades up against the blatant environmental and human-rights assault of Big Oil. As consumers we have barely started to act upon our own complicity. Oil addiction has only gotten worse, as have a number of ecological issues. Will we only take definitive action after another spectacular disaster, or after two more, or how many? Will the political distraction of climate-change denialism cheat us out of proactively transitioning to a sustainable society? When, oh when, can there be consensus that we can indeed care for humanity *and* nature?

The massive Santa Barbara oil spill happened in 1969, outraging and alarming millions of people because of ruined beaches. Fred Hartley, the president of Union Oil Company that was responsible for the spill, immediately telephoned my father Dan Lundberg in Greece. My family had sailed there from Los Angeles and we were living a beautiful life. Now it was "Dan! What do I do?" I don't recall the public relations and civics advice given that day, maybe because my father was so proud of being asked to help. He had been missing the U.S. oil industry scene into which he had successfully ascended. Hartley evidently didn't heed my father's advice, for my father wouldn't have recommended saying "I'm amazed at the publicity over the loss of a few birds." — Hartley's heartless, widely quoted gaff. It was no wonder that in the spring following the oil spill, Earth Day was born nationwide.

Though I followed in my father's footsteps, I was not called by BP's Tony Hayward to help with his Macondo-blowout PR. I have a different relationship with Big Oil than my father had (and that I once had). For I joined the environmentalist camp after 14 years' serving Big Oil.

This book recounts my personal odyssey through my seafaring youth and two opposing, high-profile careers. I traded in the first career for a real life, and an unexpected result was that I proceeded to get a far more complete grasp of the oil industry and society's relationship to oil.

Before my life-change, my life was already interesting. I had become a father, lived among other cultures, met famous people, run a widely respected family business, and had adventures at sea. It turned out to be a relatively sheltered life for my first three and a half decades. But I was dissatisfied. At that time I couldn't articulate how, nearly as well as I can now.

When I started learning about the oil industry from an insider position at age 19, I had just walked away from eco-activism at the University of California. My family was indeed unusual, and I had strong loyalty to it. One of our accomplishments was in having generated oil industry-derived income for the privilege of enjoying unique educational experiences around the world. As I later proceeded to put years of zeal into a family business that prided itself in understanding and upholding the oil industry, I found myself *en route* to joining the ruling class (or its higher managerial echelon). From the start I made the family business career part of my design to become capable of helping the world in a radical way. But after years of seeing my hopes and dreams fade, I found I had to settle for an interesting job, a business education and appreciating the fruits and comforts of money and connections.

Despite the interesting experience of being in tight with the corporate world and its handmaiden, i.e., government (that I came to service with contracts), I knew I was missing out on a life of real adventure. I was giving national media interviews, traveling to make speeches, and enjoying company perks, but my heart wasn't really in it. So after 14 years I jumped out of the inside track of "success" over to the unknown. I had to get back on a path of truth and liberation for me and for Mother Earth, whom I would now serve without turning back.

Taking the path I took meant bumping into the absurdities and disasters unfolding right in front of our collective societal nose. Being a naturally positive and curious guy, I found even the insight on the bad aspects rather edifying. But I was just starting to pay a personal price for my lessons — at the hands of corporate power, due to my family's involvement with oil money. Nevertheless, to echo folk music legend Pete Seeger, at least I didn't let them change me.

I would rather not have my sad family saga and all-too-interesting story to tell. Most people have some unpleasant, painful memories they would like to forget. But my experience is of a different order: high stakes were risked on both sides of the conflict, and there were costs in terms of people's freedom, health, security and lives. This aspect of my story is in this book, but more proudly is my work for our biosphere. This role, especially in concert with remarkable new friends and wonderful colleagues, has to be more meaningful than a mere career.

My career-odyssey and personal story may be of interest to those trying to both live a low-impact lifestyle and anticipate a post-petrocollapse future. The attempt is relatively easy compared to our ultimate task: recreating a culture for a population finding itself on the other side of an historic, watershed event known as peak oil, at a time of dire climate change. Although the challenge is daunting to "live the future now," as I advocate, there are immediate benefits to taking action for culture change.

My interest in deep cultural change for the sake of human and ecological survival developed out of extensive travels, an oil-related career, and hair-raising events during my later "eco-warrior" phase. I feel that my story and my findings make for a rewarding struggle that's still going on. Aside from my unique family's reputation, secrets and shame, for years I had to deal with the label of being "radical" or "ahead of my time." Somehow this whole process has meant I've turned out to be, surprisingly for me, a traditionalist. I show in this book how it all came about — an unusual but simple odyssey. Although I infuse some of my findings from my work, this book is not a polemic or an energy-industry analysis. *Songs of Petroleum* is how this Depaver, writer, activist, family man and musician, emerged.

Jan Lundberg
Portland, Oregon
Santa Barbara, California
Culture Change
Sail Transport Network
March 2011

Introduction to my life adventure

When I was a teenager and young man, I wanted to change the world. Somewhere along the way, four decades later, the question became: can we *save* the world?

At age 17 I became committed to social change. It was no surprise to me or to my family, considering our unusual lives and independent thinking. When I was 13 we had literally sailed away from our hip and affluent life in Hollywood, California. We ended up in the Mediterranean where I came to love my life, after I got over missing my friends and privileged life in southern California.

But the rumblings of cultural upheaval and consciousness-expansion from the West Coast increasingly affected us over in the Med, as did the world's outrage against the Vietnam War. It wasn't long before I felt pulled back to a home that was changing fast during my 4 ½-year absence.

Within months of this teenager's embracing the peace movement and rejecting capitalism in principle, I naturally thought I had the answers to warmongering, exploitation, racism, oppression and more. I didn't have much idea how complex the world was, nor how distorted was my concept of history. But I was ready to align myself with avant-garde leaders and to learn all I could by involvement, especially once I got back to the States.

I'm not sure what I accomplished in my youthful activism, other than having stood up to be counted at rallies, protests, meetings, and engaging in one-on-one consciousness raising (usually arguments). I was in awe of accomplished activists and their knowledge of the issues, and I hoped to do my part and have an exciting time at it. Few of the non-activists I encountered seriously opposed me or my stands (that I wore on my sleeve), but I did run into my share of "America — Love It or Leave It" supporters of the Vietnam War. In the mind of much of the older generation, if you were a male with long hair you were a threat to society — not so much with drugs that you were assumed to be on, but with your ideas and sexuality. And we young men for peace were often called cowards in need of discipline.

Upon reaching adulthood and feeling sure that revolutionary

change was needed and was hopefully on the way, I could not seem to ascend to much sacrifice or daring, despite my yearnings and beliefs. I'm glad that I eventually found meaningful opportunities many years later, but I regret that I was needed at all as an activist in a world "burning in its greed" (from The Moody Blues' song *Balance*, 1970).

In 1970 I found myself reluctantly back in smoggy Hollywood with my family, recently arrived from southern Europe where we had lived since 1966. I had finally decided I wanted to stay in Europe and the Middle East where I intended to "complete" my education. But I'm still not sure if I was pulled back to my hometown of L.A. for the counterculture or because I had to follow my family back across the Atlantic at age 17.

The late Sixties were for me an exhilarating time, not just because I was young. Even though I wasn't quite old enough to participate fully at first, being born a bit late (1952), I did witness and embrace my generation's radical ideas. I loved the art, the music, growing my hair long, the literature, demonstrations, the idea of expanding my consciousness, supporting sexual liberation, and stopping the war. My family was already environmentalist from way back, although my parents identified with middle-class comfort. They stood out as nature lovers, for their day, but weren't the biggest of big risk takers. I set out to take things to the next level.

But I should have seen it coming: by 1972 I was recruited into my preordained career at the family oil-statistics business, Lundberg Survey. It took me many years there to be able to say with certainty that I did the right thing "paying my dues" as an activist waiting in the wings. It turned out I was on a long break from what I really cared about. Being a young executive wasn't my preferred thing to do with my precious youth. I had to wait to content myself by being able to someday say "I could have spent my time in a worse way." At Lundberg Survey I did gather a few high-level skills and I learned about a key aspect of modern society: energy.

Meanwhile my lifestyle was easy, moneyed, and I felt special — to the point of being invincible for the rest of my life. My parents had made sure I knew the finery of European culture as well as the benefits of spending one's way to achieving the California Dream — a slightly hipper version of the American Dream. I did drift over to getting caught up in the Yuppie lifestyle, working hard enough at an important company to think the world owed me a Mercedes. I had a Diesel Mercedes for a while as my company car, and one of my main preoccupations was feeling the pecking order on the streets and freeways of L.A.

Yet I was always strongly inclined to oppose injustice and the rape of nature — straight through to my 59th year today. Rather than getting more conservative, i.e., risk-averse and more amenable to the status quo as I got older, I swung the opposite way. On that path I seemed to be "getting somewhere" throughout my forties, so I kept up the fight and stayed in the field, and didn't lose my radical edge.

One reason I've hung in there was that after 40 years from when the environmental movement took off, just prior to the first Earth Day in April 1970, activists have to wonder even harder how to change the world and heal it. In not succeeding as yet so far, as time runs out for a healthy global ecosystem, our job becomes more essential by the day. For over two decades I've been encouraged countless times to keep up my contribution, even though I've had to stretch my mind to see progress. Our ecosystem is now in far worse shape than most people in the 1970s would have ever imagined it to become by 2000, for example — this despite the environmental movement's decades and decades of effort.

When I joined it, almost everyone had a sense that there were just "environmental problems," rather than a sick ecosystem rapidly getting worse. I had just rejoined the environmental movement as an activist in 1988 when I spoke with a former client at the U.S. Environmental Protection Agency. John Holley of the Mobile Enforcement section in Washington, D.C. shocked me with his reason for approving my career change: "Nature is definitely out of balance." He was sincere, and in a better position than I to know this, but I thought he was exaggerating a little.

It was my career as an oil industry analyst from 1972-1988 that gave me a basis for starting a nonprofit environmental group benefiting from the background of my oil expertise. Having by now participated in many aspects of environmentalism and social justice since 1988, I still "put on my oil-analyst hat" just about every day to make a point as I try to inject myself into public discourse.

I would have set out differently in 1988, if I had not been

oblivious to the limitations and obstacles of setting up an office for a new organization. It was the coolest kind of office, I thought for a while, but after the thrill of commencing my nonprofit environmental career, I discovered I was caught in the same old lifestyle as the one in L.A., minus the commute and minus the big money.

With hindsight I came to see I should have proceeded with less personal sacrifice, more music making and time in wilderness. Yet, the trip has been rewarding if long and often frustrating. This book pulls together the hard earned lessons, insights and joy that working for the Earth has brought me. If I had any doubt early on that I was needed, or that more activists were needed, confirmation came in a few years:

In 1992, an historic warning by 1,670 eminent and honored scientists, including 110 of the 138 living winners of Nobel prizes for science, was issued:

> "We are fast approaching many of the Earth's limits. Current economic practices which damage the environment cannot continue. Our massive tampering could trigger unpredictable collapse of critical biological systems, which are only partly understood. A great change in our stewardship of the Earth and the life on it is required if vast human misery is to be avoided, and our global home on this planet is not to be irretrievably mutilated."

Because this warning was not heeded, major tipping points have been crossed. I see humanity and our fellow species on an alarming slide down to an unknown and terrible chasm. Few people seem to realize or admit it.

Many are racking up decades of denial, while many more of us have done much handwringing. What if the public had heard the above message in 1992 and taken effective action, such that no one could later say that the efforts were half-hearted? This would have turned the world upside down, bringing about extreme socioeconomic and political change, although many environmentalists couldn't have contemplated or signed up for the totality needed.

In my view, the chance for survival can only come from taking tough action collectively to assure a livable environment. Against their long-term interests, most people see short-term economic survival as more important — by default their long-term strategy. Their position is often a cherished attitude of discounting the possibility of a collapse of society or of the economy any time soon. Or, if they are open to it, they admit that they must keep their heads in the sand and muddle through the routine of their lives. Their tendency to ignore petrocollapse or economic collapse is reinforced by almost every funded environmental group — not because these groups can argue sensibly that collapse is not an issue, but because their funding depends on status-quo calm. They feel it is permissible for them to discuss ecosystem collapse as long as it is not identified as imminent.

By 1992 it should have been clear to anyone paying attention that the wider environmental movement was unable to sense the full, accelerating threat to the ecosystem. There were dangerous consequences to well-informed environmentalists' stopping short of embracing the depth and extent of the needed change for society. This became a huge issue among the grassroots, but the news media kept it under wraps. After all, car advertising and news about new cars were far more important to the mainstream news media than responding to ecosystem stresses. In tandem the mainstream "enviros" revealed their shortcoming in their worldview. Proof of this was their compromising on positions that seemed clear-cut to the grassroots direct-action wing, such as halting all clear-cutting of ancient trees.

When we reached the point many years ago that almost any member of the public could tell that Earth Day was being co-opted by big business and government agencies, it was clear that the thrust of mainstream environmentalism was not up to the task of saving the Earth.

It has been a disappointment to me that so many people, including all too many environmentalists, thought the spirit of liberation of the 1960s was and is dispensable. Whether we appreciate the Sixties' spirit or not, society's refusal to acknowledge the need for fundamental change has gotten us to this juncture:

> "Anthropogenic pressures on the Earth System have reached a scale where abrupt global environmental change can no longer be excluded... We estimate that humanity has already transgressed three planetary

boundaries: for climate change, biodiversity loss and changes to the global nitrogen cycle. Planetary boundaries are interdependent, because transgressing one may both shift the position of, or result in transgressing, other boundaries."

— from the study "Planetary Boundaries: Exploring the safe operating space for humanity," in Ecology *and* Society, *September 14, 2009, featured in summary form in* Nature. *The report was compiled by the Stockholm Resilience Centre in cooperation with dozens of top scientists of the world, including James Hansen of the NASA Goddard Institute for Space Studies.*

Granted, my ecological views and desire to see strong action aren't shared by everyone. Many educated, intelligent people are as well informed as their electronic infotainment keeps them. Others are tuning out ecological awareness for ideological or financial reasons. Many vocal pro-business apologists for profitable polluting believe that environmentalism has been a threat and tends to go too far. They have faith that technology can solve any limitation on the resource base. For them, news of yet more evidence of species loss and climate change can be ignored most easily when the number of corporations owning almost all the news outlets in the U.S. is down to six. And this development that severely limits free speech just happens to be unobjectionable to the apologists, for the free market can do no wrong — until their wealth gets eaten into by Wall Street sharks a' feedin'.

As just one man setting out to save the world by joining the environmental movement wholeheartedly and professionally, I soon got used to the fact that bad news for the Earth is both depressing and essential for our work. Getting the word out, even when fraught with negativity, seemed to be what I had been preparing for since a very young age. I was influenced greatly by my father's example as a reporter, author and talk show host. After ending my oil analysis career in 1988, I was soon to find that I had something positive and exciting to share — despite the negative aspects such as the web of life's deteriorating resilience — which has sustained me all these years. (I'll get to that.)

The tools of the activist are many, but aren't usually books or music. With this effort in your hand, I have finally added a book to over two decades of producing newsletters, press conferences, tee-shirts with slogans, letter-writing campaigns, hundreds of songs I wrote for The Cause, and engaging in and encouraging protest and civil disobedience. Books are occasionally credited with changing the world, and, given the increasing suppression of rebellious music on the air since about 1971, I'm putting faith in this printed effort. After all, songs and the usual activism aren't getting us very far — or so it only may seem, as countless seeds planted may still germinate and grow into a sustainable, just society. But perhaps we need a new idea, a new approach. There are days when I believe it could it be right under our noses. Can lifestyle and culture change be presented as an appealing solution, or do we have to see collapse before people go into action and cope with even worse chaos?

A book about my work was an idea I first pursued in earnest starting in 2004, when I had completed my tour of society — from materially comfortable, to living a simpler life as a nonprofit executive, and lastly becoming a very low-income writer and musician. I had accumulated not only my activist experience, but life-experience not shared by comfortable academics, for example. With my story and message I thought I was ready to be published, so proposals started going to the most likely publishers.

For the next five years, various forms of the book proposal were rejected by publishers as redundant with other peak oil books, or dismissed as a mere compilation of activist essays or blogs. Closer to the truth may be what my literary agent and I surmised, from indications from publishers: most executives in the book business are too timid (or dense) to print a book that not only challenged the American Way of Life, but took on the oil industry in such a way as to step on toes.

The way to proceed with this book during a time of rapid change in the publishing business has proven to be the separating out of my autobiography from what was an all-encompassing work-in-progress, with the working title *Petrocollapse: The Basis of Crash and Culture Change*. I've felt ambivalent about playing up my family name, having to trumpet that I formerly published the former "bible of the oil industry," the *Lundberg Letter*. Trumpeting my background was not much of a concern by itself: the messy part is my all-too-true Hollywood soap-opera, which may or may not help my prime purpose of pointing a way out of our world's energy/ecological predicament.

As much as my story and concepts may be original, the origins of a meaningful book — whether from decades of activism after a career serving Big Oil, or from, say, meditating on a mountain in the Andes — don't matter. For it is the ideas themselves and the appeal to human values that must count. My two diametrically opposed successive careers, and the personal transformation that the changeover required, might make for an unusual story worthwhile for others to examine. If you choose to come along this path with me in this book perhaps you will be uplifted, as I have been.

My post-oil industry published material has heretofore been in two forms, the essay and the activist report — about 350 published — and about 20 magazines. The latter were produced and distributed widely from 1993-2001. Of the stand-alone essays and reports, almost all online, about 250 of them deal with energy or collapse. The vast majority appeared since mid-2001, some chronicling a former industry player's rejection of materialism and his search for an environmental movement with soul. Finding that such a movement had been relegated to the fringes due to "compromisentalism," I ended up as a culture changer, if I can be forgiven for that grandiose self-labeling.

A book can be more than another tool, and activism can be more than the usual methods and goals. May this book and my next volume *Petrocollapse and Culture Change* bring to the attention of many people the possibility of liberating the mind from the dominant corporate narrative. And this book's reader goes deeper: a study of Western Civilization reveals that today's kleptocracy basically descends from the kings and despots of previous centuries' widespread misery. The tradition of democracy has been revered more than practiced, and at its best it did not place much value on nature's health. Somehow people have been talked out of revering nature as a political stance and economic policy. Before trying to improve one's lot for the long term in our fast-changing world, one might have to begin to see oneself as a victim, along with nature herself. We are victims of a society that has long been out of control, increasingly heartless and irrational. Demanding social justice is righteous, but our course must be well thought out; there are no second chances with a totally trashed ecosystem and climate. I have come to my assessment not just in my mind, based on research from various disciplines, but in my heart thanks largely to the tremendously dedicated and talented friends I have made who share my concerns and dreams.

"$ociety" is needlessly wasting our common life-support system. My stance reflects my anger and frustration, partly because simple, easy steps to begin extricating ourselves from our dilemma are bypassed both by the individual and society. We are all part of the problem as well as the solution — if there is "a solution." We each pollute more than most of us would like, and that's where the similarity or agreement ends between most people. For it is in taking action, once we become aware, that an awakened person may distinguish her/himself by embarking on a path of truth and liberation. Most days I feel this has been true for me. If one's liberation can be shared and presented widely, this aids in spreading the principle of taking action — or so I see the situation on a good day.

It has been a heavy trip for me, and others like me, when ideas fraught with nerve-wracking import collide with the world we thought we would always enjoy. It is best to at least know the truth, because some of it is so helpful. In a pinch or for a life-change, liberating and mind-blowing concepts can benefit us with lifelong alliances. Mutual aid is our evolutionary key to survival, as the human record has shown. It was refreshing for me to be able to learn this after a career of top-down executive performance. Discovering cooperative mutual aid shouldn't be such a surprising experience considering that it is common sense and attractive to all of us. But it is suppressed when someone has an axe to grind. Today this means truth is methodically obscured, from public school onward and even before age five. Television has been a great tool for brainwashing and passivity for parents and children alike, especially with the allure of materialism's gratification. Thus we are divided and conquered.

✑

Probably I'm like you: being aware, we think about the considerable non-renewable resources we use as we inflict damage on the ecosystem. We wonder how this could be greatly lessened. I happen to use far less than the average person in the U.S., but that's been my job as an activist. Moreover, what I contemplate every day goes beyond reduction of waste (especially the toxic kinds). In my line of work and from my heart, I concern myself daily with these challenges: (A) What could help people voluntarily conserve? (B) What will they do when deprived of petroleum? (C) How will climate-change alter our ability to survive?

I'm not alone in petro-pondering or wondering about the precarious state of the world. What's different about me is that I came into this activism as an oil industry professional in the area of supply & demand, with an emphasis on the pricing of petroleum products. Knowing about them first hand from an early age was disturbing, starting with the smog I had spent a decade in. As an activist I began opposing petroleum's pollution and destructive land use. This meant fighting oil industry expansion on many fronts. In the larger ecological context I have agitated for rapid curtailment of energy use through lifestyle change. This is surprisingly controversial and suppressed as it challenges the prevailing fixation of promoting replacement technologies and fuels. It isn't widely heard that there are serious obstacles to this replacement or technofix. Another controversial, suppressed concept is something I concluded long ago: the energy people really need is much less than industry and government want us to believe.

In my quest and environmental career I have adopted "simple living" and even veered toward what one might consider to be primitivism — how "green" can we be to match the ecosystem's and our species' real needs? My findings and interests in both lifestyle and cultural change came through years of promoting transport reform and land-use changes so as to end urban sprawl, which I still push as secondary priorities. As my story in this book tells, I alter my work as time goes by in order to try any promising means of bringing about fundamental change. All my work has been affected by my ongoing understanding of petroleum realities. With that basis, looking back now, I'm not so shocked at my disillusionment over a virtual religion among most industrialized peoples: the unquestioned, unopposed prowess of technology. Much activism today, especially in consumer protection, involves seeing through corporations' hype for unproven technologies, and making government agencies do their jobs. But such activism fails to reverse the trend of dangerous technologies' proliferation. The despoiling of the environment and harming public health got wrapped not just in the nation's flag but in "progress," "jobs" and scientific rationalization. Yet, despite my personal distaste for our extremely complex petrochemical and oil-oriented system running our lives, a vast array of technological applications help people arrive at sustainability via "appropriate tech." These means cannot be reasonably rejected when truly practical and verge on being completely safe.

❧

If the status quo and the direction that our world is heading in are okay with you, it's surprising you have read this far. If you adamantly believe elections and technology are the route to solving our predicament, this book doesn't gratify. I believe we have to start taking care of ourselves actively, directly, and in mutual cooperation. We can agree to disagree for now on the urgency of "climate extinction," of petrocollapse, and of impoverishment of the spirit; for first must come a much stronger sense of community and solidarity.

If you are, like most us, in need of greater human closeness and support, let me share my story with you. May you find encouragement for finding solidarity and conviviality in these pages. Some of what I've learned on my path might become part of a better way of living for you and your loved ones. Perhaps you have already been living the future as best you can. But if you are looking for a chance to move toward the transformation the world needs, jump for it when you see it. It's not all sacrifice, when deep connections and vital realizations are made along the way. One place to start entertaining life-changing ideas is CultureChange.org, to name one source. If you have any suspicion that a better world is possible, and that you might get your feet wet or dive wholeheartedly into the struggle, join us. "Us" is you and me. "It's Up To Us" happens to be a song by my daughter Vernell Zephyr Lundberg.

Jan Lundberg

On the way from Fredericksburg, Virginia to St. Marys, Georgia, Feb. 2007.
His Martin guitar traveled halfway around the world on the family's world
sailing cruise. Photo by Kevin Mullane

Part 1

My Story and the Evolution of a Message

Chapter 1

Family and the Shaping of My Being

A couple of decades ago I set upon a path of personal liberation. It is how I live and why I live.

ℒ

I was inadvertently groomed to take on a self-styled "job of a lifetime," although few of those folks aware of my "job" are in awe of it. One way we activists express such work is "paying rent to Mother Earth." It is of little interest to the average person whom I meet in the U.S., whereas my previous role as an oil industry analyst and capitalist is seen as more interesting and respectable. Whatever my second career means in the ultimate sense, I believe it serves as the main justification for writing my own biography.

As the reader will see, I came to believe "having a job" is not necessarily a valid use of the best part of one's life. Living honestly and appreciating love should be enough. I personally relate to "a life's work," while realizing that millions of people cannot relate to or have a life's work when they are perpetually trapped in the struggle for survival. I was lucky from an early age to garner exotic adventures and have two careers that could only have come from my family background. My family's extraordinary experiences in dozens of countries on a world sailboat cruise likely shaped me more than anything else. I'm proud to tell it all here.

Just as my last name is embedded in the oil statistics firm Lundberg Survey, which I once ran, my later life-experience is reflected in the succession of names of the environmental group I founded in 1988. It was my oil industry knowledge and radical parents that contributed to launching an eco-warrior career at age 36 in 1988, founding the Fossil Fuels Policy Action Institute. Subsequent name identifications were the Alliance for a Paving Moratorium that we formed in 1990, the *Auto-Free Times* magazine created in 1993, Sustainable Energy Institute (formal name change) in 2000, and finally Culture Change.

The last organizational name came to represent in part the experiences I had with my troubled family. Since changing the dominant culture is the essential challenge today, as more and more of us believe, I'm confident we'll stick with the name Culture Change until the culture really changes. I want to live to see the entire transformation, and I believe it's possible for today's generation — those of us who last — to see and live through it.

Whether one's nonprofit work is devoted to fighting illicit trade in endangered species or cutting motor-vehicle pollutants, over several years an activist reflects on any progress or, usually, the lack thereof. In my case I kept on stumbling into issues related to my original concern: smog and land use relating to transportation. The new revealed issues were overarching and fundamental to the entire reason for my work, mission, and filling in my incomplete slate as a still young man.

Although I got a unique shove onto my path due to my family's exploits and my years close to the oil industry, I felt I could not cease my own development and searching if I were to survive. I am still learning about ecology, culture, psychology, health and history. But having reached the point where the same patterns come up again and again in my observations, it occurred to me that I should pass along what I know to book readers. With the book you are holding or viewing on a screen, my odyssey and its lessons for me are offered as if they are as important as all my technical knowledge and findings regarding such matters as petrocollapse.

I've observed in these post 9-11 years some heartening tendencies in journalism and direct-action campaigns, including with Culture Change that I head today. On the whole, these efforts did not succeed — certainly not enough for me to walk away and say "I've done my bit." In Culture Change's long history, during which we introduced our readers and members to ideas that seemed outlandish or "too radical" at the time, most of these ideas have become almost popular or considered overdue. In the early 1990s, for example, well-meaning advisors told me I should not talk about depaving because it was supposedly too far out and strange. It had been my more moderate ideas that already had gotten me called "ahead of my time" and "prophetic." Unfortunately, this honor was not bestowed by enough supporters to make my work much easier!

Paradoxically, the faster that world conditions have been

changing, the harder it is for fundamental concepts for social change or truths about energy to break through. The more the whole system strains and shows its fatal flaws, the more the established order is determined to cling to its self-defined triumphs and resist fundamental change. The status quo's façade becomes more absurd but more rigid. As entrenched interests try for more economic growth — in effect prioritizing profit over the needs of the community (a town or the Earth) — the more resilient "the System" seems in avoiding serious reform. Yet, some crucial ideas and news slip through, for the truth comes out eventually. Society's failure to reform by now will result in collapse, as history has shown with past societies and civilizations that did not change and adapt. I am most interested in rebirth and renaissance, not crash. But we must first get through the present darkness and get through the collapse that has begun.

Complete ecological disaster entails unprecedented socioeconomic upheaval and injustice yet to be totally manifested. It's as if we have to try to save species and the climate by pointing out that disaster is bad business and not conducive to joyful shopping sprees. However, simultaneously, certain positive changes are underway. Awareness of critical, deep issues seems to be greater than ever. The race is between this intangible progress and the growth of destruction (and the destruction caused by growth). Regardless, the outcome depends more on the changes already unleashed, rather than the benefits of recent growing awareness. "Nature bats last" (the ecosystem's own adjustment) and the global economy's collapse constitute two train wrecks about to smash harder than anything in human experience. The culmination of my life and work would be to get this news across along with my belief in the positive opportunity we will have in a rebirth of the human experiment. We can start now.

From Youthful Rebellion to a Conceptual Contribution

The two most important turning points in my life-direction as an adult have been the years 1972 and 1988. Those pivotal times deserve brief illumination, although this jumps ahead in my life story that begins with my parents and my childhood.

It was 22 years ago — I was 35 years old — that I made my decision to get back to the activism I'd so reluctantly walked away from at age 20. As a pre-middle-age and hard-working father I turned my back on easy, big money, but didn't realize I was becoming totally separated from the wealth and estate I'd been associated with and helped create. It was 1988, my turning point.

My move in my mid-30s seemed imprudent to some. But I suddenly felt I needed to quit my oil-market analysis career and regain the idealism that was my true direction in life. I didn't set out to be some kind of eco-warrior; rather I looked for a job I could believe in. I didn't know what I was taking on in 1988, but I was to find as my new life unfolded that I would be glad to keep going with the same career despite setbacks and some disillusionment. I found that the layers of the onion of self-discovery in our complex and fast-changing world needed deeper transformation than mere environmental policy change. My discoveries felt weighty and progressively more pungent.

Friends and family members knew I had chafed in my pro-industry role after quitting UCLA in 1972. I was so unhappy that I wasn't an activist anymore, joining the Establishment and spending forty hours-plus per week amongst older people of the mainstream. I could not relate to the "provincial" people at work who shared none of my interests. I felt like I was wasting my life. Lundberg Survey Incorporated was interesting, but I'd already been too exposed to the greater world of activism, arts, other cultures, and adventure. I was a capable and hard worker, but the surroundings, especially the people and our business activities, lacked relevance to my dreams. This contributed to some depression for my spirit and my normally upbeat mien, so I was fortunate that this didn't last forever.

At the family firm I told myself I was learning so much about energy, statistics, publishing, editing, graphics, computers, anti-trust law, business management and public relations, that it was worth denying myself an activist, liberated life. But really I just wanted to live on a commune or go and complete college far from L.A. An even more important dream had been systematically stifled: my music-making — I suppressed it as had my parents had suppressed my musicality, so I wasn't aware I had submerged my greatest personal interest. I never shared my musical self-denial with anyone, including myself until very recently. Now that I see what I did (or didn't do), I'm aware I've lately been going backwards by putting music on the back burner in favor of the written word and some limited activism that pays a salary of sorts. At least I've gotten to bring the music forward over the years, and I enjoy my frequent musical dreams for song ideas.

In starting out my working career in 1972, I was active socially and my work-product was not too boring. I became aware from my first day on the job that approximately over 7 billion gallons of gasoline were being refined, burned and spilled in the U.S. each month. My reaction was that of shock, because this appeared to be so clearly destructive. I also knew it was geologically unsustainable. I had no way to act on the feeling, other than mentioning this statistic to a few people. Most were not interested, apart from my oil contacts who could only dream of increasing their companies' gallonage.

The U.S. Energy Awakening

When Richard Nixon led the way for wage and price controls — in order to deal with the fiscal fallout from the massive expense of the Indochina war, I suspected — this started the 8-year era of oil industry price and supply regulations that Gerald Ford and Jimmy Carter continued. One of the first consequences of inflation in 1972 was "pain at the (gasoline) pump," so Lundberg Survey was enlisted by the Internal Revenue Service to identify retail outlets enjoying the fattest margins. (This was before the dealer gouging of the Arab Oil Embargo in 1973 that the public encountered.) After the IRS quickly rolled back many retailers' prices at the pump, we continued to serve what turned out to be predecessor-agencies of the Department of Energy regulating the oil industry. Stanford Research Institute visited us and passed along our information in their far more expensive analytical reports to Washington, D.C.

This was the beginning of the world's great awakening on energy in general. This brought on the contest of *facing resource limits* versus *total faith in technological innovation.* No one talked about it or realized it, but the peak of U.S. oil extraction had just been reached, as predicted by geologist M. King Hubbert. Sharp consequences of high demand and dwindling domestic supply of a very strategic resource had people more concerned and angry than they ever had been, without their knowing the background story. At Lundberg Survey we didn't know all of it. We knew a lot of oil was used for the Vietnam War, but this wasn't part of the

6

competitive information we tracked. We were expert in our downstream end of the oil industry, and we were extending our expertise into additional aspects of marketing. Gouging was not only happening at the gas station level, but at the wholesale, spot market, contract and refinery levels. Our work demanded that we understand and track the vertically integrated oil industry and know every oil corporation's subsidiaries in all businesses. Hence, our Family Tree publication that classified oil companies as to level of integration. The federal government purchased it and developed sophisticated classification concepts from it for endless regulations.

In the mid-1970s I helped the U.S. Environmental Protection Agency phase out lead in gasoline. This was done by tailoring our reports to show price spreads between grades. If leaded or low-lead was too cheap compared to unleaded, the EPA had a problem, so enforcement needed to be stepped up or regulations modified. Meanwhile, the Ethyl Corporation was selling more lead to foreign refiners, escaping the U.S. market's newly enhanced responsibility for public health. Going back decades, Ethyl had run an oil-refiner statistical service based on cooperation in sharing data. This information allowed refiners and marketers to know how much aggregated gasoline sales (not by brand name) were in a given metropolitan area, by grade and by month. Ethyl lost interest in the statistical report as its business was increasingly outside the U.S., so in the early 1980s I took on for Lundberg Survey the continuation of the cooperative program for our oil industry clients. Trust in Lundberg Survey had always been high, but we were still gaining in prestige and importance.

After my first few years working in North Hollywood for Lundberg Survey, harming my health and spirit as a commuter by car, I was used to the grind. I escaped for two years while I made a foray into pop-music publishing and promotion in 1977-78, but it didn't work out (more on this phase in the chapter on the 1970s). Back again at the family business by the time of the 1978 Iranian Revolution, I found energy issues and data to be more interesting as world events and energy developments came to the forefront.

By early 1979, Lundberg Survey famously predicted the Second Oil Shock. We weren't known by that corporate name in those days, but instead by the newsletter for which I was the Publisher: the Lundberg Letter. Even more well known was the nation's "Oil

7

Guru," Dan Lundberg, our company's president. These were heady days, as our name approached household-word stature. I thought it was nice, but I needed more meaning. So my research for my firm's interesting clientele had me delving into the energy industry way beyond our original focus on gasoline and cars. What I began to learn and see implemented at our company helped persuade me that my job was too important to keep regretting.

If the reader is too young to remember the 1970s, here is an Associated Press retrospective from August 20, 2006: "During the oil crisis in the 1970s, when short supply had motorists lining up at the pumps... The fiery Dan Lundberg became the radio sound-bite of the crisis that he dubbed 'the days of lines and hoses.'"

In 1979 I learned I was to become a father. I had married my Greek high-school girlfriend Xenia Anagnostopoulou (in 1975; I was age 22 and she was 23). Bringing her to L.A. alleviated my loneliness that I blamed on what I saw as the sprawled out, disgusting, unsocial megalopolis of Los Angeles. With her as my partner I had more of a family, and with my work getting more interesting as I started to run the family business, I felt more fulfilled.

In 1980 I stepped out a bit and showed my colors: I published a letter in the *Los Angeles Times* attacking the production of nuclear waste. My father — my boss, the domineering and charismatic radical — got heat for my letter from the local head of the national petroleum lobby, one of his so-called friends, Harry Morrison. My father accused me of "trading on the family name," in my publicly railing against the idea of calcining radioactive waste as long-term solution. After several minutes of dressing me down, he concluded with, "And by the way, Jan, I'm proud of you." In his heart he hated nukes, violence, pollution and corruption. He rarely spoke out compared to his younger days, but he had earned a permanent reputation of being independent, which he kept — despite our having to be loyal to the major oil companies that were our main clients and subscribers.

As Oil Guru, Dan earned a regular Nightly Business Report commentary spot on the Public Broadcasting System television network in the early and mid-1980s. I helped edit or proofread just about every one of those commentaries, and we delighted in the occasional opportunity to attack gasohol and ethanol for causing "agricultural strip mining" (as we did in the *Lundberg Letter*). We even took a swipe at the White House policy of supporting the Contras in Nicaragua. However, when I wrote up a commentary for my father that advocated a restructuring of the work force's geographic relationship to the work place, in order to slash oil use, he rejected it as risky and too daring to pursue — even though he knew I was correct. It was at this point that we both should have had a talk about creeping conservatism in our lives.

I'll now go back in time to paint a more full picture of Dan Lundberg and our whole family:

Family of Organic Sailors

Starting in the late 1940s my father had known success as a writer and television news anchor in Hollywood, and was host of TV's first talk show — the muckraking Dan Lundberg Show, broadcast on KCOP in Los Angeles for seven years from about 1954 to 1961. The public would not have guessed it, but television was but a part-time pursuit for this energetic powerhouse. Simultaneously he had another, opposing career, serving the gasoline marketing industry as a trade-association executive and public-relations consultant. When his gasoline price survey started taking off in the late 1950s he dropped all other oil activities and found he could start enjoying the advantages of being well off for the first time in his life.

Fortunately for me, this is when I came into the world. In 1952, the year of my birth, the world had not quite yet reached the point in the nuclear arms race of being able to blow up the world more than once over (it was in 1954). So I was among the last people to be born into the more innocent, regenerative world preceding today's. I was also fortunate that by the time I was old enough to notice, my family's economic wellbeing was healthy.

I was delivered in Baja California, although my family lived in the Los Angeles area. Why have your children born in Mexico? My parents had three reasons: medical freedom surrounding birth, Mexican nationality for owning land on the coast, and being able to stay out of the U.S. military should I need to do so through Mexican citizenship.

My parents had purchased a three-acre ranch in Canoga Park in the San Fernando Valley. Paying basic bills wasn't easy for them at first, and for a while my mother cooked on a hot plate (as my father frequently reminded me in our later days of splendor). Although my father was honorary mayor of Canoga Park, he and my mother were considered by some to be oddballs, especially by the new tract-house dwellers across the street. Some of them said my parents fed their children "rabbit food" (fresh fruits and vegetables), and many criticized my mother for not using DDT on the veggie garden and orchard. I remember many fruit trees I enjoyed, such as pomegranate and white peaches. Plants and trees fascinated me, as I had my own houseplants in my room at about age 5. I planted a mango seed and was quite disappointed when it would not become a tree.

As a boy in the 1950s I had all the benefits of a good home and a loving family. My parents hardly fought at all. Nature was all around to observe and get under my fingernails. Our ranch was bounded by other similar sized ranches, all situated off a dirt road called Shoup Avenue. Our large pool had frogs and turtles living in it during the winter when we weren't using it. I had numerous friends to play with for hours, and more toys as my father's income increased. Perhaps the best aspect of childhood in that era was that children were not so closely monitored and guarded. So it was safe to wander the neighborhood all day long, eating raw corn in the cornfields or playing with crawdads in the gutters. The world seemed safe too, as I formed the idea that I lived in a great, supreme nation. I was treated to regimentation in public elementary school, as exemplified in the first grade when I saw a boy aggressively manhandled by the female teacher for having his knee on his chair as everyone chanted the Pledge of Allegiance before the flag. Another day I remember vividly was when the class spent time outside assisting with gardening. I became absorbed and realized I was the only kid left out there. When I walked into the classroom the teacher and all the children laughed because I was out of step, being so interested in plants instead of sitting indoors.

In no way could I have foreseen that the nation and the world would be increasingly torn apart, in part from the phenomenon of major conveniences I enjoyed as a boy: petroleum, cars, roads, and mass manufacturing of products and appliances. So, this song of mine that follows serves as a rude but truthful contrast with the false world I was living in at a tender age:

Song

*From a musical dream, the following lyrics were in response to the
September 11, 2001 attacks.*

Peace Now (reggae beat)

>We're on a planet that is explodin'
>In population and global warmin'
>The War of Terror is against the Third Stone*
>We need some peace now
>Don't need no jet planes
>We need more lovin' and understandin'
>But I can't say how the people gonna be saved
>
>My paranoia and desperation
>May make me crazy or even lazy
>But I don't take to no hypocritical way
>
>They're buildin' highways across the farmland
>We drive to fast food and drink a six pack
>But it won't last now so we gotta be brave
>
>We make some changes in daily living
>We say our good-byes to oil and violence
>We get together and make a culture that stays
>
>Fly the Earth flag today
>Is it American way?

*"Third stone" refers to planet Earth, as in Jimi Hendrix's song
"Third Stone from the Sun."

"Peace Now" features the bad and the good — the doom and

gloom as well as the better future that should come once the dominant paradigm is kicked over. The song has only five chords (plus variations with open-string high guitar-neck chords). I first performed it on Sept. 11, 2003 at a Humboldt State University rally for peace. My most satisfying performance of it (and perhaps of my whole life) was at a Bush Step Down rally in Hollywood in January 2006. I was lucky to do it well at those events, without screwing it up — something about the reggae beat in that song occasionally trips me up because, I like to think, I didn't have the benefit of a back-up band — not because I'm a white guy. "Peace Now" has been aired on the community radio station KMUD-FM, Humboldt County, in January 2008, when I was interviewed about my work and music.

Should one wonder about the relevance of taking music seriously when there's a planet to save and bills to pay, here are a couple of questions: What do we really feel when we clear our minds from workaday preoccupations? Do our heart-felt beliefs and dreams stand up to honesty and sanity, or do we conform and keep quiet to avoid being ostracized? Part of modern humanity's dilemma is self-denial for the sake of the delusion of conventional living, when we are all in critical times that demand a response. I'm happy to punctuate my work every day, if possible, by music. We each have our tastes, and may not like the work of every artist we stumble upon, but self-expression and honesty make for true art that all artists appreciate and encourage.

Chapter 2

The Lundberg-Hultman-Dobson Family, 1940s & '50s

What kind of man spawned very opposite children who are both known to the U.S. news media? Let us see how Dan Lundberg came to start Lundberg Survey *after* he got involved in the oil industry. These questions are answered best with stories I heard many times from my father the raconteur. I'll attempt a summation of both his effect on me and the impression he was always giving about his unlikely and harsh background. Stark details about him and especially his second wife Mesa (my mother) paint a picture of the couple's tough origins and circumstances, as my parents became up-and-coming citizens of Hollywood. As this setting takes shape I introduce all my immediate family members. Their initial lifestyle is portrayed to presage their later personal development and general unraveling. The detailed chronology of the family history is prefaced by the effect Dan had on others, as I go on to reveal his rough and colorful background.

Dan Lundberg — in a devoted, rebellious son's perspective

Everyone who knew Dan Lundberg would agree he was without doubt an extreme character: charismatic, volatile, bombastic, frightening, generous, attractive, and talented. Being close to him was difficult, but of his five legitimate children I managed it best and the longest. Nonetheless, trying to understand him and his high emotional stress and outrageous behavior reminded me of his difficult, deprived origins and upbringing.

Once in an oil executive's office I broke into laughter when the oilman said wryly, "Your father's a laid back guy." Dan Lundberg was always a man with a program, a mission. When he wasn't smoldering or exploding, he summoned charm to sweeten his intelligence and intensity. My father often gave me the sense he was mentally and viscerally still on the tough streets of his youth. At the same time, he gave the impression, especially to his family, that he knew everything of importance. His humble moments were few and therefore almost shocking when they surfaced.

Even in a comfortable, sophisticated setting with me in Europe during my unique education, or later in high-level corporate meetings with oil people, I could sense the wild in Dan Lundberg that could never entirely subside. I had seen outrageous acts of humor and ill temper. I'd heard stories of him dumping prime rib off the balcony in the Hollywood Palladium at an oil executives' gathering. In Hatton's Lebanese restaurant in Hollywood he decked a guy at the bar when the man slapped my father for drinking from the man's glass. The list goes on.

When I was very young and cared too much about what people thought of me and my father together in public, it was sometimes embarrassing to be with him. More than once he sang loudly down the sidewalk while drunk, leading his procession of family sailors at night back to the shore-boat dock or yacht club on Catalina Island.

When I was about ten years old my father entered a canoeing tournament at the Los Angeles Sports Arena. In the evening under the stadium lights was a large artificial lake, surrounded by bleachers where his family sat. We wondered what we were doing there: he was about to compete with guys less than half his age. When it was his turn to run the course he took off his coat and shirt and let hang his formidable potbelly, so some in the crowd yelled "Vic Tanny!" (a well-known gym). But my father powered the canoe like a madman and beat the pants off everyone else's time to get the trophy. I was stunned, and found there was yet another dimension to the guy I hadn't known: the athlete. When I was nine he had a wooden canoe custom built, and I had taken weeks off school to paddle it down the Colorado River with him. I only knew he could handle a canoe, and that he had written a novel about his canoeing teenage years. How many boys see their dads win a sporting event in front of a large crowd?

After I grew up and came to love the fact that my Dad was extremely different from the average Joe, I reveled in my father's antics and the stories of his crazy, mischievous behavior. I adopted many of his mannerisms and jokes, but never did get the knack of swearing convincingly in Spanish.

I have told a few friends and friendly interviewers that Dan was a street person; i.e., street-wise. His experiences growing up were invaluably instructive, but often painful for him (although he didn't ever cry about it). He must have decided early on that he wanted his own family some day to be completely spared anything resembling his old life of want and struggle. This desire, fueled by his undeniable brilliance and energy, drove him to manipulate people close to him with an obsession that undermined his children's and wives' own development. In emulating his style and values during and after Dan's living years, I obtained some disastrous results along the way. Sometimes this took the form of taking his advice to the letter; I once told a new friend with a sinister look that I had been "in jail" (which I had not) so as to scare him from getting closer to my wife at the time. Of course, it became obvious I felt insecure, and it took a long time for me to apologize to my friend. But, coming out from under my father's shadow, I became less imitative, as I was comparatively calmer and wasn't "crazy." And since, like him, I was ethical — I like to think — I can relate my own history favorably with his. One way that I am more ethical or wise is that I don't push people so much with my explicit advice for living one's life or handling a crisis (or an imagined one).

Despite Dan's accomplishments and love for his family, right after his death he was more or less dismissed by most surviving relatives as having been incredibly domineering, and, worse, foolishly leaving behind a mess. The mess fell upon me perhaps more than anyone, yet I still loved him very much — despite his being a disturbed character whose towering ego let him think his wishes would be respected after he was gone.

Today I am the only family member who upholds Dan's and his widow Mesa's traditions. To claim I carry on Dan Lundberg's spirit might be too limiting, because he had some unfortunate defects, and there was much about him that was objectionable. This anecdote gives an idea: some visiting surveyors, the Brodericks from Berkeley, came to dinner at our family home in the Hollywood Hills. Somehow I ticked my father off (no effort was ever required), and he was so tough on me verbally, eventually

15

throwing ice cubes at me, he brought Rose Broderick to tears. Little did she know he had treated me far worse on occasion, such as when roaring drunk.

But Dan Lundberg and I have in common these penchants: being the muckraking journalist, fasting for health, growing organic food, disdaining institutions, enjoying movies and plays, and setting out our individual future according to scripts we write for ourselves and loved ones along with anyone who might get close.

Today I seem to be outdoing my father in one of his favorite areas, that of being an adventurer for social and political change. He took risks, but it had to be me who would fight the good fight so as to willingly lose "on the materialist plane."

This defeat for me was several years ago, so the way I live and work as an activist is of late along the lines of having nothing to lose materially. This is something Dan could never do, ever since his first marriage in his mid 20s. In contrast, I finally shook off my career/family constraints at age 36, and proceeded to enjoy a most radical exploration of middle age that I wish my father could have seen. I owe to him my zeal, self-confidence and skills. My mother contributed to my character and my adventure as well, in different ways, as I'll show.

Dan was for a time a maestro of the oil industry as much as anyone since John D. Rockefeller. But Dan did it from the outside — and earned the tremendous prestige he craved (although he would have preferred fame as a novelist). He tended to stop short of radical actions after his Mediterranean years in his 50s. Rather than fault him for this, I can view my own odyssey as continuing the path we shared. Although he was, more than anyone else, the one who put me on my later path, during much of our time I was the one arguing for more conventional strategies: at times at our family-business years I felt frustrated for failing to cajole him into going for the big bucks by expanding our operation and maximizing our positive influence on the energy world. I tried to tell him that business needed debt to expand and just survive, but he would have none of it. I was ready to open a branch office in Washington, D.C., but I had to settle for frequent trips there for our government clients. I was somewhat embarrassed by our headquarters, an old medical building in a dreary suburb in North

Hollywood.

I didn't run the company long enough after my father's death to fulfill the possible dream with the family business. He would have been outraged by my abnegation as his successor and head of the business, and far more outraged by the way his widow, grandchildren, daughter Dana and I were treated. But he also deserved blame over it all due to his major part as a foolish Svengali (the master in the novel *Trilby* after whom he actually named his daughter).

What-might-have-been no longer matters to me, just as I got past my phase of thinking the world owed me a new Mercedes car. I believe my father would be proud of me for targeting the excesses of the oil industry on both environmental and cultural-impact grounds. He'd be too old now at 98 to depave a driveway or pedal a bike cart with Pedal Power Produce, but each generation has its duties and historic role. And he would have rather seen young people doing those convivial activities for a good cause than see them watch no end of television and bow down to politicians and corporate thugs.

Now meet the young Dan Lundberg, and learn what it was he unleashed on the world (yes, there's more) for better and for worse.

Dan Lundberg's origins and his "dynasty"

Daniel Lundberg, Jr., was born on October 24, 1912, in New Britain, Connecticut, to Swedish immigrants. Each of Danny's parents, Daniel and Freda, believed they were the illegitimate offspring of Russians: novelist and philosopher Leo Tolstoy, and a Romanov prince (whose name I did not learn), respectively. So I'm not quite sure whether I'm half Swedish or a quarter Russian.

Danny's mother left him and his father when he was a toddler. Daniel Sr., a paperhanger and musician (formerly of Sweden's popular Salvation Army orchestra), put him in an orphanage due to financial hardship. After a couple of years perhaps, Danny was able to rejoin his father in Boston and also live with Daniel Sr.'s new wife and their son Ronnie (later to become a drummer with Benny Goodman's orchestra).

The two Daniels worked in paperhanging. Danny's father was a serious taskmaster, but had a wild sense of humor. Once when calling on a new client, Danny was horrified to witness his father greet the woman with the most foul obscenities, all uttered with a calm smile. The woman was pleasantly nodding all the while, and Danny was dumfounded. It turned out the woman was deaf and it was a joke on Danny.

Once when his father was a schoolboy, he came to school one day with a cow's udder, from a butcher, sticking out of the fly of his trousers. When the girls shrieked, he took out a knife and cut off his "member" and threw it down on the ground. For me as a boy interested in mischievous fun, I thrived on such stories.

It wasn't all fun and games for the Lundbergs of the early 1900s. Once when an oppressive Irish policeman hassled Daniel Sr. on the street — not surprising, when, as he said, the less recent Irish immigrants allegedly picked on the more recent Swedish "Squareheads" — he dealt the cop a swift butt of the forehead onto the officer's nose, enabling the two Swedes to saunter off unmolested. I have not known my father to lie or even wildly exaggerate, so I report these stories in good faith if not with a little discomfort.

Danny was asthmatic — he later attributed to his mother's abandonment — so his father shipped the lad off alone to Colorado Springs for a healthier, drier climate. There, Danny enjoyed a boy's outdoor life and climbed Pike's Peak.

Back in Boston in high school, Danny got into canoeing on the Charles River. In this era before car culture, a canoe in such a place was the ticket to dates and sex, often through proving one's athletic prowess as a paddler. Danny excelled and once was finishing strong in a Marathon, but he accepted a copious drink of lemonade which caused immense cramps. This and other stories made their way into *River Rat*, a first (and perhaps only) novel he published, in 1942, that was favorably reviewed in *Time* magazine. My father showed me the magazine and pointed out that Pearl Harbor was about to be attacked, ruining many a book's chances including *River Rat's*.

Danny had taken up the trumpet in his teens and had a band that toured New England. For promotion the band would go down a main street playing in a convertible motorcar, with a band member marching in front naked but for a white flour paste. Danny was to have a later, longer adventure with music that proved to be disastrous, involving his "Jewish-mother" efforts to make his second daughter a star pianist. However, literary ambitions held sway for most of his life until middle age. And because he eventually gave up writing fiction in favor of comparatively meaningless oil-guru work, I became intent on doing a book with him or about him based on his writings, talents and adventures. I had to shelve this when he died and chaos ensued. My autobiography is probably as close as anyone will get to doing a book on Dan Lundberg.

In the 1960s my father enjoyed telling people that *The Catcher in the Rye* by J.D. Salinger was derivative of *River Rat*, ever since he met an English professor in Rome who taught his students precisely that. (*River Rat* was also the basis of the surfing movie Gidget, as Danny and Universal Pictures discovered when Dan's screenplay was commissioned for *River Rat* and found to be too similar to Gidget to bother producing.) Danny happened to be living in Rome in 1968 to produce a comedy album in Latin, featuring his children, several Jesuit seminarians, and the as-yet undiscovered Bill Conti (later known for the Rocky soundtrack) as composer. My father met him in a bar at a time when Conti, fresh out of Julliard, needed Dan's encouragement and creative hints in composing. My part on the album was to whistle through my hands clasped together.

But this digression rocketed us ahead some decades, and we must go back:

Dan had left Boston after high school to live in Los Angeles, where he knew no one, to be a writer.

On his way to reaching that goal he lived a while in San Jose or thereabouts, near to where his mother had moved. There he attended junior college (now called community college) and owned and ran a restaurant to support himself. It was just a step above a "greasy spoon," where he improvised frequently to keep it going. Around this time he had an apartment where he knew an attractive female living there as well. He told me that he and she had a comforting fling, and he lost track of her. Almost two decades later she contacted him, perhaps noticing him on L.A. radio or television, and she asked him to do her a favor. It was to visit a young man in jail and counsel him. The meeting took place in the jail (or was it a prison?), and my father had the distinct impression it was his son. My father added that the young man's mother never said one way or another, but my father felt that the age of the young man, a physical resemblance to him, and the odd request from a distant, almost forgotten liaison, argued for paternity. I don't believe my father ever saw the young man or the mother again.

Upon becoming a Los Angeleno, doing what for a living I do not know, he became committed to the Spanish Loyalist cause. But could not afford to go to Spain and join the likes of Ernest Hemingway and George Orwell. So, with his new wife Helen (Hultman) — whom he told me begged him to marry her so she could escape her parents, even though he warned her he was just an aspiring writer — he moved to Mexico with her around 1938. He figured that at least it was a Spanish-speaking country at a time of International Brigades answering the leftist call to aid Spain in its fight against fascism and the excessive grip of the Catholic church. It seemed almost laughable to me that he would just go to a Spanish speaking country, but he made it count in the good fight.

In Mexico City Dan continued to write and began working in radio for the tycoon Emilio Azcárraga Milmo, and CBS for whom he became the network's Mexico foreign correspondent. Helen bore him two children there, Guy and Dana.

Dan's best friends there were James Hinton and Rod MacArthur. I came to know both of them as a young man. Jimmy was a botanist and discovered and named many plant species in his travels throughout Mexico. His daughter Patty lived with us for a time in Hollywood. In the early 1970s Jimmy's son John was painting in the mountains and was killed for his watch. Jimmy hunted the killers down on a mule and brought them to justice. Rod was the rebellious son of John D. MacArthur, the insurance magnate who became for a time the richest man in the U.S. Rod made his own fortune selling collectible plates in the Bradford Exchange. Rod later bought *Harper's Magazine*, where he installed his son Rick, a journalist who brought back the previous *Harper's* editor Lewis Lapham.

When Guy and Dana were about three and five years old, respectively, they had what seemed to be a mortal case of amoebic

20

dysentery. After one doctor after another failed to help, Dan thought they could die soon. But he met a man named Alfred Dwynn who used to shock gringos by eating unwashed raw fruits at the open-air markets — without ill effect. Dwynn's prior history of illness and botched surgeries culminated in his undergoing fasting at Herbert Shelton's clinic in Texas. There Dwynn healed and thereafter ate very wisely, emphasizing raw, fresh and plain foods. After getting to know Dwynn, Dan was ready to try fasting his kids when medical doctors proved incapable of saving them. Dan told me he locked his hysterical wife in a closet because she would not go along with the fasting (I have my doubts he could have incarcerated her for long). Within a few days of just water, Guy was up and around again after weeks of weakness, playing on his tricycle. This brought tears to Dan's eyes, and Helen was sold on fasting as well. So the story went.

Dan had an additional job in Mexico City, at the U.S. State Department directly under Nelson Rockefeller, doing anti-fascist propaganda for "Rocky" who was the CIAA (Coordinator of Inter-American Affairs). When the war was over, Dan asked Rocky what a good career move would be. "Go into the stupidest industry in the world," said the Standard Oil heir. "What's that?" said Dan. "Why, the oil industry!" replied Rockefeller.

However, although Dan did take the advice, he never got out of important journalism. In 1945 he covered the United Nations' formation in San Francisco for CBS, and the near legendary Eric Severeid was his hotel roommate. Dan later bragged that he "kept Franco out of the United Nations" for many years by getting Latin American nations to go on record against the fascist, and then reminding them of it at every opportunity on the air.

Dan wanted to get the kids out of Mexico for their health, so he and the family moved to southern California's Kern River wilderness where they lived in a big army surplus tent. There the children got strong on the river doing poling with hand-made rafts. The family lived on bulk rice and squirrels that Dan shot with a rifle. Once he came face to face with a deer, he told me, "But I couldn't shoot it as I looked into its eyes." Dan was working as a writer there with a typewriter — a manual one, of course.

Moving the family to Los Angeles, Dan got heavily into

screenwriting (Gun Smoke, Jack Benny, World of Giants, and other productions), radio journalism, and promoting "Health Jubilees" about fasting and related modalities.

About the same time he began his oil industry activities by forming trade associations between independent retailers and wholesalers of gasoline. He was simultaneously a public relations consultant for gasoline marketers. He helped usher in self-service gasoline marketing while managing the Los Angeles area dealers, jobbers and "bootleggers" who competed against each other and the major oil companies' service stations. Dan, Helen, Guy and Dana lived in Pasadena, where the nation's first freeway was being constructed. This period and locale saw the birth of car culture and suburbanism and the so-called American Dream, and Dan Lundberg was pushing it along. Oddly, he already had strong environmental inclinations and acted on them in the 1950s onward in film and on television.

One day around 1947 or '48 Dan drove home alone in his wife's car and saw their friend Noel Charisse (brother of Cyd Charisse, actress and dancer) doing ballet moves in joyous greeting of Helen's "arrival" (as indicated by her car). When Noel realized with the evident body language of a sagging dancer that the driver was instead the husband of the object of Noel's desire, Dan surmised this and virtually collapsed. Having lost his wife's loyalty and become depressed, his health took a serious tumble and he was nearly paralyzed.

He was hospitalized against his will and not permitted to fast. But he was finally able to get out by convincing the hospital staff that they would "never get a dime."

Mesa Vernell Dobson Lundberg, farm girl who made it in Los Angeles

Helen left Dan and the children to live with Noel, so Dan called upon a friend to come help in the home. He had met a reporter and public-relations woman named Mesa Dobson who had impressed him. He had also seen her on the street when he could barely walk, and when he telephoned her for her help she had already gotten a positive impression of him.

At the house, his two children had Mesa's help during the day as she took off work, and Dan was able to resume going to work. Dan must have recovered fairly well and soon, because he told me that the lovemaking with my mother was "the best in the world." He was grateful that the children had a new caring mother figure. She was all for it, and she soon asked Helen if she, Mesa, was really going to be allowed to raise them. My mother seemed to have doubts that she could herself bear children of her own.

Dan described Mesa as someone who at a party or bar had every male in the room hovering around her. She had arrived in Los Angeles by bus from Salt Lake City as soon as she could escape her stifling Mormon family at age 18 or 21. A sister, Roberta, and a brother, Jay, who were both younger than Mesa, had joined her in L.A. They were poor, sharing a small apartment and scrounging for work.

There were eleven Dobson children originally, with some childhood deaths. The living was tough but set in nature, as the family had a sheep (wool) ranch in Idaho. My grandfather Jesse created their refrigerator by digging a hole in the kitchen and lining it. My grandmother Euphrasia Cox had her family nearly in the honey business. (We used to get large cans of solid honey that was incomparably good.) My mother was born in Shelley and remembers her early years on the farm, but soon a Great Depression-related foreclosure set the family on the road and threw them into the urban Mormon network in Salt Lake City. There, survival for the faithful was guaranteed by the church community. Jesse became a house painter, and Euphrasia kept chickens in the back yard and managed to can a lot of food. So Mesa went from the house of a housepainter to the house of a (former) wallpaper hanger (Dan).

Jay Dobson had been in World War II in the Pacific, refusing to shoot anyone, so he got to be a radio operator. There seemed to be a similarity in Jay's and my personality, as I was accidentally called Jay occasionally as a child. I liked him, and eventually learned he was also a troubled man, given to drinking. Dan employed him in the 1950s and early '60s but Jay could not stay, and he became a truck driver. He was struck down by a truck on a highway in Utah in 1967 and killed.

Roberta later worked as Dan's secretary, and eventually married

Simon Nathenson, an affable, cigar-chomping right-winger who had a career in State government. Roberta died suddenly of a stroke in 1977, leaving three young children behind: Sonya, Yolanda and David — my fond cousins.

In the 1940s, living in L.A. with Jay and Roberta, Mesa got her first major job as a copy editor at one of the city's daily newspapers. But sometimes all she got to eat in a whole day was a candy bar — all she could afford when helping to support young Jay and Roberta.

As a public-relations business woman a few years later, she and her partner Betty Lyou successfully promoted the nearby Placer River as the state's first discovery area for gold. This designation campaign was hatched because Placerita Canyon was to be developed by real estate interests who wanted the value jacked up, so they had Mesa and Betty get a park designated as the first major place in the state where gold was extracted (panned) — not at Sutters' Mill as generally thought.

Mesa was not as radical as Dan, although they had no major disagreements politically. Mesa's character was such that she could never seem to judge people. This was in great contrast to Dan, who always upheld his favored "geniuses" and then lambasted "the bastards" (one of whom, often a loved one, would always be in his revolving "dog house"). Dan dominated Mesa with his style, but deferred to her and always sought her approval. For their beginning, he liked that Mesa was an atheist and was open to his health ideas. She was turned off to Mormonism, Christianity and all religion at about age 8 or 10, because she perceived racism and sexism that revolted her. Her parents could not explain to her why black people could not be bishops or get into heaven. It was nonsensical to her that their God could only be white and male, so she decided it was all a load of horse manure. She often mentioned, until her dying day, gently as always, how much she hated organ music because it reminded her of church — even when I treated her to Iron Butterfly.

Dan and Mesa offered their children no spiritual guidance or structured learning about the mind; my parents simply taught by their actions and way of living. I was allowed to go to Sunday School if a neighbor wanted to take me, but it was for years a confusing and embarrassing subject for me when kids asked each other about their religions and I had nothing to say. Finally I asked my parents enough about it and decided, in the fourth grade, that atheism was good enough for me. I set about converting my friends to atheism. Eventually it was a revelation to learn on my own, starting at age 18, something about Buddhism, yoga, and consciousness or spirit — such was the effect of listening to Alan Watts lectures on L.A.'s Pacifica Radio station. (At the time I didn't imagine I'd be on that station years later with my ideas on petrocollapse and singing my signature song, "Have a Global Warming Day.")

My mother told me in January 2007 about her earliest times with my father: "Danny made me laugh all the time, for a man who wasn't operating right. He was seriously ill but able to walk around. It was quite a while before he really recovered." I asked her what he had wrong with him. She replied, "It didn't matter what you called it, you got sick and you got well." She described life in Hollywood in the late 1940s: "We met in Hollywood, not a very big town then. I went to his house for the first time, and a bird flew right ahead of us on the freeway to Pasadena, all the way." She continued, "I knew him a few weeks before going over there. I was living with a girl (Betty Lyou). I didn't pick up boys, although these days if I were that age I would have."

[At the time of this interview my mother was on various medications that were forced on her from 2001 until her death. At least one mood-altering drug, the antidepressant Remeron that is known for deadly side effects, prevented her from totally being her real self. Or maybe her bluntness was due to my not being her little boy anymore, so that she could be frank.]

My mother did not feel tied to her parents. Visits were not frequent, but as a little kid I believed everyone loved one another as they were supposed to, and my extended family seemed to. In Canoga Park when I was about five years old, we had my mother's mother Euphrasia (who had a little native American blood) stay some weeks in our guesthouse. It was of Spanish architecture as was the main house, with characteristic tile roofs. I lingered with my grandmother occasionally and had the tea she made me: molasses and lemon juice in hot water. From then on I liked Grandma's Molasses, as the brand's logo on the label looked like my grandmother. When I was about ten years old, my mother took me, my brother and sister to see her family in Utah and Arizona. Everyone was kind. My best memory is of a lovely, small farm we visited where one of my female cousins with strange names (normal for the area) remarked, ironically, "Y'all have such horde names!"

The Dan Lundberg Show, Channel 13

Dan, more than Mesa, had many radical friends, mainly Jewish writers and artists who were communists. Some were put out of work in Hollywood by McCarthyism's Red Scare. I met one of them in the early 1970s when he came to our family business to sell us some pencils. His daughter got a grant to produce a book that my father criticized to me as "a waste;" it consisted entirely of photographs of empty rooms.

My father had a basis to be a powerful critic. He knew fine writers, had been published in *Esquire* magazine ("Are You a Phony?"), and he was of course very well read. He told me he had read "the dictionary." There was never a word I asked him about that he did not know along with its spelling. As to appreciating art, his good sense was called into question — fittingly, by the author of the empty-rooms book — when he did his own restoration work on a very old, beautiful wooden statue of a hermaphrodite that always hung from our ceiling. Probably to save money, he had unskilled workmen do most of the job such as applying paint. It looked good afterward, but not in a real antique way to me.

But the man was an artist in other ways, and a most dynamic one. In the early 1950s Dan Lundberg created The Dan Lundberg Show, on KCOP's (Copley Newspapers) Channel 13. Every Sunday evening for seven years, this "first talk show on television" competed in southern California with the national Ed Sullivan Show. Dan's show centered around serious interviews and muckraking discussions with one to several guests. Days before each show, research was done and experts brought forth on whatever burning issue of the day was permeating Dan's social consciousness. His producer was Jeanne Brehm, whose son Dick Brehm worked for Dan in the oil trade association/PR business. I doubt that anyone in the audience would have imagined that their host spent most of the time serving the oil industry and thus contributing to the awful smog afflicting them.

As a kid I watched Daddy on TV regularly, but only for the moment he would do a subtle wave of his hand to me as he glanced at the camera. As a teenager I later learned that the show's topics included the monopolistic dairy industry that had recently put small family operations out of business by lobbying for pasteurization and homogenization. He also targeted the American Medical Association and the tobacco industry. I saw one of the taped shows decades later that dealt with radiation contamination of the atmosphere around Los Angeles.

For other shows his guests included the likes of Linus Pauling and Ray Bradbury. Back in the early 1970s, on the steps of Hollywood High School, Ray told my father, my younger brother and me that he never drove a car, despite living in L.A. This fell on my ears as if the man were from Mars and most deprived. But it influenced me years later. I have had a hard time remembering that almost every time someone runs into my car-free-by-choice lifestyle he or she probably feels the way I did when I ran up against Ray Bradbury's lifestyle.

Dan's various projects included a documentary on smog, "Smog Red," in which I had a role as a sick kid in bed suffering from respiratory illness. I had no lines, but was in bed with another "sick" child, a little girl. We were the youngest girl & boy to do a scene in bed in Hollywood, although I can't say how well the movie did when it probably never enjoyed a box office.

Dan also published books on oil marketing: "Getting Into Serve Yourself" and "The Giveaway Issue." He crowed that a professor had praised the former book as containing an original contribution to Marxist economic analysis. Another book, published when I was about age 7, featured me as a model. *How to Teach a Boy to Box* was written by his friend and my coach Frankie Goodman. (His wife Vera Goodman was my father's secretary after my aunt Roberta went off to become a housewife.) Another model for the book was my half-brother Guy who was 12 years older than I. Our outdoor boxing ring at our organic ranch in Canoga Park had a circular hole in the center so that my father or Frankie could stand in it and be at eye level with. My training came in handy when I was in the fourth grade, when two boys ganged up on me in school. I gave one a black eye and they both ran away. Years later I paid the price for thinking I could box well enough.

Years later, in the early 1970s, my younger brother Darius took many a lesson (as did I) from Frankie at his gym in Van Nuys. One day I walked in to see a publicized match and saw Barbara Streisand looking at me, giving me eye. I figure it was because of my long curly hair that she had evidently tried to achieve artificially herself. Next to her was her producer/boyfriend Jon Peters who was giving me an unfriendly stare, thereby complimenting me further in a backhanded way.

Back to Dan, who, by the way, the ladies tended to go for (all but my mother tried unsuccessfully): In the mid-1950s he started Lundberg Survey as a retail price reporting service for gasoline marketers. He sold reports mainly to major oil companies whom he believed could stop their price-fixing if they would all just buy his surveys. He found that almost none of his old trade-association "independents" would buy a price survey, as they performed their own surveys or price-fixed with each other. When Lundberg Survey started up, Dan quit the trade association posts. He gave one of the jobs to Duke Morley, who one day was physically thrown out of the building by Dan for insulting him. Duke, a big tough guy, laughed all the way being bounced down the stairs on Seward Street in Hollywood, because he had answered Dan's question, "Was that a gratuitous remark?" in the affirmative, and Duke didn't know what the word gratuitous meant.

A few years earlier at Dan's office on Cahuenga Blvd in what is now Studio City, some Teamsters who were gangsters came in to shake him down or intimidate him. He reacted by grabbing the scissors off his desk and brandished the weapon, and chased them out of the office like a wild man. They all kept going down the street while Dan gave chase while screaming and waving the scissors, and the gangsters ran for their lives. It was just an acting job for my father, and he enjoyed the subsequent adulation of his secretary Roberta and their coworker Rosemary Bloom.

My father explained to me that he had more than once written a script for himself to follow, in order to bring about some planned result, and that it usually worked. He occasionally became angry or frustrated when people didn't follow his more minor scripts, especially when it was a family member. He helped many people improve their lives by presenting them with a "script" of a concept for a business, sometimes just to "spin them off" (get them out of his affairs). His acting out could appear to be just acting up: He behaved crazy once in Cuba in a police station in 1977, when detained for taking photographs of some state installation: he started yelling for his "cerveza" and the authorities decided to let the crazy gringo rejoin his public relations group on tour. He took a lot of Super 8 film footage there, but much of it was lost by a Hollywood film developer; nevertheless a movie project was begun and probably never finished. My young cousin David worked on it.

Back in the mid 1950s, Helen came around to start visiting her children. Trilby had been born in 1949 and I came along in 1952. The times were a bit hard in the early fifties, with my mother cooking on the hot plate, but they had food growing on their acreage and had some farm animals. Mesa ran the ranch and took care of the kids while Dan disappeared over to Hollywood almost every day for his jobs. Guy milked our goats for my milk because I was allergic to cow's milk.

Guy and Dana were soon asked by their mother to live with her, and a court case ensued. Dan and Mesa thought Helen was out for money, and Dan was confident the children, if asked to decide, would choose to live on the ranch and continue their healthful lifestyle of swimming, doing chores, helping with Mesa's two young arrivals Trilby and Jan, etc. But Helen had been taking her children out for visits and giving them ice cream, which was the kind of indulgence that wasn't permitted the kids at the health ranch. So, when Guy and Dana decided in favor of their mother, Dan was caught flatfooted and felt crushed. The legal experience of discovery (seizing of private and office financial information) and onerous child support payments prompted Mesa to go to law school, which she proceeded to do at night when Dan got home.

Canoga Park was being "developed." The ranches across the dirt road, Shoup Avenue (at Saticoy street), were suddenly gone and cookie-cutter homes were to go in. One night Dan and Mesa went over stealthily and moved every single stake one foot away from their ranch.

I enjoyed growing up there, always outdoors, picking fruits, getting junk food at friends' tract-houses, playing with matches, playing doctor, looking up women's skirts, and getting taken to Catalina Island once Dan and Mesa could afford a boat.

One day Dan told Mesa he really wanted a sailboat, so she told him to go downtown and rent a room and write a screenplay to sell. This he did, and you can catch Raw Wind In Eden to this day on the late show on television, starring Jeff Chandler and Esther

Williams. I find it well done for a suspense movie that did not rely on any gratuitous violence. The boat my father bought was a Tahiti ketch called the Andra. One more movie credit: Dan wrote The Party Crashers, another 1958 movie, starring Connie Stevens.

Chapter 3

The mid- and late-1960s' Glory

In 1960 we moved to the Hollywood Hills. We got a palatial
Spanish-style mansion overlooking most of Los Angeles. It cost
us $40,000 then; today it would easily fetch a few million dollars,
despite some of the lower terraces falling away. Our move there,
to 2201 Maravilla Drive, for me at age eight eased the pain of
leaving my friends in Canoga Park. A kid could play all day in
secret passages and in the huge yard, and the place lived up to its
name in tile outside the huge wooden gates: Le Paradis. A pool, a
merry-go-round and live-in servants were some of the features of
this improved life of advantage for the Lundbergs. Four floors on
a hilltop, Le Paradis had a huge walk-in vault for bootleg booze
(accessible from the garage above through the floor in what was
designed to look like a mere grease pit).

Lundberg Survey must have really been doing okay by then.
For servants we always had a family, usually Mexican, living on the
bottom floor. For a few months we had an older woman named
Pauline as a nanny. When my parents found out she was telling
my little brother that there was an angel talking into one of his
ears and the devil talking in the other, she was fired in no time.
For a longer period we had a black couple doing the cooking and
cleaning. The man's name was James 6X, as they were a Black
Muslim family. I was a little puzzled over their prayers, but they
laid no trip on us and vice versa.

We had fancy cars such one Jaguar after another. It
embarrassed the hell out of me when my father would show them
off around my friends. Looking back I guess it was only in my
imagination that he was deliberately making me uncomfortable,
while he was only giving me attention and enjoying himself. Even
before our climb into the upper middle class, I just wanted to be a
normal looking kid: dark hair, no freckles, and be named Steve or
Mike. Why did I have to be blond, blue eyed and fair skinned? I
bought Man Tan for an overnight suntan and woke up to find

31

yellowish squiggles on my skin.

I made several friends in the hills near the Hollywood Bowl. Finding lizards and shell fossils were almost daily activities. I became an expert rock thrower. This helped me in our street games of baseball and football. In those days, affluent kids played in the streets without supervision, unlike today in the U.S. We also made forts in the hills, and sometimes watched concerts down below us in the Hollywood Bowl. I saw and heard the Fab Four, but they looked pretty small through the binoculars. I would have preferred the Beach Boys or Jan and Dean.

Each weekend a friend and I would hike all the way down the hills and hang out on Hollywood Boulevard to hit the movie houses and the Magic Shop, unsupervised at age 9 through 13 when I sailed away. We made our own skateboards because they were not yet mass-produced. We loved surf-music groups and hated the competitors, mainly the Beatles, at first. We called ourselves surfers even though we had not yet surfed.

For my seventh grade at Le Conte junior high school, girls were of great interest, but we boys were just talkers as we played out male aggressiveness. When Marianne, the prettiest girl in school, came up to me and put her arm around me, smiling at me and trying to initiate small talk as we walked, I was dumbstruck. The feeling that came over me was probably the most powerful and pleasurable in my life to date, so I was unable to say a word to her. Marianne did this with me more than once, but I was too shy and embarrassed to even think of talking with her. It was possible she was playing a game, but there wasn't anyone around laughing. Something about it was absurd, because although I wasn't bad looking I don't believe she knew anything about me or knew any of my friends. It took me many years before I could see how idiotic I was to miss my chances to spend time with her, even though I was just 12 years old. In the back of my mind then I might have suspected she was from a modest-income household and that she knew how to spot a rich boy — even before the episode when my father drove me to school late one morning and decided to careen all over the asphalt schoolyard in his new Lincoln Continental, much to my mortification.

In no time at all I went after girls less intimidating, namely Jane McGee and Roxanne (whose last name I can't recall), both of whom I was able to enjoy kissing at length at social teen-gatherings. We enjoyed the noon school dances, where a jukebox supplied hits such as The Kinks' You Really Got Me and The Beatles' Matchbox. The boys stood on one side of the gymnasium, the girls on the other, and as soon as the music started the boys walked briskly across the floor to the waiting girls to ask for the dance.

In my junior high there were two cliques or gangs: Surfers and Greasers. This was before the trend toward having knives and guns; in later years the weapons came onto school grounds and were sadly used. My best friends weren't at my school, but in my hilly neighborhood. After many a sleepover at Randy "Bird" Schneider's house, we would get up before dawn and hike down to Hugh's Market on Highland and Franklin and see the "night people" whom we found interesting. But our mission was to buy candies and soft drinks in order to bring them way up into our hill neighborhood to sell on the street. We shamelessly charged triple the cost to the junk-starved kids of the high, isolated neighborhood.

It was in sixth grade that we got quite interested in girls, although we didn't know what to do with them other than make out. We would sit down next to a strange girl in a dark movie theater and put our arms around them while we gazed at the screen. Of more interest to us was pop music. Among the crazy and wonderful songs coming out, "Like a Rolling Stone" captivated us the most because Dylan was so cool and serious with such an unprecedented length of a song. We never lacked for money to buy new records, although our purpose was not to accumulate more and more of anything (clothes, sporting goods, records, magic store tricks, etc.).

Hollywood activists

I remember seeing my first political demonstration, as we drove by a crowd of protesters with signs outside a military recruitment office on Hollywood Blvd. I was disturbed by the anger of the people with signs. Little was explained to me by my mother who inadvertently drove us by, although I would have appreciated her cluing me in. This was late 1964 or 1965, and I had by age 12 discontinued playing army in the hills with my buddies and wiling away hours with my plastic toy soldiers. I had drawn many battles on paper as well. I remember telling my father of my day's exploits in the hills with our realistic plastic guns, about killing Commies, and he said with a sad smile, "I'm one." "Whatever," I must have thought. He didn't explain anything at the time. In summer camp when I was 11 I went down a slide in the pool yelling "Kill the Japs! Kill the Krauts!" and making verbal machine gun noises. I was severely reprimanded as there was a Japanese-American boy nearby whom I had forgotten about.

For me to do such a thing may speak to the slack discipline and lack of parental attention I received from around age 9 on to age 13 when I sailed away with my family. I was the "benignly neglected middle child." Compared with my older sister and younger brother, my parents took little interest in where I was or whom I was with, although they may have assumed just where I probably was. From about age 11 to 12 I stole my parents' beer (once or twice), bought chewing tobacco and got a bit sick from it, and, at an even younger age, threw raw eggs at passing cars, and smashed streetlights with rocks. I also pulled telephone pranks with my friends whereby we made people believe we were drunk, ex-Army buddies of those we called. I caught tarantulas and proceeded to neglect them in jars in the yard until they died — I believe that a parent should monitor such things so as to spare such creatures a senseless death by stupid kids.

I was perceived as a nice kid who got decent grades in school. I did my chores at home that included yard work (even though we had a gardener and a handyman). I loved frogs and toads the most. Once my brother Guy brought me what I most wanted in the whole world: from Mammoth Lakes in the Sierras he brought several large frogs and toads that I proceeded to house in a wire mesh open-top cage in the yard, with my idea of an artificial pond in it. I was delighted but ultimately bummed out by the loss of the creatures to deaths and disappearance. Near that spot was a grapevine I planted, for I was fascinated with fruits and plants. But a gardener trimmed it back to almost nothing, angering and saddening me for a long time. It was an event that helped turn my privileged little mind against workers. It's amazing and fortunate that I was able to overcome such tendencies, but in the end it was my parents and a European education that cured me.

We had rather special guests over for dinner, such as one night in perhaps 1962 when I was ten: peace activists had sailed their boat into an atomic-bomb test area in an effort to stop the aboveground blast. It struck this child that what they did was important, and I didn't see them as helping any enemy. Meeting such people can leave an impression on a boy that shapes him. I emulated this kind of social exposure for my daughters, who through me met civil-disobedience protesters involved mainly in defending ancient forests.

I recently learned from peace activist Brian Willson (whom my daughters know) the names of those activist-sailors that had visited my family almost a half century ago; I had forgotten: the Reynolds. Nor did I know until checking Wikipedia that Dr. Reynolds was one of the top radiation scientists in the world. That Wikipedia entry is also the only instance of Dan Lundberg's presence in the website (as of this writing); my father had written and published an article about the Reynolds' voyage — news to me! Brian wrote to me on Aug. 16, 2010, about two ships and crews taking on irresponsible bomb tests:

> The Golden Rule had as crew Albert Bigelow, William Huntington, George Willoughby and Orion Sherwood. They were arrested by the Coast Guard and brought to Honolulu for trial in May 1958. A second sailboat emulated the Golden Rule a bit later, the Phoenix, crewed by Earle and Barbara Reynolds and their 2 children, along with Nick Mikami from Hiroshima. They were also arrested, tried in Honolulu, and Earle Reynolds (if not others in the case) got a two-year prison sentence. These two sailboats sailing into the U.S. atomic test areas of the Pacific Ocean were important expressions of militant pacifists taking risks that upped the world attention on the post-WWII atomic testing in the growing "Cold War."

Jimmy Fields, child-prodigy pianist

One frequent guest at the Lundberg mansion was Jimmy Fields, a child-prodigy pianist. My father hoped that his daughter Trilby would pick up some of the fatherless lad's ability and dedication. He was a few years older than me, and willing to play my games, but I felt quite superior to him because I could hike better and he was hysterically afraid of bees. He had a great sense of humor, for example referring to our fasting as "feasting." I was later to marry his former wife just after he died at age 36. He and I each had a daughter from the same exquisite harpist. If someone had predicted this for us as boys, we would have had a great laugh.

Jimmy must have been envious of me when we were lads, but never showed it. He was on a musical plane anyway, which I can't say about myself despite my full set of drums in the huge basement where I pounded the surf beat. I never lacked for fine presents and instruction. To go with my drums I took lessons at Drum City in Hollywood. One Christmas present I got from my father was his secretly outfitting a shack at the bottom of our terraces as a clubhouse for me. When he showed it to me I was awe-struck: it was a jungle-warrior hangout, with African objects hung up such as shields, spears, with some South American head-hunter fetishes such as skulls. There were South Seas tikis too. There was a rabbit hutch with a couple of big bunnies. How this man managed to take the time to do this (with help from a servant), and go buy the décor and props, didn't amaze me at the time. It does now, considering what it takes to accomplish all the things he did. People don't seem to have the time anymore that modern living offered so many of us in the 1960s.

My father even managed to be the Cub Scout leader for the dens, one of which I belonged to, meeting at my Gardner Street Elementary School in Hollywood. There he was a popular entertainer, throwing candy out into the seats of the auditorium and staging competitive games such as Shield and Hearth (or was it Knights and Hearths; he might have made it up on the spot). The school principal, the elegant Mrs. Damewood, seemed to find him extremely charming whenever he came by to tell her I was leaving school on some long adventure.

Randy Bird died in the early 1990s at the same age Jimmy did, of leukemia. He had become a tennis pro, and left behind a five year old daughter whom I looked up. I found she was his spittin' image.

By the early 1960s my parents, brothers and sisters and I frequently sailed our 50' ketch to Catalina Island across from southern California. Along the way I sometimes caught bonito that tasted great. On the island we enjoyed the car-free street in the village Avalon. We owned a mooring in the beautiful and festive harbor.

We were leading the *care*-free life of the American Dream powered by cheap oil. In that era there was for many Americans "car liberation;" indeed, it was confirmed in catchy songs sung about it by the likes of Chuck Berry and The Beach Boys. But by the mid 1970s a growing number of people didn't feel as liberated by the car as they felt over-dependent on it, as gasoline prices steadily rose and commute times grew. So, recent U.S. history is almost equally about car dependence as it has been about car liberation. It was the car that enabled my family to go across California to take the trip down the Colorado River and to get to the marina whence we set out on sailboat races to Mexico. At age five I took a long drive from Canoga Park with my father across hundreds of miles of desert on our way to Mexicali where my brother had just been born. My main recollection of our trip was that my father bought me a rare soda pop (a no-no for a health-nut family), and I didn't want to share it with him.

I didn't love cars, and never drew them like many boys did; the closest thing I drew to cars were military tanks with fire coming out of the guns. I didn't focus on cars partly because I had so many outlets of expression and amusement, such as my mynah bird Pete who imitated upshifting sports cars far below him. My parents wanted me to have everything, including ways of fully participating on the ocean. I gained the status of "the youngest celestial navigator in the world" (as my father trumpeted) thanks to tutoring. This aspect of my privileged life augured our family's world cruise begun in 1965.

I had learned a little travel-responsibility for myself by then: one voyage to Avalon saw me upset, teaching me a lesson. I left my duffle bag back home and was extremely disappointed that I didn't have it. I sobbed like a spoiled brat, "Why didn't Emma (if that was the maid at the time) bring it to the car?" My parents bought me a new set of clothes in the village, and I loved them. Another lesson I got, on a prior trip to Avalon, was painful in another way: the gangway rolled over my toes when the shore boat dock I was on lifted and dropped with wave action, below the town's enchanting municipal pier.

When I was 10 years old our family basked in my mother Mesa Vernell Dobson Lundberg's passing the California Bar, despite raising five children. I was proud of her and my family, although my preoccupations in those days were pop music, hanging out with friends, and enjoying my pets. There was another family member to be proud of: each year my sister Trilby cut a classical music record with top session people — all orchestrated, as it were, by our father. The albums were given to oil clients especially. Two standout albums were "My Days Have Been So Wondrous Free" based on George Washington's world of music (on which my younger brother and I provided dialogue), and the Shostakovich Piano Quintet; the composer sent a telegram from Russia praising the recording. We were also proud of our older half-brother and half-sister from Dan's first marriage: Guy and Dana. They were of the more Mexican side of the family, from their parents' Mexico City days. Dana was extremely fun loving and wild in a sweet way, whereas Guy was serious and sullen. These differences between them caused some people to jump to the conclusion that Dana was not nearly so smart as Guy, as my mother explained to me. Guy was 12 years older than me, so anything he said was weighty and memorable. One of the few times we hung out other than the occasional family meal was when he drove me around the adjacent neighborhood where the new tract houses were being built in Canoga Park. He pointed to a brown house and said, "Niggers will live there" and I had no idea what he meant. Guy was groomed to run the family gasoline-survey business, and Dana left her theatrical talents to become a young mother. Her husband of course joined our family business, and despite his lack of formal education my father was able to utilize him in various ways.

Regardless of occasional minor lapses in behavior by family members, and their incipient problems that a wise observer might have spotted, I saw the family as the greatest in the world. I now see that it could only be so or appear so because of my father's energetic will and his creativity, coupled with the support from his female other half. My proud family-assessment as a child was also bolstered by my parents' imparting to everyone a concern for the planet and humanity. Discussions at dinner or in the living room were often about racial relations, health food, the dangers of medical drugs and hospitals, avant-garde films, and concerts. We were well off, people knew it, and I couldn't help admiring my parents for it. Life was easy and the future seemed to have infinite pleasures and many rewards.

Right before my father went full-time with the gasoline survey, in about 1960, his news anchor job at CBS TV's Los Angeles affiliate, KNXT, was abruptly terminated. It happened upon his exposing anti-Semitism by the chief of police: Dan's report finished with, "Tomorrow's likelihood of protest, however, is discounted by the police chief because it's Yom Kippur." An influential Jewish viewer called the station demanding my father's head. It was Jerry Lewis, who I heard was too drunk to get straight the fact that the anti-Semitism of the *police*, not my father, was what was exposed.

Sail to Greece

As an aspiring 13-year old surfer enjoying Hollywood, chasing girls and loving my comfortable, exciting life, I heard about something strange I could just make off in the distance past Hollywood: the Watts riots in 1965 vaguely awakened me to mass injustice and discontent. The riots made my parents all the more aware of the less than ideal environment for their children, and it gave my parents a kick in the pants to follow up on their daydreams of taking their children around the world for an educational cruise and life of adventure. One night my mother said to my father, "Put your money where your mouth is." So they sold the house, put a piano on our 50-foot ketch, and we cast off.

Why? My parents had always been anti-medicine, having raised five kids on fasting and organic food (and smog). So when they said they wanted to get their kids out of "the drug culture" it wasn't just cigarettes, marijuana or pills — we had never had a vaccination among us, and we kept it that way even as we entered country after country. To this day I've never had an aspirin. I think my parents not only knew of depravity and unhealthful environments; they thought the moral fiber of society was poor and getting worse. To give their children all possible advantage, it was clear we had to get out of the U.S. for a long while. My parents also must have wanted to assure our togetherness. A small floating home can help.

As the summer progressed in 1965 I was more sad than proud that my family was moving onto our custom-built steel ketch, the Passat, to sail around the world. I hated to leave my friends and my junior high school life of girls (that I still didn't know quite what to do with). Our fantastic house was sold soon for double the money my parents paid for it. On the afternoon of September when we cast off from San Pedro, my sister Dana jumped off the dock in her clothes to bid us goodbye. Off we went, loaded with Tang and a small piano and other instruments, first stop: Avalon, 26 miles off the coast. As crew on the Passat we had Ron and Val Sewell who had bought our 36′ Tahiti ketch, the Andra.

We moored in every anchorage and harbor on the west coast of Mexico, and Trilby began playing piano recitals and concerts that our father organized for the next year in various cities we traveled to or got near. Practicing on the boat's piano was not all that appealing to Trilby, so often my father would get out his violin and he would force her to rehearse Mozart, for example. I played nothing for five years: I hated leaving my drum set behind, and refused to touch my snare drum as inadequate. My mother's Martin guitar came with us, but no-one played it. I had no idea it was a great guitar until decades later.

Experiences were given to me that few 13-year-old boys, and the vast majority of adults, ever get to have. Some of my family's sailing and creative exploits were not especially remarkable in themselves, but when strung together, one right after the other, a few days' adventures packed as much as what most affluent jet-airplane travelers get only after several extensive vacations. In Baja California's very large Magdalena Bay, frequented by whales for breeding, there was no settlement and our boat was the only one visible for many miles. Going ashore with our Boston Whaler outboard-engine skiff, we swam off a quiet, deserted beach where rusting old whaling equipment lay. My father, Ron and I had snorkeling equipment, but for me the super clear water with large fish near the shore spooked me, so I timidly stayed near the steep-sloping beach. I did appreciate the stark, lonely beauty of the huge, wild bay.

As it was only 1965 and not 1995 or 2010, Cabo San Lucas was not yet overdeveloped. We loved the small bay and the luxury hotel on the hill where we enjoyed fine meals not possible on the boat. From Cabo San Lucas we sailed around the tip of Baja California and moored at La Paz. The town wasn't very impressive to us, but our high point was worth the visit: a huge fiesta on a hillside. I don't know what the occasion was, but there were the best tacos we had ever had: sea turtle with jalapenos. At the time sea turtles certainly seemed abundant, but nowadays it is rare that they are eaten, or maybe it's that people rarely admit to eating them. At this same fiesta were cockfights, which I had never witnessed before.

We crossed the Gulf of California to Mazatlan. One calm, sunny morning while we were at anchor a motorboat about 12 feet long pulled up to the Passat. My father woke me up to tell me I was to go shark fishing. My father knew I was interested in sharks, and here was an unusual opportunity where I would also have to practice Spanish. I went along reluctantly; I was a spoiled kid who sensed a little bit of possible discomfort at sea with these strangers, a Mexican man and a boy. They were probably illiterate and knew harder work and more deprivation than I could imagine. They were quite patient with me and were able to do their usual job without my being much of a distraction. I joined them without my packing a lunch, so I later shamelessly shared their meager food on our long day catching sharks. (It occurs to me only now that we could have enjoyed sashimi or sushi on the spot.) We went a few miles out from the harbor and used hooks and bait to haul in various kinds of fish, mostly sharks. I still don't know how we attracted them in such variety. I was glad when my mild ordeal was over and we returned to the Passat at anchor in the harbor. The fishermen were well compensated by my father for putting up with me, and one reward was a Polaroid snapshot taken of the fishermen on the deck of our boat. The fisher boy's mind was delightfully blown by his instant image in his hand. As I witnessed this I sensed the privilege my family and I had as to technological products, our not having to work, and our good fortune in meeting interesting people. This was un-humbling for me, as I appreciated my advantages more and more and believed we were deservedly the greatest or luckiest family in the world. Seeing how others peoples lived was interesting, but even more significant to me was how my family and I were able to do what we were doing. In the months after Mazatlan I saw many poor people in different kinds of environments. It would be decades before I sensed that they were enjoying some social or cultural advantages over my materially fortunate family. It was easy to tell that the local scenery beat smoggy, sprawled out L.A., but the cultural differences I could detect at age 13 and 14 were mostly limited to our material sophistication and wealth compared to others' deprivation or simplicity.

The biggest contrast between rich gringos and the

impoverished local people came when a yachtsman named Captain
Horace Brown happened to be visiting Mazatlan when we were
there. He had been married to an actress who had been one of
William Randolph Hearst's consorts, Marion Davies. Captain
Brown seemed like a nice guy, a common enough boozer with
excess money. I already knew the type. We were all at a fancy
restaurant and exited together, satiated and (some of us)
inebriated. He stood at the door on the sidewalk where dirt poor
Mexicans stood amidst stray dogs, and called for a waiter from the
restaurant. Captain Brown proceeded to place an order for the
most expensive cut of meat that he specified as raw. My family and
I stood off to the side and began to worry as we watched our
drunken friend. The plate of meat was brought out the door, and
Captain Brown set it down in front of a small dog he fancied, and
said "Eat up, Pooch. Eat up, Pooch." This misplaced generosity
shocked everyone around, and as the dog finished up, my father
said to me that Captain Brown could get himself killed by the
angry, hungry crowd around us. I was so clueless at that age I did
not realize how terrible and stupid Captain Brown's action was, if
not for my father's observation. My father was disgusted to the
point that we no longer could tolerate this drunk who almost got
himself knifed. The Mexicans were not poor because they were
stupid or lazy, as I might have assumed when I was 13, but rather
they were in their state from being on the receiving end of brutal
exploitation by upper classes. Their condition was connected to
the reasons some rich fool like Captain Brown could have money to
burn.

One of the most pleasant times of our trip to date was our
day's walk down the coast from Mazatlan. We went along a wild
area with coconut palms growing by a beautiful beach. The clean,
blue waves were beckoning all during our relaxing stroll. But they
were not perfect for body surfing, so I passed. I don't remember
swimming at all, for I was spoiled by that time in this regard. The
highlight of the afternoon was having my first coconut milk and
the wonderful-tasting nut's young, soft white flesh that we
harvested. To me, this was real living and I wanted more of this.

So far I had been gone from L.A. for two months, and I had
almost nothing to complain about. On the boat I looked forward to
still more interesting landfalls and mahi mahis for me to catch just
by trolling along.

Lovely anchorages beckoned that I couldn't have anticipated. We stopped at Islas Tres Marias where the tropical sea life was beautifully abundant in the clear waters right around our boat. We next sailed to Puerto Vallarta, quite undeveloped then, such that dugout canoes brought yachtfolk to shore through the breaking waves. So we commissioned a dugout canoe to be made from scratch. We were in no rush, so we enjoyed Puerto Vallarta. I was developing as an all-around useful mate, happily letting my family off at the beach for dinner and then going back past the waves to drop a small anchor. I then swam in towards the lights on shore in the dark, and after dinner I swam out through the waves to fetch our skiff.

When we sailed down the coast I was delighted to see jungle for the first time in my life. There were Indian villages such as Yelapa and Jalapa. My father and I went ashore with my .22 rifle to go hunting. We didn't find anything to shoot but it was a lovely hike through the forest. Looking back, it was a stupid thing to hunt without permission or without the knowledge of the Indians. One day at anchor my father gave me the job of unfouling the propeller. Over the side I went with a knife and wearing a faceplate. There was one other sailboat nearby, and its captain called to us that he had just seen a shark's dorsal fin. So I calmly exited the water. I had learned from Ron Sewell that sharks are generally not dangerous. Indeed, they kill about four people annually in the whole world. My father and I told Ron, who had Montezuma's revenge something awful, that I had postponed the propeller job due to the presence of a shark. Ron jumped up out of his sick bunk, started swearing, took the knife and went over the side to do my job. His anger could have been attributed to being ill, but since there was no rush he may have relished making a macho point. He had done so back in Mazatlan where we stayed at a lovely hotel: he saw a man looking at his wife through the window and he chased after him like a ferocious madman.

From 1965 until we all returned from Greece in 1970, we did a lot as a family in our own fashion. We appeared normal and respectable, if a bit odd and ambitious in our seemingly strange way. I grew up being stared at by a new set of locals sometimes every day, which might have contributed to my sense of individuality that I'm still continuing to develop. What are you lookin' at?

No matter what my parents could have promised me in advance about our trip, I would never have gone on the voyage voluntarily, having to leave my friends and my privileged lifestyle. Today when I hear parents in the U.S. say they don't want to move anywhere because of their children's schools and the kids' school-friends, I don't see the wisdom of such a decision. Years ago I became convinced that my parents did the right thing by uprooting us from U.S. culture, from an educational aspect and to become world citizens. There are even more important reasons today to leave for a while or forever, as the twin threats of petrocollapse and climate disaster gather steam: if one is able to move out of a large city, one strong argument in favor is that it is always safer in low-populated areas, and that's where property is priced lower. I believe that mediocre schooling, especially public school with large classes, should by bypassed, in favor of useful skills and knowledge of the world. For these and other reasons, it is more than ideal — even essential — that other countries be experienced when one is young and impressionable. From what I have learned, removing one's family from consumerism and finding a functioning community where the people are closer with one another cannot be accomplished in the U.S. Even in rural USA, families are not as close as other nations' families, in my experience.

I had no choice but to sail along and learn, so I made the best of it. At least I had my little brother Darius to play with, constant wildlife observations such as sea snakes, and lots of mahi mahi for fresh ceviche. I had many other duties on the boat besides fishing and cleaning the fish. I took my tasks seriously, and was very seldom ordered. I don't believe I ever complained. Tasks on a boat are endless, but it's nevertheless relaxing almost always — even filling the battery cells with water. Unlike chores at a house or apartment, any and all jobs on a boat are essential to the crew's survival. The rewards were obvious to us: anchoring in idyllic spots, becoming familiar with dugout canoes, meeting kind and interesting locals, and being masters of our own destiny. We knew it was an enviable existence — if we stayed safe. My main problem was that I missed California and the U.S. on an emotional level, as I realized from time to time what I was missing out on. The new pop music was barely getting to us, but I had known since age 12 that it was clearly part of a cultural wave building. I also longed for other aspects of plain ol' American culture.

Sometimes they were the furthest from our minds. Mexico City was stimulating, and my father was able to show us the ropes and the sights. We visited Jim Hinton and his family in charming Cuernavaca, where we were reminded a bit our affluent existence in the Hollywood Hills. We were on our way back in our rented car to Acapulco on a dark night when we smashed into a parked truck that had stopped in the two-lane road with no lights. I was amazed that we were all apparently unhurt. Nearby the truck's occupants had a bonfire going, and they didn't even apologize. I thought they, and by extension a lot of Mexicans on the roads, must be incredibly stupid and thoughtless for parking in the highway, but many years later I learned of lead exposure being a severe problem that reduces intelligence. Mexico City in particular suffers from lead, primarily from gasoline. We somehow made it back to Acapulco, where we learned that the police investigating the wreck said the inside of the car looked like a pig had been slaughtered. Such was their attempt to get a major bribe, called *mordida* (bite), but my father knew how to outmaneuver them.

We reluctantly sailed away from Acapulco, which I had found to be quite beautiful and fun. We headed south without the Sewells and with the addition of a young Canadian sailor named Doug Benjafield. I'm not sure why the Sewells had quit, because they did so in a diplomatic fashion. The exotically beautiful Hawaiian Val had become moody to the point that I once went crying to my mother, who advised me to tell Val, "Keep your distance." Val was supposed to be my main teacher for my Calvert School correspondence course for the 8th grade, but the only thing I remember her teaching me was that large papayas we were getting were considered in Hawaii to be "Opala" (garbage). She was also offended by my eating the hard inner core of pineapple. (Psst — kids, this is how to get rid of your teacher!)

A couple of days out from Acapulco one moonless night our crew enjoyed seeing high levels of phosphorescence, a strange but beautiful condition. The white caps and jumping fish were bright green with darkness all around. Looking down into the water near the boat I saw some very large fish or cetaceans, visible by their strong phosphorescence, which I would otherwise not have detected.

Destination: Salina Cruz in the fearsome Gulf of Tehuantepec. We had already seen dismasted vessels from their adventures in

45

that Gulf. It is situated against the Isthmus of Tehuantepec, Mexico's southern region that stretches east and north to the top of the Yucatan. Winds all the way from the U.S. Midwest blow across the Gulf of Mexico and funnel through the Isthmus, out into the Pacific at great velocity more often than not. We eventually had to make a break for it sometime, especially as bleak Salina Cruz had almost no appeal. So off we went in a strong breeze. The first night out saw us in a storm. We stayed relatively close to shore, where waves would not have gotten a chance to build much. We thought we were avoiding sand bars of rivers coming out of Chiapas and Oaxaca. We were able to make progress thanks to our powerful diesel motor and keeping some sail up. I still have the image of my mother and Doug at the bow taking down the jib, with the wave action throwing them up and down. With the spreader lights brightly illuminating the deck, I saw her grab hold of Doug to keep him from rocketing up and over into the black drink. Back in the cockpit we noticed a flashing light out to sea and behind us. It kept on flashing for quite a while, following us, until my father noticed a pattern. He found a table of maritime signals, and the light was found to be giving us a U. He looked this up in another table that indicated U to mean "You are standing into danger." My father flashed the boat following us an acknowledgement, and the light out to sea disappeared as the boat must have turned around. We altered course as well, steering widely of a probable sand bar that had likely shifted from a spot where our chart had marked it. The bravery and selflessness of the unknown fishermen (probably) who saved us made a positive impression on us regarding the Mexican people; it was not the first time.

Our first country after Mexico was El Salvador. We tied up at an exposed pier for big ships at Acajutla. From there we toured the country, learning that six families owned it all. We drove up to Guatemala City. It had some appeal for me for some cosmopolitan culture. My father and I visited Turkish baths. The Guatemalan countryside smelled better than in El Salvador's, where my father joked there was a common drink: "They drink it twice."

Back on the ocean I recall taking a watch with my mother in the middle of the night off Costa Rica. We traded off at the wheel and kept each other company in the cockpit while the others slept below. I don't remember which of us had the canned tomato soup and who had the instant hot chocolate, but it was a bonding experience that I felt other mothers-sons seldom got. In the same part of the world my father and sister were on watch when we came close to being run down by a freighter. The faces of the crew could be seen looking down at our boat. As any yachtsman knows, the big ships never change course; might makes right despite right-of-way rules.

A few days later we pulled into what looked like a perfect anchorage on the chart. It was nighttime, and I believe the radar was working for a change. In the quiet morning where we saw no civilization at all, we heard a small motorboat in the distance. Three men were headed toward us. My father told me, "Jan, get the anchor up. Tell me when it is." I was doing so, stepping on the electric foot switch for the winch, when the *hombres* neared our vessel. Any boatman knows the etiquette that you make a greeting and do not put your hands upon another boat or board without invitation. But as these men lacked these manners, and possibly any good intentions, my father stood up over them as they put their hands on our rail, and bellowed, "Que quieren ustedes?" (What do you want?) Prominently hanging out of his belt in front of his big belly was our huge brass flare gun. These fellows probably had not seen one before, and as they reflexively let go of the railing I shouted "All clear!" and my father put the Passat in gear, and we began to pull away. The *hombres* could have taken us but they held back. Maybe they were nice guys, who knows. Several days later in Panama City we were informed, "Coiba is a prison island!"

In Panama City we went on a U.S. Canal Zone military television talk show, and we were well interviewed about our whole voyage. My only line was "Yeah, I clean the head." (The head means the toilet.) I was too shy to talk about the other stuff I did on the boat, such as crawling into the water tank to scrub it, as I was small enough to get in there. That task wasn't fun, but one takes these things in stride when you have a captain and you're a loyal shipmate.

One day at the yacht club in Panama my mother and I were watching the long pier going out to the big harbor on the Pacific side, and saw my father walking toward us. We were struck at his thinness and ease of step. His belly was still bigger than young men's, but he looked better than ever. My mother and I both knew then and there that our living afloat was good for us all, if Dan

Lundberg lost the gut and would live longer.

Once in Panama at a U.S. government cafeteria, I felt comforted yet homesick when I saw the large stainless steel and chrome milk dispenser. The industrial-agriculture, long-distance shipped, cold product tasted just like home. I realized that only an outpost of U.S. society would have such a fancy and wonderful machine, and it was not something the Latin American countries that we were visiting could or would ever have. I knew I would not see such a machine or that kind of affluence or enjoy such a proud product for a long time hence. I had been weaned on goats milk on our ranch, and my parents later got regular supplies of raw cows milk, so I knew that the pasteurized and homogenized mass-produced milk was unfit for anyone, but on a world cruise by sailboat I sure missed the taste of that milk along with other consumer products that had formed my identity. Levis jeans and rock 'n roll records were probably the top two, and they had of course obtained by shopping with our huge station wagon now sold. This longing for American products as symbolized by industrial, cold mike was the influence of the technological culture on my boyhood consciousness. My industrial mind in boyhood was so firmly formed it would not be fully revealed and undone for decades.

A vivid scene and sound from my Panama days lingers inside me, when hanging around the yacht club in Colón. The rains came like clockwork each afternoon. I saw my first barracudas lurking near the docks. On the juke box was "There But for Fortune" by Joan Baez. The haunting, exquisite song is still with me. I'm amazed to think that this boy would meet her thirty years later when her son Gabe, who was her drummer, introduced me to his mother backstage in Humboldt State University, Arcata, California. The performance had been flawless, yet I was not simply there as a fan — I was there as a father making sure my ten year old daughter got a taste of excellent folk music. My main hope was to get Joan Baez interested in singing a song I had published, "Mother Earth First." I did present it to her, but what sticks in my mind is her approaching me with an unexpectedly sensual glow and palpable beauty.

After passing through the Panama Canal, we sailed to Columbia, the Dutch ABC Islands, St. Thomas and St. Croix. With us was our Mexican sailor Ruben Martinez, whom we called Teddy because he resembled a servant in Hollywood; "Teddy" didn't mind, and was a reliable crewman. My father, possibly fearing pedophile tendencies, stopped him from playing with my cute little brother.

We found ourselves going against the trade winds, having to motor constantly against a near gale. I wish that had been our biggest mistake. For we nearly destroyed ourselves, harming the family forever: we were fed up with having a few cockroaches on the boat, so we sprayed the interior on two occasions, with Shell Oil's pesticide. We soon got reactions of strange sickness. We figured it out: oozing boils and pain meant toxins were going through our bodies and exiting dramatically. This taught us what we already knew about non-organic methods, a hard lesson as my mother was incapacitated. She eventually had to have a tumor removed and a hysterectomy by the time we had sailed to Greece. She never got her full strength back. In 2001 I quoted her in the first *Culture Change* magazine at the front: "Shell Oil is why I don't walk today." She could walk, but not well at all.

Still, there was nothing that could stop us as a family seeing and enjoying the wide world, or so it seemed to me.

Aruba, Bonaire and Curacao were exquisite for their swimming, but other than the turquoise waters these islands were not among the richest in the cultural sense for us to experience. I was intrigued by the local language, Papiamento. The Shell Oil refinery on Curacao was an important stop-off for my father, and we visited by car the execs and their families on their idyllic tropical lagoon south of the main town. A day on the water there was extra lovely, especially with the company of U.S. kids my own age. It was sad to leave, but we had to get east to Bonaire. Our boat was moored just up the coast, and our departure had us heading by the Shell execs' lagoon. The weather started turning bad, so we decided to tuck into the lagoon to anchor and move on the next morning perhaps. Before we could find a spot to anchor a Dutch coast guard boat approached the Passat and ordered us out of the lagoon. My father tried to explain that we needed the shelter due to the weather, but the officer in charge had no patience, and coldly ordered us: "GO NOW!" We did so, reluctantly and with anger. At the next opportunity my father wrote to the Queen of the Netherlands to complain about this shoddy behavior, and he got a nice answer.

From the Netherlands Antilles we crossed the Caribbean northward and visited the U.S. Virgin Islands. I enjoyed the quasi-

U.S. culture to be had. A cute American girl living at the marina where we stayed captivated me as no other girl had, and I embarrassed myself by doting on her while refusing to admit to her little brother (my playmate) that I had a crush on her. I was evidently on the cusp of openly and uncontrollably pursuing girls, about to abandon the tendency to cling to solidarity among boys. At another Virgin island, we were at a public dock where another yacht was near us, whose occupants looked like they enjoyed life a little too much for prudish observers. A dockworker made a remark to my father about their being degenerate sinners. My father, who should have known better than to go along with a stranger's biases, agreed that the other yacht's crew was to be avoided. I saw them getting off their boat in a happy mood. Their dress was quite casual and Bohemian, and the women were sexy. Heaven forbid, maybe they weren't normal scotch drinkers or they made un-American comments on the dock.

Trilby got boyfriends instantly wherever we went, which I could not quite relate to, being pre-pubescent. If my parents thought that taking Trilby out of Hollywood and her series of boyfriends was going to change her life, they were wrong. I was shocked by a spurned lover's slashing his wrist one night at dockside as Trilby and I sat on deck near the bow in the Virgin Islands. He unexpectedly approached the boat with a friend and called out to her just before the knife sliced. She did not move a muscle as the spurt shot high, other than to quote a song to me, "What now my love." He lived, but it wasn't because she took any action. Maybe her pattern of self-gratification influenced me to be a bit cold in the romantic realm as a very young man, which I often was.

We sailed to Bermuda and had hired an additional hired sailor from the U.S. to help (Doug quit in Puntarenas, Costa Rica). The man was in his late 20s and was giving a massage to 16-year-old Trilby on deck one night in the Sargasso Sea when her father discovered this foolishness and broke it up. There was never a word about it afterwards. Only upon recent reflection, it occurs to me that my parents habitually failed in both discipline and wisdom-imparting regarding their artistic, beautiful and spoiled daughter.

After a visit in Hamilton, Bermuda from Dan's Boston working class buddies Stanley Carlson and his brother, we left racist Bermuda behind — the "Darkies" were not allowed in the yacht

club, and they had their own beaches. We were finally off to the
Azores. We spent 18 days at sea, in part because of a fearsome
storm that the U.S. naval base in Bermuda failed to anticipate for us
when we picked their brains for our passage. Besides Teddy for
crew, we had Peter Henderson the Englishman whom we borrowed
from Cunard Lines.

Hurricane Dorothy came on a beautiful afternoon, July 21st, my
sister's 17th birthday. We put up the spinnaker for a change, and it
was fabulous sailing. But the wind gradually strengthened, and
strengthened, until we were down to storm sails. Within two days
we jury-rigged a sea anchor to slow down our descent down steep
waves, the tops of which were breaking due to 70 knot winds. I
calculated the waves to be 39 feet high. We didn't know we were in
a hurricane, so we just hunkered down as usual and did our jobs,
mostly bored. It was a little scary looking down the troughs of the
waves, but our boat, 39 tons, was built for safety. And the 371 GM
diesel never gave out. One of the few concessions to the storm was
that I didn't have to check the oil (not easy with the motion); my
father amazed me by just pouring a quart in every once in a while.

My mother was in a bad way with oozing boils from the
pesticide poisoning, and the rest of the family had milder
symptoms. My father's hand was very swollen and red. I had one
boil after another on my hip, and still have the scars today. My
mother could not move; her pain was so great. I know this because
if I touched my leg or bumped it, my boil on my hip would create
spasms of hurt. Nevertheless, the main task I had when I wasn't
conferring with my father on navigation or adjustments to our
storm sails, was to amuse myself with drawing or reading.

My 8th grade correspondence course was really "Micky Mouse"
so I had to pursue other mental stimulation. During my first year
at sea I drew quite a few diagrams of ranch houses, yards, orchards
and bodies of water. I also made up baseball statistics, imagining
team members' accomplishments that broke records in hitting and
pitching. I pictured myself as a team member. Other times I read
the World Book Encyclopedia, reading about farms, for example.
We had several good books for a 13 or 14 year old lad, and a decent
library as well. I read about sharks, solo circumnavigations, and
baseball. [When I read on Aug. 21, 2010 the news story of Laura
Dekker, age 14, setting off on a round-the-world sail, I can totally
relate: I wanted to do it too at that age, and felt I could be ready

soon.]

My daydreams for my whole 14th year were mainly of sailing in the South Seas, swimming in lagoons behind coral reefs, and not being afraid of sharks (which by now I wasn't terribly). Too bad we had headed the wrong direction, failing to benefit from trade winds, because my parents were Eurocentric. We could have first hit the Marquesas, Tahiti and innumerable islands with their tropical fruits, fresh fish, stupendous swimming, diving without scuba gear, and canoeing. I wanted nothing more — living in that way was all I desired. Despite my infatuation in the Virgin Islands, girls were not on my short list, as I had not quite hit puberty.

After the hurricane was over, one night Teddy who was on watch woke up my father to tell him we were over a shoal, according to the waves and the depth finder. We all had to pass it off as either erroneous or an uncharted mystery of the Atlantic. I think Teddy would have had more credibility if he did not regularly play the drunken sailor in port. During his almost one year with us, upon docking he would prepare himself for a night on the town by greasing his hair into a bright, slick pompadour, put on clean clothes, and go out drinking and looking for sex. We only knew what a night he had when he came back drunk or badly hung over the next morning, in a taxi. His practice was to ride in a cab all night, spend all his money, such that he was broke and my father had to pay for the cab. Teddy didn't say much, but one thing he was good for was keeping our Spanish up. This served me well over the years, off and on, for I barely studied the language formally.

I was so glad to spy the Azores' volcanic peaks on my 14th birthday after 18 days at sea. The Azores were charming, friendly, and beautiful. At Horta de Faial, our landfall, we saw the same villagers in a picture from a book we had, *Half Safe*, by Ben Carlin (about an amphibious boat that passed through the Azores). They were extremely kind, and showed us the lovely volcanic crater high above their small town. Even more mind-blowing to me was the long ascent past high banks of hydrangeas. We had many tour guides, all full of hospitality. They wanted nothing from us but our company, perhaps in part because of the sameness of the days and years they had in their paradise. I toured the whaling station after a hunt that our Peter Henderson went on overnight. At the scene of the carving of whale parts I stepped over a massive blob of flesh, and was told it was the penis. Another memorable trip was to the island nearby, Pico. I climbed up most of the way up the volcano, in awe of the scenery. I was hoping to get onto the U.S. military base on Terceira so I could buy some American clothes and drink cold U.S. milk. We chose not to make it to that island, and I'm glad now we didn't, for I so appreciated what we did: visiting Azorean villages, enjoying the beaches, seeing the wild, semi-cultivated hillsides, and participating in Punta Delgado's busy town promenades at the end of each day on the island of São Miguel. We met families who sadly had their young men forced to go to war in Portuguese colonial Africa. We visited a docked Pakistani freighter where we were treated to a fine lunch, and the kindness of the crew is still with me.

What turned out to be a four-and-a-half-year voyage outside the U.S., missing the 1960s' turmoil and hippie revolution at home, gave us a unique exposure to the world, with much togetherness on our ship. My brother and I went to mainly European schools, fulfilling a dream of our parents — how high could we climb? I sometimes suspected that my father in particular wanted to see us consorting with the aristocracy and other bits of la crème de la crème such as great artists. This came true somewhat, such as meeting the Swingle Singers, a jazzy classical group in Rome after their concert. (One of them does a great job on the Procol Harum album from 1973, Grand Hotel.) In the arts Dan attained his objectives, especially as Svengali or impresario for his Trilby. He was always active, planning, and accomplishing. To avoid being a total drain on the business back in Hollywood, my father did a little oil industry consulting and kept tabs on the family survey business.

On the entire cruise I joined in all the navigation and sailing decisions with my father, even though I was only 13 for the greatest distance of it. It was in my interest to survive, and he was a loving and fun dad most of the time. Our efforts were made especially worthwhile whenever, for example, we made landfall. If you're a sailor, you know the satisfaction of dropping anchor in a secure anchorage, or tying up at a well positioned dock, and being able to disembark and explore your conquest. The land always rocked under your feet a bit at first. If I had to pick one place that sticks in my mind as perfect, I would say Portofino, Italy, where we were in August 1967.

On the way to Gibraltar in September 1966 we hit another bad storm with no name, almost as bad as the hurricane. A few days later, going through the Pillars of Hercules, I felt a kind of historic and ancient vibe.

It had taken us a year to sail from Catalina to Gibraltar. The town and Rock were interesting — anyone had to admit it. One of my first experiences there was to view a den of wild Barbary apes. I can still see a dominant male, between grabbing quickies with females (apes, not humans), seizing my *Mad* magazine. I could not give up that vestige of Americana, so I grabbed it back. He got quite angry, looking me in the eyes from less than two feet away. Fortunately, he decided to let this go, and my face was spared a possible rearranging.

I entered British Grammar School, a year behind because my correspondence course was not up to snuff. Enjoying English and Gibraltarian friends, and spelunking in the Rock of Gibraltar, walking the streets and buying goodies, I was a happy laddie. But strange things happen even in idyllic days and places: my mother occasionally flew off the handle, which my father said was from "the change of life" (menopause). One of my biggest troubles in Gibraltar was that I had bought a light blue jacket or anorak, finding that my schoolmates in the all-boy school were puzzled over my choosing a "girl's color."

My father wrote a novel in Gibraltar, *A Hurricane Makes You Think*, based on our sailing and travel experiences. However, his literary agent in New York said it could never sell because it had been written with the concern of the author for what his children might think of it — where was the sex, etc.?

My father worked on journalism and the book on the boat while we had an apartment in town. When writing his book, he often listened to the Beatles' Hard Day's Night on our 8-track stereo on board. We also had some of Trilby's classical albums, some jazz, and the Surfaris. I inadvertently taught "Wipe Out" to some British boys who heard me hum it and pound out the drum solo without any drums. With one of them, Steven Odgear, I alternated being the boyfriend of the lovely Cheryl. The only thing I can remember her saying to me was "That bloody well hurt!" Well, we were finding ourselves, along with Steven's little brother Gerald who was on top of Jennifer, next to us on Jennifer's living room floor. We were all clothed. We all got along great, especially after I adopted a "to-ally Bri-ish" accent. I had "Gibbo" friends too, who were rather hip with their "hipster" pants. Everybody's favorite songs seemed to be "Black is Black" and "Yellow Submarine."

Trilby's old boyfriend Alban back in Hollywood sent her a 45 record and an album that arrived on The Rock in fall of 1966. The group was Love, and I already knew Alban was the drummer. I was impressed with the single "7 and 7 Is" and I was sure the voices were yelling "Hey Jan!" I found it hard to believe the vocals were not by Alban. He was the group's drummer on their first album (and keyboardist on their second), and Alban is one of the only surviving members of that celebrated interracial psychedelic-folk-rock group.

From Gibraltar it was time for the Lundbergs to resume the round-the-world voyage and fulfill one of its main purposes: to stick Darius and me in a fancy French boarding school. I knew a little French from my Gibraltarian tutor. My parents found L'Ecole des Roches, "the best school in France," in Normandy. My father and I first flew to London, took a day's tour with a private car and driver, and went off to Paris. We saw the sights and eventually made for Normandy. After treating Mrs. Dassonville, the school's Maitresse, to some restaurant trout, discussions were concluded and I was accepted at the school. After a short intervening time back in Gibraltar, Darius and I dutifully went off to be lonely boys. Darius was put in a part of the school for younger boys about a mile away on a country lane from my "House" (Maison) called Le Valon.

The school was and is just outside Verneuil-sur-Avre on 148 landscaped acres, with several large Maisons serving as dormitories. All Houses met at the main House for meals and teatime. It took me some getting used to; almost everything done was different from what I knew. For example, I finally learned I had to go to a village to buy some jam so that I could be like the other boys with their personal jars in a cupboard in the large tea room at Le Valon. This House also had the physical-education locker rooms, showers, and large alcove where we students were called out to receive letters from home (although the school was our home). There was one other American boy in the school, whose last name was Buchanan, a friendly enough sort who was into the Electric Prunes. Many of the boys liked "A Whiter Shade of Pale" enough to hum that new hit. A boy named Carlos was

none other than my playmate from Acapulco a year and a half
before. But he soon became unfriendly at L'Ecole des Roches,
probably as part of his attempt to become Frenchified. My brother
and I spoke unpardonably poor French. But Carlos may have
instead picked up on the idea that French boys shouldn't like
Americans because of the Vietnam War.

It was here that I was awakened politically. I was asked by my
dormitory leader Michel Blanc, "Que penses-tu de la guerre au
Vietnam?" (What do you think of the war in Vietnam?) I replied,
"Je n'aime pas la guerre." He retorted, kindly enough, "Il n'y a
personne qui aime la guerre." In other words, English words, I was
not being let off by saying I didn't like war, because Michel was
pointing out, "Nobody likes war." I realized that I had to be against
what the U.S. was doing in Vietnam, but I knew almost nothing
about it. His not letting me off easy taught me that a discussion
on sensitive subjects of great import has to sometimes be
relentless.

In my dorm was Louis Dani from Corsica. He was getting it on
with a maid at a teacher's home, although he was just 14. He tried
to set me up with her — a good looking woman of about 20 — but
I passed. Chalk it up to being a slower-maturing Scandinavian
blooded boy compared to the quicker-maturing Mediterranean
lads. Louis invited me to come to Corsica for the summer but I
passed on that too, which I eventually realized was a mistake. I'm
sure I would have lost my virginity under his excellent tutelage,
while enjoying great beaches and Corsican food and music. But I
knew that the French and Italian Rivieras were ahead for me.

Missing our mother badly in boarding school, my brother and I
were glad the family drove up to visit us from Marseilles. Our
mother was ensconced in the village at a hotel on the main square,
and Dan and Trilby returned to the boat where a crew from
Gibraltar awaited. Darius thenceforth stayed with my mother in
the village, partly because he had had the mumps at school. I had
tried to get the nursing staff to allow him to fast, but after some
days of my trying to bring this about the nurses explained to me
that the kid was eating willingly, ignoring my efforts by deceiving
me that he would fast. This was one of my first times in life where
I tried to bring about or force something for which I was quite in
the minority, and failed.

My mother's presence was delightful, and we enjoyed the

French country-village atmosphere. The Idaho farm girl had come a long way! She was somewhat ill from the pesticide poisoning on the boat, but she was a fully devoted mother and was able to enjoy being so in a charming locale. On the square outside our hotel, near the cathedral, was the regular outdoor market. It wasn't the first such market I had seen, but I began to appreciate its dependability and the vendors' unique sausages and cheeses.

When the trimester was over we hired a car to take us to the Passat in Cannes.

Upon arriving in town I saw my first long-haired hippie guy, and his mane was a shock that attracted and intrigued me immensely. However, more on my mind than meeting funky travelers was water skiing, canoeing, and ordering fancy food with my passable French. The summer of 1967 on the French and Italian Riviera included a visit from Jimmy Fields in Cannes. My sister performed Mozart at Monaco's outdoor Palace court, and it went well. Nevertheless, Yehudi Menuhin's pianist-sister Hepzibah gave Trilby an evaluation my father requested, based on a recital on the Passat's excellent piano. My father and Trilby were not pleased that Hepzibah basically said, "The kid doesn't have it." I felt the disappointment too, but I was happy-go-lucky. I treasured Sgt. Pepper's Lonely Hearts Club Band that my sister gave to me for my 15th birthday in Monte Carlo. We had a good record player for the stereo system on the boat.

We sailed along to the Italian Riviera, bound for Rome's port Fiumicino, for my enrollment in an American day school. On the way we enjoyed San Remo, Genoa, Portofino, Livorno, and Porto Santo Stefano. We hit Rome's Via Veneto and found an elegant pensione nearby. Right away I was off each weekday through Rome's northern suburbs to the Overseas School of Rome, a kindergarten-through-twelfth-grade private school. There I skipped up to my grade/age level. That I had missed ninth grade was meaningless then and forever. We soon found an apartment that was near the Vatican. Our landlord was singer Emilio Pericoli who had the hit Al Di La. Our next door neighbor was a pop star called Little Tony; our young but old-looking maid was quite impressed. This tiny young woman with the salty, raspy voice and dark, southern Italian skin made an impression on me when she showed up once with a black eye. Her husband had done it, the first time I had witnessed the results of domestic violence. I guess my mother's giving my father a black eye once in the Caribbean, when he was too drunk to sail responsibly, gave me the idea that it wasn't such a big deal because he was a man and so much bigger and stronger than she. But a man hitting a woman? Good god.

During the period between summers we seldom saw our sailboat (by then she was like a family member or protective spirit) tied up way down the Tiber River. Fiumicino wasn't an ugly town, even with huge water rats, and dead cows and used condoms floating down the river. We had a Norwegian sailor living on the Passat who had been recruited in Gibraltar. Reidar Lutnes was an iron Viking who didn't talk a lot, except to say to me whenever he saw a female in my age bracket "Therrre's a girl for yeeeewww." Fiumicino is where my father and his new assistant Vincenzo Daniele taught me to ride my new compact motorcycle. I accidentally rode it slowly up a dog's back as he (or she) walked in front of me, and I can still see its expression as it looked pleadingly into my eyes. Miraculously, the dog wasn't hurt. The end of that session was lightened by enjoying on the street a vendor's raw mussels with fresh squeezed lemon juice.

My year in Rome was no more than okay, as I made the mistake of gravitating toward certain popular American kids instead of being open to wonderful Italians I didn't bother to know. On my motorcycle I ran around Rome, but this didn't make me popular. And it was dangerous; I got in two minor wrecks that, surprisingly, now that I think about it, didn't bother my parents at all. I felt I needed the Italjet 50cc bike because many kids in my school had motorcycles, although mostly older kids. I longed to fit in well with the American kids, but I was an oddball who had sailed from California. I would have preferred to be like them, having parents who were bureaucrats or in some part of the military. One of the popular boys was named Charlie Band, who became a Hollywood filmmaker of horror movies. He married a stunning girl of our grade named Hermida. When I ran into her ten years later in Hollywood at the old Erewhon health food store, she barely acknowledged me; she only wanted to know if I knew the location of her old flame, our friend from our school, Jim Alpert.

I met Xenia Anagnostopoulou, whom I was to marry, in Overseas School of Rome. I can still remember sitting next to her by chance, during our 10th grade first-day orientation when we were 15 years old, and asking her name. Translation of first name:

"hospitality" or "foreigner"; last name: "belonging to Anagnostopoulos." Her exotic beauty and name weren't a bad beginning for me at the OSR, although we didn't hang out that year. Our high school romance began a year later when we coincidentally ended up in the same high school in Greece.

I wasn't sad to leave Rome at the beginning of the summer of '68 to sail to Yugoslavia. It was there that I first realized that a place like Dalmatia, not Hollywood or the U.S.A., was the kind of stomping ground for me. I looked up an Overseas School of Rome classmate of mine, in little, quiet Cavtat, south of Dubrovnik. I can still see beautiful Melitza stretched out in her bathing suit as her 45 of Jimmy Hendrix's "Stone Free" came to life with its sensuous cowbell. Her other favorite song was The Tremeloes' "Silence is Golden."

I no longer wanted to go back to the States! My realization came while riding my motorbike back from Melitza's to Dubrovnik — it hit me that I was probably having a better time than my friends whom I left behind in California. I was in a better world filled with charm: the rail tramway from the yacht fiord to Dubrovnik, the Trappist cheese, Slivovic wine, musicians and intellectuals visiting us on our boat — the list goes on. One evening as we strolled giddily through Dubrovnik's ancient main street (car free), my father started chanting a drunken "Slobodna China! Slobodna China!" simply because it sounded like "slow boat to China." Our Dalmatian friend explained to us that surrounding pedestrians thought the concept interesting: "Freedom to China" was what my father was obliviously spouting. This was one of his more harmless bouts of Scandinavian benders.

We were a little nervous to be in Yugoslavia in August 1968 because Soviet tanks had invaded Czechoslovakia and snuffed out Prague Spring. What we could learn about Yugoslavia impressed us, and we hoped it could endure.

Jimmy Fields visited us again, and while on board with conductor Zubin Mehta, my father asked Jimmy, "So you played with Mr. Mehta." Jimmy blushed and stammered to clarify that it had not actually happened. At any rate, it was a great summer of music and new friends. Trilby gave a good recital in Dubrovnik in a fine old building with a good crowd. She made a friend that kept in touch for years, Jasna Golub. Darius, our 11 year old blond darling, had met Jasna first on Dubrovnik's harbor-beach and brought her all the way home to the boat to our fjord moorage north of the city.

I was seeing one great country after another as a sailor and student of culture, and the U.S. was not stacking up well in my mind. How can you beat trying up your sailboat to an island's pine trees (on the way to near Split), and having a lamb roasted over a spit next to the boat, and the next morning exploring the island on your motorbike? There was endlessly more to notice, and compare.

At Split's annual pop festival at Diocletian's palace, I learned something about police and resisting them: an Italian pop star was being let in through a crowd of fans to the main hall, passing through a metal gate. As he entered, the guard in uniform was too rough on an innocent fan, so the Italian took the cop (or the soldier) by his shirt and pushed him up against the wall in a flash while uttering a warning. The crowd cheered as the Italian walked away in disgust toward his backstage dressing room. I had the feeling that the locals or the whole nation was somewhat under the thumb of uniformed thugs.

In Rome I had seen drivers, male and female, cuss out cops with impunity when traffic conditions were being worsened by traffic cops. It strikes me that the Italians in general don't take any shit from anyone on a given day, compared to today's U.S. population living in fear of a getting a ticket or a beating.

The end of the summer of '68 was encroaching. As the Suez Canal's closing the year before caught us up in the Mediterranean, preventing our circumnavigation, we sailed to Greece where surely another English speaking school existed for the boys. Trilby didn't have to go to school, and never did graduate high school. None of us thought there was anything wrong with that, considering the education we were getting as we continued to see the world. Her piano lessons and performing continued, but as a sort of typical teenage American girl she was mainly a romantic and often promiscuous. Her volatility and temper might have seemed rather artistic at the time, when our parents appeared to condone her behavior and did not clamp down. Her mother didn't control her at all, partly because of illness from the pesticides. (My mother's health was still so-so as we left Dalmatia.) Dan Lundberg seemed volatile with his daughter, as he was with others, but somehow he must have coddled and spoiled her. One of my ex-wives observed in the mid 1980s that he inflated her self-importance.

Our ketch gave Albania a wide berth, as we were wary of getting impounded by the most notorious Communist nation to mariners. Along the way my father entered into a depression and treated me to verbal abuse and coldness for a few days; why, exactly, I never knew. Accepting the bad with the good was my lot, just as other boys in the region had to do things like lead a mule through their village when they might have preferred to go for a swim.

I took an instant liking to Greece; the whole family did. The people were even more friendly than the Italians. Corfu was okay; nothing compared to Dalmatia. We kept on sailing, through the Gulf of Corinth where we pulled into Patras. The lack of vegetation in Greece, so far as I had seen, at first was uninviting. But my parents' gratitude toward an old man who cashed a check for them in Patras impressed me, as well, as to the potential for kindness and acceptance.

Our idyllic life was going well, despite our concern over Mama's health. I was on top of the world in Greece: I had friends who'd lived in Afghanistan, Iran, France, and I was at liberty to go anywhere and do anything without supervision. I made my way to nude beaches on Greek Islands by age 17; my parents didn't care where I was, as I was trusted. I sampled the wines, the girls, the languages, and tried to monitor the anti-war movement and psychedelic art back in what I would soon regard as the imperialist homeland. I didn't want to return to the States, having already reached that liberating decision. The English-speaking high school I attended and the jet-setting social circle I enjoyed were exhilarating, while I learned languages and believed I would always taste the delicacies of life.

We first lived in Kifissia, a lovely suburb near Athens on the way to Marathon. *Kifissia* had become a famous retreat of philosophers during the reign of the Roman emperor Hadrian. For my 11th and 12th grades I went to the American Community Schools, situated toward Athens in an area called Xalandri. There I was glad to run into Xenia whom I'd met in Rome. Her father Theodosios Anagnostopoulos had retired from the Greek diplomatic corps in protest when the fascist colonels took over his country. I began seeing a lot of his daughter, Xenia, but he did not like boys coming around with flowers in their hair as my friend (and Xenia's) Peter Blood and I once did. Theodosios's wife and children seemed to be afraid of his dower, authoritarian manner. But many years later after his divorce he was a lot nicer to me and to everyone in his family, and offered me a valuable dowry when I eventually married his daughter. I declined the dowry because I would have had to convert to Greek Orthodox Christianity, and I wanted his daughter to own the property instead. He was extremely happy when we presented him with a granddaughter in 1980. Zephyr is our daughter's middle name, after my mother's childless sister; by chance it's a Greek word.

In our Greek-American high school, at first Xenia and I didn't know anybody else. We played Jumpin' Jack Flash on her portable 45 record player on the school grounds, and everyone left us alone. Along with her charming younger sister Katy we soon hooked up with some American Embassy kids, enjoying the pool and other amenities of Ambassador Talbot's residence. Xenia's and my romance was brief, but afterwards we kept the same circle of friends. (Xenia and I of course rekindled the romance, got married, divorced, and are friends today; this summer of 2010 I received a packet of Greek music CDs from her from Athens. Next time, Xenia, please try harder for instrumental Zambetas!)

In 1969 for our family's lovely villa household (*ecos*) in Vouliagmeni southeast of Piraeus we had a nanny from Ireland, Olive Hannon, later Olive Bozorghmehr. Her job was to help my family members in general fashion while my mother recovered from surgery for a tumor and hysterectomy in Athens. My mother's plight and recovery seemed thankfully brief, so I was able to just enjoy my Halcyon days. Our villa was above the beautiful bay, and at night I could hear the wavelets breaking on the shore not far below. I used the dugout canoe and went waterskiing in our Zodiac skiff with the 20-horse outboard. The Passat was at a charming nearby marina where a small restaurant made wonderful kalamarakia and other simple dishes. Behind the marina was a tiny, pretty cove where a Greek friend taught me to catch small shrimp from the tidal pool and put them into our mouths to eat on the spot. A luxury hotel, the Astir Palace, was around the bend. It was there a friend of mine named Henney (or Henny) saw Brigit Bardot on the beach and said to her, in French, "You've never had a vision." Maybe she already had; she became an animal rights activist. Perhaps he couldn't think of anything more profound to say, while hoping he would be rewarded by not saying the obvious,

"Bon dieu, tu est belle!"

One family voyage to the Greek islands Hydra and Spetses in spring of 1969 took us through the waters of the Battle of Salamis where the Greeks defeated the Persians. Off the island of Poros, just south of the Saronic Gulf, we had a close call. Sailing along on a splendid afternoon, well away from land, we were jarred when the Passat's keel hit ground. My friend Chuck Wertime was most of the way up the main mast, sitting on the spreaders, and the impact almost knocked him off to fall to the deck. The boat stopped abruptly, leaned, and stayed leaned over. My father, who was in command, was drunk as a skunk on ouzo. I have always blamed him for the accident, but now that I think about it I wonder what a sand bar was doing far from land where there were no rocks or buoys. I have to blame myself for being too relaxed and not checking the charts and our position carefully enough. In a short time a large motor yacht came by to help us. We threw them a line and they pulled us off. We were on our way, putting Poros behind us, when a naval skiff caught up with us. Without permission, three officers boarded. They ordered us to turn back and follow them to port, and I knew it was because the motor yacht owner wanted to claim possession under international marine law of salvage. However, we were uncooperative. My father was still drunk and was probably useless and intimidating to talk with. Our Greek friend Vasili Condoyannis (now a successful chandler, broker and charterer) was at the wheel, but he would not let go of it as ordered, even when an officer tried to wrest it from Vasili's strong hands. One of the officers spoke to my sister, a big mistake. She let him have it on the face with a hard slap without a word. After a while, as we were continuing on our way and taking the skiff and its crew far from Poros, the intruders gave up and got in their boat and went home. I don't remember if they had guns, but I know that elsewhere in the world such as the U.S. we would have had guns pulled on us. The next day in Hydra my father and I went to visit the motor yacht's owner to thank him, but he would not deign to show himself.

Later that year was an event that shaped me just as much, although at the time it seemed like just another day in Greece with my father and school buddies:

World renowned architect and town planner Constantinos A. Doxiadis was to give a luncheon talk in a downtown Athens

hotel ballroom. On that autumn 1969 day, students of our high
school economics class (taught by Prof. Econopouly, of course)
went to hear Doxiadis. My father had spoken of him for years so it
was great we could go hear him. The talk was interesting enough,
and in those days everyone was in awe of computers — one of
Doxiadis' cutting-edge specialties. But my father stood up at the
end, causing me to go pale in embarrassment, and asked a question
of Doxiadis. It was something like, "Aren't you condoning or
contributing to the industrial destruction of the planet by paving
over nature? Don't we need a little nature?"

It was a heartfelt and reasonable question, I realized right then,
characteristic of my father partly for its strangeness. (Doxiadis'
answer seemed to me off the mark.) That was my old man, way
ahead of his time. His questioning a great man influenced me to
think independently for myself as well, challenging conventional
wisdom or even the progressive wing of the status quo. Very few
kids' fathers were similarly engaged with society. I had forgotten
this event for over four decades, until just before this book was
going to print. Clearly, my father's question to Doxiadis,
remaining in the far reaches of my mind, was a seed for my later
sentiments and career.

❧

By the time our Hellenic adventure was getting going in 1968,
we had started receiving disturbing letters from Guy in
Hollywood. He wanted no more interference in running the family
business as we were "gallivanting around the Mediterranean with
cancer" (an inaccurate reference to his step-mother). In 1969 I was
faced with my father's needing to return with all of us. I stayed
until February 1970, and until then I made the best of my
disappointment by envisioning L.A. as the center of Western
Culture and the growing counterculture. What with Hollywood's
film industry and rock groups like The Doors, Steppenwolf,
Canned Heat, and Iron Butterfly, it wouldn't be so bad to live in a
major fount of radical creativity. Before my return to the U.S. I
made excursions on my own in the Eastern Mediterranean. I
appreciated immensely the foods, music, all kinds of spices, and
sights — not a bad time for a 17-year-old on his own. My
escapades were made easier by my father's absence, as he and my

sister returned to L.A. in November 1969. My mother didn't bother to get his approval for my wide travels, and he stated a bit after the fact calmly enough that he didn't approve.

My mother, brother and I had left the Vouliagmeni villa and moved back to Kifissia. We lived in the Hotel Cecil, an old fashioned elegant place with fine food and a kind manager, George Petrov. He admired my mother, and once took us all to Delphi where the pagan oracle dwelt.

Reluctantly letting go of my beloved Greece of 1 1/2 years — despite its having a fascist dictatorship at the time — I made my college applications for the U.S. If I could have remained behind by myself I would have, but I was too shy to recruit any friends' families for a foster home. So I landed in New York in February with my mother and brother.

It was a fiasco as the pressure change during the flight caused my nose to bleed. This set off a long illness exacerbated by U.S. smog. At the airport my mother had an oily mess due to her cherished Greek olive oil bottles breaking. I was startled that I had accidentally brought in undetected some hemp seeds — they were sold in Greece as bird seed, and my friends and I got a kick out of seeing the marijuana-relative planted in places such as the American Embassy.

But what about the Passat, our faithful, stalwart home? On an autumn day in 1969 my father called me up at school in Athens and said "Spiro didn't make it. Do you want to sail with me and Trilby to Malta?" I said "Sure," and I hopped a cab for the coast. On this voyage we had the help of a Greek Navy officer as crewmember. One night I came up into the cockpit in the moonlight when he was on watch. Suddenly I had to grab the wheel from him, as he was steering almost right into the lighthouse we told him to steer toward; I saw rocks in the swells near the boat in the moonlight as we plowed along at 7 knots. My father told me it was a wonder the officer did not get more mad at me than he did. I was amazed that a Navy man could be so stupid on the sea.

We almost sunk the next day too. My father and I were relaxing on deck lying down next to the fore cabin's hatch when my father happened to look down into the cabin, and shouted "Jesus Christ!" The officer had left the fore cabin's toilet valve open, and water had filled up the cabin almost to the battery bank under the bunk. We pumped the water out. The real crisis was, my father explained, that if the water had reached the batteries there would have been a chemical reaction to create mustard gas, and we would not have been able to stop the water from flooding in all the way to the deck.

We steered erroneously southward and were nearer to Africa than Malta. So we corrected course northward on that calm hazy day. Landfall and docking must have been uneventful, because the next scene in my memory banks is seeing the island's museum with Crusaders' suits of armor. The Crusaders were evidently small men compared to most Europeans today.

The best thing about Malta, I decided, with its atrocious cuisine, was that John and Yoko Lennon's "Give Peace A Chance" was on the air and in the air. We flew back to Greece, having been preceded by our Greek officer who left us tearfully and with gratitude (which my father and I really couldn't fathom, when we were just glad to see him go).

So the Passat had moved to what I assumed to be a better long-term port prior to our family's return to the U.S. I hated for us to quit the Med, but Guy was acting up back in L.A. He wanted Dan and Mesa to shut up and stay away from the business that Dan was still president of. Wrong thing to pull with Dan Lundberg! Once back to L.A. he never returned to Greece. Taking Trilby was probably a bad idea, considering that the culture that she was re-entering was what the whole (aborted) trip around the world was largely for: to get away from its influence. Looking back, I don't know that the whole voyage did Trilby any lasting good, but she did pull her weight on board. I didn't mind hearing her perform Sunken Cathedral on the ship's piano.

I visited Istanbul and Palestine and Israel at the end of 1969. Outstanding trips at the age of 17, as if I were an adult, served to eventually set me apart in my mind from most people I met who were more stationary and less daring. I discovered with my friend Chuck in Istanbul how glorious it was to see the ancient city's sights and sample the food (even better than Greek, we agreed). Negotiating the selling of my tape recorder in the Bazaar, sitting on a traveler's eye-glasses by mistake, running into hostile Marxists on a bus — all these experiences opened my eyes.

When I went to Palestine and Israel, the trip was largely funded by my high school's Archeological Society I had co-founded. The club was a joke, serving to create a good looking affiliation on college applications. But as we had made money selling hard-to-get Coca-Cola to Greeks, and the semester was over, with no one interested in making an archeological field trip, I made a one-man trip to another ancient land with the cash. I rode a freighter from Piraeus. As Cream sang in Tales of Brave Ulysses, "You thought the leaden winter would bring you down forever / But you road upon a steamer to the violence of the sun." It was a wild voyage with nice people on the freighter, mainly funky travelers a few years older than I. The old freighter's public address system played Everyone's Gone to the Moon. One woman at dinner seemed promising for possible intimate times in the evening, but when she rose from her chair, with difficulty, it was clear her legs were badly damaged and deformed. I became speechless and embarrassed at the unspoken understanding we had: I was no longer interested in her physically.

After landing in Haifa, two fellow passengers and I agreed to first visit Nazareth. There some Arabic men walked up to us and said, pointing to one of my companion's long brown hair, "Manson. Manson." That was all the English they knew, so there was no point telling them how peaceful we were. In those days in much of the world, whether a young man was peaceful or not was not as important as the length of hair and the presence of a beard.

From there I took a bus to the actual Walls of Jericho, although like with almost all ancient sites they are built upon by less ancient structures. Thanks to a contact in Greece, I obtained a scholarly Catholic priest's kindness in the form of a personal guided tour all day of the ancient sections of Jerusalem. Except for my first night's stay in a fleabag hotel called the Columbia, I stayed in the Casa Nova, a religious hotel in old Jerusalem. I went out of the gates of the old city one evening to see a movie, Ice Station Zebra, but was not allowed to leave the theater before the show ended: my way was blocked by a soldier in uniform with a gun. His job was to make sure the moviegoers left all at once, and not before the end of the show. This was a problem for me, as the Casa Nova's curfew was upon me. I had to wait, but fortunately I was able to gain admittance through the gates and to my hotel. I vastly preferred the old city to new Jerusalem in every way (except for a modern movie).

I went to Bethlehem where I was most impressed not by the tourist spot, having to do with the famous manger, but by the clay

oven in the town plaza where local pita bread was being made by
one baker. He just stood on the dirt in the open. It tasted so good.
Years later I thought of this "bakery" as a model of efficiency,
simplicity and sharing, whereas modern consumers don't share
their ovens and thereby waste much energy.

It was on a bus on the way to Tel Aviv, New Year's Eve 1969,
that I had to bid the groovy 1960s (and my exalted family's status,
it turned out) goodbye in favor of the dreary, less enlightened
1970s and the family troubles that started to smack us harder and
harder.

Within six weeks I was back in Hollywood, feeling lonesome for
my friends in Greece, as well as alienated and non-American. I
wanted no part of a lifestyle that lessened my freedom that I had
enjoyed in Greece, even though we drove no cars there. In L.A., as
anyone knows, daily and nightly life was and is about driving cars,
but I resigned myself to my "new" surroundings and followed my
glorious family in its ways. Guy had gone to UCLA, so I assumed I
should go there too. (Oy veh!, as it turned out.) The schools that
my friends and I discussed back in Athens were not nearly so
appealing to me as UCLA, but then I knew very little. My parents
didn't care where I went to college of if I went at all — they were
above formal education, it seemed.

After some months I could not wait to get my driver's license.
I took my first long road trip in the Fiat my father had gotten in
Rome and had shipped to Greece before importing it to L.A. My
destination was Arcata, California in the coastal redwood forest.
Highway 101 was still a country road, with a lot of ancient huge
redwoods around. Near Arcata I visited Trilby and her first
husband Alan Garber, who both lived in a communal house rental
where a sail boat was being built for a voyage they did not take.
The household had little else to do but to cook, smoke Humboldt
herb, and listen to Buffalo Springfield. Trilby, to the
disappointment of my parents who tried everything to keep her in
L.A., was living as a non-political hippie. She was sweet to me and
I appreciated her and Alan's showing me the stupendous seashore
of the region. When I got back to L.A. my carefree, traveling
youth was basically over from then on, although I did not know it.
If my parents or anyone else I trusted had pointed it out, I would
have rebelled. I was not afraid of work, but it had to be
meaningful in a political and cultural way.

❧

It is fitting that I write this chapter while a 1960s-format radio station in Portland, Oregon covers the hits for my nostalgic ears. "Lightening Striking Again" (Lou Christie) is one song I imagine that captured my late half-brother Guy's feelings of lust and his part in the sex-crazed youth culture.

❧

When I visited Guy at the family business prior to his final departure in early 1970, he told me that he represented revolution whilst our father represented the Establishment. I had been studying Marxism, so I thought my brother was a superficial revolutionary at best since he just wanted capitalistic control. He didn't bother to hang out with me, which I would have liked to do if he asked. But he was caught up in his Yuppie world, self absorbed, and I didn't feel he had much to teach me except to occasionally show how clever he felt he was.

Dan, with the help of his daughter Dana as a stockholder in our family-business, had beaten back a stock ownership/board of directors challenge from Guy. I was disturbed and saddened that two people I admired and loved, my father and brother, were at odds. It was a lesson to me that for some people, namely Guy Lundberg, money and power were more important than loving and supporting the family. My victorious father then transitioned into day-to-day management again, which ultimately drove him to an early grave. For his health my father might have done better to let go of the company and his ego to go into writing full time, if it had been financially feasible (which I did not know). Without the family business under Dan Lundberg's firm control, we might not have been able to buy the fancy house with the pool that we were soon to move into. It was sold to us by Derwood Kirby (of Candid Camera television show fame), and was in the Hollywood Hills above Universal Studios: 3347 Bonnie Hill Drive.

I had lost respect for Guy because I had heard he engineered a strictly optional divorce from the charming Kathleen McCarthy, mother of their cute kid Erik. My father's and Guy's falling out lasted several years, while Guy fared well as a computer consultant using the name Lundberg Research. The oil industry in those days did not like the idea of a family schism, but after a few years, with all Dan's other children helping out at the business, the disgraceful crisis involving Number One Son was forgotten. Who would have thought that years later it would be far surpassed in another family-fight? But society had changed enough by 1986 onward, when my father died, to just pass off what was happening in our family. So the oil people we dealt with could just ignore a disgraceful changing of the guard.

Back in 1970 before the disturbing schism became final I had looked up to my older brother, enough to try to enroll at his *alma mater* UCLA. My scholastic record barely allowed it: in the SAT exams I scored like a girl: high verbal score, lower math score. Through tutoring I had achieved a math score of 503, while the threshold for the UC system was 500. At my Hollywood High graduation, at Hollywood Bowl (sitting next to the late Janet LaLanne, daughter of television's Jack), I hadn't the coveted honor-roll cap. When I got my UC acceptance letter, my last choice for a campus, Riverside, was what was offered.

There I was dismayed that the anti-war protest movement had peaked in May of 1970 after the revolt over the Kent/Jackson massacres had died down. And here I was in L.A., most reluctantly, wanting most of all to join the counterculture and fight the war machine. The decline of the peace movement was sadly underway, even though anti-war sentiment overall was building, and Nixon finally had to wind down the slaughter and defoliation. Fortunately for my enjoyment and inspiration, new rock albums coming out were still infused with rebellion and creativity — lamentably, this was not to last much longer.

The 1970s started idealistically enough, it seemed, to a seventeen-year-old who thought he was a Mediterranean in an exotic former homeland. But things seemed too tame and calm in L.A. — where were the student riots and love-ins?

Just a few weeks back from having spent 4 1/2 years afar, I was walking on Sunset Strip one evening in early 1970 with Olive, on our way home. We were near the "Psychedelic" head shop was that still attracting hundreds of hippie kids, when a fat Sheriff's deputy yelled — as I crossed a street legally — "Hey kid, get over here!" I approached him like a good, meek citizen and he proceeded to frisk me while telling me to give him "no lip." I just looked up at him

while he fingered my testicles through my pants, while he
repeatedly warned me, "Don't gimme any lip boy!" I knew that if I
had resisted it would have been his field day to crack my head and
charge me with "resisting arrest." My hair was longish, and I wore
a headband I had picked up in Palestine several weeks before. The
experience with this evil cop told me volumes about the generation
gap and the city fathers' real policy about kids hanging out
peacefully in public. Could anyone blame me if I continued on my
way across the street disgusted and muttering "Oink!"? For the
cop's part, he was no doubt following orders to clean up the streets.

I was inspired by the student backlash to the Nixonian
expansion of the Indochina War in May of '70, such as UC Santa
Barbara's Isla Vista community's complete shutdown by resident
protesters. It was covered 24/7 by KPFK (Pacifica Radio) in
Studio City, which inspired me onward in my dream of radical
student activism. It seemed we had media, art, love, and a message
with expanded consciousness. At Hollywood High School I was
meeting with anti-war/leftist organizers and sympathizers both on
and off campus. One of them was to become my girlfriend, the
beautiful Carolyn Ristuccia. She was one of a few fine women I
"let get away."

Alban (alias Snoopy) came by our temporary rented home in
Hollywood in 1970 on Ogden Drive, bringing his home: a VW
van. He seemed as cool as ever, and he and Trilby and I went out
to see The Magic Christian starring Peter Sellers and Ringo Starr.
After Alban's visit, another great musician walked through the
same house one afternoon, unannounced, when our landlady
decided to show off Ravi Shankar. My main thought at the time
was that I just wanted to finish my blueberries in the kitchen as he
walked by me, even though I really loved his work. Being young is
to make mistakes.

I made two big mistakes after the spring of 1970. That year
turned out to be the high-water mark, or ending of the '60s
revolution as well as the Lundbergs as a great, cohesive family.
That summer was mostly wasted on getting my driver's license,
something I had not cared about whatsoever in my first six months
back in the States. I was buying into the L.A. lifestyle, without
knowing I would become stuck in it for many years. My other
error, I saw later on, was to pass up an invitation to go to Colombia
with Steve Tarnoff, a Hollywood High classmate whose late father

was a friend of my father's. My parents did not want me to go, so I did not go, thinking it was no big deal — I had already sailed to three dozen countries. Little did I know that I was succumbing to my parents' new trap of L.A., and that I would soon long for travel and adventure.

My summer of 1970 was notable only for driving, such as to Arcata. As time went on since arriving from Greece I felt more like an American, and I did mind having a car. I got into the spirit of trying to consume my way to happiness, as I saw no way of returning anytime soon to the Med. To ease my longing for my friends and my fun in Greece, I basically signed up for fun on wheels, going all over California, taking girls out on dates, and becoming... a consumer! After all, where was the revolution? I couldn't see it.

Chapter 4

The 1970s' Slide of the Lundbergs and Fame of Lundberg Survey

For the Lundberg family the year 1970, compared to the 1960s, typified the overall change in U.S. society from the 1960s to the entire 1970s: hope, energy and enlightenment diminished. Dreams were still pursued, but were more frequently compromised or abandoned as difficulties and disunity mounted. In the 1960s our family had unlimited horizons and the course was set together to attain greatness on our journey. It's true that Dan Lundberg's personal power and charisma were at a height, but he had a healthy, supportive wife, and his five children were pretty much where he wanted them to be. This changed rapidly as the new decade opened, and each family member started into his or her own direction. Our individualistic tendencies strengthened, to almost everyone's detriment.

Yet, the accomplishments continued, primarily the ascendancy of the *Lundberg Letter* (the flagship publication of Lundberg Survey Incorporated). This weekly newsletter of the family business's data and analysis made the name Lundberg a household word by the late '70s, and our prestige grew to its maximum. A plateau of our fame and success was eventually reached as oil prices stopped going up and oil regulations came to an end under the Reagan presidency.

But before any of this fame came about, this young man had some more intensive development:

My next big mistake after passing up the Columbia adventure was to actually enroll in the University of California, Riverside, campus. I stayed two quarters, living at the dormitory. The campus was, like all others apparently, losing steam in anti-war protesting and general radicalizing. I felt like I missed the big student revolt, and was let down when students did not want to organize demonstrations again. In response to my efforts, I was told things like "I did that last year, and now I have to study."

My roommate was Kirk Hayward, from Orange County. We liked the same rock music, so much so that he kept my Savoy Brown album and I still want it back. Kirk was a mediocre guitarist who gradually inspired me to play because even he could do it; I finally got an acoustic Epiphone guitar. Probably the worst thing about my life in those days was whenever I forgot to bring a fresh bath towel from Hollywood, and I had to use Kirk's raunchy old red towel. (Poking fun at a guy is a good indication he's a cherished friend.)

We had party buddies in the dorm, where I stole Bob Palmer's girlfriend Laura Alster. But it was to her Syrian-American friend Michelle that I gladly relinquished my virginity. (Michelle and I never became an item, maybe because I was looking for adventure in the way of politics, and she wasn't.)

Kirk, a physics major who regaled me with tales such as The Twins Paradox, was addicted to surfing, but he managed to get into UCLA's doctorate program. But he came up short and ended up working in a weapons/aerospace corporation. It wasn't too surprising when he asked me, mystified, during the Iran Hostage crisis, "Why do they hate us?" That sums up the stereotypical Orange County political consciousness. He had an Orange County girlfriend named Janis Hart whom he eventually married. She had, and probably still does have, a heart of gold. She was a nightclub singer in the tradition of Doris Day, but to supplement income she taught aerobics.

My other main friend at the time was John Cartaya who had a large Cuban family in Santa Ana. I did most of my weekend carousing with him as we plied the freeways to go skiing and anything else the car-lifestyle affords. His family didn't think I understood Spanish, and they referred to me in my presence as "El Rico" (The Rich One). Among John's attributes were changing his mind and flaking out on social arrangements, so a verb was coined by friends; he "Cartayaed." After graduation he got into the medical field and is still there. Despite his getting hit by a car in the 1990s and sustaining a serious leg injury, he became a concert violinist and he takes trips to Kenya to do volunteer health care.

In 1970 I was involved in the UCR school newspaper *The Highlander*, where they published anything I wanted to print except for an article on fasting that one editor called "bullshit." That was fighting words, and I retorted, "You're bullshit." My, was

I having to grow up. One of my colleagues' favorite articles of mine was actually written by my father, at his instigation, about Ralph Nader. I had not asked him to do it, but it looked okay to me so I published it under my name in *The Highlander*. I would not raise a child that way; instead I would rather see if I could interest the kid in Ralph Nader enough to write an article about him. I was later to have positive encounters with Ralph, who liked my work against road building and globalization, after my father's death.

Several months before my *Highlander* rejection on fasting I ran into the same censorship on the topic of fasting, for my 12th grade health class in Hollywood High. We were told to pick any topic relating to health, and make a report. I told the teacher my subject was fasting, but a few days later she came to me and said the Principal forbade it. However, a classmate overheard my thwarted intentions and decided to do a fast unbeknownst to me. She was an overweight and homely girl, and I was surprised she had embarked on a fast with no convincing and no background in fasting. Every day in class she would tell me how many days she had gone, and I knew she was doing a long fast by the telltale smell of her breath and her weight loss. After perhaps 10 days as her energy, looks and smell improved, I began to regard her as more vibrant, shining, and cute. By then I already knew that very few people are inclined to try something culturally and radically new, despite clear benefits and verifiable logic.

From UCR I transferred to UCLA, thanks to a little string pulling by my father. The campus had been my first choice only because my brother Guy had graduated there and had been a star oarsman on the rowing team. But I soon found UCLA to be a dull commuter school, uninspiring and a bore, with student demonstrations practically nil by the time I arrived. At least the fraternities were all but out of business, thanks to the recent youth revolution emanating from places such as Berkeley. I didn't miss UCR, but all in all it was, in hindsight, a better experience with smaller classes.

In UCLA I was encouraged at my Orientation by a student-government activist named Bruce Givner, to get involved. Givner's "fifteen seconds of fame" was his being the last person to leave the Democratic Party office at the Watergate in 1972, as the White House burglars had to hide as he flew down the stairs. At UCLA I formed the campus chapter of People's Lobby, which had the Clean Environment Act on the state ballot via initiative petition. It was defeated, really creamed, by negative corporate advertising, mainly by the American Automobile Association. I've hated the AAA ever since — it's not so much an emergency repair service but a huge insurance company.

The UCLA Environment Club was part of Student Government, where the campus chapter of Peoples Lobby had its desk. The club was headed by a pro-nuclear power activist named Paul Silver. I was astounded that he and his flunky could be pro-nuke, but his ponytail gave him enough credibility to call himself an environmentalist.

I appreciated People's Lobby immensely, and I liked the founders Ed and Joyce Koupal. Their funky office over in Hollywood was their home too. But when their campaign became focused on Chevron's allegedly bogus F310 additive, I felt I had to bow out in solidarity with my father. He was working eight days a week to revive Lundberg Survey after the damaging departure of Guy Lundberg in early 1970, and Chevron was the biggest client. I don't think Dan or any family member appreciated my sacrifice and loyalty to the firm when I quit Peoples Lobby. I gave the reins over to fellow UCLA student Ted Bavin, an orchestral percussionist who found a career in renewable energy installation.

One vivid moment I retain from my final tabling for People's Lobby on Bruin Walk at UCLA was a volunteer's excited attempt to have me join an experimental orchestra for class credit. I was convinced I had no capability to do anything musically, so I declined and declined until he gave up. I realized many years later that my gutless and stubborn refusal was a regrettable mistake.

I eventually came to see my parents had got their son and daughter mixed up, when they groomed me to be an executive and tried to create a musical career for Trilby. Those decisions were based on gender stereotypes, even though Dan and Mesa were right that I had executive talents and Trilby was musical. The paths of brother and sister, however — to get ahead of our story here — were for me to reject corporate administration and for Trilby to all but abandon music, as I gravitated toward music and she embraced corporatism with a vengeance.

At UCLA I flunked the only course of my whole academic career: PL1 computer language, although I made my usual academic effort. I just could not accept arbitrary code at face value, such as the critical placement of a comma. The disappointment of an F-grade led me to try my father's suggestion that I take a break from school and help out at the office. Besides, I was unable to find inspiration or solidarity at the campus due to its lack of radical activism, so I took a leave of absence and began to work for the family business.

He made me perhaps the highest-paid 19-year old in L.A., at $1,000 a month, in part to keep me from wanting to return to school. I found that my new job compiling national gasoline sales and market share reports was interesting. Soon my mind was blown over the oil statistics that I was responsible for, when the ecological implications of petroleum were considered. But with this meaningful work, while lacking a groovy scene elsewhere, I was getting roped in to the corporate world. My father's employees resented the nepotism. And I resented their resentment.

My Share of Market Department calculated state-by-state monthly gasoline sales by brand. This was when I noticed that the grand total for the year was a statistic available nowhere else: the sum of the gallons burned and spilled for the year in the U.S., was, as I recall, about 90 billion. This was pollution big-time. With nary a comment on such massive gasoline use by anyone I'd ever met, or any writer I'd read, I knew my new position of knowledge had potential importance. Looking back, I see that I lacked the skills or experience to do something with it from an activist standpoint. Even more remote was the possibility of making a big deal over depletion from a crude reserves standpoint: I also wondered how such huge consumption was geophysically and ecologically possible to occur again and again thereafter. I would not have imagined it would go on this long and get past 140 billion gallons burned and spilled in the U.S. each year. I don't think environmentalists such as Denis Hayes and his 1970 Earth Day crew would have imagined it either.

Speaking of imagining, a fond memory of about 1971 was Trilby's teaching my John Lennon's song Imagine on piano.

College did not strongly beckon again for a long time, except for short-term needs. The most telling experience for me at the UCLA campus, as to the loss of idealism and student fervor, was about seven years later during a night class. It was a course on the Common Market (now European Union), and a young man was making small talk about "money markets" in such a way to be

almost drooling over high interest yields. I was almost sickened as
I lamented the complete fading of the dream to change the world
that students had been known for. I did get something out of
other yuppie coursework, actually enjoying Managerial Accounting
as well as Business Law. Good teachers were the key.

All this added up to two years of UC, and I was too busy
helping to manage a prestigious company to take time for more
classes — for what, a credential to get a job? Nevertheless, I
regretted not staying in school, mainly because I could have been
far away from L.A. in, say, Vermont. My other big daydream was
that my decision should have been, from 1970 or '71 onward, to go
live on a commune in the countryside. But I had bought my
father's pitch: "Be financially independent and you can change the
world. You can't do it by handing out leaflets on the street corner.
But if you think of a way to bring about a revolution, I'll follow
you." (He was my original introduction to Marxism when I asked
him about it in Greece.)

I took him at his word, and it was with reluctance I took the
college track and, more reluctantly, the family-business route. To
back up his radicalism and socialism, he came up with a profit-
sharing program called Merit Award. Unfortunately, this bonus
system was still a capitalist's scheme, and the workers took it for
granted almost with contempt. It certainly did not stop many of
them from treating me rather shabbily. I was not only the boss's
son; I was a bit too zealous about business and our statistics.
Maybe we all felt a little shabby due to our physical environment:
The offices out in smoggy North Hollywood were on the way to
nothing except equally smoggy Sun Valley. The toxic air and the
lack of any parks or groovy shops made for a miserable
environment. Good restaurants were not nearby. A small pool and
garden on our premises was meant for worker relaxation but
almost no one approached it; people just worked, ate, flirted with
the opposite sex, worked some more, and left. Indoor smoking
abounded, adding to my needing to take a mid day nap on many an
occasion. There was a funny-smelling couch-bed for the janitor
that I used, but one day my father pointed out that the wall I was
laying up against was packed with electrical equipment that could
affect the body.

Our "crew" was typical for early '70s pop culture: one employee,
Pierre Guertin, who thought of himself as a swinger, invited the

straight-laced accountant Lance Morrison to swap wives, bringing it up in a meeting at our conference table. Lance didn't go for it, and to his credit, even though I didn't respect his office-politics, he did not attack Guertin physically or politically. Guertin started out as an assistant printer in our print shop, and was promoted up and up by my father who no doubt saw many young people as he once was, ambitious and blocked by society. Guertin married one of our employees, Barbara Smith, who was demoted to make room for me as Manager of the Share of Market Department. Needless to say, the couple did not like me at all. When she told me I had "no class" (in the presence of others) all I could think of was her misfortune in not understanding the real meaning of the word (in a socialist analysis). Guertin and another employee, Ken Cox, eventually tried to go into business for themselves against Lundberg Survey by making arrangements with a Dept. of Energy bureaucrat named Bill Gillespie. Dr. Gillespie and his associate Peter Antonelli made our lives miserable for a while by being unfairly critical of our work we did for the government. They all saw themselves as better than the Lundbergs and in line for the same dollars. Then again, my father's manner and style may have been off-putting, combined with any negative talk from Guertin and Cox. On an occasion when I was visiting Gillespie in Washington, he stepped out for a while as I waited for him. I got out my camera to change rolls of film; I was new to Washington and was taking tourist pictures. When he opened the door he topped his rudeness of the whole visit by asking me, in an accusatory way, "What were you taking pictures of?"

Generally I was treated well with my sales visits to the federal and state agencies. Once I called on an energy regulatory administrator, Hazel Rollins who later became the Secretary of Energy under Bill Clinton. In the meeting, with a large number of staff members around a conference table, she began by saying to me, "You're so slick. You're so slick." She was smiling, so I smiled back. I'm not sure what she meant, and I was happy to cinch another contract and go on with another profitable visit in Washington. On a later visit I met the Interior Secretary James Watt. I could hardly believe that someone could be so smilingly hateful of nature and conservation. When around him I could think of nothing intelligent to say, so I remained a closet environmentalist in his mind.

I wasn't doing my health any favors in the "SmelL.A." environment, sitting in a car and at a desk so much every day. I had fallen into an existence that I was in need of rebelling against. After my parents had led me across the seas to bliss, I foolishly followed them into their North Hollywood hell. To some people, it was all good, when one considered other kinds of work and environments that were far worse. But I was a young man of the world who wanted to change it and taste life — now. For me the years 1972-1979 were like "lost years" for the prime of my remaining youth.

I went up to a major peace march and rally in San Francisco in 1971. On the march an anti-Castro Cuban, "Paulo," walked with us, a friend of my friend John Cartaya. Paulo was inadvertently holding up a Viet Cong flag, not caring about the Vietnamese or anything other than the girls on the march and the bands that would play at the rally. It was then that I realized the anti-war movement was relying on an unsteady base. How many people were really committed? During the march I wanted the crowd to take a direct route to a federal government building instead of to a park, but I thought that I had no power to bring it off, and I was not yet aware that march organizers are almost always compromisers with the authorities. The most memorable part of my trip was afterwards as I drove around the Embarcadero: I had brought an Army-surplus gas mask in case there were to be tear gas directed against protesters. I was not even sure it worked, so just for the hell of it I decided to drive with it on, in my Fiat 124 Sport Coupé. When I took it off several minutes later my nose and lungs were assaulted by gasoline vapors that were in the interior of the car all the time, but I had never noticed — the gas mask obviously worked. Many years later, post 9-11, I was interested to learn that the government decreed that possession of a gas mask at a demonstration meant engaging in terrorism.

My brothers and sisters and my parents did not attend anti-war rallies. Needless to say, my coworkers at Lundberg Survey had no interest in peace activism. This was unfortunate because my work-environment was my world (except for day dreams). I stayed long hours and had family there. In the early '70s, no other siblings were at Lundberg Survey on a steady basis, although at some point in their lives they all were staffers and stockholders. I was the only Lundberg kid to ever go into the firm voluntarily to learn long-term, as opposed to reluctantly accepting a job to make some money short-term (and ending up there for years, as the others usually did). One of the more enjoyable periods was when our dear family friend Jimmy Fields, classical pianist, did a stint of receptionist work for us between his concert tours. He would occasionally tickle the ivories in his masterful way on the player-piano that graced our lobby. When he played Brahms it was like a bomb hit, Bahms!

My first job at the firm was actually during college, part time, 1970-1971, on every Friday night. Our team had to write down over the telephone the gasoline station survey-data from around the country, mostly just price changes for the grades of gas. It was an easy job and was suffused with camaraderie and free food. A minor nemesis for me was Mike Clark who was a card-carrying conservative with short hair, but without him I would have been in a false bubble of mostly hip friends at our job. I ultimately came to manage the night operation, having to deal with any missing surveyors who might need to have last minute replacement in their city. Such breakdowns and the possible "kitchen tabling" of gasoline station data (fraud) were the big worry. It was late-night work, bad for one's health, but somebody had to do it.

In those days we surveyed over 10,000 stations per month, whereas now Lundberg Survey is reportedly down to 5,000 that are surveyed less frequently. To most of the oil industry, the retail end of oil is of less interest than oil wells and refineries. Selling the gasoline was once a barely respected role, especially before the oil price shocks and gasoline lines in the 1970s.

My father told me repeatedly that the real profit in the oil business was not in marketing gasoline but in "monetizing crude." One way this was done was through the oil depletion allowance that made for massive profits with little work. John F. Kennedy reportedly wanted to end the depletion allowance, the way he reportedly wanted to end the Vietnam buildup (another oil-profit bonanza both in military-operations and in the resources to be gained in Vietnam and offshore). But Kennedy was struck down before those policy changes could be made. My father pointed out to me that much jet fuel was being used for the planes involved in the Vietnam war, and he did not approve. But he did not speak out.

My oil work was more interesting than the pay, although at first I couldn't complain about the latter. After I started to feel trapped and longed to be far away, nothing could buy my satisfaction in southern California. The success-track for this hip young executive was excruciating. One major instance was when I attended IBM's corporate campus seminar for one week, at the time Richard Nixon was re-elected. If you weren't alive yet or old enough to experience it, take my word that this period in the U.S. was a time of division and hate between many citizens. As a slightly long-haired, barely concealed radical hippie, I smoldered when the IBM course showed film clips of animated exploding hippies as the staff's way of announcing the end of a session. When Nixon gave his acceptance speech on the tube, I bitterly blurted out to my fellow corporate classmates, "Yeah, bombs!" They fell silent until I went back to barracks.

I was meeting quite a few oil industry characters, most of whom were quite genteel — "friends" of my fathers. He knew it was part of his game to consider them his friends, although they were simply Philistines or cogs in the machine. He genuinely liked some of them, as a union organizer might like fellow workers who aren't really in the labor movement. Around this time he explained to me how he got things done throughout his life: writing the script in his mind and making sure people played their parts. I didn't suspect he was writing my part, but I knew him for being a well-meaning, manipulative impresario who would run anyone's life if he could get away with it.

One of Dan's friends was Mark Emond, the West Coast Editor for National Petroleum News, owned by McGraw Hill. My father encouraged me to ask Mark about meditation and Buddhism, as Mark was well disciplined. I did so, but perhaps teaching was not Mark's strong point, or at age 20 I found the whole subject totally mysterious. Mark had three children and a wife in a lower-middle class Orange County enclave. One day my father told me that he was going to get a major article out of Mark on our company's gasoline station classification and market research system, Comprof (Comprehensive Profile). Comprof expanded on our current database of prices of gasoline, brand, location of retail outlet, and little more. This system (or "product" of Lundberg Survey) was meant to keep us competitive with fancy models used by more mathematical research services.

My father's scheme to get the article was to make Mark's dreams come true by jointly buying a beautiful piece of land in the

Rocky Mountains just west of Fort Collins. My father made it possible to buy the place, 134 acres bordering U.S. or State Forest land, and let Mark (who either put up some of the money or owed my father money on the purchase) prepare pleasantly for his future retirement: hunting, fishing, building a house or cabin, etc. Yes, the article did come out, most favorably. This isn't to say Dan didn't think of Mark as a friend, but it shows that Dan mixed business and pleasure and would manipulate.

We traveled to the land a couple of times, the men of both families packed with hunting rifles into in a pick up truck with a camper. The vehicle was itself a family business purchase upon the need to make the trip. We enjoyed the land and the surrounding community. My father liked it all just fine, but my brother and I loved it and intended to spend a lot of time there. We rode horses, caught trout, and I was intrigued by the proximity of a Buddhist community nearby in Red Feather Lakes. What a change from smoggy L.A. and the grind there! I never did spend much time on what we called "the Colorado Land" but I obtained literature on soil, growing high altitude fruits and vegetables, greenhouses, etc. as I built my back-to-the-land dream in my mind. I looked forward to going there to homestead and visiting the neighboring ranchers again. One friendly neighbor was a kind of cowboy hippie into horses.

Being caught up in my L.A. life, and later when I lived in Virginia, I eventually found myself cut off from my future dream-home possibly forever. The land was sold out from under me in secret in about 1987. My brother Darius felt the same way about the loss. At least the buyer of the Lundberg Survey half of the ownership was Mark Emond, I heard, whom I never saw again. Every few years I think, "What if I returned to the Colorado land and wanted to live there. Could I?"

≈

My first business trip far away was to go off to Iowa to hire a state capitol lobbyist for our gasoline-data needs — I got the job done but it wasn't fun. Then my father substituted me for him at the Oklahoma oil jobbers' convention as keynote speaker. I met my first governor and marveled that the state's population was heavily of native American blood. I was a boring speaker, but I was getting experience. Too bad the reason for the speeches and networking was worthless activity, I felt in my heart. I couldn't relate to the business of wholesaling gasoline and other petroleum products, but in time I could more easily understand the overall industry from oilfield to refinery to gas station.

My father's penchant for self-education was being transmitted to me, but by giving me a management position over the heads of his other workers and paying me well I was missing out on the tougher education the average person gets in the proletariat. I was in no way among society's poor intellectual hipsters having to manage without a rich Daddy. But in addition to the great learning opportunity that I soon sensed was superior to college, I was getting business experience form an owner's standpoint: caring about whether the lights were all turned out at the end of work became part of my routine, which doesn't necessarily happen with even an important job that someone can get.

The price of such an education and comfortable paycheck was high when I was really not my own man. Under someone else's power one can be degraded or abused. A vivid example was a dinner my parents and I had with two oil executives in Beverly Hill's L'Escoffier restaurant. It was enjoyable enough, with stories to enhance enjoyment of the drinks, fancy meal and deserts. My father told the clients of our near scrape in the Corinthian Gulf as the Greek sailor steered for the lighthouse on that perilous night in 1969. I interrupted and corrected my father on some of the details of what happened. I must have done this at least three times, but all was well and the evening ended. It was on the way home with my father at the wheel that he berated me for contradicting him in front of our clients, even if I was right. I should have yelled, "Look, I saved your life you fool!" My mother just sat there, presumably agreeing with him. I took his criticism and wondered why I was wasting time with these people in a negative, draining situation — and I was thinking not just of the evening but of the years I spent in frustration and boredom so far at Lundberg Survey. My captain was losing my respect and my awe for him. However, the closeness of a family in a business or work-environment together is real and an advantage that most families in the modern world lack. I still appreciated my family more than most young folk seemed to do in the U.S.

A small foray into a business I was interested in, that of opinion polls or surveys on social issues, was People's Research. I headed this project up with Bill Keane, a Share of Market Dept. researcher that everyone liked. He reminded some of us of Star Trek's Mr. Spock. The only poll we did was in advance of the 1972 presidential election, and it sampled the population of Los Angeles. I can only remember that our survey covered Nixon versus McGovern. Upon completion of conducting the poll based on a representative, random sample of local citizens, we tabulated the results and put out a press release. I had to go out of town, and Bill was not around, so my mother handled the one radio interview we got.

In summer of 1973 I enjoyed one of the perks of my family-business: a trip to the Hawaiian Islands with my younger brother, ostensibly to survey gasoline stations. It was a present for my 21st birthday. I was not able to appreciate my life much in those days, not finding much going on in L.A. and still missing Greece. An indication of my feelings in 1973 surfaced during the Hawaiian vacation: I felt most hopeful and pleased whenever the new Pink Floyd album Dark Side of the Moon came on our rental-car radio. Little else around me interested me at first. Darius and I did have a thoroughly good time, breathing sulfurous fumes on the Big Island's volcano, looking up Ron and Val Sewell in Hilo, and hiking the Kalalau Trail on Kauai. It was there that we exited civilization and had to forage for food such as wild mangos. The beach where most of the hikers gathered saw no clothing on anyone. Once every several days a helicopter dropped someone off. Once on the trail my brother almost fell backward with his big backpack off the trail to the rocks and surf far below, but I grabbed him and pulled him back. It was on this trip that I was treated on three occasions to disrespectful behavior by older (but young) women at their jobs. I knew it was because I was clearly young and could be slighted. One of these instances was when I was at a beach nightclub in Honolulu, and was rudely advised by the waitress "Time for your second drink!" I suppose most of us middle-aged or senior people today would love to be back in a position of age-discrimination of the young, but at the time it added to my unhappiness and my longing to be back in Europe.

By the time of the 1973 Arab Oil Embargo just a few months after my Hawaii trip, I had a busy social life that still included driving all over California for my "outdoor" recreation. But I only wanted to be back in Greece. I finally made it back in the summer of 1974. On my way there, in various countries from Canada onward, I felt like a normal human being again. I constantly encountered the kind of friendly people who didn't seem to exist in L. A. I was on a Eurail pass and checked out alternative-living scenes, made love with Nordic beauties, listened to Procol Harum in record stores, passed out anti-nuke literature in Denmark, and visited our old floating home in Mallorca. The Passat was in good condition, but I didn't even think of taking it out for a sail by myself.

In Spain I enjoyed the close company of an Australian girl in Barcelona and a French girl in Palma de Mallorca. With the latter, whose name I forget, I had a close call in the Royal Yacht Club. I risked jail by the repressive Franco regime for the crime of co-habiting without holy marriage. I had taken many a meal at the club's restaurant where the headwaiter, Manolo, consistently treated the customers shabbily. I had had enough, so I upbraided him. That next night I slept with the French girl in her room in the club's hotel, and I stupidly made a call from her room at dawn, alerting the management to my presence in the room. Fortunately, no one told Manolo. Most nights I slept on the Passat that was moored close by. One of my memories I have of the French girl on board was when I served her a bottle of beer without a glass. Her way of saying that she would not drink it without a glass was to say to me, snootily, "I am not American."

Something momentous happened while staying on the boat: I had two intense musical dreams, my first such experiences. In one dream Donovan was performing via the radio or a cassette player. It was electrifying: the power and harmonic sweetness of his music was like an orgasm of the mind, a rapid cosmic flowering. I woke up pleasantly stunned, but unable to retain the music or the words of the song. The next night the same thing happened: in the dream I was in Lundberg Survey's computer room when a fellow worker, John Shelton, mounted a disk onto the drive (massive things back in 1974), as if the disk were a vinyl record. He put the stylus on the disk and intense, beautiful music came out: Jeff Beck. It was powerful and electrifying in such a way to immobilize me in jolting ecstasy.

For days I was amazed at these dreams and their possible

meaning. I knew I wanted more such musical experiences. I got my wish, as more musical dreams followed, but never as intensely. I was soon able to capture music and lyrics from dreams of all kinds of music and dream scenes, such as live performance, John Lennon singing his latest song to me over the phone, or just vague music and/or lyrics in my head as I woke up. In the cases of the first two dreams, the music was new and unknown, rather than being actual works of Donovan and Jeff Beck. In my thousands of musical dreams I may have only once heard an exact rendition of an existing song. This and my songwriting while awake tell me that music in its variation and permutation is infinite, no matter how many composers are writing or will ever write — much as fingerprints and voices are all different from one another.

In 1974 I could barely play the guitar, and in my life I have always been more interested in songwriting than performance. In the 1990s I got into performance and recording as a means of getting across a message. I haven't gone more than a few days without a musical dream since 1974 except for a hiatus when I was married to a classical harpist for a few years. The fact that music is infinite and cannot be exhausted in originality has made me understand the spontaneous creation of music as the channeling of the universe's essential vibration and harmonic energy. Mathematics are involved, as well as a homing in on a receiver (the composer).

[As I write this, August 7, 2010, this morning's musical dream is in my head: on a radio in a dream was Traffic performing from its album Shootout at the Fantasy Factory. When I figured the music out on guitar, in the key of B-flat minor, I could tell the beat and music didn't resemble the actual album. A line of verse came with it: "Have you seen in her grey eyes". I've noticed that right-hemisphere statements are less normal or typical in their construction and choice of words than wakeful, normal left-hemisphere language. I've stopped using tape recorders to preserve the dream music, so I operate nowadays with the hope that my notation on paper and my memory will save my little creation until I can complete the song. Lyrics and finger-position on the guitar help me remember the music. As my tools include only my guitar and voice, I conform many dreams' instruments such as brass to voice, writing some words when I wake up, sometimes to go with original lyrics from the dream's images.]

I have days when a new song I'm writing or practicing is the only thing that keeps me going.

In Greece at the end of summer 1974 I met up with my old high-school girlfriend Xenia. In no time she and I arranged that she would come and stay with me in L. A. on an open-ended basis. In Athens we went back to our high school where everything seemed the same. In those days and in those parts, an adult could just go onto the school grounds and walk the halls without some security-minded authority challenging you. Apart from Xenia there was practically no one for me to see in Athens from the old days, as people had scattered. The U.S.-backed fascist Colonels and their dictatorship had just been sent packing by the populace, but there was no revolutionary fervor to really change society, that I could detect. Anti-U.S. sentiment was fairly high so I sometimes pretended to be French. An improvement over the just-concluded political era was that people were a bit more relaxed, after what seemed to me an already relaxing period under the Colonels. Greek culture has to do with closeness of friends and family, so any fascistic aspects are of little concern if one can ignore unpleasant realities. Then again, I did not know anyone tortured in the jails.

Xenia joined me a few months later in the Hollywood Hills. She was accepted by my parents, with whom I was still living at age 22. Xenia's presence in L.A. was comforting to me, but it did not give my life in the States any more sense, as I only sunk deeper into the quicksand of my sell-out at Lundberg Survey.

Between the time of my 1974 trip to Europe and the arrival of Xenia in January 1975, my father became ill with the terminal disease called myasthenia gravis. He quickly became paralyzed and was informed by doctors that the tests showed he would die. But he always had little use for doctors, so he went on a fast of just Perrier water for 40 days. (See more on his amazing recovery in my treatise, Fasting for Healing and Inner Peace, in this book's appendix.) Xenia's arrival to live with us was about the time my father was just starting to get around normally again.

I was delighted to have Xenia with me — good-bye lonely days. We acted like normal 22-year-olds, such as driving to the Shrine Auditorium to see Genesis perform with Peter Gabriel as their front man. She and I got an apartment in Malibu right over the surf, where we reveled in the non-North Hollywood, misty environment. I tied the family canoe, River Rat, under the building to some pilings. We were visited once by Guy who kept a Hobie Cat catamaran nearby. I remember his dropping by my living room and sneering over a Genesis album cover he saw, "Nursery Crime." He prided himself on being a classical-music snob. The only other time I saw him in that period after not seeing him for over a year, was on Pacific Coast Highway. I walked up to him as he fastened his boat to his car and said to him with a grin, "Spare change?" But he looked right at me and said No, pretending to not know who I was. Maybe if I had mugged him he would have openly recognized me.

Xenia and I got married in July of 1975, largely because her visa had run out and the U.S. government was not easy about letting foreigners stay long openly. The U.S. Immigration and Naturalization "Service" caused us to lose a lot of sleep, partly because the INS staff in downtown L.A. was abusive and rude as a matter of course to the public.

The post-honeymoon (we had gone to Catalina Island) period was stressful for me due to two factors. The nasty INS still refused to recognize my wife as deserving of staying because, though married, they now claimed I might be Mexican (despite my U.S. passport, apparently just a State Dept. document in the eyes of the INS/"Justice" Department). I also was finding that my possessiveness and insecurity as a husband meant I was not really ready for marriage. I became depressed and unsure of myself. My work suffered, and I felt trapped in the marital contract and relationship. It took me months to get back to functioning with some peace of mind. I did not particularly care about the nice regular paycheck; what disturbed me was something worse than the lack of meaning in my work: my marriage was unenjoyable. I was clearly too immature for a relationship when trust, for me, meant control — but I hadn't thought any of it through; I was just bouncing down a bumpy road. So the marriage — imposed by the government — was a fixture or a habit that I was too weak to just break off. I just lived from month to month in an unhappy state, disgusted with myself that I allowed the marriage to go on, as if I had no strength. If I had been very attached to and dependent on Xenia, that would be understandable. She was a friend I was getting along with, but after enough years a forced union can ruin a friendship as well as any trust.

I must have been rather typical in one sense: one weekend in

1976 when Xenia was out of town on Lundberg Survey business, I happened to meet a delightful woman. We gallivanted around town until the wee hours, and ended up at my place where she would spend the night. The mood was good with Peter Gabriel's first album on the stereo; it was important to me that she liked it. But I was soon kicking myself for saying too much through the evening about my circumstances, because she said she would not sleep with me because my marriage was not something to tamper with. This was the swinging '70s, pre-AIDS, and sexual gratification in my mid-20s was often all-important.

At first I thought the lesson to be learned from my failure to seduce my beautiful new friend was to be more careful in future about what I disclosed. She consented to see me again for a few minutes outside her dress-shop job, and it was the last time we saw each other. She would have no reason to remember me now. I probably offered very little to her of any substance in terms of originality or idealism. These were carefree days for me and most people I knew, but I yearned for something different than the commonplace (more sex, more music, and getting drunk or high). I needed real adventure, sex with new partners, new music, and involvement in politics — in that order. What the episode with my sexy, vivacious date really indicated, upon reflection many years later, was that I was one of those people needing to go from one relationship to another. Such bouncing to and fro, instead of ending a poor scene, prevents taking stock of one's own situation and identity. One needs to be able to establish a new relationship with a little care and good sense.

In 1976 I was feeling better about my work, beginning to take care of client relations. It was still one of those lost years where I did nothing creative or important. Yet, I was transitioning from the young sprout of the office to important manager. My co-workers remained cynical about my father's and my idealism, and two or three were still surly about my working there. By 1976 I was ending my phase of hated boss's son (even though I was far from a jerk, I felt), no longer thought of as a counterculture liberal who should just "love America or leave it." Sadly, few people cared about or were bothered by "the cause," and the movement to change the world was dead. So I appeared to be more of a regular guy, a member of the staff who ran one department after another. I had the inside track for transitioning to the top executive role. It was hard to have to recall that in my first years the better I performed in the office the less friendly was most of the staff. After enough years of proving myself, all employees became my staff for all of the firm's activities. The results of my work eventually became universally appealing for everyone's welfare.

In the '70s I dabbled in high society; my Los Angeles FILMEX contribution of $100 listed me in the program with famous actors. Another year I backed Tom Hayden for Senate, although it soon seemed he was counterproductive in doing away with the decent incumbent John Tunney — California ultimately got the right-wing joke Senator Hayakawa. I was disappointed that Tom had almost nothing to say to me at a fundraising reception he held. I brought my sister Trilby. We were unhappy that Tom's wife, actress/activist Jane Fonda, was absent. He did have Bette Midler on hand for support, and Trilby gave her one her own classical albums; it was politely accepted. I had a similarly unsatisfying experience when attending a Bella Abzug fund-raiser; perhaps she was shy, but she walked right by me at a garden party when I was there as her supporter. (Two decades later Bella supported me at a United Nations meeting in New York, by clarifying publicly the position I was stating on the need for a road-building moratorium, when Brazil's Environment Minister sounded more like a *Development* Minister.) I was clearly wasting time, not finding myself. It would have been different if the '60s movement had not died out.

I also backed former U.S. Attorney General Ramsey Clark for Senate (to represent New York). At a fund-raiser I met his son Tom, who was living on Venice Beach with his girlfriend. The two of them joined Xenia and me for a "Seventies" evening, and Tom followed up with a thank-you note, thus showing the "good breeding" my father was teaching me.

By 1977 when I left Lundberg Survey for a year, I was still miserable with my job, my routine and my lifestyle. Part of my frustration was that I could not understand how an immensely capable man like my father could waste his time in a smoggy megalopolis serving the oil industry. He later confided that he felt he sold out, yet he still wanted me to work myself into the ground along with him, believing our business was the best security we could devise. He also imagined he could do some good as an activist liberal on occasion. This he did, but less and less so as he became a bit conservative as he got older. He was ambitious in achieving Oil Guru status, but he let almost all other talents and dreams sit on the shelf. He also neglected his health, which he expected his family and our employees to do too. A man who had had a hard life until early middle age, and fought for and reached a position of national respect, had to be a driven and intense operator. He could not be deterred or influenced, which cheated him out of enjoying others' potential. His way was the only way, in his mind, even though he knew he was not measuring up to his intellectual potential in fields that held greater appeal and meaning for him and his true admirers. His peers in Hollywood became distant, although he kept up his membership in the Screen Writers Guild that screened monthly movies we attended.

Memorable co-workers and strange characters at Lundberg Survey

In 2010 my brother Darius wrote to me and recalled a woman we knew, Linda Lervold, who worked for a year or two with Lundberg Survey. She was somewhat strange, but kind, and surprisingly joined a community theater group with my brother. She was killed by a car in the mid 1980s right after she lost her mother. I had forgotten about Linda until my brother mentioned her. I can think of the many times I had her perform a task. I went on,

> "You and I certainly knew some interesting people thanks to our parents. Like Bill Keene — the guy was like a Mr. Spock on many an occasion. I often thought of him as a good advisor, were I to be the President of the U.S. The fact that I was born outside the U.S., preventing me from ever being president, was compartmentalized elsewhere in my mind.
> "Many of the people we were thrown in with were, to me, not so nice or worthwhile. Daddy assembled people around him (and us) who were in some cases a real a drag, who had limited consciousness and often hated me because I was the boss's son. But some were nice. It was quite an assortment of people. We had a blind fellow named Dave who had permanently lost his sight on the 405 Freeway.

We would try employing a highly educated PhD on occasion, but they never lasted. More often than not our hires seemed to need a break in life, so our father gave them a chance. Dave, being blind, was one. John Ayling was another, and he was not only grateful but a pleasant workhorse.

"We had Florence Klein ("Flahrence") and her son and daughter, all favorites of mine. I had a thing for Stephanie Klein but we never acted on it. After she left our employ she developed a strong dislike for me and Daddy because she felt her mother was underpaid. She certainly was if we compared her to the laid-back, boss's son-in-law Bob. Other workers we had were relatively underpaid compared to Bob who had been with the firm longer than almost anyone. [Seniority counts for something, Stephanie!] Flo Klein's son David Klein got angry with me because I didn't go to his father Jesse's funeral. I liked the old guy but had only spoken a few words with him; he was a retired furniture salesman. David was a part time printer of ours (having done Friday night phone survey work too), and he eventually married another printer. I thought he was a cool guy because he liked some of the music I did, such as Procol Harum, and he had some of the best looking bell bottom pants obtainable.

"I really had a thing for Ginny Seigel, and she liked me. I was married, though. At that time we hadda guy who worked with me named Greg Cook, formerly with the U.S. DOE, and he and I often played racquetball as I did with Raul Riutor. One time I told Ginny in the hallway of LSI that something that had happened in her car would make it smell as bad as her house. Greg said, 'What a shot!' I'm glad I got out of the habit of being the occasional jerk with poor attempts at humor."

Many of the LSI employees with whom I worked from the early days came to accept and respect me as their leader. I was finally enjoying the work after my first five years there. Unfortunately almost all of the people on staff were eventually fired or they quit, after "Tribully" Lundberg seized the company in 1986 — but we're getting ahead of the story.

Living in L.A. had some advantages, but the inefficient layout of the streetscape and the smog rendered the place unpleasant and depressing. But "Smel.L.A." is tolerable for those having their creative juices flow and getting paid for it. I wrote a short story, "Even the Valley's Okay after it Rains." I showed it to my father who was alarmed, adamant that I not try more such works. He didn't say it was badly written, but rather I believe he did not want me to get sucked into poor-paying work. To be an artist was okay for a female in our family, he thought. I can only wonder today: was his lack of interest in my music, the time I played him some of my tentative guitar compositions, about not wanting to give me any dangerous encouragement? I wonder much more whether he would have liked my later works that got on the radio with a strong social and environmental message.

With the oil shocks of the 1970s I learned about other energy technologies, and I longed to concentrate on those instead of the dreaded gasoline. I associated the latter with urban sprawl, too much driving, and the scattered, inferior social scene of L.A. I was interested in solar energy, but the installers I met were seldom stellar fellows. Solar, diesel, wood waste, liquefied or gasified coal — these were worth studying to escape the boredom of gasoline surveys. I escaped to Washington, DC and other towns for seminars or sales calls a few times a year just to get out of L.A.

One visit that stands out was to go to a fort near the Pentagon to see my customer at the Defense Fuel Supply Center (renamed the Defense Energy Support Center in 1998). It was (and is) the biggest fuel purchaser and, as the Pentagon's buyer, the biggest consumer of oil products in the world. I wanted the agency to continue to use Lundberg Survey's reports, and not other sources, for their contracts. As a peacenik I somehow justified this relationship with the war machine as one to be proud of. At that time, 1977-1980, the U.S. had been fairly well behaved on the world stage for several years compared to the Vietnam War days. I am *not* now proud of my old work such as catering to the Pentagon's subscriber status, but I justify it as part of the period of my life: Lundberg Survey was like a graduate school or apprenticeship for the most meaningful work I could ever do later in life — against fossil fuels and motor vehicle domination.

94

Chapter 5

Plateau of Prestige Gives Way to the Worsening of the 1980s

The decade had begun with some hope and pride for Dan and Mesa when they got their first joint grandchild, Vernell Zephyr Lundberg. My having a baby daughter anchored me to the ground right away, for the first time in my life. I was troubled no more about philosophical or psychological questions. Early in the decade I also found purpose in the family business, as energy issues and market surveys proved to be a challenge I was up for. By 1984 I was running the company, with Dan doing less and less except for some continued media exposure.

For my nearly 14 years at Lundberg Survey — for my young manhood — I was stuck in a land of cultural deprivation that was less convivial than almost everywhere else in the world I had been. No matter how excellent was the L.A. Philharmonic with Zubin Mehta conducting, no matter how many Hollywood stars and producers there were on the west side of town, and no matter how mild the weather was compared to the rest of the U.S., I needed something more in order to hack it. The great rock bands of L.A.'s late 1960s flowering were gone or in remnants unappealing to my nostalgic heart, hence my obsession with music. But I was neglecting my own musical creativity. Sucking the corporate teat of Big Oil's money and forgetting my dreams of changing the world, not imagining I was an artist, I suppressed tension brewing inside me that I would be forced to act on.

To justify my "choice" to stay in L.A. – I somehow felt like I had no choice — I thought of my devotion to my father, and I was waiting to see if our family was going to resume fulfilling its greatness together. The justifying became harder after the novelty of working at an important firm in the early 1970s wore off and my rapid learning curve leveled off along with my wages. I was ripe for something more than being a good executive. Visible activism was practically nowhere, and almost everyone's lifestyle I could see was just a variation of consuming and short-term gratification. By the mid '70s I was slightly less on fire for social change and to save the environment, and my attempts were far from all-out. I seemed to have very little outlet. So I began to think mostly in terms of acquiring an excellent girlfriend (or wife someday, before my first marriage and after it ended). I worked so hard I felt I ought to just enjoy a laid-back life of weekend leisure, music and recreation. But bringing Xenia back into my life in 1975 through to 1983 had been disastrous in large part, for both of us and for our innocent child. Then again, Vernell's arrival into the world brought happiness for all of us.

Xenia stuck with me when I left the family business for over a year in 1977. But rather than find my own way and do my own thing, I got caught up in another one of my father's programs: a new pop-music newsletter called *Offbeat*. It was a business failure, such that it folded by the time the first subscription came in. I sought to guide the music industry in taste, because it sure needed it: the fare on the radio was the pits, and I took the Punk or New Wave trend about as seriously as I did Disco music. *Offbeat's* high point was an interview with rocker-turned-record-producer Spencer Davis, where he said, "America has poisoned the media for the Western World." The statement was the caption for his photo. After the newsletter was published I called him up at his office at Island Records, and he said right off the bat, "I didn't say that." I was too disappointed in him and too gentlemanly to say, "Well, listen to the tape!" so I let it go. How can you get tough with the guy who brought us "Gimme Some Lovin'"? Spencer, I've lost the tape, so you're safe!

I met some interesting Hollywood women (such as Gayna at the Grammy Awards) who made me increasingly feel chained to a marriage that was less than joyful for me. As it turned out, Xenia and I stayed together long enough for me to get back to working at Lundberg Survey and become further tied together. Xenia had been working at Lundberg Survey a couple of years, and was my father's "right-hand man." However, Trilby began to get jealous and demanded that Xenia be fired. This my parents did, and I held them in enough contempt for it to contribute to my quitting on my

way to doing *Offbeat.* Xenia went to work at a law firm in
downtown L.A., which didn't fill me with confidence or trust.

A making of enemies

Instead of fretting about my marriage and my less than joyous and
uncreative life, I would have done better to wonder more about my
sister Trilby. I guess it would be healthy for me to do that now:

One could still talk to her openly through the mid 1970s, but
she increasingly exhibited out of control emotions and unmeetable
needs. She seemed to have reserved a great deal of hostility and
other complex emotions about me. Years later it was clear to my
brother and me that Trilby was hostile also to other people, or even
people in general. Darius and I have speculated that Trilby's near
fatal dose of ant poison as a toddler, prompting her stomach to be
pumped, may have affected her brain.

On the Passat two events stand out that should have been dealt
with, perhaps with therapy or separating the two of us. In the
Caribbean she was having a fit and brandished a large knife at me.
Once in Vouliagmeni when we were having a social evening with
friends she snapped, without warning, and slammed me on the side
of my face with great force. I had said something in jest that as I
recall was hardly outrageous. I forgave these acts quickly and
resumed what was supposed to be a loving relationship, and until
about 1976 she was nice almost always. One reason she seemed to
be a normal loving sister and daughter is that she was mostly
living in northern California, and absence made the hearts grow
fonder. She was living poor as a church mouse, and I was glad to
help her occasionally. I was as surprised as my father, who
occasionally helped her too, when she said to us that nobody helped
her.

During one visit to Berkeley when I was about 19 or 20, I tried
to talk to her and Alan about the Vietnam War, not for the first
time. I got his standard reaction toward anti-war organizing, "I'm
not into that." Neither was Trilby into that, but she called our
parents "pigs," which in my opinion did not place her in the activist
column. Twenty years later I was to reflect that she was to change
places with me: I was living in Arcata as a foe of the oil industry
while Trilby was in L.A. as a servant to the oil industry, which I
was myself from 1972-1988 except for my feeble musical break

1977-78.

Trilby's activities as a pianist in public were few and far between, and basically ended, from her last gig on Greek radio our father arranged in 1969. Her dropping music disappointed everyone in the family although we didn't hold it against her. I was visiting Berkeley in perhaps 1971 when she had a gig at a women's political center in San Francisco. These were radical young women, and no men were allowed. Because of this I became fixated on somehow entering the building and seeing everyone, but I didn't quite do it. I examined my reasons and my urge, and the explanation must be that my being excluded for my sex (or race, or age, etc.) provoked a reaction to overcome the discrimination. I was unreasonable, for even though I was young and inexperienced I knew full well that women needed to organize and improve both their world and everyone's world. I was proud of Trilby for her connection with these hardcore women's liberationists.

When Trilby moved to North Hollywood from the San Francisco Bay area in 1976 she needed help. She could barely function, so Xenia and I helped her with favors such as errands, money, and socializing. We were three close friends, and we were glad that Trilby got a filing clerk's position at Lundberg Survey. This was probably the greatest mistake the family ever made: hiring her. She had a hard time getting into work, so we would help her driving to her apartment to pick her up. During this period she spent a lot of time with Darius's friends in North Hollywood, breaking hearts. She was not happy at her job, in part because she was beneath everyone in experience. She began to become surly and complain to her parents, who had the executive offices, about employees including Xenia and myself. Trilby's jealousy was out of control, as it focused the most on Xenia who enjoyed a comfortable position in the family.

One day in a relaxed mood I called Trilby up from my office when she was at home, and I said I needed to start getting back some of the money she had borrowed. Her response was "Stick it!" and she slammed down the phone. I was totally puzzled. It wasn't clear at the time, but it was from that moment that she treated me henceforth as her enemy. I wouldn't have been puzzled if she simply had little use for me or her nieces, and she just wanted to do her own thing. But what has been hard to wrap my mind around is the level of hate she has acted out towards me and the rest of the family. It took many years for me to see I had too long been unable to judge her objectively. For my own protection and for the sake of the family I needed to make a decision, many years before I actually did, that she had to be treated only as a foe that could never be expected to treat people right. But I didn't take that prudent step when it could have helped.

With the loan issue unresolved and spiraling into greater division between us, it should have been predictable that Trilby's and my relationship only could go downhill. I insisted on the money while she went to great lengths to convince our parents and her boyfriend Scott McCreary that she owed me no money. What she was also doing simultaneously, that Xenia and I hadn't expected, was to try to diminish us as workers and executives at the family business in the eyes of her somewhat sympathetic and therefore vulnerable parents. Unfortunately, they could not be objective about their daughter, and they promoted her over the heads of competent people who had seniority (as my father had done with me). Conflict became the rule of the day within the family and at work, as Trilby constantly went to her parents to complain about me, Xenia and other workers.

The rest is history, as coming pages will tell. Eventually Trilby's tactics and designs got her severed from the firm, a year before our father died. However, she was by then far too close for too long, such that people's fates were sealed. I have come to learn that when you have a conflict with someone who cannot be placated or reasoned with, and the person wants to only take from you and gain at your expense, the only sane course of action is to totally cut yourself off from that person. If that is not possible because the person is entrenched in your world, it is important to neutralize the person as much as possible by securing your rights permanently. Giving in and practicing appeasement and compromise only encourages your foe.

From Whiskey-a-go-go to the mansion to the skateboard commute to Pacific Palisades

Xenia and I were living in a rented house next to the Whisky A-Go-Go on Sunset Strip in 1978. I put a black light in our front porch light fixture. At the nightclub I met quite a few musicians, but didn't believe I'd ever be a performer. After less than a year there, during which time a childhood playmate moved in across the street (Paul Kassler, a talented animator who died a few years later), we were tired enough of the neighborhood to jump at a free rental, a mansion offered near downtown L.A. All we had to do was furnish it. My brother Darius joined us. It was a lovely three-story home with an old carriage-house in the back. It was surrounded by a dense low-income Latin American neighborhood. The Latinos used our unfenced front lawn for lunches and picnics, as we had some of the only green area around. I'm ashamed to say I didn't really like them to do it, even though I knew what it was like to lack natural surroundings. And I knew about being unwanted in one's own neighborhood:

A year or two earlier, within a few doors of my parents' house in the hills, I would pause on my way down the next street (Adina) where there was a break between the houses, where I'd look out over Universal Studios. The lot was small, steep, and all it was good for was sitting on the edge of the curb with one's feet hanging down the hill. As I was doing so one afternoon I was joined by the resident of the house next to it, who began a friendly conversation with me. We talked for a while, but eventually his real purpose became clear, which was that he wanted me to leave. He felt threatened that I was near his property. The poor jerk. Fortunately for the neighborhood's partial redemption not long after, a woman a few doors down from him had the opposite reaction to me as I picked berries across the street from her fancy yard: this hot, blond wife of a nightclub owner was flirting with me.

Back at the mansion in the Latino quarter, Darius proved at age 20 to be less than tidy. This was the only time to date I thought of him as someone I could not always get along with. His artistic cleverness left little patience for me as a manager type. He was by then a receptionist at Lundberg Survey, and I don't think he enjoyed it. Before a confrontation might have developed between us over housekeeping, the neighborhood proved too much to tolerate. When an intruder came in when my wife was sleeping, and I talked him into leaving, this became reason enough to move out soon.

Our property manager, Mary, was a lawyer, having recently graduated from USC. She said to us in a letter that my story about the intruder was a lie, fabricated so our lease could be broken (even though the rent was free). Eager for her first legal fight, she never got the chance: the owner of the property was supposedly a mysterious celebrity. To get through the veil and stop him and his mean lawyer from screwing with us, all I had to do was call up a city property-records office and get his name, Ray Briem. He was a local talk radio host I'd not heard of. (Wikipedia says he was "noted for his conservative viewpoints.") I got on his show and told the call-screener I lived in his property and wanted to talk about gasoline prices, the topic of his show. I was put on the air and alluded to his property, and we commenced to have a good discussion about the latest gasoline crisis. The next day Mary called and said Ray was furious, and that we could leave freely. Maybe my stunt was one of Mary's first real-world "legal" lessons, but through her anger she may not have learned that one should not be a hard-ass and doubt someone when safety is claimed to be an issue.

When I went to pick up the last items, L.A. policemen were there moonlighting for security pay. They handed me my items which were for a costume I'd used for a party where I was the "Electric Priestess," consisting of a Catholic bishop's hat and frock, a gun belt with live ammo, a large, garish marijuana-leaf/coke-spoon pendant, with my electric guitar slung over my shoulder that I played with a battery operated amp. The cops handed over the items at the big ornate door, and I mused that they might have thought I was some kind of a druggie. But we had a good chat, about how the lawyer was acting like "I'm a big lawyer."

Xenia, Darius and I moved to North Hollywood right across from Lundberg Survey, at a tacky apartment house that nevertheless had the usual southern California amenities. It had eaten up some of the last open space in the neighborhood. I skateboarded the few yards to work, right at the time when the Second Oil Shock was going into high gear. It was when we were living here that Xenia and I learned she was to have a baby. This changed my somewhat aimless and dissatisfied mind-set to focusing on clear objectives and to "cash in" on my parents willingness to make our lives more comfortable for a growing family. We were ready to get out of the apartment, actually two separate ones occupied by both of us simultaneously, one above the other. It was a good thing we had the one above when the lower one was flooded by sewage.

It was here that a redneck neighbor wanted to dismantle me because I asked him to turn down his music. Xenia defused the situation and saved me. The next day I visited him with my brother-in-law Bob Sharp who was a reserve Deputy Sheriff — another one of my father's ideas. The redneck (not Bob, the other one) was calm and all was well again. But what was I doing in such a dreary place, when I had known the beauty of swimming in the electric turquoise waters of the Blue Grotto at Capri and babbling in Italiano? Probably more important was that my family was quite together, as shown by Bob's reliability and bravery. He and Dana had gotten a divorce, but her manic depression tended to make Bob more essential than otherwise.

In business there were enlightened moments in those days. My father, my sister and I took Daniel Yergin, from the Harvard University Kennedy School of Business, co-author of *Energy Future*, to Hollywood's classic restaurant, Musso & Frank. After a lovely dinner and stimulating conversation, as we all talked in the parking lot, I could see Daniel was sweet on Trilby. They were both young and good-looking, and she had a father famous in the world of energy. I wanted to see them get together, but Trilby had a habit of rejecting or even being rude to perfectly nice men just because they were good looking, intelligent men. I don't know if this happened then with Daniel, but I was especially impressed with him when he invited me to come to Harvard to lecture to his class (which I failed to follow up on, for reasons that will become clear in the pages ahead).

My daily musings and concerns in those days were not to be found on the scale of "catastrophe living" that I was later to know. A topic popping into my head frequently in my easy days was how people got around so inefficiently in the land of the Little Old Lady from Pasadena and original home of the hot rod. During all my working years in L.A., not just when I was cutting back on driving, I increasingly thought of L.A. as in dire need of light rail. I realized it would take an incredibly large investment to replace the extensive Red Car system that had been trashed decades before. But I was excited to learn of the first subway project on the drawing board to go from downtown L.A. out to North Hollywood. Many years after several lines were built, I used the system around town, but found it to offer too little for a vast area such as metastasized Los Angeles.

In October of 1979 Xenia and I were between homes, staying at my parents, and she went to Greece for a family visit. I took a vacation and joined her by flying the opposite direction so I could fulfill my aborted yacht-trip around the world, and circle the globe albeit by jet. I visited my high-school buddy Peter Blood in New Delhi, as his father Archer Blood was Chief of Mission for the U.S. Embassy. When I got there, Archer, the hero of East Pakistan (and nemesis of the vindictive Henry Kissinger) had suddenly transferred to Afghanistan as Ambassador due to the Soviet Invasion. Peter had the run of the house, where John Kenneth Galbraith had lived as Ambassador. The grounds were my first view of Untouchables who were guards and lived in the back. The property was sort of magical, with the large pool, the strange air and light of the city, and the smell in the garden from the non-potable water — more tainted than what North Americans think of as grey water. For our morning papaya and American breakfast Peter and I enjoyed daily privileged State Department briefings on, say, Cuban troop movements in southern Africa. Peter and I had a good time in Delhi, where I bought a sitar, and we soon flew off to Katmandu for adventure in the Himalayas.

Our week and a half there was not a pleasurable venture into Shangri-la. Our stay started out well as we explored the city and bicycled out to an incredibly green edge of town in the golden sunshine of the late afternoon. If seeing tree-temples, wildly decorated public buildings and small plots of land with lush crops growing, this place appeals to anyone wanting an exotic experience. But we had to agree that the food was predominantly poor tasting. From Pokhara we hiked up to an ancient mountaintop temple where I performed a sacrifice of a goat to the god Shiva. Here's how this unanticipated act came to pass: in our hut the night before, a seer strongly recommended that I sacrifice a goat to Shiva for my health. The old woman, grandmother of our Sherpa, had been right in her palm readings about Peter's life and my life, so I was convinced in her ability to advise as well. Two days before I'd caught an intestinal bug. I noticed it the moment I downed an old can of Indian orange juice, which wasn't tainted or bad, but was dead as any kind of fresh food. For whatever validity there was for the power of Shiva's hearing or seeing me, the truth of the matter was the family got to have a goat stew out of the deal. I was pleasantly astounded that my health immediately took a marked turn for the better, which I cannot explain. I wrote the whole trip up in the short story "From Nepal With Blood," but couldn't get it published, to Peter's and his family's relief.

I picked up Xenia in Athens and flew back to L.A., where we moved to a nice rental house in Pacific Palisades. The backyard was mostly paved, so I put up a hydroponic veggie grower that didn't work. We knew almost none of the neighbors, par for the course. But when one has a new life to nurture — our baby about to be born — a helpless human being to care for and raise takes precedence over community or cultural issues.

Although I had been trapped for nine long years at Lundberg Survey and in L.A., something finally made up for the gap in my life after losing an enviable existence in the Mediterranean. That something was also the only thing that suggested there were benefits to a marriage such as mine: the gift of Vernell Zephyr Lundberg being born to us in 1980.

Prior to that great day of April 26, 1980, Xenia started staying at home while I drove to North Hollywood five days a week. She had stopped smoking. Vernell came into the world with the help of a midwife in a birthing center in Culver City. After a few days of getting used to bringing a new life into the world, I was in seventh heaven to think of my beautiful, lively little girl right there in her crib every day. Xenia was a very good mother and was entirely in accord with me about avoiding unnecessary medical industry procedures for our daughter. Ultraviolet radiation was prescribed by our pediatrician for mild jaundice, but as the condition was of no seriousness and the UV was only for appearance, we declined. But the doctor thereupon quit, seeing us as unprofitable. Vernell was breastfed a year and a half, which I believe guaranteed a strong start for her health. A vivid memory I have is when I fed Vernell her first solid food, some organic orange-colored melon. She loved it, and to witness it was a great experience for me too.

I played guitar a lot in my spare time and Xenia was, as always, tolerant of it. Vernell's soundtrack as a baby and toddler was my guitar playing, plus albums such as Pink Floyd's The Final Cut, Five Miles Out by Mike Oldfield, and Bach conducted by von Karjan. In those days we had a television. The series Dallas was one of the few shows we watched.

In 1980, life had plenty of leisure time for music, movies, etc.

Looking back, those days were less hectic for society at large (compared to what was ahead). But not all was perfect with my little family. Xenia was of course tied down much more than I. She resented it, which I did not understand; everything was provided for, and I was not running around town socially. She had wanted a college education ever since her father forbade her from applying to U.S. universities, and lately she had blamed my father for somehow stopping her from going to college as well. I didn't believe this, but in any case I told her I would be glad to take over child-care duties for any and all night classes; Xenia doubted me. Xenia and I each had in-law troubles, and I was not as patient or as easygoing as I could have been.

For a while my home life was enviable and sensible. Our charming house in Pacific Palisades was in northwestern, smog-free L.A. I was a member of an exclusive men's club in downtown L.A. that had a fancy beach annex not far from our house. (I walked to it once but that's not done in L.A.) After Vernell was born I felt like I was on top of the world, and I didn't mind the commute to LSI quite so much anymore. I found time to take night classes at UCLA that cut into my time at home helping to care for a baby. To me the arrangement seemed unavoidable, but my wife seemed to be somewhat unappreciative of what we had, and she had not made friends in the neighborhood. Yet, it was a stable time for over a year.

During this time came the shock of John Lennon's assassination in December 1980. I recall taking the day off in his honor, just walking around the garden. I called into the office and told my father why I wasn't coming in. He didn't like or respect it, but he didn't throw a fit.

My calm, affluent existence came crashing down in 1981 when my wife decided that I could not lay down the law on how long we could spend in Greece for a holiday (six weeks minimum was her demand; I said three perhaps). I was thinking like the dutiful executive and not what she wanted or needed. I was in no hurry to make the trip. I could not understand the deep need Xenia had to go there for a several weeks. Ultimately our argument resulted in her agreeing to a shorter time for us there. After all, I wanted to see my daughter every day, and it had not occurred to me that Xenia should go with just Vernell. Many years later I could tell that the more extended family Xenia had was an attraction for helping to raise a child. I was a nuclear-family American.

One day when I had been fasting a few days I had a very fitful morning in bed, and when I got up my little family had disappeared. There was a note that they had gone on a long errand. I got a call from Xenia in New York and was devastated that they were on their way to Greece. I felt like a brick labeled "divorce" hit me on the head, although I didn't want to face it. Xenia later phoned me up and said I was welcome to join them. At first I demanded that they come back, but in the end when I recovered from my fast I went there for a visit, at the urging of my father. Vernell, at just over a year's age, was shy around me at first. Our visit was not so bad, as we enjoyed Marathon and a Peloponnese beach resort called Tolon.

We came back together, but we never recovered from what I considered was a betrayal. In a few months, after another stay at my parents in Hollywood Hills, my little family moved to our own home that my parents helped us buy in a distant, countrified suburb. The huge back yard, with a prolific white nectarine tree, was the best feature of this ranch-style home in Saugus. The upper-desert town is now part of Santa Clarita. I became even more unhappy in the marriage, particularly as I saw my daughter being raised somewhat contrary to my experience. We were there until 1983, when I was forced to file for divorce (so it seemed) while I attempted to stay in the same house together.

Our relationship had deteriorated but I had stuck it out in order to spare our daughter a broken home. This worked for less than two years, as I became increasingly unhappy, thus making my wife less happy. She had not found her own life's purpose or made friends once again in our new "community." Saugus was okay for suburbanites commuting and doing back yard barbeques. At least it was basically out of the smog.

Owning our starter home, at a 16% interest mortgage-rate common then, we were supposed to be content. I was a car commuter, but proud enough, and relished being the father of a wonderful little tyke. Our yard had lizards and occasional raccoons. This was the edge of the L.A. area, culturally as well, with some good aspects, but hardly anyone to relate to. One neighbor's bumper sticker said, "Sierra Club — Go Take a Hike!" My days there were calm but not happy, due to the failing marriage, and I gave myself added pressure that my daughter deserved better than the fate of my father: the product of a broken home.

What triggered my divorce action was Xenia's announcement that she was going to Greece again with Vernell alone, with no return date. She allowed no room for discussion or negotiation. So, acting quickly, I disconnected the spark plugs on our Mazda Rx7. The domestic atmosphere steadily deteriorated, despite my joy of still being able to take my toddler out to the park. Worsening matters was the surprise arrival of my Greek mother-in-law who came to the house to stay. This was in order to shore up her daughter in what was becoming a state of war. With some heavy scenes in front of Vernell, they managed to physically kick me out.

In seeking a restraining order to keep Vernell from being taken out of the County without my permission, I had to be by law filing for divorce. So I had done this. I was relieved that my father was quite supportive. I did not intend to follow through with divorce, but Xenia and her mother wanted me out, and their behavior hardened my attitude such that I decided to let the divorce ride on through. Many years later I realized that it was a mistake, when for Vernell's sake I might have tried much harder and avoided the wrenching psychic pain for her. The arguing, the uncertainly for a vulnerable child, and permanent separation of parents are the worst thing that can happen to a child short of being maimed, physically and badly abused, or being stunted by malnourishment. In retrospect, I might have somehow established a double life for my own needs, possibly coming to some accommodation with my old friend Xenia, while keeping the household and family together for the sake of my child. However, I felt strongly about things being only "right" or "wrong," and I believed I could soon reestablish myself in a calmer household for the best interests of my daughter. I partially succeeded, but the emotional damage to a little girl was done. Unfortunately, her mother eventually proved to have difficulty as a single mother, after her mother left, despite my generous financial support and visitation arrangements for our daughter.

I was warned by my sage lawyer Marshall "Rusty" Sanders that Vernell's unhappiness at three years old, with fighting parents who were to be separated, which showed in her eyes, would affect her the rest of her life. But I could not really tell for many years, such were her efforts to be a good child, top student and member of her community. I realized I had been the one mostly responsible for bringing matters to a head because of my domestic dissatisfactions and concerns, but I justified it in my mind. Bolstering my self-confidence and resolve was my belief that my actions were necessary so that I could raise my daughter the way I had been taught to raise a child, without the interference of my wife or her family who had more permissive cultural values. It was disturbing to me that my wife included our daughter in the Greek practice (over in Greece, not so much of Greeks elsewhere) of staying up very late. In Greece people commonly have super after midnight, one reason a siesta is necessary the next day. Over two decades later I decided that I was wrong to divorce my wife, due to the harm to our daughter. Vernell's family stress that I allowed, at her tender age of three, had to verge on the emotionally traumatic.

I moved to an apartment down the road for a few months before moving to the Lundberg Survey-owned "Halfway House." It was a penthouse condo over the hill from the Hollywood Bowl. I saw Vernell frequently, but it was a few years before Xenia would allow Vernell to spend the night away from the Saugus house. I finally broke this pattern when I learned that Vernell's emotional pull to return to Saugus seemed to be based on a promise of dollies; I told her that she and I could stay longer in Catalina Island because I would get her the same dolly. I fondly remember bicycling around with her seated behind me, as she inadvertently picked up from me some of The Final Cut that she sang with me around Avalon.

I was the visiting dad, and it was miserable although I made the best of it. My soon-to-be ex-wife's non-cooperation in our daughter staying overnight with me seemed to be just for the sake of maintaining control. It thus took a few years until I could really be a 100% dad. I wanted custody, joint or full, but had to wait years before achieving it. (My daughter later chose to live with me when she was eight.) An unhappy single parent can easily blame the ex-spouse for any misery, but one must always put oneself in the child's position. I was able to do that sometimes, such as when I asked Vernell what she thought of my daily routine, as we drove down the freeway in my fancy Buick Behemoth: "Do you think that every day I go to the merry-go-round or the zoo?" She said, "Yeah."

That's what a four year old can think. My father also helped me to put myself in her position: when I had buckled her into the car seat once in his driveway, I slammed the door shut in a normal fashion. He told me, "Be gentle with the loud noises you make around her." I would not have thought of it, perhaps. It was many years later that I came to strongly dislike the artificial environment, such as hard and dangerous surfaces made of materials that involved much entropy and toxicity, and noisy trucks and buses. Such thinking made me appreciate nature and natural materials all the more, and I passed this along to my daughters.

Even as a fulfilled father, in the '80s it gnawed at me that I was failing to "make a difference" for the workers of the world and for the environment. I was still living a lie. Regret for not leaving L.A. for good after high school was still my major lament. I was partly hooked on a regular paycheck, and I had little concept of truly living on my own (without my father's help). I didn't have significant debts, but there seemed to be invisible bonds tying me to L.A. and therefore Lundberg Survey. Despite the increasingly interesting work, the truly meaningful thing in my life was being a father. I did sense greatness ahead for the family firm, on top of our established success, but what was this compared to two higher purposes: the responsibility and joy in connection with having a daughter, and realizing my most cherished personal goal of a life of adventure?

Little Vernell and I were in the glitzy Centrum restaurant in Studio City enjoying brunch when I noticed at the next table the actor Ed Asner, the "Lou Grant" TV star. He had several younger adults sitting around him. At a lull in their conversation, he said, "There's a demonstration tomorrow against U.S. support for the El Salvador death squads at the (so-and-so building). Anyone game to go down there with me?" No responses. I nearly blurted out, "Hell, I'll go. What's the matter with these friends of yours?" I felt sorry for his disappointment but I admired his fighting the good fight. As for me, in those days it was a big deal to be a father and run an important company, so I wimped out on Ed's call to action just as his young friends had done.

The freedom and adventure that I still craved was self-denied. I was sucked in by family concerns and our capitalistic venture towards greater and greater prestige in the energy field. I began to see that my parents' less than high confidence in their children discouraged their leaving the nest to go out and struggle or succeed on their own. (I was the only one to permanently move away from southern California, in 1986.) Maybe this was not a big deal to my siblings, because they were not out to "change the world" or have a grand adventure of life.

The way it worked out for me, my whole time in L.A. after living in the Med was a time of paying dues: I was learning rare professional skills and developing a track record more valuable than any academic degree – if, and only if, I used it for the greater social good. My education was also in the area of "human nature," and I was being prepared to take action in my life at every significant, future turn. My "School of Hard Knocks" was ahead for my middle age. I can blame my parents somewhat, but not hate them, for my later hardships and my roller-coaster life. I must thank them for their originality and focus — and love.

Lundberg Survey at its height

Apart from some meaningful work for the Environment Protection Agency to help phase out lead, and some interesting work for the agencies that would make up the Department of Energy, the important data our company had was going to waste. Where was the knock on the door from the Sierra Club that could make use of our data and expertise? Why wasn't my father being sought after by the Secretary of Energy or the President, so that meaningful policy changes could be ushered in?

These frustrations and misgivings faded when the Iranian Revolution of 1978 had its tumultuous effect on gasoline prices, and our firm predicted with fanfare the Second Oil Shock. Also in 1979, our data became essential for the California Public Utilities Commission to set natural gas prices based on our alternative fuels surveys. This prestigious and socially charged role, like all the company's departments (except for *Energy Détente*, a money-losing venture for keeping Trilby and Germán from moving to Venezuela), was my responsibility, as I was my father's prime collaborator and executive. For example, the weekly *Lundberg Letter* saw me as "final editor," safeguarding client concerns, data integrity, and other aspects of our business. Trilby was frustrated at my abilities and jealously wanted me to receive no bonuses. The only other person who resented my role, only in part, was Mark Emond, our star editor of the *Lundberg Letter* in its 1979-1980 heyday. He felt forced to have a young man – Dan's kid — come to him, a veteran professional trade journalist, with editorial changes; this ruined almost every week for him. But more often than not I prevailed. Mark vastly preferred our statisticians Lynn Beavers and Harry Ash, young guys but with masters degrees who didn't argue policies with Mark or edit him. It was, despite everything, a brilliant crew, and the results were obvious. The nation's press was forced to pay a subscription for the *Letter*; we issued no press releases although my father, and occasionally myself, did consent to interviews.

Despite our triumphs, it was hard for me to rationalize that we were really independent analysts and commentators when the major oil companies were paying 90% of our bills. Worse than this, the purpose of our reports was generally not noble: serving to increase the gasoline sales of each competing corporation using our reports. I eventually realized that my market reports that I tried to sell so hard, as we competed against other firms offering similar services — firms we hated and feared — were all about growth: more gasoline sales, grown of oil company profits, and of the whole urban sprawl lunacy that involved constructing more gasoline stations (using our data) and generating still more motor traffic. I hated the effects of my work but I loved my job and our prestige. Crazy, huh?

Meanwhile, because I couldn't stand L.A.'s sprawl and my being car dependent, I started living in parts of L.A. that featured some denser neighborhoods. In Sherman Oaks and later in Studio City I could walk to nearly everything I needed — even though this was L.A.; it made a great difference to me in tolerating the daily grind.

By the early 1980s Dan's health was going steadily down, what with his routine of the short commute in the smog and a sedentary lifestyle for too many years. Instead of living intelligently for the long haul, his habits and lack of vision got the best of him. His heart began to fail him and he used nitroglycerine pills and later a nitro patch, and he used a wheel chair. He had been looking for a new sailing yacht, but the search went on for years while his health worsened. His chosen boat, a 44-foot motorsailer he named Comrade, was only a few months under his command. He lived his last days on it at Catalina Island while I ran the business. Trilby had been severed from Lundberg Survey the year before, as her jealousy of me and her schemes with her OPEC-loyal husband, previously severed, had created strain and craziness in the family.

The year following my separation and divorce from Xenia I met up with a woman I'd met years before when she was married to Jimmy Fields. The occasion was a sad one, Jimmy's funeral. But I hooked up immediately with his ex, Heidi Lehwalder. We soon formed a new nuclear family with their daughter Polly Fields, Laura, another one of her children from her intervening marriage, and my five-year-old Vernell. The joyful fantasy of this union seemed most promising, and I didn't think I minded being stuck in L.A. anymore. As plans solidified for a life with Heidi, there was a warning sign that our relationship might be rocky. I chose to ignore the incident that was her flying off the handle with me on a long-distance call. I just wanted the happiness she had started to give me.

Our daughter Bronwyn was soon on the way. Her birth was in early February 1986. With this delightful new anchor in our lives we seemed to be on top of the world. By this time I was running the family business, as my father was finally where he wanted to be: living on his new sailboat forever.

On August 3rd of that year, 1986, he died. I was caught off guard, or had been in denial about losing him and seeing his dream-projects unfinished. Instead of his potential having been fulfilled, or at least his exploits being celebrated in a book I'd write on his life, his death unleashed all-out family infighting and disgrace.

From the *New York Times* archives online:

> WHOLESALE GASOLINE PRICES JUMP ... " said Jan C. Lundberg, president of Lundberg Survey Inc. of North Hollywood ... prices. Mr. Lundberg said that prices from refiners ... August 13, 1986 - By LEE A. DANIELS (NYT) - News - 699 words

> DAN LUNDBERG, OIL ANALYST, DIES; FORECAST 1979 GASOLINE SHORTAGE.. Dan Lundberg, the oil industry analyst ... attack. Mrs. Lundberg said he died in a ... , when Mr. Lundberg was among the first to ...View free preview August 6, 1986 - AP (NYT) - Obituaries - Obituary - 396 words

My father's memorial service was at the California Yacht Club. In attendance was Fred Hartley, CEO of Union Oil Company (Unocal). My brother Guy read a long poem by an Englishman that failed to move me. At the closed family dinner after the memorial, present were my mother, Trilby and Chacín, Darius, me, and Heidi. It was clear from the tension in the room, as Heidi observed to me afterward, that Trilby and her husband were in opposition to me and trying to play up to my mother.

Leaving the Fold

Things got crazier and hellish after my father's death, and never abated except years later in my successive world of activism, music, learning about ecology, and rare, wonderful relationships. I became grateful that I was subjected to pressures prompting me to leave the family business, despite the stress and troubles in and out of court later on. After all, I escaped "Smel.L.A." and gained much.

It took Trilby and her husband Germán Chacín, a Venezuelan whom she had met in Caracas when he was an OPEC official, only a matter of weeks to gain total control of Lundberg Survey. How they did it was not to be read about in a typical business-press article or MBA textbook.

They had been together five years, and toward the end of their employ with Lundberg Survey, Dan and I had learned to ignore their dreams, demands and incompetence. So they increasingly concentrated on Mesa, who had had her first stroke in 1984. By the time Dan died his widow had become very sympathetic to her daughter's and son-in-law's complaints and dreams, and the relationship between Dan and Mesa was under stress for the first time ever to my knowledge. By 1984 I was becoming the closest confidante of Dan, who was becoming depressed about his family due to his daughter's loyalty to the troublesome Chacín. Still, he thought he had the future mapped out for after his death.

Trilby's attacks on the family could be out in the open after her father was out of the way, and as the attacks escalated the "soap-opera" gained momentum. Ultimately it cost Heidi and me our marriage, and eventually Trilby's campaign cost two Lundbergs their lives.

As hellish as the disaster was following my father's death, the changes that his passing triggered set me on my own true path. I was finally out from under his script, although I've always credited him for most of what I am. In order to emphasize the positive aspects of my family's disintegration, I have gotten ahead of the sequence of developments. Back to the take-over:

I had to write and publish the *Lundberg Letter* with my "In Memoriam" for my father; arrange for my father's ashes; get the

White House to send my mother a telegram of condolence, and continue to confer with department heads at Lundberg Survey. I soon found it hard to continue my management of the company in the media spotlight and trying to keep the departments on track, because of a sideshow: a circus atmosphere was being created in the work place. This was solely due to interference by a determined outsider, Trilby Chacín, who had reentered the firm just to help our mother open condolence letters.

Trilby and Chacín were nearly openly carrying out their long-planned move. They had nothing to lose as they overtly dominated my befuddled, bereaved, ill mother Mesa Lundberg. With her recent stroke, the lasting effects of her pesticide poisoning, and being distraught and dazed about the loss of her husband, she was a sitting duck without him. My father and I should have faced this two years before and dealt with it strongly, but we must have been clinging to the illusion of family togetherness. Dan had in recent years become more protective of Mesa, and despite his declining health he was still outgoing compared to her in her passivity. When he moved onto his boat it was like a break from his wife that might have set a new tone for their marriage. Regardless, she was not prepared for his death, as it was a total, devastating loss for her. She did not grasp where she stood legally, so she started to make confused "decisions" she had no right to make. I would correct her and gain her understanding and cooperation, but she changed her "decisions" day to day due to relentless pressure from Trilby. I could not offset the mischief by trying to stay with my mother constantly; I had not the time.

During their banishment from Lundberg Survey, Mr. and Mrs. Chacín had been working with my former wife Xenia Lundberg who offered expertise such as office skills, knowledge of legalities, importation, telexes and other communication. The three of them were trying to do some kind of business I knew nothing about. Xenia was actually secretly playing a part, unbeknownst to her partners, to help the cause of her daughter, Vernell Lundberg as heiress. Trilby and Germán assumed that Xenia hated me as they did. But they were dealing with a Greek, and no one in the world puts family first more than a Greek does.

When my father died Xenia became very agitated, but at the time I misinterpreted it as a chance to interfere in my life and my marriage. Xenia had some information for me, however. I received some of it on paper and the rest of it verbally. The latter was Trilby's cold statement, upon the death of Dan Lundberg: "One down and one to go." The information on paper was copies of telexes of business between Chacín and traders in weapon systems and oil. Xenia had to account for the missing copies, so she told them, with my secret permission, that I had stolen them from her. Their reaction was to pressure her almost to the point of violence to have me charged and jailed for theft. The information I had was further proof that Lundberg Survey could be in danger of antitrust violations by having someone in the company involved in taking a position on oil prices. I eventually found that no one really cared, for the oil industry turned out to be less and less genteel and honorable than I had thought. It took me many years to accept that corruption is more than likely the norm in big business, and that objecting to it or fighting it is mostly limited to movies.

In September 1986 I gave the keynote speech for the Renewable Fuels Association in Washington, D.C. for its annual meeting. As President of Lundberg Survey I was sympathetic yet skeptical about the industry group, but the audience wanted oil insight. It's impossible for me to remember what I said because of two shocking events right after my speech:

Following me on the stage was the man I sat next to, C. Boyden Gray, Vice-President George H. W. Bush's legal counsel. This regulatory insider (and later Neocon) spoke at length about the need to support the Administration's Contra policy in Nicaragua, seemingly connecting lobbying well for renewable fuels with killing Nicaraguans. I was amazed and disgusted. I got up and asked the first question: "How are these ladies and gentlemen before us supposed to go about their business with the added obligation of doing something they may not believe in?" — I don't recall my exact statement. Gray was caught off guard completely, and answered me at the podium: "I don't understand what you said, but I agree." I remember that clearly, partly because it was so stupid. Only now do I see that the answer may have been clever: to get everyone off the subject and instead wonder about C. Boyden Gray's IQ.

When I got to my hotel room, I got a call from my mother who said I was fired. She didn't have the authority to do it, but was being used by my sister and her husband as a brainwashed weapon. My mother seemed like an automaton in the sense that she had a telephonic message for me and nothing more. It was a bit ironic that I had just defended the people of Central America downstairs, while two supposed foes of U.S. Imperialism, champions of Latin America, were gunning for my job.

I was unable to stop the domination and abuse of my mother and of our company, even after weeks of additional effort and patient dealings with my confused mother. My lawyer and I met with my mother, sister and their lawyer Michael Markovich. What was strange was that weeks before, Markovich as lawyer for the Lundberg Family Trust, being created by Dan and Mesa, told a meeting of the survivors that it was clear I was to continue running the company. But now here he was as my adversary without explanation. The meeting resulted in a triumvirate management team, something I agreed to because I could veto any of Trilby's moves. But that evening Trilby forced my mother to sign a letter to the effect that I was still fired and not to come into the office. The letter was delivered to my home. I called my right hand man, Bob Sharp (former brother-in-law), and before I could tell him the latest on Trilby's games, he surprised me by threatening me with a "class-action lawsuit." He somehow switched from disparaging Trilby's actions to joining her.

My mother did not like what was happening with her children in a family business, but she was physically and emotionally unable to cope. She tried when it was too late to keep me in the company, by arranging a lunch meeting alone with her at a North Hollywood restaurant. She offered me a position as sales manager of Lundberg Survey. She (and Trilby) knew that I was needed to keep up client relations and government contracts. However, with the OPEC allegiance and antitrust elements that the presence of Trilby and her husband meant for our family business, and likely fights over editorial policy, I could not accept any position, be it sales manager or president. I felt sorry for turning my mother down, because in her heart she just wanted her children to be happy and do well. She was completely incapable of doing the right thing in her state of health and confusion without her protective husband. I knew I was walking away from financial security and the chance to make more money than ever. But I instead felt less secure, and proceeded to scuttle the purchase of a fine house for my wife and me in Woodland Hills near Topanga Canyon.

Trilby could dominate my mother almost 100% of the time (as could anyone given enough access, at that point in my mother's condition). My clean-break departure from the firm was part of my "peace in the family" policy. I negotiated with my mother (within her marching orders) an extremely modest severance settlement. My stock in Lundberg Survey was purchased from me at "book value" rather than the vastly greater market value. The main material assist I got in my settlement was worth about $85,000 which was my father's boat, the spiffy 44-foot Lancer motorsailer Comrade. Its draft was too deep for the Chesapeake so I reluctantly sold it within a year, all the while paying slip fees and membership in the California Yacht Club.

I had just chosen to ignore my father's last will dated in the early 1970s that gave me owning control of Lundberg Survey (with Darius's stock proxy which I had). That document appeared to have been damaged and thus weakened, and a newer will was suspiciously missing. So my abnegation was assisted by hurdles and closed doors, although knocking them down could have been possible. Firing family members or suing them, I felt, would have ruined the sterling reputation of Lundberg Survey, and more importantly, the family name.

With all confidence in my abilities I moved on, stripped of my legacy that I was groomed for. A judge running for re-election told me at a party, "Your name is like gold, like the Kennedy name." Soon our name was to be tarnished, making a mockery of my sacrifice for peace in the family and to protect the family name.

My lawyer was Michael, a wimpy Harvard law sold-practitioner. He could only advise me to "hang out [my] own shingle. This was intriguing, so with dismal prospects to keep my rightful position I decided to quit Lundberg Survey. I began to work from home and see what client arrangements could be had. With just enough encouragement from a couple of major oil companies I resigned from Lundberg Survey, obtained the aforementioned settlement, and proceeded to create a new market-research firm. I made preparations to move my family and myself to northern Virginia to start afresh. I flew to Fredericksburg, Virginia and found a fine, historic home in the Tidewater region, took pictures of its inside and outside, sent them to Heidi and got her approval, and leased it. When I returned, my wife and I arranged for a moving van, packed our two cars with all our kids,

and paid a visit to my mother. We crossed the U.S. with cold
weather that, along with poor air in the heated cars, did not help
Bronwyn's health. It took her weeks to overcome earaches, which
we fought with antibiotics even though I did not approve of them.
Heidi was insistent on them, having no faith in my assurances that
a fast would cure Bronwyn. (Heidi had suggested, and I had
agreed, before Bronwyn was born, that I would be in charge of
health and she in charge of music.) For a long time after our
cross-country trip I blamed Trilby and my mother for causing our
departure to the detriment of Bronwyn's health.

Upon our move to Fredericksburg in 1986, we thought we had
relocated to almost a different culture. As for me, inside I was the
same: I did the same kind of oil company work, and my guiding
life-purpose was to do a job that I had pride in as Dan Lundberg's
son. I knew I would keep doing it well, hoping for more meaning.
I had a couple of major clients, and thought that I could build from
that. I kept busy, my wife less so.

In the coming months I started to become aware once again
that the life of adventure I craved was a dying echo of a 17-year-
old's forever-lost dream. I had sold out, but with good intentions,
and besides, I'd gotten deep into serious stuff, as the "soap opera"
unfolded. I thought I had to keep going with the cards I had been
dealt, to survive.

At least I was finally out of L.A. for good, with a great wife and
my sweet children. From my vantage point as I pictured my new
home-to-be in Virginia, Fredericksburg seemed to be a suburb of
Washington D.C. But we found out when we got to know our new
home town at the end of 1986 that it was more like the Old South,
at least in the minds of most of its citizens. I had done much
business in Washington for Lundberg Survey and enjoyed that
town 50 miles north of Fredericksburg.

Bronwyn didn't have the healthiest childhood compared to
Vernell, so I felt helpless and afraid at times especially when her
mother and I didn't agree on health. We had two pediatricians who
alternated. Seth Craig was understanding and patient, taking my
side regarding what I thought would have been unnecessary x-
rays. I liked him as a citizen as well. The other doctor, John
Painter, was more conventional. A letter of his to my soon-to-be
ex-wife was used against my having custody of Bronwyn, alleging
I had interfered in antibiotics. Sadly, I had dutifully given them to

her, when her mother was on the road for concertizing, one after
another as Painter experimented and got poor results.

In late 1986 I had formed my own company, Lundberg Reports,
without one bit of business from my old firm as Trilby insisted. I
was to find out that this was as generous as she could get, as she
soon wanted what I had and wanted me out of the way.

Yet, in Fredericksburg my little family and I enjoyed the snow
as we anticipated living through the four seasons. We also
appreciated the ability to walk around a small community for our
needs and pleasure. My main client was Mobil Oil, before its
merger with Exxon. My new firm proceeded to survey about 10%
of all the gasoline stations in the U.S in the less than two years I
operated it. Truly out on my own, I was still walking in my
father's footsteps and, like him, had assembled an interesting crew
of workers that I sent around the country. My views on the oil
industry and U.S. society were nothing remarkable, and I had no
idea they would start developing rapidly as I was approaching
major changes in my life and career.

A client of mine wanted to join me in business in order to
improve on what marketing information was being generated by
Lundberg Survey and others. I was quite interested, and we got far
into collaboration and negotiation. But the attempt to come to an
ownership agreement came to a halt: both of our egos wanted
majority control, so we dropped our plans immediately and never
spoke of them again. Looking back I should have given him what
he wanted, considering that in a matter of months I simply
dissolved Lundberg Reports.

My last public testimony as an analyst *for* the oil industry was
when the U.S. Environmental Protection Agency held hearings to
decide what method of vapor recovery was best for gasoline
vending. I happened to care whether cars would have canisters to
capture the carcinogenic benzene and other poisons, or if gasoline
stations would have to install vapor recovery hoses and sheaths.
The latter is the far less efficient system, allowing fumes to escape
into our air and into our bodies. And, that system was costly as
hell. None of this seemed to matter, as the car industry won the
fight. Anyone who has bought gasoline in the U.S. and used
modern nozzles has seen, without being aware, an interesting
example of the car lobby's being more powerful than the oil
industry (at least on occasion). This oil boy wanted our side to win

along with the atmosphere and public health. But instead the nation got "No, let the car companies save money and stick it to the oil industry and our lungs."

After I testified I happened to phone my mother to let her know what I had just done, and when she heard I had done something involving the EPA she sounded as happy as if I told her she was getting another grandchild. She jumped to the conclusion that I was changing careers and going over to the environmental side. This was right before I myself knew I would do that.

After less than a year into my Lundberg Reports venture, Trilby became more paranoid of my abilities. With stealth she sued me fraudulently in federal court, while I was in Singapore at an oil conference. The false complaint was that I was illegally using my own name and competing (although I had written permission to do both from my mother, Chairman of the Board), and allegedly possessed proprietary information from the "family" firm. I still don't know exactly who came up with that smear or the rest of the perjury, but it was likely a combination of Trilby, her husband Germán Chacín, my former brother-in-law Bob Sharp, and their lawyers. My sister's declared worry, as a justification for injunctive relief, was that my selling my boat would provide me cash for my competing business. This aggression was part of an attempt to ruin my financial capability, as it was timed with a letter to our client base that claimed I had been "duly terminated" from Lundberg Survey. The suit didn't go anywhere, but accomplish its main result by costing me many thousands of dollars in part because I countersued. My sister and I settled out of court without ever speaking with one another. It was my countersuit that brought an end to her and Lundberg Survey's aggression. So the skirmish stopped then and there. I regretted that I could not pay my lawyer, the able Bob Besser (related to The Three Stooges' Joe Besser) another large retainer to pursue the case. It might have destroyed Lundberg Survey — something that years later, I realized, would have been best for the family. Besides Trilby's concerns over my making a living at her perceived expense, it was clear to some of us that her jealousy of my having children and having succeeded in business was too much for her nerves.

Soon after the federal court incident I was visited in Fredericksburg by the chief executive of E.K. Williams & Co., a service-station accounting company in Santa Barbara that we at

Lundberg Survey had respected and feared competitively. CEO Keith Hamilton had taken a liking to me and felt I needed to know a couple of things. He told me that when he visited Lundberg Survey in recent time, he asked Trilby Lundberg about all the barbed wire on top of the fences around the property. "It's because of Jan," she told him. When he told me I was stunned, and informed him that the barbed wire had been there for many years before. As he learned more of the problem I had with my sister, he advised me, "You can't help who you're related to. Their problems are their own. You are not responsible for your sister." David de Rothschild, of the banking family, is an environmentalist who put his situation this way: "I cannot be held responsible for other people's actions despite my best efforts, even family members." He opposes Israel's intention to mine oil shale in the Biblical valley where David fought Goliath.

Keith's suggestion was a revelation to me, easing the burden of shame and frustration over my family's breakdown. What I didn't realize for a good while longer was that my assumed life's work and ego were only causing me trouble. A different character might have sidestepped not just the conflict on the mid-1980s but the entire 1970s. What if I had ignored my parents and gone to Columbia and discovered Gaviotas, South America's gem of a showcase for sustainable living and ecological restoration? Trilby might have followed me, but any might-have-beens have little value when the stakes have gotten higher still today.

Chapter 6

Rehoisting the Banner for Social Change

My Career Change

By the time the federal court case was settled, I had recently become totally disillusioned in paying people to do work I myself did not enjoy doing, i.e., market-data gathering and processing. This prompted me to almost overnight make the career jump to environmental work. There was additional impetus from others equally bored with gasoline station information: on two occasions in Washington, D.C., when recruiting surveyors and filling them in with details of the job, each applicant literally fell asleep, nodding off in the middle of my spiel. I can't say I blamed them. I was getting closer to confronting the question, "Do I want to build a business and career based on meaningless drudgery?" Too many capitalists have gone before me, and since, in offering people "shit jobs" without qualms.

The final straw had occurred when I was surveying a gasoline station in Baltimore. I looked up at the sign with its gasoline prices, clipboard in hand, and said, "That's it, no more." There was no going back, and the world opened up for me.

With the spurious lawsuit against me settled, I could start transitioning out of the private sector and begin the adventure I had craved for almost two decades. Although it was clear to me that I was less and less satisfied with my oil-statistics career, I had to yet make the break and land somewhere. My jumping-off point came at a speech I made on the oil market for the U.S. Department of the Treasury in December 1987, where I advocated higher taxes on oil consumption to bring about conservation. I also predicted that the oil price would spike sometimes but not rise enough to allow alternatives to gain dominance, until the final spike when it would be too late for them to step in coherently. *National Petroleum News* covered the prediction, but not my suggestion on taxes.

I set about looking for a job in environmental action, or to create a joint venture with someone in a renewable energy publication. I got only one job, a temporary slot at Renew America (formerly the Solar Lobby). Commuting with me on the Amtrak run north to D.C. was Bob Gettlin, who was researching Richard Nixon and Watergate for the book he co-wrote (*Silent Coup: The Removal of A President*) that made a good case for the Watergate scandal being a planned changing of the guard. But politics of that sort held little interest for me by 1988, no matter what polluting wing of the two-party system was on the way out or on the way in.

I made a point of visiting the Sierra Club and offering any help as an oil-savvy activist, but I was received bureaucratically and unimaginatively. I never heard back.

It hit me that if Lester Brown could start up Worldwatch Institute, I could found a nonprofit institute as well. Having thought of the environmental crisis in terms of smog, dating back to my eye-watering short-of-breath childhood in Hollywood, I set out to focus on petroleum, alternatives and energy policy.

I was encouraged by Norman Cousins, who soon joined our Advisory Board. He told me my plans were of "a noble calling." My father knew him, and I wanted to too. A giant intellect of the 20th century, Cousin's wisdom deserves contemplation today: "We come of age as a cosmic species when we accept the fact that the universe does not exist for our exclusive convenience." If only he had lived longer. I never met him. Before I left L.A. he put on an exhibit of his photography, but I was having too hectic a time to attend.

Despite the intent of the new organization, my purpose was amorphous. After scribbling out a couple of dozen possible names for a new group, I settled on Fossil Fuels Policy Action. I was open to almost anything, but my preferences began to come through quickly when joining activities and making statements were called for. At the time I wanted in on cool politics and to join the club of the greats. I dabbled in motor vehicle fuel efficiency standards, Amtrak support, and raising the gasoline tax. I visited Capitol Hill and spoke to reporters in need of an environmental sound bite. As a neophyte I was proud to introduce the VP of Worldwatch to the Editor of *Harper's* magazine, and they hit it off.

When I found out about the present danger of global warming it was on a sweltering evening over dinner in the summer of 1988 in Washington with the chief economist of the Environmental Defense Fund, Dan Dudek. His bad news made me feel as if I lost some innocence as a child of the Earth. Yet this spurred me on to jump into the movement with all I had.

Fossil Fuels Policy Action Institute was founded in August 1988. In announcing a newly formed organization, the national press was kind to me; it helped that they knew well who I was. My well-attended press conference in Washington's International Club resulted in reports on my starting a "global warming center." I blew it at the podium when I betrayed my embarrassing ignorance of the Windfall Profits Tax having already gone out of existence. So my best publicity was by a reporter who hadn't attended: *USA Today's* headline with my photo was "Lundberg Lines Up With Nature." My wife said my picture in the story looked like I was a fascist, but it was an executive mug shot. Same thing?

Because this story was seen on an airplane by the editor of *Population and Environment* journal, my life's work was to take a significant turn. That journal's editor, Virginia Abernethy, an anthropologist teaching at Vanderbilt University, enlisted me to review *Beyond Oil: The Threat to Food and Fuel in the Coming Decades.* For my extremely long review of that book/econometric model, I learned about peak oil, net energy, and the lack of practical substitutes for cheap petroleum. I seemed to have accidentally hit on something big about the oil industry on which I was supposed to be so expert. The information was not strange, as it fitted with what I had known. My review began, "Party's over!"

A note about peak oil literature: the first popular peak oil book was published in 2003, *The Party's Over*, by Richard Heinberg. ("Great minds think alike," as the saying goes.) He had been a reader of the *Auto-Free Times*, which was running my columns on oil depletion and crash in the mid '90s onward. Richard has written that he woke up to peak oil from Dr. Colin Campbell's and Jean Laherrere's groundbreaking article in *Scientific American* in 1998. Peak oil is now almost a publicly known fact — along with other such kinds of heavy, new insight; there's a lot to go around — thanks especially to these writers. Other top authors on peak oil, James Howard Kunstler and the late Matthew Simmons, have been like generals with their own armies, with powerful presentation and legions of followers. I enjoy picturing myself as their grand old man of peak oil, seein' as I was into it long before they were — even though I'm a lot younger (just more hair on my head).

When I served the major oil companies, I had the sincere notion that they consisted of honorable gentlemen (and a few ladies in lower echelons). I believed in their sincerity when they explained how ethanol was a joke compared to the high net-energy of gasoline. Yet, when I later asked about peak oil, it meant nothing to them. This didn't conform to my previous experience with them as professionals and researchers. The biggest clue I had for rejecting their dismissal of peak oil was in knowing their corporate focus was very short-term. Planning allowed for five years at most, although certain major investments take longer. An exception among my oil contacts was Larry Sakai of Standard Oil of Ohio (later BP). He had kindly sent me a copy of the libelous letter about me sent by Trilby Lundberg that urged no oil company client of Lundberg Survey to do business with me. His parents had been interned in World War II in the Southwestern U.S. in the government's racist concentration-camp system. We kept in touch even after I left my service of the oil industry. In 1988 I told him I penciled out how long the U.S. motor vehicle fleet could operate on the best case scenario for exploiting the Arctic National Wildlife Refuge: less that two years if all the oil dreamed of were turned into gasoline. He just said, "Wow." He, like the rest of the industry, was not paid to worry about the future or the welfare of the nation, its people or nature.

I had always received good treatment at the family business from the marketing end of the oil industry we served, until I left Lundberg Survey in 1986. It had been engrained in me that if there was sharp practice or chiseling, the guilty ones were usually independent oil companies. The cheapskate among the majors was Texaco. I was glad not to be in other industries that I saw as sleazy. However, I was in for a "crude" awakening. Not long after leaving Lundberg Survey in 1986, I learned that my good service was barely appreciated. There was no concern over the "OPEC takeover" of my former firm (Trilby's husband was a Venezuelan OPEC official).

My best oil-industry friend turned out to be Frank Breese, retired editor-in-chief at National Petroleum News. He knew my family and tried to help me in my struggles. After I became an environmentalist, which he did not hold against me even though he was a Reaganite, he sent me occasional cartoons he drew, depicting such things as my opposing the wimpy, "compromise-entalist" Sierra Club.

Apart from Frank and a couple of others I rarely heard from, such as Keith Hamilton, the oil industry fraternity of gentlemen that my father and I cultivated let me down. Nevertheless, after of the loss to the nation of an important public service known for its integrity, I set out to fight pollution, not oil people.

The personal life is affected too

Meanwhile, my wife's tenuous standing as the top harpist in classical music was not improving due to her less than optimal location: neither L.A. nor Fredericksburg was Manhattan. I saw that with her moves with me, "for" me (she had always hated L.A.), and my failure to remain the affluent L.A. executive she had married, the marriage was, unbeknownst to me, quickly getting rocky. For a challenge and a creative outlet for us both, I encouraged her to start her own music festival. By 1988 we got it together and treated the town to a series of fabulous chamber music performances. Via WETA-FM, the DC radio station, National Public Radio broadcast the performances from the first, and ever since, thanks to producer Deb Lamberton. Just as I was working to create a nonprofit organization for music, I found myself creating another one for environmental advocacy. Between them I had a job or two and a livelihood, I thought. I was half right: as my advocacy for Heidi's security and dominance within our new board of directors was too strenuous. So someone or some persons had me back off 100%, immediately. I was out.

After the spurious family-business lawsuit and my decision to change careers, my wife suddenly wanted out of the marriage. She gave me the news in a curious fashion, when I told her Lundberg Reports might have to declare bankruptcy. Her reaction was "Serves you right!" I had lately irritated her by not being an artist, and she made clear repeatedly that she wanted a new partner who was a passionate, top performer. She and he, whoever he would be, had to live in Manhattan, the center of classical music for the U.S.A. My finances and security had changed markedly from when we got together in 1984 to when I moved us to the Washington, DC "suburb" of Fredericksburg. Heidi had stood by me in awful

126

turns of fortune, but she understandably could take no more. She reminded me that a promise to her from my father and me that a nanny would be hired was never fulfilled.

Heidi was so talented on the harp that she hardly ever had to practice or rehearse. Bronwyn was at baby sitters much of the time, but what can go wrong will go wrong: she suffered two severe accidental blows to the head, but she recovered. This was largely my fault, as it hadn't occurred to me to tell my wife I would not pay for child care elsewhere when she was the mother at home. My wife did not really understand my work in petroleum. I once overheard her telling someone on the telephone, "He's an economist." We didn't quite have enough in common.

Our celebrated chamber-music festival was not enough to save the marriage, which devastated me mainly on behalf of our children. I tried to hold on to our joint collaboration, but she affirmed I had no place in the festival. I was busy enough, as I was just launching Fossil Fuels Policy Action, which was of little interest to her. She took a trip to Seattle in the summer of 1988, and when she returned she suddenly had me go live in my office. I was forced to do so, for when I tried to remain in the home I had bought for us, she ran away with the children and would not return if I were there. This was puzzling and depressing, but there was no discussing it; her mind was made up. Yet I hoped that the marriage could be salvaged, for two reasons: I was in love with this charismatic woman, and, more importantly, our children needed us together to offer them a good home.

I made the best of living in my office without the building management's being aware. I was really getting some overdue experience in the real world. Besides the building's restroom down the hall, I bathed in the adjacent Rappahannock River, when it wasn't too cold. I was lucky to have a Greek Cypriot diner across the street that sustained me. The new Fossil Fuels Policy Action Institute kept me stoked on life, and I saw my children and soon-to-be-ex-wife a lot. When she went out on concert tours I got to stay in our house and take care of the kids; then when she returned I was back in the office on my futon (usually after dinner at the house with her and the kids). We had many long conversations about her career and her favorite interests. My patience paid off when she told me that a marriage, such as ours, could be based on just friendship and respect. She was trying to do the right thing even though she was conflicted inside. But with her misery in Virginia summers and her missing her hometown of Seattle, she decided to end our marriage. New York never happened, for she took up with a conductor based in Seattle, a good man. His train route as conductor was nonexistent, as he conducted ballets.

I blamed my sister and my financial demotion for the ending of my marriage. But Heidi and I were not suited for each other, as it became clearer. It was a kind of blessing that my loss of both position and inheritance helped liberate me from a possible lifetime with someone who never could have stuck with me into my uncertain, changing future. It might be asking too much.

Discovering what kind of environmentalist I was

When I formed the new nonprofit "energy information/policy group" I assumed I would work with some of my old associates in petroleum, albeit at arms' length. I immediately paid a visit to the American Gas Association (AGA) and its top public affairs people who had been much interested in my previous career. (As mentioned earlier, it involved helping public utilities commissions to set natural gas rates based on Lundberg Survey's alternative fuels surveys.) Nelson Hay, director of communications for AGA, had me come to his favorite after-work watering hole with his boss to chat about my new venture. After our visit it seemed clear I was to receive one of those fat grants the AGA had been handing out to environmental groups (such as the Sierra Club) to promote the idea of natural gas as a "bridge fuel" to renewable energy.

However, the paying-for-policy-positions disturbed me, and I thought about the basis of the policy: competition between the natural gas industry and the heating oil industry. I decided to create perhaps the only journalistic exposés on this conflict and on the fact that the natural gas industry was buying environmentalists' cooperation or silence about natural gas being petroleum and a fossil fuel. I sent a copy of this *Fossil Fuels Action* newsletter to Nelson, and his reaction was to call me and leave this message on my answering machine: "What are you on, Jan, acid?!" I didn't return the call. I remained glad that I rejected this money in favor of seeking and spreading the truth as I saw it. I was truly in my new career for the fun of it. Another reaction I got was from Joe Browder, a well-known energy-policy environmentalist near Capitol Hill: he admonished me that I should take the money, "because all money is dirty." At the time I didn't quite believe that.

Around this time I attended a Climate Institute symposium in Washington, D.C. Its finale was Al Gore's addressing the usual grouping of luncheon tables, except that he was at one of the tables and stood to speak with no microphone. He sounded reasonable except for his stand in favor of nuclear power. When he finished and the crowd could ask questions, I stood and asked how he could justify nuclear power when the half-life of plutonium is so many thousands of years. His only response was to tell me, with his hands raised in resignation, "I'm sorry, I'm sorry!" This was so astoundingly incompetent that everyone including myself was speechless, although no doubt many attendees were pro-nuke.

The first call I had not returned upon forming Fossil Fuels Policy Action was from the head of the nuclear lobby. Maybe he hoped to rope me in to their schemes. I was quite put off to the point of fear. Other folks' reactions were more welcome, such as the friendly letter from the president of World Resources Institute, Gus Speth. Former Congressman Dick Ottinger, D-NY, was kind enough during our first conversation to go through his Rolodex over the phone and give me his best contacts in energy conservation, such as the philanthropist Jay Harris IV.

Jay had made his mark with an historic project: funding *Beyond Oil: the Threat to Food and Fuel in the Coming Decades.* An early peak-oil activist, Jay was also a technofix-oriented activist who believed strongly in solar panels and electric cars. In our dealings Jay donated many *Beyond Oil* booklets to our office and sent a check for $1,000. One time he told me he did not want to contribute grants to Fossil Fuels Policy Action because he felt I was irresponsible to start a nonprofit career when I had two young daughters. He might have added that people going through divorce should also not start organizations or be rewarded with funding. Or, that blue-eyed people shouldn't be in the sun, due to ozone layer depletion, and the sun is usually out on Earth Day. He may have been right about my risk-taking, but perhaps my daughters now, as adults, should be the ones to judge. My feeling is that for Earth's sake someone has to take risks. And, despite some inconveniences and worry, I've been supported by being rewarded with staying power. I guess I've done what I loved.

The romance of activism fueled me, but the dollar wasn't quite being reckoned with. How my new career choice would affect me financially was something I just had to find out as I went, and I worried none. I felt confident that funding would happen just as it did for other DC institutes (grants, donations, contracts, subscriptions, etc.). I still felt this after telling AGA to go fly a kite and getting nowhere with Jay Harris's grant making. In my beginning couple of years as a professional environmentalist I must have thought I would always have a semblance of family to be a part of and fall back on to a degree. Certainly the family home in Hollywood would always be there; I assumed this without even thinking about it. I could not separate my idea of life from a stable family and house we could always share.

My mother helped me on my way right after I formed Fossil Fuels Policy Action by sending a donation of $4,000. My former CPA at Lundberg Survey, Dolph Kornbloom, now working for my mother — so he thought; he was answering to Trilby before he wanted to face it — told my mother and me that it was good for her tax returns to make tax-deductible donations to the Fossil Fuels Policy Action public charity. I took this in stride and thought there would be more donations. There were, but not enough for me to let up on seeking grants and other sources of support. I didn't express my gratitude to Dolph, nor did I appreciate enough his backing me as CEO after my father died. He was caught flatfooted by the unfriendly take-over or usurpation, but continued to serve Lundberg Survey until he retired. He was always able and a friend of the family. His son Irving took over the CPA business but it was years after I left Lundberg Survey. I would bet he was envious that his father got to work for the firm when it was a real family business. No dummy, he must have made out well and knew how to handle Trilby.

The single dad

Before Heidi left, I had her attend mediation with me with a prominent lawyer in the town involved in our chamber music festival. The mediated arrangement was that Bronwyn would live with me for two years at age nine. (I thought this would work based on my trust in Heidi, judging from her apparent arrangement with her previous husband David Singer, who had custody of their daughter Laura.) For good measure, our mediation was signed by a judge.

By 1989, with Heidi permanently in Seattle with our daughter, I was back in my home raising Vernell alone. How it came about was potentially fraught with pitfalls. She had joined Heidi, me and our other daughters on her own accord. She made her decision known when she was eight years old, and I was able to bring it off with her mother's assent when Vernell was nine. But I was sleeping regularly at my office, involuntarily. Vernell was happy to live with Heidi, who encouraged Vernell to call her "Mom." Vernell was in good hands, and I was there a lot. I never told Xenia that Vernell was not actually living with me, and it seems Vernell did not say anything. When Heidi drove off to Seattle for good, Vernell and I were left alone, but we were doing alright.

I was enjoying being a full-time dad, enrolling her in elementary school, and we made the most of our town life together, going to the library, watching War of the Worlds on television, etc. We had a comfortable car-free existence, as I'd gotten rid of my Buick Behemoth from Lundberg Survey. Bear the Bagel Eating Beagle, rescued from the pound, lightened our lives. Our problem was that Bronwyn, starting at age 3, was in Seattle with her mother. Vernell and I missed Bronwyn, but at least we could look forward to the arrangement whereby Bronwyn would live with us for two years at age nine. (Unfortunately for everyone but Heidi, this agreement wasn't honored.)

All seemed to be well at first with my acceptance of Bronwyn's absence, but one day a volunteer in my office told me her mother was obsessive about neatness. When I told her my ex-wife was the same way, she said, "Do you really want your daughter to be around that all the time?" I realized that I had buried that issue in my mind along with the idea of living without Bronwyn. So I started fighting for joint custody to begin immediately, which ultimately caused the mediated, court-approved agreement to be voided. I also made an enemy (for a while) out of Heidi, which I could have avoided by letting her have my daughter on whatever terms. But I was successful for a time in my effort to gain shared custody. So Bronwyn divided her time equally, a few months on one coast and then a few months on the other coast. This worked for a couple of years.

It was almost time for her to enter kindergarten (home schooling was never on the table, unfortunately), and it was my turn for a custody period. However, Bronwyn was suddenly hidden from me in a remote part of the Pacific Northwest, and I was forced to give in to agreeing to no custody, just so I could see her. At the time I was low on resources such as a car to find her and enforce my rights, but I also did not look forward to having to sock some in-law, perhaps, in the jaw. With the deal I was forced to sign I was on the way to losing all decision-making over health or education matters.

How this happened was, as is often the case, because nice guys "finish last" — my lawyers in Fredericksburg, Ferris and Lucy, were about as tough as 15 year old cocker spaniels, and in this regard they gave me poor advice. Among my other lessons learned was that meditation is not in one's interest unless both sides wish to be giving and can be counted on as totally trustworthy. Ultimately, Heidi and I opted for a psychologist's final recommendation on where Bronwyn should live. Thanks to negative input from Xenia about her frustration over her daughter Vernell not living with her, the scales were tipped against Bronwyn living with Vernell and me. The psychologist, Marsha Hedrick, confronted me about three bad things I did or supposedly did that she wanted confirmed or denied: that I had taken Bronwyn out of Kindergarten for her birthday to go ice skating; I made Bronwyn take fresh vegetables to eat on an airplane, and that I had yelled and misbehaved in a supermarket when Heidi bought some candy for Bronwyn. There was even an alleged witness for the last allegation; a friend stepped in with a plausible sounding accusation. My ex also described me as jealous of her new boyfriend and that I wanted her back. I'm sure Dr. Hedrick had bought into these plausible indictments. It was true I had tried and tried to keep the family together, but I owed that to my children. Marriage to Heidi had become my least preferred situation. (My true preference was, rather, for full custody that I foolishly passed on obtaining automatically a couple of years before, when I could have, when Heidi disappeared from our home with the children.) It all worked against my, and Bronwyn's and Vernell's, favor, as Dr. Hedrick gave all authority to Heidi except for my visitation rights.

One has to go on, somehow. My new life in 1989 saw me happily caring for my older daughter full time, I had my stimulating work, and I picked up the guitar again — and have not put it down since.

Chapter 7

The Lundberg Soap opera heats up

This chapter tells of my eventual relocation in 1991 to Arcata, northern California, and peaceful days establishing myself there with my child, my work and music. In 1994 my mother had a major stroke, and a second round of problems in L.A. began. Mesa lost her financial independence at the hands of Trilby who took control of our mother's checking account at a vulnerable moment. This is why, by 1995, the household of Mesa and Darius Lundberg was under siege, being starved out, by Trilby's refusal to cover basic monthly bills. Conservatorship was sprung on Mesa literally overnight, and the nightmare of family strife began in earnest. Darius lost his home as a result for six months, and secretly removed his mother to where her care was a slight improvement (she had not yet gotten care befitting a stroke victim in need of aggressive therapy). She resurfaced with Darius and they lived an uneasy existence in the same house until 1997 when he and I, with my older daughter, had her join us in Arcata. Her first home there was actually with her former daughter-in-law Xenia, who had moved there to be near Vernell.

Based in Virginia far away from Los Angeles, visiting my mother and brother by train for holidays and summer vacations, I was not fully tuned into their suffering at the hands of Trilby. Darius was starting to complain about it but could not cope with it well. I had first thought that my mother had 'retired" and that she was simply not going to the office anymore.

Trilby would not talk with Darius or me, nor was she ever present for holiday meals. I had only two conversations in the early 1990s with Trilby, who finally assented to visit our mother's and Darius's home when I was there with my daughters. One conversation was in passing in the kitchen. I said, "How about if we have a family conference?" Trilby barked, "No family conferences!" and walked away. The other conversation was when she had an office-boyfriend named Aaron along, and the family was sitting in the living room on Bonnie Hill Drive. I mentioned that I had hiked up the road to the outlet to the canyon, and was shocked to see my wild hiking trails being developed by roads and housing in what was a beautiful, roadless area. Trilby floored us with "I did not come here for preaching." Her lack of concern for nature was almost as shocking as the destruction going on in a beautiful, wild canyon. She was a Lundberg? Something twisted had happened with her. The canyon was the only substantive discussion of that brief meeting, besides introductions. I would have liked to discuss peak oil with her. But Trilby's agenda was hard set. My new work was completely outside the one in which we had been competing, but this didn't soften her in any way. And she took no interest in her nieces whatsoever.

❧

I was not very surprised or upset about Exxon for its Exxon Valdez spill in 1989; rather I felt there was an overall ongoing disaster of oil: for example, much more oil was being spilled deliberately by ships at sea when regularly emptying bilges over the course of a year. This was one of my big turn-offs for globalized world trade. As for Exxon, it wasn't any different than any other major oil player. It was my last client; in 1988 I terminated my firm's lubricants survey contract for Exxon and gave them back their money in the form of reports on gasoline markets.

It was when Shell Oil was tainted by the Ken Saro-Wiwa execution in the 1990s that I began to revise my view of genteel, honest oil industry people. Since then, many instances of violence, corruption and environmental harm have become commonplace or better known, in part because of the rising competition for megabucks and the dwindling finds of major oil fields. The oil wars (The Gulf War, the Iraq and Afghanistan Wars) and their architects the Bushes, Cheney, Rice, Halliburton, and the ecological and cultural damage to Nigeria's and the Amazon's environment from major oil companies' operations, have led up to the final disgrace known as BP. Until the early 1990s the oil industry was better tolerated by the public; it had "only" caused oil spills, engineered price hikes and shortages (so people believed), and contributed illegal election campaign funds (e.g., to Nixon).

134

Culture Change (formerly Fossil Fuels Policy Action) has monitored and run many news stories on Big Oil's missteps, greenwashing and crimes. Non-major oil company crimes occur as well, carried out as part of the "oil fraternity" that I used to know and trust. Oil exporting countries, independent oil companies, and Big Oil are one big, friendly trade group that cooperates across borders on a daily basis. Regardless of the malpractice inherent in any fossil fuel business, the approach of our nonprofit organization was to demonstrate alternatives to oil dependence while warning of oil's devastating environmental effects. I can say my job has been a gas, in the good sense of the phrase and the bad as well. But I've gotten ahead of the story:

During my post-marriage period in Fredericksburg I "lived for" encouragement coming daily in the mailbox for my new activities. I continued to receive professional assistance, *pro bono*. A couple of kind CPA firms and nonprofit support groups helped establish Fossil Fuels Policy Action legally. Our CPA Bob Bishop was a pleasure to know. Forrest Craver, well-known DC nonprofit fundraiser, provided a professional visioning retreat for our new group. I accepted these kindnesses in stride and should have expressed much more appreciation, which would have been easier with better funding for Fossil Fuels Policy Action.

My small organization soon found its purpose: to understand why the nation was not conserving energy, and what could be done to change that. Taking direct action along those lines came later. Here is the origin of the earliest vision of Fossil Fuels Policy Action, up until the "ultimate" big picture analysis today that must include a critique of Western Civilization:

The first impression I had of the funded environmental movement in Washington, D.C., as I re-entered the movement in 1988 after an absence of 16 years, is that the many nonprofit/lobbying players I met were part of a "green industry" circle of socializing professionals . I wasn't overjoyed to learn this, because I had approached them with total admiration. I found that they seemed to be mainly waiting around for a more beneficial business environment, through politics, for their superior, cleaner-energy profit-seeking/nonprofit income. This does not mean that they were not good people trying to make improvements in people's lives, our nation and the ecosystem. But I came to feel this professional circle was unimaginative or even deluded. I became disgusted with many of them over the next two years when I saw how they dealt with the Gulf War: pushing improved fuel economy only, which bought into car and oil domination. In their minds they were the new paradigm. I had wanted to join them and find a job, but if I had gotten a good enough look at them in my several weeks at Renew America.

Soaking up breakthroughs and creating my own world

But in 1988 didn't I, like these respectable professional environmentalists, imagine that this technocratic environmentalism could reform the system? Was this was our common goal? It seemed so, when there seemed to be no alternative. In a few years I came to the conclusion that their propping up the system with more technology and policy reforms was a waste of time and effort. One book that steered me toward this realization was *A Green History of the World* by Clive Ponting. Beyond the unmitigated ecological disaster, Western Civilization has been an Age of Lies and theft. Just when in my early eco-activist career I made the shift away from believing in mere reforms might have been the morning in 1989 I woke up and felt there had to be a "conservation revolution." My disillusionment with the D.C. green-industry operatives was imbedded even before I started Fossil Fuels Policy Action in 1988. It was because I could not fit in, though I tried for months, that I launched my own organization.

At first it was intended to be an information and policy clearinghouse regarding energy, but soon I was grappling with the questions of why conservation of energy wasn't happening, and what could bring it about. After "reinventing the Green Party" and gravitating unknowingly toward Earth First!, I was glad to discover those movements. I believe I made my intellectual contribution to both, and kept going. From the start I was fortunate to have good colleagues' inspiration and authors to draw upon, such as Jeremy Rifkin (*Entropy*). Soon I didn't want to fit in; I had to do my own thing. I dropped in on Rifkin, and it was great to meet him, but despite all his great work I cannot get behind his technofix approach for the world's crises that he keeps promoting today. But hey — and not to pick on him — he has to pay his bills; to do this one must play the game.

When I was starting out in full-time environmentalism in my late thirties, it was an exciting time for me on many levels. But soon Fossil Fuels Policy Action had almost nothing to do with the nation's capital and all its organizations and agencies' regulations. I had gotten a post office box in Washington to have an official address there, but closed it within a year. Down in Fredericksburg was where I had all the excitement I needed, in my own little world of activism. What gave life even more meaning for me was being a single father. I was able to achieve a wonderful dream in having my older daughter, then nine years old, live with me instead of with her mother in California. My younger daughter was with us half the time, and her rapid development with us was a marvel to behold. Fredericksburg, however, was not a great place to be single or to operate long-term a nonprofit environmental group. My activities were so unusual in our conservative, still Confederate minded town that I was able to attract most of the potential volunteers for miles around. Washington, D.C. was close by, but becoming irrelevant to our original, grassroots-oriented work.

Our first editor, besides myself, was John Robbins, not to be confused with the founder of Earth Save of the same name who rejected his Baskin-Robbins Ice Cream legacy as a vegan. John (of Fredericksburg) wanted editorial independence, but I didn't think it was justified, so we parted ways but remained friends. He had had a transplanted liver and died several years later. I assume he lived out his last years on the traditional Japanese futon & tatami mats that I gave him.

My post-industry life was a major departure from the corporate culture, and I don't mean the suit-and-tie uniform. I adopted a strategy which holds for me today: I'm always trying to attract helpers. The help I need, that Mother Earth needs, I feel, is two-way and builds energy by collaboration. A movement starts with just two.

By about 1990, despite the novelty and thrill of my activities and new contacts – no more oil people except for John Lloyd Davies and his wife Patricia Morrow who were supportive friends — my new glorious job for changing the world appeared more and more like a different version of the same old culture: paperwork, deadlines, stress, money, and technology such as phones, faxes and computers. I realized I had not really made a significant change in lifestyle, despite the nonprofit aspect and new set of goals and associates. Our cause was wonderful, and our purpose was becoming clear. But there was no end to the office work and city living. I began to see that my ego and distaste for the Lundberg Survey takeover had pushed me into not only continuing in the same line of work for almost two years, but had helped propel me into starting a nonprofit office. The new stream of paperwork and archives was endless. I realized I had made a mistake: I could have and should have used the settlement from Lundberg Survey to exit the business/nonprofit culture entirely. I could have bought a farm and got close to the land. However, in 1986 and through perhaps 1992 I would not have known enough about how to make a rural transition in the right fashion, such as by selecting the right location.

The Gulf War was building by the time our little group had publicly explored a national paving moratorium (on new roads and parking lots). Our main project, EcoDemocracy, resulted in one magazine with the theme Revolution for Conservation. It was an immersion in "deep ecology" that we were reinventing with an energy twist. For example, in a letter we published in *U.S. News and World Report*, we asked why society should be choosing between natural-gas fueled and nuclear power generation, when the right question is "Why have either?" That insight was courtesy Robert McConnell, geologist from Fredericksburg's Mary Washington College. He was on our new, small board of directors. The letter was seen by a rainforest activist in Bellevue, Washington who called me up — thus beginning my lifelong friendship with Lonnie Maxfield.

Our next editor besides myself was Bill Van Doren. A talented graphics artist, painter and musician, Bill was a Los Angeles-savvy resident of Charlottesville. He had worked with the Primal Scream Therapy founder and created a fine, huge color map of L.A.'s old Red Car rail passenger system: "The one that got away." I liked and admired Bill as one of the few Virginians I met who could relate to me.

The most defining lessons I got during my time in and around D.C., prior to moving back to the West Coast in 1991, were shocks from what some would consider the left-wing enviro-establishment. It was their non-focus on energy that made me believe there might be a role for me to play with a new organization.

When Iraq invaded Kuwait and a U.S. military response looked likely, I was appalled that President Bush used a "Cigarette Boat" that guzzled fuel to speed. It was then that I realized he could be called a redneck: part of the larger segment of mainstream culture that was oblivious to conservation and pollution.

When the Gulf War was ramping up as Operation Desert Shield — in large part manufactured by PR and Great Game politics — I organized most of the national environmental groups in D.C. to band together to oppose war for oil as an energy policy. Before our grand press conference, however, an executive of one of the Nader groups told me he was going to hold a similar press conference immediately — just to promote better fuel economy for cars. At this press conference, which attracted most of the colleagues I'd lined up, I took exception to their grand claims for cars' cutting back oil consumption. My public question put me on a black list for the majority of these D.C. environmental groups — given their funding from those believing solely in technological solutions and regulatory reform. I still put on the intended press conference, with only the participation of Worldwatch's then-Vice President of Research, Christopher Flavin. We had eight television cameras on us, earning me a telephoned death threat when a nut in TV Land didn't like what he saw on C-SPAN. As the press conference wound up, I was accosted by the host for the venue (Communication Consortium, funded by Jay Harris IV who had funded the *Beyond Oil* project). He said, "I heard you say there's no technological fix. We'll never work with you again," and he walked away.

There was seldom any debate allowed in such circles on bringing about energy "conservation" via lifestyle change in order to simply slash energy use, or to provide the greater change society needed. The same holds true today. The difference with Worldwatch was then and is now that they liked my ideas. Their the entire staff in 1989 signed our national paving moratorium petition. A few months after my press conference with Flavin we arrived at a global oil-use spike for the Gulf War's devastation. A year later they adopted the substance and some text from my office's "Conservation Revolution" out of our *EcoDemocracy* magazine. In another example of taking a cue from us, a few years later they backed off their electric-car advocacy when we critiqued it in our *Auto-Free Times* magazine. Recently they created a culture change project for their State of the World 2010 (see CultureChange.org, "Musical Message: Singing Our Way to the Next Culture Change," Feb. 7, 2010, the article they requested of me). Flavin became president of Worldwatch a few years ago, and his VP is an expert on population — Robert Engelman, whose landmark book *More: Nature, Population, and What Women Want* was enthusiastically reviewed in 2008 on the Culture Change website. Worldwatch, although very much on board for the technofix as part of policy reform, was and is clearly the exception (besides Friends of the Earth-U.S. chapter) to the average environmental group's weak approach to energy issues and climate protection.

The other lesson from the Gulf War that my office learned was from launching the Alliance for a Paving Moratorium as a peace proposal and energy-security initiative. As war relies entirely on supply lines, it made sense to me that the U.S. should not lengthen its oil supply lines with more and more roads. I enjoyed making the argument even though I was not for any war. We also appealed to environmental and architectural preservation by promoting a paving moratorium. Unfortunately, despite our Gulf-War efforts to make a logical case for a sane energy policy without war-for-oil and to encourage alternative transportation (AMTRAK, especially), the anti-war movement's leadership wanted nothing to do with energy/environmental issues. Instead, their message was "No bombing!" and little else.

At a big anti-war demonstration in Washington, D.C. in 1990, which I attended with my older daughter and my assistant Andrea Vella, three sights and exchanges stick in my mind. Joining the marchers from a side street was a large contingent of women, whose huge banner was "Chicago Lesbians Say Lick Bush." Next, at the rally near the White House, I happened to walk by a group of people under a tree interacting with each other. They were dressed in black, circling around and chanting: "Tanks, no thanks, we'll burn your fucking banks" — real tough kids who could have chanted to themselves just as effectively in an empty parking lot, as they were, with their body language, closed off to everyone around. Perhaps they were rehearsing, or being led by an *agent de provocateur*. The last memorable experience from that whole rally was my engaging a mainstream reporter who had a camera crew. He was demonstrably bored and contemptuous of the whole protest, and could not care less about issues I brought up about energy.

Despite my small group's setbacks in trying to provide leadership for the environmental movement's energy and pollution clean-up sector, we learned about additional efforts that fired our resolve and idealism to new heights. In generating our own energetic sense of purpose, it took us nearly a decade to really burn out with our roads & cars focus. Major twists in our development were our participation in the timber wars and in efforts to "Reclaim the Streets." In 1990 we were not particularly anti-car or actively against modern society's consumption of tree-based paper, nor had we taken many positions on issues beyond those strictly environmental. The crystallizing moment was when our Fossil Fuels Policy Action and Alliance for a Paving Moratorium got a call from a retired geologist from NASA's: "Do you know about logging roads?" He was Bob Mueller, the first Earth First! organizer I was to meet.

It was through Earth First! and David Brower, founder of Friends of the Earth, that I was ushered into the greater ecological awareness I needed. I met Dave in 1991 in the Shenandoah Valley where we were both speakers for the Preserve Appalachian Wilderness (an Earth First! affiliate) conference organized by Bob Mueller. The first thing Dave said to me was in regard to the national environmental groups: "They need a testicular transplant."

At that conference I was introduced to what I call eco-rock, when Dana Lyons brought the house down with "Turn of the Wrench." I suddenly knew what I could try do with my decades-long habit of composing fragments of music: write protest songs! I had done the unpardonable thing for that conference, flying from California where I had just moved, but I was fulfilling a promise to appear — and I didn't regret it when Dana performed for Earth First! It was life changing for me. The music and singing were so stimulating that the audience used the plastic chairs of the hall for passionate percussion, resulting in happy blisters on many a finger.

Chapter 8

The Nicer, Natural Nineties

My new home by the time of the Shenandoah Valley gathering, for
my older daughter as well, was Arcata. It is in northern
California's Humboldt County redwood country, a different climate
and slightly different culture from the rest of California. I picked
the town because it was small enough to walk to everything we
needed; it had a university where volunteers for my projects could
be recruited, and it was halfway between my two ex-wives'
respective towns (in fairness to my kids). I got into bicycling for
the first time since age 13, just as a way to rush to the post office
before closing time. My family in Hollywood heard I was using my
daughter's toy bike, so they sent me an adult bike from L.L. Bean.

In Arcata I was at first only writing, leaving office management
to my staff back at my townhouse-office in Fredericksburg. After
several months they began to treat me as unnecessary and
bothersome. Eventually they refused to work with me. A
ringleader is always involved. I smelled a power play, and knew I
had to react decisively. So I shut down that office without warning
by having a realtor friend change the locks, and I accelerated the
sale of the townhouse. I reestablished the office in Arcata in a
shared space with Citizens for Social Responsibility, a peace group.
Next-door was the Redwood Alliance, an anti-nuke group whose
slogan was "Split Wood Not Atoms."

My daughter and I were living in a very modest two-bedroom
apartment next to the railroad tracks, but I felt it was perfectly
fine, as if I were living in Manhattan as many there feel they must:
I was very much where I wanted to be. After four years we were
able to buy a cute house a bit higher up from the flooding and fog,
thanks to my mother's financial cooperation with funds in her name
that I had done much to generate at Lundberg Survey.

I was offered a spare desk to use in the Plaza offices of Citizens
for Social Responsibility in 1992 because I had donated a fax

machine (I didn't want such a thing in our home). The desk had been vacated by a famous character, Rick Springer. His project was the "100th Monkey" that had received a donation from Jimmy and Roslyn Carter. Springer soon became well known for leading a large anti-nuclear procession in the desert to Las Vegas, only to see him go off and unilaterally confront Ronald Reagan and smash his award to bits before a national audience. The award was a glass eagle from the National Broadcasters Association, and Springer thought it was sacrilegious from an American Indian standpoint.

I had already allowed our office to take on Springer's Community Service obligation that was associated with a milder charge connected to protest, and I believe he completed the work for us. But in connection with his Reagan action he decided to become a fugitive and not follow through with his jail sentence. So, during his flight two young U.S. Marshals paid a surprise visit to the *Auto-Free Times* office, saying, "We're looking for your friend Rick Springer." They used "your friend" in order to scare me by trying to connect me to his actions. I told these two greenhorns I had no idea where he was, and, "I have an appointment in Eureka, and cannot miss the bus. Goodbye." I turned and left them standing in our office with our able staff ready to answer questions about the evils of road building and car dependence.

I had been learning more about energy issues beyond transportation. I was active on the Advisory Board of former Congressman's Richard Ottinger's Pace University Energy Project, in White Plains, New York. It pioneered demand-management so as to thwart new generating plants via utility hearings' interventions. As part of my energy education post-oil marketing, and my transportation focus, I thought more and more about my living habits concerning energy use.

I had a fascinating experience as a homeowner paying energy bills from 1995-1999. Never mind transportation; we needed no car, and even depaved the driveway to create a fine garden; it appeared in National *Audubon* magazine and the *Utne Reader*. As for our monthly electric and natural gas bill from Pacific Gas and Electric, it was $5.00 (five dollars) or a tiny bit more each month. Why:

- No TV; we read books, played our musical instruments, talked at the dinner table, living room or in the yard, and best of all had quite a few parties. We went to movies, concerts, lectures, meetings, etc.

- No refrigerator; we did not need one, as we frequently biked to the co-op and grew some vegetables and raspberries. When our vegan dishes were covered on the stove, they could stay that way for 24-hour intervals if brought to the boiling point once a day.
- Our heating was from one natural gas wall unit that was rarely used (Arcata, northern California, has the moderating ocean climate). No wood stove, and the fireplace was non-operational.
- Cooking was with natural gas.
- I did have a small home-studio for recording eco-rock, and we did have lights, but that was it.
- Computer was at the Alliance for a Paving Moratorium office downtown, where it belonged.

I got invitations in my PG&E bill to get a discount if I were to get an efficient refrigerator. But I was just a marginalized consumer paying the minimum PG&E bill — five bucks is what the bill would be even if I used zero energy. I asked the utility for a break because I was conserving even more by having no fridge, but they wouldn't bite.

Arcata enacted a visionary impermeable surface tax to cover storm water costs. But my depaved driveway did not save enough money for the city to give me a break on the city tax. The tax was so low it didn't result in depavings around town.

Our house was a three bedroom small house, single-story, that was medium-well insulated. I thought, "I should get solar panels for the roof." But then I realized the payback time would be forever when my bill for electricity *and* natural gas was only five dollars a month. And the energy-use involved in the mining, manufacture, transport, packaging and disposal of the panels and batteries would have been self-defeating.

We gave up the house in 1999 because it was not in a close community, being in what I fondly call the United Paved Precincts of America. If I thought we would stay indefinitely, I would have gotten one solar panel and batteries for the lights and sound equipment. The panel, lights, batteries and sound equipment were all toxic entropy gizmos, truth be told, so if that global system crashed for good it was a good thing that we really enjoyed acoustic instruments, books, bicycling, and each other.

One reason that consumers, rural or urban, do not invest in renewable energy is because they are consuming so much energy — vastly unnecessary and gluttonous amounts — that they are told by the solar panel salesperson that the cost will be many thousands of dollars. What the salespeople and municipal or rural government people don't do, and this goes for most environmental organizations too, is advocate that the homeowner opt for a very modest system that would just power some essentials (e.g., lights). When this minimalist approach is bypassed in favor of big profits and convenience of appliances and machines, what do we get? — the status quo, through no action taken.

What I've almost never seen from environmental groups or politicians is the idea of curtailment as the true, low-hanging fruit for energy conservation and climate protection. There are great benefits to curtailment — pulling the plug on global warming and consumerism — apart from the obvious ones of saving money and cutting emissions. It originates from and helps bring on simple, more convivial living. In my many years' efforts and being ignored, I finally got a mainstream environmental group to modify their technofix-program for a campaign. In April 2010 the 350.0rg group headed by Bill McKibben announced its Great Power Race, "a clean energy competition between students in America, China and India." The group modified its press release and instructions to students based on my input urging gardening, depaving and other action having nothing to do with solar panels. I was hoping this augured a trend, but at this writing in November 2010, it seems not be happening yet.

≈

In Arcata I had been attracted to the presence of numerous nonprofit groups, cultural projects such as ethnic dancing, art workshops macrobiotic cooking, and programs by activists of various sorts. The plethora of organizations and informal groups was such that Humboldt State University was not the source of much activism. Rather, the town exerted activist influence on the college. At that time and through the 1990s Humboldt County had the highest percentage of nonprofit groups in the nation, per capita. Our office kept up the national paving moratorium campaign and became a kind of Earth First! liaison with an anti-logging-road-building emphasis. Our group's development veered toward car-free advocacy when our newsletter, *Paving Moratorium Update*, adopted the better name *Auto-Free Times*. We never got the support of the rail industry, as we originally sought, so by default we became the pro-bicyclist/pedestrian leader in fighting road construction and car domination around the world. The Alliance for a Paving Moratorium soon included forest-defense groups, animal-rights groups, bicycling advocates, recycling businesses, and more.

How did my small group and I become anti-car? It stemmed from one strategic realization: fighting road construction was not altogether comprehensible or seen as having appeal to the populace. An AP reporter named Mike Feinsilber in Washington, D.C. had challenged me, after receiving several Fossil Fuels Action newsletters and Paving Moratorium Updates, "what is your alternative to building more roads?" He saw that I was on to something, but not quite there yet. He seemed to be asking if we had anything to offer to take the place of or cure endless road building. I responded, "Well, not having a car is one alternative." When I told him that, something clicked in his mind. He soon did the feature story I wanted. However, each newspaper in the nonprofit AP co-op gets to pick, for any article, the newspaper's own headline and the place where to truncate the story starting from the bottom. The following version is from the *Philadelphia Inquirer*, which had the funniest headline of the hundreds around the country:

One Man's Cry: Pave No More *(excerpt of beginning)*
Mike Feinsilber, Associated Press

"Jan Lundberg, a visionary, has a simple idea likely to irk anyone who has been stalled in traffic and can't find a parking place upon arrival.

"He wants the nation to stop building roads.

"And parking lots.

"And thus to stop chewing up the green space that remains beyond city and suburb.

"In the process, he thinks, America will rediscover the city and reinvent the future."

In 1997 Feinsilber published a book revealing that "Gerald R. Ford took pen in hand and changed — ever so slightly — the Warren Commission's key sentence on the place where a bullet entered John F. Kennedy's body when he was killed in Dallas. The effect of Ford's change was to strengthen the commission's conclusion that a single bullet passed through Kennedy and severely wounded Texas Gov. John Connally — a crucial element in its finding that Lee Harvey Oswald was the sole gunman."

The *Auto-Free Times* was therefore our best means of fighting road construction. After the magazine was born out of the Paving Moratorium Update we kept developing our overall concept and philosophy. Our rag was turning into an all-around radical journal for fundamental socioeconomic change. We never lost sight of the petroleum basis of what we as eco-warriors were up against: runaway consumption of greenhouse-gas producing, habitat-destroying infrastructure.

We eventually wrote off the big environmental groups, as not one of them ever joined our Alliance for a Paving Moratorium after repeated invitations. Meanwhile, the Sierra Club, for example, launched a big anti-sprawl campaign, but their road fighting was limited to occasionally trying to move a particular road's proposed route somewhere else for slightly less damage. We increasingly rejected piecemeal governmental reform, and we supported indigenous, traditional ways as the real answer to ecocidal consumer culture. Our readers and members were mostly active foes of urban sprawl and clearcuts, but we showed them the bigger picture along with visionary tools for sustainability such as depaving parking lots and driveways to create food gardens and wildlife habitat.

Such activities and related projects made me a natural from the early 1990s onward to get involved with the Earth First!ers' fighting road construction and blocking roads. In fact, the *Auto-Free Times* encouraged it by running cover stories such as the indigenous Borneo roadfighters' blockading logging roads to defend their forest homes.

For most people, roads and cars were only issues to be considered in relation to one's own convenience or needs. But a big question for back-to-the-landers — latter day hippies in Humboldt and Mendocino Counties and Oregon — was "How can people live in the countryside without having to drive, even with the 'electronic village'?" Our readers wanted to know. One, Bud Hoekstra, moved from Humboldt to the Yosemite area and became interested in road building without the usual asphalt or gravel surfaces. I visited him and checked out a formula and process for natural road surfacing, and was impressed with the method and results. But I couldn't get excited when it still meant car dependence. This drawback of country living therefore had me living in Arcata rather than some other part of Humboldt where narrow, harrowing roads would have been my bikeway.

Bud had me come to speak to the Audubon Society's Yosemite Chapter, in May 1995. I accepted in part because I had never seen Yosemite. My talk went well I suppose, but I remember my ending the evening with a performance of several of my songs. I included Englandtown Motorways, my road-fighting ditty that I had recorded with brass in Hollywood. I got a good review in a local newsletter by Bob, the ancient cowboy of a folk festival organizer.

I hiked up above the Yosemite Valley past the famous waterfalls into the wilderness where snow was on the ground. I just managed to spot the campground I was seeking before nightfall. I joined a campfire gratefully, and reflected that people one encounters in wilderness are almost always going to be kinder and saner than city folk. I unknowingly got within two feet of a black bear who was sniffing my backpack that I had put down next to a tree. When I was getting into my pack, unaware of the bear's presence next to it, the animal shot off so fast I didn't have time to get scared. That night it rained heavily, so I allowed a fellow camper to come into my small tent to be dry. This is how I learned that when anything touches the side of a tent when it's raining, water will pool and come in to soak the occupant(s). Next time, no more Mr. Nice Guy.

I camped out also in the crowded valley floor area next to other tents. In an instance of overcrowding or overpopulation, my presence was greatly resented because I was next to other tents; it was the only spot I could get for the night. Belligerent campers stood outside my tent in the dark and wanted me to leave, but I ignored them, just as everyone ignores overpopulation.

$\approx$

We at Fossil Fuels Action were hard working and jazzed up with the knowledge and insight we were getting, and we were well received by an international audience who cared about forests, rights of bicyclists, biodiversity, peace, and related issues. When I say "we," I might be more honest to say "I." The office had a staff of only two or three, as funding was limited to a few daring donors and foundations. Our readers and members covered about 40% of our minimum expenses when we really milked the direct mail fundraising. The other 60% was met by grants and donations. I also proved to be "the it" of the organization as three take-over attempts — designed to suddenly wrestle control from me and eject me from the organization — took place, in 1992, 1994, and 1997. Each time I had to regroup and reshape the organization, and reaffirm "our" anti-car, non-economic growth philosophy. In the first two organizational crises "we" endured, economic growth and electric cars, respectively, were issues of contention (besides gaining organizational control). I would not promote either idea, but my soon-to-be-ex-colleagues did so at the end of our association, for the sake of wider appeal in the funding world.

I have recounted the first take-over attempt, in Fredericksburg when I was 3,000 miles away concentrating on writing (when I changed the locks on my townhouse). The second event was a plot by an executive director I had hired who connived with two Board members of our organization to remove me. I was being encouraged to go off and do my writing (for whomever). I wouldn't have minded a kick upstairs if their intention had not been to alter our stand on electric cars in order to qualify for funding from the huge Energy Foundation. I disagreed vehemently, and in the long dispute over who was in charge I was attacked for wasting money: $300 for a mailing list — all that my foes could come up with. I was tenacious, as I heeded advice from veteran activist Richard Register who later joined our Board: "Don't quit; destroy the organization before you let others take your work and twist it." I kept this in mind in the grueling Board of Directors fight that wasted much money and time. It ultimately resulted in the insurgent faction quitting in order to start its own organization. This would have been unobjectionable, but they took our main funded project, the road-fighting wilderness protection campaign, as well as that project's grant we had just been awarded. So it was not a happy ending of the dispute over control of our office.

The grant in question was controlled by the foundation's head. He apparently saw the opportunity to bring our project and some of our people into his stable of activist projects that included Dave Foreman's *Wild Earth* magazine and the Wildlands Project. Foreman was co-founder of Earth First! When I refused to step down and the organization split, the foundation head wrote me a letter chastising me for not giving up the organization I had founded, because, he reasoned, he had quit a media center in San Francisco that he had founded. He and his foundation seemed to bring about a similar "funded split" of Earth First! by creating the new publication *Wild Earth* whose first editor was the just-departed editor of the *Earth First! Journal*. In that years-long dispute a mostly artificial schism distracted people with notions of "hippies versus rednecks" in the Earth First! movement. In reality it was just the newly funded, academic-oriented and non-direct action wing, attacked by northern California Earth First!ers who had the inside track for the soul and leadership of the remaining movement. No one seemed to notice that the Alliance for a Paving Moratorium soon endured a similar "funded split," fragmenting the road-fighting movement in the U.S. The new group published its newsletter titled *Road Rip*, which I privately called *Road Rip-off*. Our office kept on doing our same work and did not miss the would-be usurpers.

The final take-over attempt was in 1997, engineered ironically by the lone staff member from the previous episode, even though it was his job I had protected. On some poor advice whispered by a part-time consultant in our office, my young assistant was overcome with desire to bask solo in the glory of our work. When he demanded I vacate the office and work from home (which I was starting to do more and more), I told our Board member Lonnie Maxfield about the situation. Lonnie immediately said, "Fire him now." I reluctantly realized this was necessary, so I let the young man go. In retaliation he had a friend of his working for us in the field quit, stopping our fight against NAFTA Superhighways. My departed prodigy took our art and contacts to start a competing magazine. As in previous take-over attempts, he tampered with existing funders or proposed grants, and he spread negative gossip and falsehoods about the office going out of business. He was talented and competent, but had come to see me as a fifth wheel due to my reduced time in the office. I thought we were making organizational progress as I wrote at home, took part in depaving, etc. But he had been oblivious to my new projects, Pedal Power Produce and Sail Transport Network, which may have seemed to him irrelevant to road fighting.

It was after this episode that I realized how much the dominant culture's values had poisoned my former protégés. I learned from these take-over attempts that corporate values were alive and well in the nonprofit sector. These episodes taught me much about the Earth's foe: the culture of power and ego, prompting individuals to behave ruthlessly for purposes having nothing to do with the ostensible mission of the activist non-profit group.

In a backhanded way I was also complimented by the three take-over attempts' implicit acknowledgment that I had envisioned and created something worth trying to seize. There wasn't much money involved (on average $60,000 revenue in a good year, almost all of it taken up in printing costs, postage, telephone, and rent). So the real issue was power: try to control a project, an organization or a movement.

These prominent disputes can obscure the fact that dozens of helpful volunteers and colleagues had shared the work and triumphs with me since 1988. Some of these became wonderful friends and roommates, and I learned from them all. My lifestyle and life-purpose were becoming honed joyfully. I was learning invaluable things about ecology, "primitive ways" such as wild food foraging, appropriate tech, direct action, and personal relations. For example, as my former executive self I merely had to request or tell people what needed to be done, and it would happen. Now I had to get the voluntary cooperation of equals. It helped that they were there because they believed in saving the ancient redwoods, for example. Socially we also had reason to stick together. There were many good times and quite a few lasting friendships made. This would not have been nearly so likely in the corporate suites or cubicles.

In my environmental activist career I have always tried to

attract help, the kind that's two-way and builds energy, collaboration and friendship. A movement starts with just two. Attracting collaborators is in contrast to having a corporate or specialized job involving a limited function day in and day out. A non-social pattern can emerge. Getting the paycheck can seem the only really necessary objective, although this doesn't mean such a person isn't someone who gives and receives a lot of love and has creative interests to enjoy.

Between my work, my music and being a single dad, I didn't pursue romance from 1988 through 1997. Years later I came to think of this as a mistake: everyone, especially children, needs community that has as its basis the couple. Community in the form of a loving couple in one household would have been best for my daughters, for a female role model. It was clear to me that I had obstacles to achieving this, mainly that of my status as an activist following austere principles of simple living. The average woman in the U.S. who has become a consumer, especially one past her idealistic and experimental twenties, would be uninterested in such a man. This went against finding a woman of my age bracket who could embrace my low-cost, bicycling-in-the-rain lifestyle. Many times I recoiled at an attractive, intelligent woman upon seeing her with her car, much as a smoker turns off many otherwise admirers. However, two girlfriends got past my defenses in 1997 and 1999 when I initially thought each was car-free; by the time I discovered I had made an erroneous assumption, I was hooked and then unconcerned over the car. By 1997, however, my daughters were not as in need of a female presence as they had been a few years earlier.

Elder abuse still ratchets up

In 1994 the Lundberg family scandal/soap opera went into high gear and commanded my attention when my mother had a serious stroke. My brother's girlfriend Vanessa Douglas reported to him that Trilby arrived at the house, threw a fit with her mother, yelled and slammed the door, taking all the family photo albums with her. A few hours later my mother was found on the floor of her bedroom mostly paralyzed. (This seemed to echo my father's paralysis in the late 1940s when he too was shocked by a loved-one's behavior.)

According to my brother, who had moved in with her after our father died, she was regularly preyed upon by her daughter Trilby. Darius has stated publicly that Trilby pressured her mother to visit Dr. Kevorkian (the assisted-suicide doctor) and sign up with the Neptune Society for cremation. My mother did do the latter, but when she would not go the Kevorkian route, Trilby said to her (according to Darius, who overheard), "But you promised!" Darius, my mother and I saw no reason for Mesa Lundberg to need or want to "check out early."

The household was soon being denied its income under "Tribully"'s control, and attempts to work it out met only her intransigence. When we forced the issue with a lawyer's help who sent a letter demanding the rental income for the family business property ("unlawful detainer"), the response was maximum escalation: Trilby filed *ex parte* to become conservator. Anyone can claim anything to get a preliminary hearing, and the burden is then on the innocent to respond most competently and ruthlessly. Darius was made out to be a wastrel wasting his mother's money. Trilby was claiming there was no indebtedness to the proposed conservatee, which was patently untrue and therefore perjury. She also claimed that our mother was never going to recover her health (proven wrong later on). My mother did not fight back hard at all, because she would not bring herself to tell someone, perhaps even herself, that her daughter was "a lying thief."

Thus began my new, part-time and unpaid job that I did not welcome. Not only was the crisis a huge drain on my personal time, robbing me of togetherness with my children, my friends, and energy I had for music, the family crisis also interfered in my work and career. My activism and fundraising suffered. Neglecting the latter is considered worse than failing to pursue relevant activism in the professional nonprofit field. Some well-meaning friends, family and colleagues thought I was simply wrong to "fight" with my sister. One *Auto-Free Times* employee quit because I occasionally got too animated on the telephone regarding my family issues. To some who have been spared the kind of family conflicts having to do with money and power, the idea of fighting amongst family is incomprehensible and unforgivable. Fortunately, few people treated me as tainted by the doings of my sister and the wrenching trouble she was causing the family.

India again

A wonderful respite from the family soap opera and the whole U.S. scene was the trip my daughter Vernell and I took to India. I also invited my younger daughter Bronwyn to come with us, but her mother wouldn't let her. Vernell and I landed in Madras via Tokyo from L.A., after a flight marred by pesticide gassing in the airplane. We enjoyed Madras, although we didn't quite succeed in keeping the pervasive, uncontrolled vehicle exhaust out of our lungs. We hired a car and driver to pollute us along the south seaside highway, where we saw coconut-palm fishing boats, stone sculptor work going on, the Auroville community (a model of land restoration), and finally the charming former French city of Pondicherry. Vernell, about to turn 16, was a great travel companion and happy to see and learn. We returned to Madras and caught an overnight train to the other side of the subcontinent, the state of Kerala. I had heard that this state was exceptional for high literacy, low infant mortality, and women's rights, due in part to independent communist leadership. Vernell and I enjoyed it immensely, and learned about its political and environmental issues. Noam Chomsky had recently spoken in Kerala and was well received in the press. I felt a connection to him since he had placed in one of his short books a mention of Alliance for a Paving Moratorium as a good resource for his readers.

A recent book on India was in error on a few points on Kerala, so I later wrote up my critical review of the book in the *Auto-Free Times*. The author saw it and sent me an angry letter, sort of a backhanded compliment that our magazine seemed so important to a successful writer. The visit Vernell and I enjoyed included special access to the upland wilderness and tribal areas, thanks to my going up to the Kerala minister of tourism at a party. I told him, "You don't want to build more roads so that people trying to get away from big Western cities find just what they're trying to escape. By the way, I want to visit wild tribal areas." He responded positively, telling me someone would call me in the morning. We got the call, and our time in the Wyanad region soon began. First stop was the top administrator's headquarters in Sultan's Battery. He told Vernell and me, "I have the power of life and death over you." I took this as a humorous comment on the organizational set up in this remote area, but I wasn't one hundred percent sure. His tribal manager made sure we saw everything of interest: a government tea plantation and factory protected by Ghurkas (closed to the public); a holy stream where wishes are granted to supplicant bathers, and craftspeople making "khadi" — the cloth Gandhi spun for his own garments. We visited tribal people who were only allowed to access their former wilderness home to gather honey. This tribe was practicing their own permaculture, such as the guild of pepper vines crawling up coffee bushes. A member, a quite ancient woman with a silver ring in her nose, came up to my daughter and offered to sing a song. This was readily accepted, and my daughter stood face to face with her as the traditional song was given. Her voice was good and the sound of the tribal language (probably an endangered one) was something to savor and try to remember.

Back on the coast, Vernell and I got to know a family running a yoga and massage center. I lay down on a huge slab of wood while a young man standing above and hanging on to ropes applied ayurvedic oil onto by body with his bare feet. The family was wonderful, and I had half a mind to import the beautiful, sensitive and intelligent Maya to Humboldt to live with me, if I could afford to do so. Vernell and I were in India only 3 1/2 weeks, but it felt like much longer, and we wanted to stay. So it was no wonder that upon our arrival at Los Angeles International Airport our immigration man got a shock: He said to me, "So, a few weeks in India. Business, right?" I said 'No, vacation." He laughed, as if no one would willingly go there for vacation. Thereupon Vernell piped up, indignantly, "It's better than this place!" He looked crestfallen.

₰

At this moment in creating this book I happen to be writing on a plastic table. I am on Amtrak, having just crossed the Willamette River through Eugene. Plastic — that toxic product made from the stuff that at this moment is gushing out of the BP Macondo well in the Gulf of Mexico — surrounds us and touches us, contributing to fatal diseases and alienating us from nature. I resume my story now with a plastic-society twist.

&

By the time my family crisis reared up again in 1994, I was well aware of society's being "plastic" — as the hipsters in the 1960s called the Establishment. This description eventually applied to much of my family, as I started seeing myself as the only one taking many of my parents' teachings and example to heart. What I was learning and feeling set me apart from almost everyone in my family, as my growing awareness shaped my new life. Knowing that society is "plastic," for example, is a bad enough feeling without adding a personal disaster such as my own family's disintegration.

This plastic-family ordeal, however liberating or instructive as it has been for me, has been everything that any major soap opera tries to depict about family greed in our culture. I brought the saga on myself in large part myself, because in 1986 I would not abide by the presence of my sister and her husband in a respectable family business. From that point on I seemed to seek out opportunities to take a stand on ethical matters, environmental policy, and political issues — regardless of consequences such as effects on my finances. I was not plastic enough; I was not bendable or pliable.

Timber wars and road fighting

The science of ecology became an abiding interest for me in the early 1990s, borne out by our efforts in the trenches. In our arguments and testimony we passed along what information and findings we could, both to friend and foe (road builders and their government buddies). It's impossible to say how many roads and parking lots we really stopped. The Duluth-Manitoba truck-only toll road comes to mind. The northern California forest road known as proposed Highway 162 was another. We did get the word out globally about stopping urban sprawl and rejecting the car. One reason that our message and constant efforts were important was because road schemes that got defeated could rise up again, requiring a massive effort to stop them all over again. Our Road Fighting Network, our Fact Sheets and magazine aided many activists in the U.S. and beyond, but eventually it seemed we were not winning the overall fight.

We were determined to show what we meant in our personal lives to uphold and fight for, via projects as well as in our newsletters, magazines, speeches and interviews. The projects from 1990-1997 were road-fighting through our Alliance for a Paving Moratorium, and targeting the car (or, promoting car-free living). We had no cars, we promoted depaving, we held public events such as rallies, we concretized, and we protested. I rarely got out into wilderness, having made the mistake of starting a nonprofit organization, but my friends were often at action camps, tree-sits and reconnaissance that have been a way of life for two generations of forest defenders in Humboldt County, Mendocino County, and Oregon. For our efforts we got free donations from sympathetic workers at the food co-op and other expressions of kindness from citizens and country folk who wanted us to keep up the fight.

After hearing disturbing first-hand reports of Sheriff's Deputies' brutality against nonviolent forest defenders in 1996, I spoke with the Sheriff by phone. I told him about the heavy-handed tactics, but instead of denying them he complained about what protesters were doing to hurt Deputies. I scoffed at this and prepared to hold a press conference on October 4. The night before, I received a phone call in my office from Arcata's token right-winger on the City Council, Carl Pellatz. He objected to my holding the press conference (even though it was not an Arcata matter) and told me in an unfriendly tone, "You're going to get your fingers blown off on this one, Jan." This was indeed "the Deep North."

The press conference had others more nervous than I was: hastily scheduled was another press conference by the Sheriff at the same time and day at the Court House/Jail. Near the room of the press conference a young forest defender, Timber Wolf, locked her neck to the west side of the building's main entrance, disrupting or enhancing the press conference. My press conference on the Arcata Plaza went without incident, with the presence of my daughter who had been mistreated in her removal from a tree sit such as with nerve damage from tight plastic handcuffs. The way some people even in Arcata regarded these protests was with hatred. The nurse at the Open Door Clinic attending to my daughter's hands told her, "You're paid to do these protests, aren't you." If only!

Fall of 1996 had feelings running high as the last of the ancient redwood trees continued to be clear-cut, often on steep slopes. Later in October about 50 of us got arrested for riding our bikes in a big "Critical Mass" protest in support of defenders of ancient-redwood groves. The day we picked was the National Day of Protest to Stop Police Brutality, Oct. 22, 1996. On a rainy Tuesday afternoon, almost 200 of us set out from the Arcata Plaza for the courthouse in Eureka, the scene of much injustice toward our brave friends: Crow, Nature Boy, Spirit, Dijon, Garlic, Grasshopper, Dirt, Pond Scum, River, Ayr, Timber Wolf, Buckwheat, Screech Owl, Sleeper, Lizard, Sawyer, Felony, Almond, Peanut, Josh, and many more. (Why these nicknames? Protesters feel that FBI or police informants or *agents de provocateur* don't need to know identities of those planning to trespass onto corporate timber land, for example.) New eco-warriors were in the very making as we streamed down Highway 101 with excitement, as the cows in the pastures beside stampeded in the same direction just for fun. We were taking both lanes as well as the bike lane, blocking the speeding polluters behind us. But we *were* traffic. Ahead we saw a strange sight: coming at us going the wrong way was a mass of Highway Patrol cars and motorcycles. They came up and stopped us right there, violently grabbing and slipping in the rain on the oily road, herding most of us off the G street exit that was the last one for Arcata. Many arrests were made, and video cameras seized when our participants attempted to document the arrests. I was caught by the arm of Patrolman Clocker (of course), who later testified that I had pushed him ten feet with my bike(!). He let me go after issuing a citation, but made me promise not to get back on the freeway (even though there's a bike line). If he had checked my pockets he would have found fliers for the Critical Mass that my office had done up. Free to go, I rode with another protester to the meeting-point in Eureka, going the long way around. When we met up we proceeded to the Court House/Jail on Highway 101 that is the main street in town. We circled this building, the biggest in the county, a few times, getting picked off by arresting officers directed by a senior officer. Police usually don't take kindly to protests unless they are totally laid out and authorized, even though we all have the right of free assembly and free speech.

I was cuffed by an officer named Lawson, appropriately enough (although Liarson would have been perfect). Dozens of protesters who had not been arrested were around me, glad to see me finally arrested instead of sitting in my office. My daughter Vernell (forest name, Spring) was particularly happy, as she was at age 16 a veteran arrestee. On the bike ride, she had said, "This is cool, Dad!" (That night she and our friends held a Jan's In Jail party, which I wish I could have attended. But then it could not have happened.) I went peacefully into the bowels of the Court House building to be processed. My charges included "resisting arrest." Gosh, why would police officers lie? I was put with all the other male protesters, two dozen others, in the maximum-security wing. This was so that no other inmates could be infected by our subversive ideas. As arraignments and hearings took place, we noticed wife beaters and car thieves getting low bail amounts compared to us. We had simply ridden our bicycles legally. In jail I fasted, not trusting the food. The water from ancient pipes probably was leaded. At least this old section of the jail had the televisions all out of kilter, so we could talk, howl and talk on the prison phones. I called Associate Press, ultimately resulting on a big feature on me with my photo, by Martha Irvine, that appeared in hundreds of newspapers. I decided to make bail because I heard a brutal Sheriff's deputy McAllister with a thing for my daughter was looking for her because he knew I was her only guardian, and he could pick her up as a minor. So she was on the run, no big deal for her. I was visited by volunteers organized by the jail support group; one was named Rabbit. So I had my office assistant pay $10,000 (for the crime of riding my bicycle) and I got out after three days and nights. When I got my clothes and personal items I saw that no one had removed the protest fliers I had come in with. I was met by an Earth First!er when I was released and debriefed.

I went home and fasted another day so that I could get the bad water from jail out of my system. The experience in "the can" was a little stressful due to the headache generated from my internal outrage of my freedom taken away. But I read lots of books in jail, made a new friend (cellmate Steve), and when I was called to leave I said "But I haven't finished this book!" I eventually had a trial. One woman on the jury had the power of independent thinking, and did not believe the police. The judge, C. Michael Brown, was quite disappointed in the hung jury. He later got back at me in

2003 by refusing to recognize my response to a motion to steal my family home by evicting me. This had to do with fraud and elder abuse against my mother. But I don't want to get ahead of the story...

Around the mid-1990s Britain became a hotbed of anti-road activism, giving rise to Reclaim the Streets demonstrations in London: two junked cars driven by activists would deliberately collide in a busy intersection, enabling the drivers to get out of their cars and pretend to dispute hotly. This would create an instant traffic jam, whereupon the rest of the demonstrators arrived to begin a street party. A large battery-operated sound system would be biked in, and a large puppet danced. Under the skirts of the puppet would be a jackhammer to rip up the road (don't say pavement; in Britain that only means sidewalks). The music and commotion supposedly drowned out the depaving machine. Meanwhile, more and more pedestrians, bicyclists and motorists joined the party.

But our decade-long approach to the ecological and socioeconomic crisis ultimately had little immediate or perceptible effect. We were not sure of our progress, or we didn't want to admit our doubts. At the time we were caught up in our zeal and solidarity with other eco-warriors, and we believed there was a crying need for our message.

Always will to try new tactics and strategies, after living in Arcata a few years I felt I needed to take my message out on the road (or the rails). I became more connected to what I called the activist network. I knew that I could go almost anywhere and receive cooperation if not support. Such a way of life was the best possible adventure in my estimation.

By this stage in my development I was becoming "self-contained." I had some skills and interests that gave me pleasure and purpose, making me feel independent of "Babylon" (conventional modern society). As already mentioned, knowledge of wild native plants for food, medicine and other uses was a fascination, although my learning was far from accomplished. I was at least finding out what I didn't know and should learn about. To pursue my interests I did a lot of reading, listening to experts in their fields, and hiking. I also contented myself with music making and keeping in close touch with friends and family. Especially after my full-time child-rearing days ended in 1999, I found I could just easily be alone with my projects and hobbies as be with others.

I was trying to emancipate myself from the market economy and dependence on technology. This sounds insane or impossible to some, but I was only pursuing my step-by-step personal growth. Those who have tried this path toward self-reliance and liberation in these times reap rewards. However, we can only go so far without a tribe or close community. We bump up against the need to have substantial cash. Less is more, but only up to a point.

Chapter 9

1990s Learning New Concepts in the 1990s

Eco-rocking from the Redwoods to Kyoto

By 1997 I was in my prime as an energetic activist, loving the simple life with little materialism, and enjoying a kind of leadership of the road-fighting, anti-car wing of the environmental movement. My favorite project was Pedal Power Produce, based on bike-hauling farm veggies grown at our own farm to the Arcata Farmers Market each Saturday. (I was a minority partner with a local hip landowner known for planting thousands of trees.)

My lifestyle and activism affected my music greatly. Music itself had begun to be more important to me and my work, and this resulted in an eco-rock album by our band The Depavers, titled Have a Global Warming Day. The title cut was my contribution to the Kyoto meeting of the United Nations Conference on Climate Change. Despite feeling guilty about the jet fuel I used, I went and participated. Japan was a treat, although the lack of fiber in the food was no treat.

My conference activities were an eye opener in two ways: (1) Our music was far more appreciated than our literature or my willingness to be interviewed, and (2) my sharp questioning of U.S. officials at press conferences was not much appreciated, especially by one Associate Press reporter who felt there can be no activism involved with journalism. So I was glad my song got airtime on National Public Radio and that I was filmed performing it by CNN-International. Our fliers and networking did not seem to accomplish much due to the tonnage of paper offered by so many groups. Making the paper route even tougher, a Japanese pollution institute tossed our papers into the trash when we left our table alone.

Music was in 1997, and remains, probably the best way to get our message out in various settings and media. We needed all the tools we could apply for our no-more-roads/car-free cause. I had growing disillusionment with the funded environmental movement and its connection to Wall Street's priorities. Any funder or foundation has holdings on Wall Street that depend entirely on economic expansion. (The book *The Revolution Will Not Be Funded* discusses the effect of funding on nonprofit groups.) So I reasoned that a song could do the most good if it could only be heard. After hundreds of songs I've written, many performances, airplay and sharing songs with other musicians, I cannot say I have done much for the movement through my music. But my faith in its potential is as high as ever, especially as the world seems trapped in continuing war, destruction and exploitation, while activism, books, elections and religions seem to make little headway.

Music helped us get through our activist struggle. Despite the obstacles my office faced in the late 1990s, which are similar to the ones today, our work and our movement were exhilarating. We felt we were on the cutting edge on multilevels. I was learning a lot from my ever-broadening network around the world. My reading and learning from other activists and writers were expanding my mind, and it all found its way into my work, my music and my lifestyle. My daughters were affected indirectly and we enjoyed our time without sacrificing anything; indeed we gained from the simple but engaged lifestyle.

A time for woolens! Cool, damp Humboldt County, required that I wear long underwear eight months a year. For my daughters and me Humboldt proved to be not a bad place at all, relative to other parts of the nation, in terms of weather, opportunities, interesting people and high quality food, drink, etc. When my mother joined us in 1997, my home and family were in good shape in many ways. I was now fulfilling another purpose, that of eldercare management, with no difficulty, and I enjoyed my mother's presence. She was always there to help edit the *Auto-Free Times*, hear a new song, or participate in a discussion such as on her granddaughters' activities.

But by 1999 I could tell I had gotten my fill of "cArcata" when I hit the wall of mainstream culture Humboldt-style. It was better than Hollywood-style, but as long as I was still in the United Paved Precincts of America I began to feel that I might as well go off to a big city to be in the belly of the beast, if it made sense doing something there. Arcata was getting steadily more expensive, less funky and artistic, and anti-homeless. City council policies increasingly permeated government and law enforcement with fascistic tendencies wrapped in liberal rationalization.

So activism in Arcata and Humboldt County began by the end of the '90s to seem not so worthwhile as pursuing something else somewhere else. I did have personal needs. Why not make "a career" out of taking excellent care of my multi-level self? I needed that. Due to a boxing match knockout at age 12, I should have had physical therapy on a frequent basis. By the time I realized in middle age that weekly chiropractor visits did me no lasting good, I seldom sought therapies because of the time and expense required. In the twelve years I lived in Humboldt I never made it to Heartwood Institute, the celebrated healing center that offered me an open invitation for the complimentary Activist Weekend for burn-out prevention.

On any given day, if one takes care of one's body, there isn't a lot of time for conventional work or wage slavery. Instead, certain things that need to be done are skipped: yoga, exercise, creative arts, rubbing oneself down with olive oil after a bath (or having someone else do it for you), getting a massage, giving a massage, reading, writing letters, visiting friends, cooking, gardening, mending socks, going out to the co-op, and less pleasant stuff like putting a check in the mail to some corporation. The list goes on. The business of life leaves no time for giving one's day to someone else's business, not to mention being exploited and sacrificing one's health. Once one gets used to relative freedom so as to call one's time his own, it's difficult to imagine going back to a job-job. In Humboldt, straight jobs have always been hard to get. I was to find this out when desperate, but it's even harder to land a job when one is over 50 and over-qualified. Still, taking the time for one's true interest is a habit never forgotten no matter how tough life seems to get.

In Humboldt my little universe was normally, 9 out of 10 days perhaps, spent within the confines of this triangle of walking or bicycling: house, office on the Plaza (until 1999), and the Co-op, all in downtown Arcata. On those meridians were the post office and the bank. If I didn't visit friends somewhere along the triangle, they would come over to my house. At first my home was my small family, a daughter or two, and later my mother. Later when they left I had just a roommate or two, and no wife or live-in girlfriend. The word "girlfriend" is politically incorrect for many in Humboldt and elsewhere on the West Coast; preferred terms are "partner," "significant other," "mother/father of my child," *ad infinitum*.

My music making was almost always at home, often every morning and evening, and I was almost as happy to do it alone as with another friend or bunch of friends. It was special to play with family, meaning my fairly famous daughter Vernell whose stage name was Spring. She was too busy building a big repertoire of folk songs to spend time learning many of my rock-twinged tunes. Her powerful voice and strong playing supported her determination to sing about fighting for protesters' rights and the cause of the threatened ancient redwoods. She was in high demand as an entertainer and speaker. Her occasional national media interviews were not surprising to me, although her age (16 onward) astounded some people. Sometimes it wasn't so pleasant, as Rush Limbaugh made fun of her name: "What kind of a name is *Spring?*" he asked rhetorically with contempt. Despite her opportunity to meet and enlarge the demand for her voice, spoken or sung, she was first and foremost part of a movement with its own social circle. Almost no-one in it was distracted by looking for individual fame or success as an activist. Few worked alone or with their own program, as Julia Butterfly later chose to do. But if it worked for her and Mother Earth, who couldn't be glad?

There would have been more emphasis on family and music for me if I had not had to go to court in L.A. every few months in regard to my mother's difficulties. Fortunately, my work, adventures, and conceptual breakthroughs were fulfilling and open-ended. But they eventually led me to give up on Arcata and intensify my own growth on my idealistic path of self-liberation.

One avenue of discovery was to explore community preparedness for Y2K, the Millennium Bug. I wasn't sure if Y2K would be a big deal or not, but the study of complex systems on which the consumer population depends was worthwhile. Few people had given this much thought, and when they did they sometimes got scared or depressed, especially when Y2K was considered a real threat. My investigations and conversations about preparedness and community resiliency contributed to my becoming fed up over Arcata's lack of interest. I held meetings at city hall, announced by the newspaper. But nothing changed. To an activist, this is par for the course. Oddly, as the end of 1999 approached, public interest in issues of community preparedness steadily went down instead of up. A few people instead just stocked up on food, water, weapons, etc. How many times were you treated to some excess food or other items that had been stored in 1999 and finally let go of by the owners? Probably not many, and few talked about it. People did not want to feel foolish about worries over Y2K, and almost everyone wanted to forget about complex systems away from our control.

By mid 1999 I was ready for a major change, aware that I might have reached the end of what would later seem to be a good period of stability and security. I put my house up for sale, as my daughters hadn't any interest in spending much time there, and I was suddenly rather free. Free to find a more community-oriented, more natural home environment.

After Seattle-WTO: from *Auto-Free Times* toward *Culture Change*

The highlight as well as end of my decade-long Arcata comfort and relative calm was when I left Arcata with my girlfriend Erika "Juniper Elk" Lorna Kraft to buy a sailboat in Puget Sound. On our way we participated in the "Battle of Seattle" and helped shut down the World Trade Organization meeting there on November 30, 1999. (I was later surprised to hear Trilby disparage my doing so. She had changed since her relatively recent bumper-sticker politics: "No Vietnam War in Central America." You can bet there is no "No Vietnam War in Afghanistan" on her famous Mercedes featured by Associated Press (see photo section). We did get the boat, but as I will explain, we did not stay long away from Humboldt.

By early 2001, after seeing that the anti-WTO demonstrations in Seattle did not include much awareness of our core issues, my close colleagues and I were ready for a change in strategy and lifestyle. In the past we had not gotten quite enough indication that we were on target or that our issues were more widely recognized. An exception was my 1994 paper "Beyond GATT." It was distributed by Ralph Nader to Senators in his effort to derail the General Agreement on Tariffs and Trade (GATT) that gave rise to the World Trade Organization (WTO). I described in the paper the gross dependency on oil for world trade. But other than these occasional exposures and examples of solidarity, we were a figurative and sometimes literal voice in the wilderness. Fortunately for our story and this autobiography, forging ahead doesn't necessarily depend on getting clearly positive signals. Only an activist would understand that — as perhaps too the champion of an activist which you might be turning into!

The *Auto-Free Times* took an interest in the Battle of Seattle because of the interrelated issues: vast amounts of dwindling oil for world trade, economic growth and consumerism that meant greater urban sprawl and greenhouse emissions. Also, social movements converging for the protest against the WTO was unusual, something we all needed more of. Despite the bad press over a small number of broken windows in Seattle — that the corporate media emphasized without covering police brutality and violations against freedoms of speech and assembly — Seattle was a victory. Juniper and I were pleasantly surprised, and part of it was from participating: during the action we locked arms to help keep WTO delegates from their meetings. Humboldt activists were coordinated by Direct Action Network (DAN) to take over a key intersection, Sixth Street and University, to block access to the Convention Center. I was disgusted to see jets of pepperspray shooting into protesters' faces as they sat on the road. Phalanxes of 'Robocops" came at us, and we smelled teargas. Our mandolin player was shot by rubber bullets and beaten by police when he mounted an armored vehicle, but he escaped. He, my daughter Vernell, Juniper and I went to Juniper's house that night to play music, shocking her Republican parents. Their only comment was that Ayr didn't smell good — a badge of honor for many eco-warriors, but I never did go that far. During that week Juniper and I played our songs for free dinners at a vegan Chinese restaurant. Only one diner objected to the lyrics (about resisting the police state, for example).

Because my office's effectiveness had peaked by 1999, thanks to so many issues demanding everyone's attention, I had begun to prefer setting up projects and communities to weather the coming storm of radical change and upheaval. We promoted many "tools of sustainable living" and visualized "models of sustainable living," and we pointed to some of our projects. But we could not break through to a large segment of the population. Reasons included obstruction by the corporate media, lack of interest by comfortable academicians, and government leaders who could not grasp peak oil or the global impacts of petroleum and fossil fuel dependence. If we had more grants, we would have gotten the word out more thoroughly, but if it all depends on money, what kind of a movement is that? Not a grassroots one that will really change things.

In 1999 we would not have thought the consumer economy had much of a chance for many more years of global growth, and were amazed and disappointed way that the economy kept revving up. However, perhaps with the recession that began in 2008, the zenith of oil consumption and "peak everything" represented the turning point: the end of the corporate Waste Economy was at hand.

At the risk of making a prediction that could appear inaccurate, I believe that in mid-2010 as I write this book, we are seeing the inexorable beginning of total socioeconomic collapse. My reasons for my opinion are grounded in oil-industry realities and the overshoot that Earth's population has temporarily achieved. Many who deny the possibility or likelihood of collapse engage in wishful thinking, in part from great hope for a non-wrenching post-peak oil future. However, their opinions do not seem to take oil industry realities into account. It is hard to tell at the moment what is in store in the short term, for only a future looking-back perspective with hindsight can see how fast developments are taking place today to bring about the historic change we have been anticipating. [We do not want to see pain and hardship, but discussing it may help people understand what is happening to them. They need to coalesce and plan for the dissolution of the United States as we know it when plentiful oil supplies can suddenly dry up. Gorbachev had no choice but to oversee the collapse of the USSR, and Obama may find himself in a similar position after wasting much effort and resources on propping up the status quo and Wall Street profits.]

I saw our office's work as more relevant than ever, but in a changing light. The ceaseless "paving over of paradise" served as the main factor in choosing the new name of our nonprofit group in early summer 2001: Culture Change. I had suspected for years that the root problem society had with mistreating nature was cultural. But I increasingly connected anti-nature predation to predatory behavior within families. It had to do with materialism that meant exploiting nature and workers to achieve the false wealth that today's society condones. Materialism and overwork are notoriously virulent in the U.S., but they are held up as virtues or "human nature." Long before 2001 I had already been thinking that most of the malevolent behavior one encounters anywhere has to do with the perpetrator's perceived material insecurity. Taking this further, I eventually saw not just a psychological defect, but a culturally taught phenomenon shot through the entire population of modern humanity (especially the U.S.).

After a few years of living the personal lessons of the culture's nastiness in my own family after our courtroom disgrace starting in 1995, it was a natural transition to put my personal and professional energy toward fundamental change in the culture. Addressing ecological and social issues simultaneously was satisfying, for one yearns for meaning in trying to understand a changing world. I will return to the birth of Culture Change after describing events in my life leading up to far more than a name change.

Chapter 10

Elder Abuse & Paving of the Planet
Fuel *Culture Change*

In 1999 I had concluded that Arcata was neither a real community nor progressive enough for me to live in. The changes that I kicked into motion for me and my family may have been justified, but a heavy price was paid. Leaving Arcata was fairly easy, but I had mounting misgivings over leaving my mother without as much family support as she had had. I justified leaving her behind because she had her own good home, mostly excellent caregivers, and a granddaughter several miles to the south in Humboldt County. When I saw that my mother's situation wasn't as good as it had been under my roof, I had already sold my house and was committed to stick to my plan to leave Arcata for good. One reason for my move was to be nearer to my younger daughter Bronwyn, who lived with her mother in Seattle. Bronwyn liked sailing, which I offered in the Puget Sound, but we enjoyed each other's company under any circumstances. Seattle, that I have nicknamed SeAngeles for its L.A.-type drawbacks, was a place I wanted to avoid, but I was in sailing and bussing distance to it when in Everett or other moorage.

Living on a 30' sloop in Everett meant having as neighbors a U.S. naval base and a Kleenex factory — both of which are hugely polluting and generate motor vehicle traffic. My daily routine by myself was okay, but not tolerable forever in that spot. Too much of the cold, rainy winter weather is also a bring down. At first I had Juniper on board, and our good times and plans for extensive sailing together made for a most worthwhile period of my life. But she decided to return to Humboldt State University, and I was confined to the small but ship-shape boat alone. I wasn't sailing much on the Sound due to winter weather and insufficient contacts, but I kept busy and had a new friend on the same dock. I missed Juniper partly because we shared interests such as performing eco-

170

rock together and brainstorming on the fledgling Sail Transport Network (STN). On my own on the boat, STN was my main project, but its acceptance was handicapped by very low oil prices at the time.

I began making more visits to Arcata than Juniper was making visits to Everett, and I ended up living in Arcata again. I lived for a few months with her in the Earth Church, a small compound not far from the University. I stayed in Juniper's room, and we were good friends with three other roommates: Kerry Liz, Tofu Mike, and Dragonfly. I wasn't delighted with being back in Arcata when I felt my destiny was on my boat up north, but some cool events happened in Arcata. I finally met Julia Butterfly when she briefed the public on her two-year tree sit. Angela Davis visited and gave a talk in Arcata's downtown theater, packing the house. She spoke mainly about the imprisoned population of women. For the question & answer period I had a point to make, so I sang a verse from one of my songs: "We're cut off from the land / It's all been fenced or paved / The corporations say 'just keep on buying junk' / Just to make us think we're free." Davis responded, "I think that covers it!"

I wasn't with joy or a feeling of close community that I began my final phase with Arcata and Humboldt. I dug in, however, when I had to take over my mother's house and start living in it. A con man had befriended my brother and was benefiting from my brother's taking my mother on a long vacation to Santa Barbara. I kicked the man out of our family home with the force of law, cleaned up the place, moved in, got comfortable, and commenced the process of bringing my mother back home. Where I truly wanted to be was back on my boat for the sailing season and to be out of Humboldt with or without Juniper. I don't think my brother or I had an idea of the extreme danger our mother was now in due to Trilby's proximity in Ventura.

It was when living in my mother's house, now my family home, during 2000-2003 that I became dissatisfied with the "four walled prison." At first it was more than tolerable with Juniper in the guesthouse and I got the organic veggie garden into shape. But the novelty of living in this house, and having jam sessions with my friends there, did not constitute an adventure or my real future. I was working on the computer for the *Auto-Free Times* (soon to be *Culture Change*), usually 12 hours a day, without exiting the premises for 48 hours straight oftentimes.

I enjoyed gardening, which I knew my mother was sorely missing. I surprised myself by bringing fresh cut flowers or greens to the farmers market to barter, and was rewarded by generous exchanges of excellent peaches or home-grown eggs.

But my sense of suburban oppression and lack of old-fashioned neighborliness made me want to escape. Much of the time after a long day's work with no planning I had nowhere to go but to walk to a huge health-food market to buy some organic food. This was true for most citizens (except they drove) unless they were going to a music venue or to friends' homes. One can have a busy social life, but one shouldn't have to work at it so as to not be alone (if one lives with no family). I felt surrounded in my neighborhood by pavement, cars, and isolated consumers watching their private televisions. My biggest desire was to be sitting on the side of the road with my guitar, not knowing where my next meal was coming from. For some reason this had greater and greater appeal compared to sitting up on my boat alone as I slowly put together a sail transport community.

My dream as a troubadour was coming true, thanks to a good deal of white collar crime that served to reinforce the elder abuse of my mother. To recount her second phase of elder abuse after the mid-'90s pains me greatly. I have trouble to this day believing what was done to my mother and by extension her granddaughters. I certainly hope that her being dispossessed, the main effect of which was to shorten her life perhaps by many years, does not necessarily mean that my daughters' and my being dispossessed will shorten our lives. We are indeed struggling, but somehow managing for now. I have tried to see the inadvertently healthy aspects of our struggle, but this might be partly a mental exercise to assuage my feelings of failure. How I could have been so ineffectual in my efforts to fight it sometimes fills me with hate for my mother's perpetrators, whom she called "attackers." She suffered the consequences of their greed and her life was clearly shortened. This awful story has to be told in context with decisions I was making with my work and lifestyle:

As I mentioned, I had returned from the boat life to Arcata for family reasons and to spend time with Juniper. My colleagues and I were still putting out the *Auto-Free Times*, but, without enough positive signals from the public that our cause was on the rise, we ran out of enthusiasm for the same old approach in activism and publishing. So we laid out our plans for dissolution or scaling way back.

Before implementing this, it became clear that what we really needed was to find a way to inject more relevance into our efforts and our public image. I was deciding to reformulate my own work for personal reasons, for the long haul. It would be based on what I enjoyed doing most: direct interaction with people who were engaged in sustainable living as they consciously resisted the mainstream corporate economy. This was the birth of Culture Change.

By the time my staff and I started Culture Change we had brought our land-use and transportation issues to a certain level of public awareness. But in early 2001 we perceived that our road-fighting and car-free activism had reached a saturation point. We had to make a change. Not knowing what to do besides shutting down our magazine and monitoring the post office box, we were going to fold. I thought about what I really wanted to do that would be effective and true to my values. I had been brooding for months, building on years of vague desire for deeper involvement.

Surprisingly, we had an exhilarating rebirth of our message and mission. What started out as a grant proposal to the (Ted) Turner Foundation, which had funded us in the past, became our new purpose: Culture Change. As stated above, it came about from my desire to pursue activism in a more direct fashion with people face to face. The limitations of sitting in an office and putting out magazines, when we were no longer growing as an organization or movement, made me just want to hit the road and find opportunities to work with cutting edge activists. I most admired those living with a minimum of money and a maximum of tribe-like support. I wanted to become houseless or homeless and go wherever I could make a difference. Not having any family to take care of was my new status, although if my mother were to resume living with me I would be a homebody, or home-office body.

The Turner grant proposal was declined, but we had by then decided to give our magazine one more try with a new name. So our issue #19 was *Culture Change* rather than *Auto-Free Times*. I wrote 20 out of its 25 articles, whereas our prior magazines usually had one or two articles or editorials by me. In exploring the ramifications of culture change there was a lot to think about and address with our wider, deeper focus. As distinguished from *cultural change* we began to publish on the need to recognize the need for *culture change*. It is healthy to promote cultural change, but if it's not realistic to do so when a massive change in culture. By this we meant replacement of a culture with a new one, or the total overhaul of a culture with a return to ancient traditions. We saw this clearly as the only reasonable outlook or hope. The aforementioned aspects of our culture — society's perversely valuing the paving over of the best farmland, and society's permitting and even rewarding the theft of family inheritance between family members — seem so basically wrong that cultural change (e.g., respecting grandparents' rights to see grandchildren impacted by divorce) is too superficial to assure the health and longevity of such a culture.

Our new approach made it easier to explore in a unified fashion issues such as species extinction, peak oil, feminist health care, overpopulation, and "organic" food shipped thousands of miles. Ten years later, these are fairly popular subjects. In my experience, questioning a culture and sketching a sustainable society sheds light on the deepest origins for society's ills.

My questioning an ecocidal society's legitimacy and rejecting the conventional wisdom of living only under Western Civilization have made it easier to spot narrow reforms and shortsighted campaign-based activism. Thus our activism gave way to projects that tried to convey a message on the bigger picture. This presented difficulties when such concepts as "the market" were questioned when the alternatives are not in place. But we could still write about these concepts and try to present ideas critical for a sustainable culture. Some hands-on, practical demonstration projects lent themselves to photojournalism and musical expression. Utilizing media was our main tactic, but we were not and are not limited to media. We were and remain open-ended with our approach.

Even though our specifically fighting certain roads was abandoned in 2001, my projects and those of Culture Change since then encompassed our former emphasis, to address more and more precisely a future society's practical needs and ways of operating. Looking at land-use and energy for transport can be done in such a way to question the entire petroleum infrastructure and the profit-based, growth-oriented system.

Culture Change's work has always pertained to oil or petroleum in some respect. The energy and materials from oil had served to vastly expand material goods and wasteful consumption. What I had noticed before I perceived the complete cultural impact of petroleum, after the oil industry stopped paying me, was that the use of energy had everything to do with harmful land use, technological food production, war, and vulnerability of society to oil shocks and overpopulation pressures. I offer here my energy-related chronology to get us up to the present (2010):

As far back as my 1988 exposure to *Beyond Oil* for *Population and Environment*, all my activism has been based on an understanding of peak oil. My particular grasp of the petroleum business (price & supply of refined products) became my basis for predicting collapse. Again for *Population and Environment*, in 1992, I roughly assessed the Russian people's ability to deal with their Soviet-system collapse favorably compared to the U.S.'s massively precarious petroleum dependence.

In the mid 1990s I stumbled upon *Eating Oil*, written by British petrochemist Maurice Green in 1978. This gave me a clearer idea of agribusiness's and the food system's extreme dependence on oil and natural gas. Why such a book was and is basically unknown, and the subject of little interest even today (although more than prior to 9-11), tells volumes about the propensity of the population to simply consume without awareness.

When I became a partner in a certified-organic farm in 1997, we found to our disappointment that the operation used "outside inputs" with a high carbon footprint. The soil was not being built, as chicken manure was being trucked in, and mulching was not done — tilling was done intensively without question, with a petroleum-powered tractor. When we took over the farm we made positive changes. This project encompassed more than its name Pedal Power Produce: the seven-year running effort taught us a lot about permaculture, river erosion near our farm, bike cart technology, and having fun. I can still hear the mice running around at night in the walls of the little ramshackle farmhouse with its woodstove crackling and bunches of garlic drying. Unfortunately, farm output was lower than it might have been because I mistakenly allowed our project to become foremost a community rather than a project with a goal. So this tiny community did not maximize farm work or expand service of

Pedal Power Produce beyond one farmers market (Arcata Plaza). The farm's community felt that their Earth First! activities, involving sacrifice such as jail time, justified taking it a little easier on the farm than professional farmers would. Still, I always found it a beautiful place and a nice scene to enjoy and work at. One song I wrote was about the bears and other creatures that would come through our fence to take our melons and other food in the fields: "You stalk through the night to find a good meal / The tear on your coat from barbed wire you feel."

Throughout the 1990s our publication *Auto-Free Times* (formerly Paving Moratorium Update) pointed to the unreliability and of the petroleum infrastructure and the vulnerability to "depletion" of fossil fuels. Rather than keep to the Establishment view that "energy security is national security," my concerns were increasingly with nature, and tribal inclinations, not the market or assumed needs. Thus my academic/industry skills in numerical analysis were mostly left behind, as I opened myself to relying almost solely on others' calculations and often their interpretations. I felt I could tell what studies and authorities could be relied upon as I found them and considered them. A great deal of interesting material was mailed to our office. My analysis became more intuitive and from the heart.

In recent years some peak oil writers have had a hard time agreeing with some of my positions, at least publicly. Besides my blunt conclusions and faith in non-market, low-tech culture, my analyses have been discounted because they are not loaded with numbers and graphs. (More often than not, my dire prognosis for the consumer economy and maintaining over six billion people is something people cannot agree with publicly.) I can't help it if I am imbued with definite feelings and realizations that seem more urgent than refining more facts and figures. Some readers do appreciate my approach and give me encouragement, but the higher they are up in the Establishment, the less interest they feel they can show in my work. When Culture Change columns started appearing in 2002, some readers had not seen such a critique of society that combined so many disciplines and findings to reach radical conclusions. The first two online essays released, in summer 2002, in June and July respectively, were "Alternative to techno-enslavement" and "Hunting and gathering in Ecotopia." My first essay as an aspiring columnist marked a hopeful career move. My columns would elevate me to syndicated status if I only kept at it. I was putting my faith in the familiar professional drive for success and material rewards befitting a concerned intellectual. Although I didn't intend it, my content and focus excluded me from mainstream media opportunities. Still I would not give up my delusion of desirability for newspapers that part of me knew were hopelessly corrupted by car advertising revenue. My very first paragraph still rings true for me today, in terms of what people need to face:

Culture Change e-Letter #1 [paragraph 1]
Burned up about planet burning up?
Alternative to Techno-Enslavement

As technology advances, we have less security and less freedom in our daily lives. The nuclear threat is the best example. But nukes are only one manifestation, and are not separate from the general technological and wasteful nature of our artificial (e.g., paved) environments. It is the workplace, residential and four-wheeled environments that dispirit our animal selves as much as nuclear holocaust that hangs over our heads. Our true selves need more than a cold beer and television — or even more than a great book or being loved by one's chosen mate.

It can't be stressed enough that in the U.S. we have evolved a culture that paves over its best farmland — my favorite example, like a mantra. Destroying living soil and creatures that depend on it (humans do too) is a nonsensical way to treat the land, except for the few making short-term gains at everyone else's expense. For centuries, most likely, Society has needed to examine itself and change its value-system. But there has been little evaluation or acknowledgment of our destructive nature by the mass of people, despite the environmental movement's long and hard efforts. Then again, the environmental movement was hijacked sometime around the 1980s by compromisers seeking Establishment approval and paychecks within shouting distance of a corporado's salary. I was naïvely seeking such a paycheck while pursuing inconvenient truths.

After battling ten years to change policies on land use and energy, hardly making a dent, I saw that the "pave paradise" syndrome was not only at the root of the environmental crisis but also at the heart of our culture. Unwise land-use, however, increasingly appeared to me as but a symptom of flawed human relations under a system relying on oppression and exploitation. Finding these truths came naturally for me. The cultural critique regarding "paving paradise" fit with first-hand knowledge of my own oil-soaked family and its division over corruption regarding money and power. A third factor in birthing Culture Change was the three take-over attempts of Fossil Fuels Policy Action; these reminders of desperate, corporate-minded values were helpful for my seeing the need for fundamental change in society beyond, for example, redistribution of wealth.

My previously great family was now drowning in problems of greed, materialism, mutual alienation, and mental illness. Since my family was not unique with problems regarding inheritance, theft and elder abuse, I saw a pattern that was related to the false values of ruining farmland and wildlife habitat for exploitative gain. My growing feeling was for the need for a change in the dominant culture and dispensing with "alleged reality." The two crises, environment and family, had a common denominator of *defective culture.* On occasion I also threw in "materialist illusion," which I wrote about on occasion as if I were taken over by metaphysical or Tao-of-physics revelation.

A change of culture thus became the clear mission of our office's work. This meant we left behind the road-fighting and anti-car activism in favor of addressing general petroleum dependence in the context of culture more than of politics. It got deeper than that, with the personal element and the arts more integrated into our mission.

Funds allowing, we would have been happy to continue the *Auto-Free Times* and the Alliance for a Paving Moratorium, but on a shoe-string budget we had to continue on our way: sink or swim, as it were. We had to choose our activities carefully and emphasize whatever could "lead somewhere." We had broadened and deepened our focus, but we had to "narrow it down" as well, in order to be clear in our message. The public still didn't seem terribly interested in our issues: charitable funds went overwhelmingly to churches and hospitals. One wealthy person's spare million could have allowed our work to make fabulous progress around the world. But our time for pursuing grants and donations was limited, when the staff consisted of me and two part-timers (besides our many collaborators and friends).

At this turning point in my development I believe my father would have been fascinated with my work and be in support of my activities. It's too bad he never got to see what I later did with the education he and my mother gave me. He got a taste of it occasionally, but he probably thought I would take the safe route and be responsible. After all, I liked money and doing business, and I had two children. But he didn't quite have me pegged correctly, or he would have warned me to suppress my activism in future. He would despair over my later financial difficulties or even consider me impoverished. My response might be that I didn't intend a life of struggle, but it might be part of obtaining a life of adventure. I was a bit naïve, at first, to think that there was "a market for the truth," or that the "truth business" could pay. For my hardships my father might blame my sister and my ex-brothers-in-law, or perhaps himself. What he would think of the treatment his Mesa got is like contemplating a nuclear explosion; indeed, many people have observed that he would be turning over in his grave if he knew what was happening to his widow.

I made two miscalculations in making changes in my life, regarding my mother and the legacy we were trying to protect. First, I kept pursuing her lost stock instead of cutting our losses. With great effort I hired lawyers to get Lundberg Survey back in her name. It was a good case, as proven in part by the aggression against her in court; her position of rightful ownership explained much of what happened to her in the last quarter of her life. But I wish I had not tried to go after the stock, because it made us vulnerable to devastating attacks on our flanks. My mother paid the ultimate price and did not need the money and power, but she went along with my attempt to get back the company for us. She made her wishes clear, however, in her quiet way. My brother Darius was certainly all for it, and I believe his and my efforts were for each other as well. The other error I made was to leave Arcata by selling my house after moving her out of my home to her newly purchased house down the street. It allowed for a slick con man to move into her house, at first as someone helping me on the case who needed a temporary place to stay. I believe he encouraged her to leave to Santa Barbara, and she never saw her home again.

As my mother's troubles in Santa Barbara deepened, and her property and savings were seen in southern California as something to liquidate and divvy up as fast as possible, the authorities in Arcata and Humboldt did not seem to mind the loss of a property-owning resident. Many locals knew and respected my daughter Vernell and me, but they did nothing to help. The *Arcata Eye* newspaper, despite its honorable stance on diverse matters, never seemed to believe that what I informed them, that oil money was attacking my family, was anything more than a figment of my imagination. During the early part of this phase of the crisis, 1998-2000, I had no idea that my mother's plight would some day be so serious that what befell her — and my daughters and me — was the worst disaster that could happen to any family short of a U.S. troop raid on an Iraqi house with women and children inside.

Thrown into the Briar Patch

How I like to live means being a seeker. It's not just a lifestyle of no car and enjoying flexibility and freedom. The additional and most essential element is that I "live the revolution," whatever that means. With respect to funding, when it comes in I don't save it or direct it just to myself, but rather "invest in the revolution" by paying others to enhance the website, for example. I feel part of a cause, despite my feeling isolated when working on my own. My role on a given day may be to just quietly keep looking for the truth, and frequently sharing my thoughts and analysis. George Orwell said, "In a time of universal deceit, telling the truth is a revolutionary act."

Much of the time we activists perceive or fear that "there's no movement out there," but we still have a sense of purpose and a grasp of history that tells us major change eventually comes. We usually don't have much of an idea of what will be the catalyst we're trying to bring to bear. So we acknowledge as promising any significant event or trend from any quarter. The personal and the professional spheres of our lives increasingly blend, so that we are always on the job, yet always being ourselves. Most people cannot relate to this, as they are content to perhaps work at the post office for decades or join the military. After all, having enough money on a constant basis, without any other real freedom, is of prime importance, particularly when trying in our consumer society to attract a mate or gain casual sex.

I have brought in over one million dollars in donations to Culture Change, but when averaged out over 22 years it is not quite been enough to run an office, pay staff and other bills — although at times it was enough to cover such costs with volunteer help and the zeal that seekers possess. Thus I have consistently "funded the revolution" by continuing my work, as opposed to opting out and making money for my material security or comfort. I could have had things easier if I had not sold all three houses, that I owned throughout my life, at the worst possible time in the up and down housing market. But even when financially broke, my overall outlook has always been optimistic enough that I knew I had a greater calling than just survive. I could not rest, for another reason: I needed to find a great living-arrangement with maximum community. These realities and feelings were at work in my final years in Arcata and Humboldt.

Despite my enjoying Culture Change and writing up a storm, it was becoming intolerable for me to be stuck in Arcata. If I got my mother back into her own home, and I had to be there as full-time care-giving manager with few breaks away, I accepted that responsibility. I would have had an easy but tame, stultifying life in some respects. My life purpose was, I felt, to engage in culture changing activities out where people were gathering. I was ready to go to them wherever they were. This need contributed to risking everything to bring about changes in my life. My colleagues and friends had similar feeling for their own circumstances, although I was the only one to take the steps to alter my scene to the point of upheaval. My urge to stay on my path of personal liberation did not contribute to keeping my mother's house for her and the family. But there was probably nothing I could do, considering the back-room deals apparently at work in and around Santa Barbara. I did not fully understand this at the time, because, having been raised in the United States of America, I still thought justice was often obtainable from the average judge despite gross inequities between opponents in court. A "fully informed jury" (one that knows and exercises its true power and independence) is one's best hope for justice.

I did know vaguely where my life-changes were heading, and

even though it offered little attraction in the usual ways, I kept going. I wanted to get rid of the house and other material things in order to be free. I believed I could rely on people and nature. I got my wish and lost the roof over my head with a little help from my relentlessly selfish sister, the drooling lawyers associated with her in various ways, the conservators, and their medical-care cronies. I was nevertheless feeling alright with my less certain circumstances. Before tracing the exact steps, I'll continue to paint the contextual picture.

Chapter 11

The Messy New Millennium

Guy Lundberg

If the "selection" of George W. Bush was a tough pill more many of us to swallow in December 2000, I lost my brother Guy on the 24th of that month and year. He succumbed to brain tumors and cancer after a few years' fight. I intended to visit him in recent years but unfortunately had put it off due to my change-laden life. Just as unfortunate, our relationship was all but cut off due to our lack of appreciation for one another, although there was some affection deep down.

Several weeks before he died we had our last conversation. I was checking up on him by phone when he was sailing his yacht with his son Erik. Guy had endured some rough medical treatment and I believed he might be on the mend. Before we could exchange some good words, he lectured me after I said "Hi Guy!": "When you call someone you always have to ask, 'Is this a good time to talk?'" I knew he had undergone pain, drugs and radiation, so I didn't cuss him out or hang up on him. But it was an example of his cleverer-than-thou ego. It was so clever he was not allowed at Erik's wedding years before, although one reason was that Guy's second wife was widely seen as a risky guest anywhere.

Guy's favorite kind of story: Once upon a time, business consultants were hired by a firm to solve the problem of slow elevators that employees complained about. The consultants insisted on this stipulation: "No matter what we do to solve the problem, if we eliminate the complaints we are to get paid in full." Upon acceptance of this, they proceeded to install mirrors around the elevator lobby, halting all employee complaints. The fee was reluctantly paid in full — such a story could pass for Guy's whole philosophy as far as I could tell, although he had early on adopted conventional beliefs about religion and the medical industry.

The last thing Guy said, that I heard about, was to our sister Dana who died in 2007. Guy told her, she told me, that what I had previously informed him about Trilby and the swindle of stock in Lundberg Survey was going to shake things up. I was glad to hear that he was thinking straight and seemed concerned.

Back in 1987 he made a mess of things by talking to a *Los Angeles Times* reporter about the conflict between his brother and sister, Jan and Trilby. The reporter called me and made a special trip to Virginia to interview me. He repeatedly said I could trust him. I did not, but hoped for the best. My hopes were misplaced, as the article missed major issues and gave a free pass to Trilby and her husband, while I was called "immature." I did not blame Guy, and I kept in touch with him.

The coverage was at least more honest than the *Washington Post*'s, which blared the headline "High Octane Family Feud." The reporter had phoned me to interview me about my business, he said, but the story he was really working on, unbeknownst to me, was about Lundberg Survey and its conflict with me — which I found out when the morning paper came out. The newspaper refused my repeated attempts to clarify issues with a letter to the editor. Friends comforted me by saying I had gotten my picture and name in the paper. The Treasury Department saw the article and gave me a speaking job, as described already.

Guy always "looked out for number one," as our father told me, and I found out the hard way that this was true. The one time I asked Guy for help, he refused, telling me, "It's not necessarily good to own a house." He owned quite a fancy one, though I never saw it. He knew what was going on with "the Trilby problem." But at the height of the conflict in 1987 when I was sued in federal court, Guy sent a letter to Trilby and me castigating us for fighting. I was thoroughly disgusted at his cover-my-ass attitude. Later he supported my environmental efforts a little bit. He told me he coined the phrase "poplution." Soon, however, he disappointed again when our 99-year-old grandmother died and he and his wife walked off with every cent of the estate. He probably had no idea he was setting the stage for his son Erik to be left with nothing, not even the sailboat the two had enjoyed. I did not know my grandmother Freda well, but one of my few conversations with her sticks in my mind. I had to inform her that her son Danny had died. I identified myself as his son, and that I was the brother of Guy and Darius. All she had to say to me was, "You call those brothers?" Apart from her cold reaction I thought it was weird because she knew Darius even less than she knew me.

The Lost House of Mesa Lundberg

In 2001 my mother was re-institutionalized after leaving my
brother's care in Santa Barbara. There was apparently little
disagreement among concerned parties over that fact that she
needed to be back in her own home in Arcata with good care-
giving. A mediation meeting was held at her lawyer's office, but it
wasn't clear to me, her, or my brother Darius what was really
taking place. I was under the impression, as was my mother, that
she would soon return to Arcata. The conservator was replaced,
and I went along with this in order to protect my mother from the
con man in Humboldt who had tried to steal her house. I felt sorry
for my mother when at the end of the mediation, she said to the
assembled, "So when do I go home?" I thought things were
moving in the right direction for her, and that most people
generally do the right thing when the facts were known. But I was
way behind their scheming, calculating minds and secret
agreements. My brother and I were also not working as one at
that critical juncture, which was mostly my fault.

Our mother was stuck in a Kafkaesque trap that enriched others
at her expense. A neuro-psychological exam showed she had some
dementia when she had lost the ability to walk in recent time, but
the dementia was seen as of a probable temporary nature. The
report called for a follow-up study along with her full participation
in her legal affairs. My mother got neither. As she moved from
one institution to another, slowly improving despite not being in
her own home getting the best care, she reached a hopeful point:
she was scheduled to visit her home under my care in June of
2001. However, she fell to the floor in a personal-residence nursing
home and broke her hip. For an elderly person this can mean that
death follows soon.

I had plans to go to my first Rainbow Gathering, a bartering
and mutual aid experience for thousands in a different forest each
year. I could wait and go another year, but this summer I was
starting to go out with a lovely musician whom I could fall in love
with. When I had to bow out and rush down to Santa Barbara, my
attractive, outgoing friend found another guy to accompany her to
the Rainbow Gathering, and we never got back into dating. At this

time I hired a caregiver to stay in my mother's guesthouse, a lovely artist sharing custody of a young son. She was a tempting and vivacious young woman but we managed to keep things on a just-friends basis.

My mother squeaked through her crisis and healed well, but by that time she was barred from returning to her home despite her desires — even though I got a letter from her hip surgeon that she could travel.

In June 2001 after my mother's hip surgery I filed a motion *in pro per* to move Mesa Lundberg back to her own home. The judge was not impressed with my arguments and was unconcerned with what my mother really felt. I would not have filed the action unless I knew what she wanted and needed. Our opposition outnumbered us and my motion was defeated. Outside the courtroom the Conservator Mary Lou Parks, standing with her lawyer David Turpin, told me "You'll have to get another free place to live, Jan!" I told them I had basically bought the place and was paying their fees, because I had made the money my mother had as part of my previous career's success. I was a fool to think this made any difference to them or any of their associates. I barely had any idea yet how comfortable and skilled Parks and Turpin were at separating elderly, rich people from their money and their families. Other victims came forward to me but without enough specifics to be of help to me. I was barely beginning to learn that the judge was entirely supportive of the local cabal of well-dressed fraudsters and scam artists in the legal and medical community.

An attorney in Ventura, Christoph Nettersheim, informed me in 2009 that Santa Barbara Judge McLafferty and his colleague Judge Anderlee constantly made crazy and unsubstantiated rulings that they always got away with. Interestingly, Nettersheim had seen wrongdoing against his family by a previous conservator of Mesa's, Frumeh Labow in Los Angeles, who had been my mother's unkind foe. But Nettersheim's stated interest in our case to claim the wrongful death of my mother dissipated when he found that a Deputy District Attorney in Santa Barbara whom he respected, Mary Barron, was stonewalling that there was any wrongdoing of any kind regarding my mother at any juncture.

I decided to go to the press after my failed 2001 motion. I had lunch with a Santa Barbara *News Press* reporter named Josh Molina. I gave him all the background and urged him to go to the

courthouse file on the case. He sent a photographer to the nursing
home where my mother was currently being fleeced. The picture
landed on the front page of the newspaper. Unfortunately, the tack
the reporter and his editor took was evident in the first line: "Jan
Lundberg is living large in Humboldt County as guitarist for the
Depavers." Later in the article I was mentioned as having
possessed stolen information from Lundberg Survey, based on a
false declaration among court documents dating back to 1987.
That (lie) was inserted, as editor Alex Rose later explained to me,
"because no one would talk to us except you, and we had to print
something negative to balance it out." The night before the story
came out, the reporter called me up with a vague apology, but I
didn't know what he meant. The accusation against me was in the
1987 declaration of Bob Sharp, former husband of my late sister
Dana Lundberg. He had been reporting to me regarding
alternative fuels surveys at Lundberg Survey at the time when I
left, and his declaration that I had proprietary information was one
of the only ways the 1987 case in federal court against my using
my name in business could have any hope of getting heard. If the
Santa Barbara newspaper had asked me about the accusation I
could have responded, but this was their idea of balanced
journalism. I tried to get a letter printed in the newspaper in my
defense but failed. The worst aspect of the newspaper's coverage
was that the reporter did not "follow the money." It was as if there
is no white collar crime or fraud going on against wealthy elderly
people, or that an old woman's stock in a famous company could
not have possibly been swindled from her. I had clearly advised the
reporter of the basics of the case. His and his editor's lack of
interest to follow the money was possibly because the money led
ultimately to entities such as Chevron and other major oil
companies that Trilby Lundberg prominently served. The *New-
Press* article's summary on the newspaper's website is:

The Lundberg Saga
January 6, 2002: NEWS-PRESS STAFF WRITER
Jan Lundberg wants his mother to come home. His
siblings think that's a bad idea. So where is home for 81-
year-old Mesa Lundberg, matriarch of the family behind
the Lundberg Survey Inc., the Camarillo company which
publishes the newsletter regarded as the bible of the oil

industry?

I have come to believe that Lundberg Survey's clients cannot be ignorant, and were not ignorant, of Trilby's persecution of Mesa Lundberg and me. The oil companies certainly did not slack on tracking their opponents and the environmental movement, especially one who got much coverage on radio and in the newspapers from time to time. They also have institutional memory, and knew who was the chairman of the board of Lundberg Survey: Mesa Lundberg, after Dan Lundberg. The oil companies' ass-kissing facility that Lundberg Survey became did not want it to be under the control of anti-oil Jan Lundberg (via Mesa Lundberg).

All during my efforts to return my mother to her home, I had a professional caregiver living in her guesthouse. After my debacle in court in 2001 I was fortunate to meet Barbara Shults, a registered nurse who was also a legal-nurse practitioner. She testified well in court in 2002 on behalf of my mother, whom she met, and had the temperament and training necessary to spot fraud and incompetence. Unfortunately, the facts of this case were of little interest to the judge, and he might have been swayed by Trilby Lundberg's fabricated assertion that Barbara was my girlfriend. If she was, which I'm sure her boyfriend Jim would have disagreed with, what could this have to do with her competence? Barbara's efforts on behalf of my mother were strong, and as I came to know her I could not imagine a better person to have on one's side. Barbara's passion over medical justice was immediately clear when she was shocked from the start that my mother was installed in an end-stage facility.

I visited my mother when I could, but hundreds of miles each way was not easy for a man on a low, sporadic income. I wanted her to visit me and her granddaughters in Humboldt. But the Conservator and my mother's usual MD, Michelle Armet, claimed my mother was unable to spend the holidays in her own home. What I noticed about their casual, unfounded but binding assessments was that my mother was claimed to be generally "doing very well" as a justification to keep her in the lucrative Santa Barbara "care" environment, but whenever the subject came around to visiting me she was described as "very frail." Which was it? Not one of my mother's enemies ever came to see her Arcata home or met the professional caregivers I identified (some of whom knew my mother well). My presentation could have been better than what I managed in the way of photos to show we was a nice home. The Conservator told me she heard the house was "ramshackle" but she and her cronies sold it against my mother's clear wishes, for $350,000 in 2004.

More than four times that amount of my mother's dwindling funds went into the pockets of Conservators, lawyers and nursing homes in Santa Barbara. They claimed Mesa Lundberg belonged there instead of her home, but the medical basis and legal arguments were weak. All they needed was a compliant judge, who along with our opposition always did whatever Trilby Lundberg requested. My mother's wishes and health needs were ignored, even though there was no basis whatsoever for my mother to be in a *"hospice-respite" home for seven years.* The Humboldt County Court Investigator determined my mother should be back in her own home under my care, but the judge ignored this finding as he gleefully ordered sold my mother's "Golden Years" home in her presence (with me was my older daughter who burst into tears). I appealed this decision, with zero help from my mother's attorney, and I lost on a technicality. My appeal was called "dead on arrival" as my mother supposedly had no rights when a judge decides on conservatorship in Superior Court, even though my case had been accepted and assisted by the top appellate law firm Lasher & Lasher.

The Appellate Court was in Ventura, where Trilby Lundberg lives. Her attorney Gary Faulkes appeared at the hearing and got to speak for a while, but the judges figured out he wasn't really a party to the case, so he was asked to go back to his seat. Meanwhile, he managed to put the judges on notice that his client was Trilby Lundberg, who everyone knew as Big Oil's famous market analyst right in town. I was in court most urgently to stop the sale of my mother's house, but right before the hearing the house was sold unbeknownst to the court, to me or my mother. I found out when visiting my mother after the hearing, and her Conservator walked in to my mother's bedroom and sadistically told us of the news as if it were wonderful. I brought to the court's attention the secret, premature sale before their decision but they didn't mind the questionable tactic at all.

Such "legal" decisions were part of a pattern: no matter what the facts were, no matter what my mother's rights were, Trilby Lundberg prevailed at every turn. As the Humboldt County Court Investigator told me, "Money talks." It was too bad the investigator had injected irrelevant information into her report on my mother's home that my mother's enemies could seize on for their arguments for selling the house out from under us. These centered around the question of mildew in the home, which the Humboldt Environmental Dept. later certified was not present. This evidence was ignored by the judge, but he had the right to ignore evidence because the case was a conservatorship trial, and, as I vaguely understood the Court of Appeals' logic, it does not need to question a lower judge's decision involving ignoring evidence. I brought up my mother's Constitutional rights but apparently the Constitution is not the last word to these judges. When I made my case before the judges one of them gave me hope by observing, "It's expensive in Santa Barbara." This was the only honest comment that anyone affecting my mother's fate had come forward with.

At the very beginning of my mother's seven years incarceration at Toltec Living Center, I had first visited my mother there in October 2001. The day after I left she went on a hunger strike in order to return to Arcata. I didn't find that out for months, but she was put on a powerful drug to keep her quiet and subdued. My sister approved of this along with every other tactic, some that she devised, to limit her mother's rights. This was most cruel when she knew her mother did not like drugs or non-organic food. One of the drugs my mother was forced to take was Remeron, which according to www.Drugs.com, is "used to treat major depressive disorder." My mother never had depression, and if she did she never would have voluntarily taken a drug for it. She and her husband raised a drug-free family. In this respect she and I were vulnerable to attacks from conventional or fear-mongering enemies who painted us as extremist health nuts. Fasting, for example, was something my mother tried a few times in her incarceration but she was forcibly stopped, and I was falsely blamed. Trilby Lundberg pandered to the conservative judge's likely ignorance of fasting by claiming that I would fast (starve, by implication) my mother. In a court hearing when the judge ordered an investigation of our Arcata home, my mother lucidly assured fended off the attacking lawyers' claims (David Turpin's and Gary Faulkes') that I would force my mother to fast. The judge was even friendly to me, calling me Jan. Months later he became much less friendly and respectful.

My mother would not quite counterattack her firstborn child. This sealed my mother's fate, or seemed to support the need for conservatorship). But when my mother told me "This judge is bought off" she must have known where the money came from (besides her own personal money being drained by his cronies).

The U.S. is a nation of drug addicts — users of mainly legal, petrochemical medicines that are freely (but very expensively) prescribed when a healing, preventative approach to disease would be far more effective. Better nutrition and other methods are safer and cheaper than powerful drugs, many of which have been poorly tested. Meanwhile, the term drug addict is applied only to users of illegal drugs, and not cigarettes or alcohol. The Toltec nursing home owner said he learned Chinese medicine and got my mother onto that alternative regime for several weeks, he told me, but she could not stand the taste. She therefore stopped it, he told me, even though she was making progress with her physical ailments such as respiratory congestion. I was contacted by the Conservator to see if I could talk my mother into going back on the Chinese medicine, probably just to save money. I could not convince her.

The journey for personal and culture change unfolds

With the creation of Culture Change, my team and I identified our real goal: a way of living in harmony with nature and in a "freedom tribe." We've had a taste of it, to an individual degree among us, more or less, and we wanted more.

I was soon to find out what my impulses and yearnings had in store. Things got rougher for me, but I eventually noticed something fascinating: somehow, no matter how unlucky I was in fundraising or in obtaining life's necessities, I was always doing alright. My health was good, I did not go hungry, and I had my music. I didn't mind if I had to meet Food Not Bombs on the Arcata Plaza and enjoy a vegan stew. In fact, I preferred this way of living "on the edge." I was "surfing my cosmic wave" and not wiping out, year after year. One can call it Providence, or the result of a fortunate, privileged, educated white man's determination to obtain minimal food, lodging and clothing. But I saw that whenever I was in dire need of a little money, a small donation materialized in the post office box, cash handed over in my office by a supporter, or a PayPal donation happened. Somehow, Culture Change kept going, although often on a minimal basis. It helped that I was used to stress and could handle it, partly because I saw it as "noise" in the bigger picture.

After my early years of privilege and trouble-free living, the late 1970s saw infuriating and hurtful instances of conflict with my sister that produced severe headaches. I simply got used to them. She frequently would go cause some trouble with my gullible parents, painting me as a meany, forcing me to deal with the latest lie or scheme. My frustration eased with practicing patience with my repeated disappointments. But I lost what some call innocence, that as a sheltered, fortunate young person I had enjoyed so much.

❧

I'll backtrack a bit further before bringing my personal story up to the present. I'll spare the reader many more painful, minor details of my ongoing family soap opera such as every legal motion and further betrayals by lawyers.

After the tumultuous conservatorship of my mother starting in 1995, I had to cut back on being the activist/artist/nonprofit executive I had been before. To continue on my path I integrated into my life the extra job of trying to protect the family from itself. As I previously bitched in this memoir, the traveling I did for a decade was almost all related to the family's court activity. I even moved down to Hollywood for a while. In early 1995 Jimmy Hinton, my father's best friend from Mexico, visited my mother and brother. He called me up and informed me that "Darius stands no chance against Trilby, so you have to get down here." Jimmy saw Trilby manipulating and abusing Mesa and the household. I followed his advice, and settled in to help. My mother was not quite strong enough to help me help her; she could offer no resistance to Trilby of her own. For two months while in Hollywood I left my 14-year-old daughter Vernell in Arcata in our rented house, moving one of her favorite teachers in temporarily as a live-in babysitter. This period of frequent travel on behalf of my mother went on for nearly a decade.

After the "death sentence" ruling in 2002 whereupon my mother lost her house and freedom, I was just visiting her as opposed to appearing in court. In Santa Barbara I usually stayed with my sister Dana, who was raised for years by my mother who was the stepmother. I appreciated the extra time I was spending with Dana and her three children, and our nephew Erik and his family. This would likely not have happened if my mother had not gone to Santa Barbara to lose her freedom and life.

In connection with the stress over Trilby's earlier motions in southern California over the years, we soon had new family difficulties in Arcata. This eventually resulted in my mother's and brother's departure to Santa Barbara without my knowledge. To try to return her and reestablish the family home, I moved into my mother's house a few doors from my old one I had sold. Our office soon followed — the whole move was accomplished by just pedal-power carts. I remained in that home from summer 2000 through early 2003, and, as I have previously bellyached in this memoir, I was soon feeling stuck. My floating home in the Puget Sound was neglected, so I eventually gave it to my older daughter who moved it to the San Francisco Bay in 2002.

By then she needed a temporary home base for her federal court case in San Francisco against Humboldt law enforcement agencies for their torture of her and our friends. *Lundberg v. Humboldt County* came about from pepperspray being applied to the eyes with Q-tips during sit-ins for the threatened ancient redwoods.

The case took eight years and was finally decided in favor of the plaintiffs (our side) in 2005. The outcome is that you will almost certainly not be tortured for non-violently resisting arrest, especially if the police remotely suspect you can get a lawyer and sue them. Curiously, it was the post- 9-11 Bush Supreme Court that upheld the Fourth Amendment (search and seizure) for the Earth First!ers in Lundberg versus Humboldt County. Excessive force was found to have been applied to the plaintiffs in this precedent-setting case. The County had to pay the plaintiffs' legal fees and pay each plaintiff one dollar. The latter aspect should not be considered a defeat for the protesters, when their stated goal had always been to stop the practice of putting pepper spray in the eyes of nonviolent protesters. The lawyers for our side included Tony Serra, Dennis Cunningham, Bob Bloom, Bill Simpich, and Ben Rosenfeld. The support team was strong too, and I believe all concerned credited my daughter Vernell with doing a great deal of the work for the case. Her grandmother and namesake was quite proud, and of course there was no dementia associated with grasping or remembering any of the matter.

༄

The world event known as the 9-11 attacks served to focus almost everyone onto issues of terrorism, war, politics, election fraud, and related issues. The issue known as the environment, or in activists' terms the defense of nature, was suddenly of much less general interest. Yet, it was clear that the nation's system of violence and dominance needed to be addressed. If the connected issues of ecocide and genocide were aided by reining in the system (e.g., via whistle-blowing), we understood and supported this in the spirit of general positive change. However, impassioned polemic against Bush and his cronies usually served to obscure more fundamental issues or specifics about energy that people needed to know. A radical critique was missing, so Culture Change endeavored to fill this gap. Others were trying to do so as well, but we were all few and far between, and silenced willy-nilly in part by those who should have been our allies. A comprehensive, unified analysis wasn't being widely sought, and when we offered it, it was limited to the ephemeral internet world rather than in a prominent book or musical album that could reach more people and do so more deeply.

Finding no more family obligations to deal with face to face in Arcata on a daily basis, I then got one of my top wishes: living in nature. This was aided by my opposition in southern California and Lundberg Survey, which succeeded in evicting me from the family home. Despite my mother's stated desires to move back there with me as her lead caregiver, and for me to stay there if I wished (I even paid some rent to the banksters in charge), the house was ordered sold in order to fund her care-givers in Santa Barbara. Thankful to them on some level, I began almost two years of sleeping on beach dunes, in my office, on friends' couches, on Amtrak, Greyhound buses, and elsewhere once I hit the road with my guitar. In 2003-2004 I loved living in my crude but sturdy hand-built log shelter in the redwood forest, for four months (photo in this book). In early 2004 I moved away from Arcata and Humboldt, to Virginia for several months before settling activist-style — i.e., no house purchase — in the San Francisco Bay area.

I missed my older daughter Vernell who was not to be seen except in federal court fighting Humboldt cops. As I was not needed as her single-parent Dad anymore, and she took pride in not needing family help, I had more leeway to be anywhere at all and with modest means.

When my work failed to provide a modest living after the downturn for funding due to 9-11, and the family home was stolen in court in winter 2002-2003, I finally achieved my goal of going totally broke. I really wanted to live without a house and without money, to be closer to the more tribal activist friends I had who relied on each other and the community rather than money in our effort to stop corporate deforestation. I went often to the Food Bank, ate the vegan Food Not Bombs meals, got a few odd jobs, did some house-sitting, and raised a few hundred dollars every several weeks from my Culture Change writings to pay some minimal bills.

I was broke, and it was a little weird and difficult — but what's really broke is the world around us. I continued my activism, with minimal volunteer staff, and was a semi-skilled "internet geek" activist. My music continued for my own sake, as recording and performing were mostly put on the shelf. Despite hardship and uncertainty, I felt as much at peace as I had ever felt — even compared to past periods with my own home with family present and I had more tangible accomplishments to point to. This goes to show that what I was really looking for was the experience of the adventure and the revealing of the truth. The reason I didn't get depressed or frantic when my financial collapse descended on me is that I was now more connected to the reality of living in our times. I accepted the need to struggle to make my way in a community (or the closest thing to it). Finding the community for the remainder of my days has proven elusive, and I knew that Northern California didn't quite offer it. I had to uproot myself from a house in Humboldt, and then Humboldt entirely, to really live.

It wasn't easy, but I took it in stride. In Arcata my itinerant lifestyle was enforced partly because two of my friends, with whom I was staying for free in exchange for continuing my activism, were kicked out of their old Victorian rental in spring of 2003. Our virtual eviction was along with the other tenants who were activists or students at Humboldt State University. For gentrification and profit, prominent liberals got rid of students during final examinations, and some of us didn't get another roof after that. Landlordism became more repellent to me. That spring and summer I was fluid, moving around, but sticking to my lifestyle out of sheer need — financial and spiritual, one might say.

On the day the North Country Fair started on the Plaza, the husband and wife team who were central to founding and running the Redwood Peace and Justice Center caught me sleeping there on my office floor. I was taken aback that they treated me as typical (sub)landlords would. I was threatened with Board of Directors' action, even though I explained that I moved around a lot and was in a transition. I believe that more humane and homeless-friendly treatment was in order, especially as I thought we were friends and collaborators. They offered me no help or sympathy. I had been swallowing the disappointingly high rent for the closet-sized office, but the situation worked for me. My older daughter visited me there and urged that I center my lifestyle around sleeping on my office floor and engaging in dumpster diving. She approved of such a strategy with all sincerity, as she, like me, rejected many conventional norms, and she appreciated my growth.

Eventually when I left Humboldt for good, the Center terminated Culture Change's sublease unilaterally. This had nothing to do with my being busted for needing a floor to sleep on, but perhaps my presence was not missed by some. And someone probably wanted Culture Change's office space even at high rent. The Center eventually closed entirely, which due to my treatment did not invoke any sense of loss or nostalgia in me. The location was handy for downtown amenities, such as Arcata Pizza and Deli when I had lunch money. The oldest operating cinema in the U.S., the Minor Theater, was just down the block — my memories of seeing movies there with my daughters in better times pulls my heart strings. Primarily, I appreciate my office at the Center as my base for living outdoors. For there I kept my work materials, most of my clothes, my extra food and nothing more. I lived on my bicycle and was a free man.

At some point in my eco-warrior life it has felt like I am on a spiritual journey of some kind. The term "spiritual warrior" comes to me, but this is probably silly when no one has called me that. When I speak of spirit or being a warrior I don't feel apart from ecological concerns. Nor am I a destroyer except of injustice (if and when I am that, and if so it's so rare). I am on a quest, and

action-oriented quest. I date this to 1988 when I formed Fossil
Fuels Policy Action, although at the time I would have laughed
nervously if someone warned me I was to become a spiritual
warrior or that I would call myself such.

♄

During 2003 the issue of peak oil began to get traction.
Richard Heinberg's *The Party's Over* showed so clearly what we as
clever technological humans had done to our energy future. The
respected oil-industry geologist Colin Campbell founded the
Association for the Study of Peak Oil and Gas in 2000, and the
2003 meeting (which I was invited to but could not afford to
attend) was a success that reverberated globally. Dr. Campbell had
given Culture Change an article on peak oil that we published in
the only printed *Culture Change* magazine in 2001. As right as he
was with his message (title: Peak Oil: a Turning Point for
Humankind; we substituted Human for his Man), it was just more
of what our readers mostly knew. So I did not even deem the piece
deserving of a place on the cover's partial list of contents. Such
was the general lack of interest in oil in 2001. I was glad to see
this change in 2003, as the invasion of Iraq awoke interest in oil
and energy.

London calling

In February 2003 I was brought to London by The Institute of
Petroleum to speak at its annual meeting. In a prior meeting of
the Institute, the future U.S. Vice President Richard Cheney gave
his oft-quoted talk admitting, in effect, that peak oil was real. My
assigned topic was conservation, which I delivered with
exceptional veracity: "conservation" was an easy topic for me when
I had to couch surf every night in order to have enough to eat
during my two-week stay.

I imagined there was great opportunity for collaborating in
London with Greenpeace and Friends of the Earth, such as a joint
press conference on oil issues after my speech. But I found they
were not interested in working with me in the slightest. My
deflated activist dream and the lack of solidarity were offset by
receptivity by the Institute of Petroleum's head for an idea I

197

broached in my speech: Community Petroleum Councils. The head, the gorgeous Louise Kingham, was about to preside over an institutional merger creating the Institute of Energy. Not far from her mind were the recent petrol and lorry (gasoline and truck) riots in England.

I believe that the U.S., with its vulnerable populations — rich to poor – so dependent on petroleum, would likewise do well to engage in public meetings on oil and related issues. Food security, heating and air conditioning, and fuel for transporting the workforce to jobs, are currently and carefully off the table for discussion in the corporate media and public schools. When the next major supply crunch hits the oil market, riots will break out if preparation has not been made both individually/family-wise and collectively; there won't be any patience for dialog or planning as a citizenry then, I fear.

Two days before my speech in London I marched with two million people against the Iraq Invasion, and two days before that I had suddenly become homeless (houseless). Thus began my exalted education or adventure to live by my wits and within the wider activist network. But, thanks to my eviction by the oil-funded thieves in southern California, the possibility of family continuity in northern California was probably forever dashed. [Now, October 2, 2010, everyone in the family lives in southern California except for two of us out of state.] My mother was heartbroken by the apparent loss of the family home, but proud of her son for imparting his message at The Institute of Petroleum. Such a sentiment can cause one to be called "demented," when that someone is the rightful owner of Lundberg Survey and who came to reject the oil industry on ethical and health grounds.

In East London I fulfilled a fantasy by giving a performance of my eco-protest songs at a bustling activist center. I stayed at a squat in Hackney, a former workingman's club for snooker. It was established by the local elite many decades ago in order to distract the radical workers from following an East London fiery preacher. The ringleaders of the squat were quite sociable. When I saw anti-landlord graffiti around town I had a feeling they had done it. I also stayed with journalist and author Robert Allen in Ipswitch, enjoying his and his wife Ann's kind hospitality. Robert and I plotted collaboration between his BlueGreenEarth.com and Culture Change. The only thing that came of it was his website's posting of each Culture Change article, thanks to the graphically talented Tim Barton, a colleague and friend of Robert's.

My group's website culturechange.org had become, along with our email list, our only showcase. Needless to repeat, here were times when the lack of funds for staff, and a weakening of the volunteer spirit for our unusual work (compared to Earth First! forest-protection or anti-war organizing), made me the only part of "we." An attempted campaign we half-launched flopped: Committee Against Oil Exploration (CAOE). Its formation did receive an emotional complaint from Colin Campbell, but I didn't hold it against him. Attitudes have hopefully changed for most people, after the BP Macondo oil rig and well explosion in April of 2010. President Obama's advocacy of expanded offshore oil drilling, right before BP Macondo, blew up in his face, and caused the public to search and locate CAOE (pronounced K-O) online. Its logo is on the back cover of this book, and is used by World Oil Reduction for the Gulf (WORG), a de facto outgrowth of CAOE.

A few months after the monthly Culture Change e-Letter's launch in 2002 I made it weekly. It became less and less suitable for corporate media op-ed pages, as I enjoyed developing my critique of the corporatized power structure and materialist culture. One of the few columns that appeared in newspapers was a speculative piece on Teresa Heinz Kerry as the first "green" First Lady. That's how impressed I was with her when we met in Knoxville in 2004. She steered me to her son Andre who was there, as he was involved with the Natural Step sustainability project. A reason I was never able to follow up with him might have been because I absent-mindedly asked him if his last name was Kerry. He probably thought I was one of the dumbest, insensitive people he ever met. His father, former Senator Heinz, had been killed in a plane crash. In the late 1990s I had been critical of the Senator for advocating and funding more road construction. I wonder if that would have counted as another faux pas in Andre Heinz's mind.

By 2003, when web activism and lack of funds made untenable Culture Change's old formula for activism and publicity, we were able to gauge mass consciousness growing quickly regarding climate change. It was finally coming to the fore. But the ecological noose was tightening up for everybody. But this took a back seat to outrage over the Iraq War and vote fraud. A whole new set of writers and activists, with a few holdovers from previous decades such as Noam Chomsky, pushed political issues deeper and harder. They did a fairly good job. But their focus helped to temporarily submerge everything else that was unaddressed. Events and crises sped up, so that awareness of peak oil increased — but not as fast as paranoia about evil-doers who were mostly in government. Instead of radical journalism stepping up front and center for the issues that we at Culture Change cared most about, a milder critique of the crises — that appeared hard-hitting — gained dominance under the banner of the progressives. They looked at disjointed symptoms of a larger problem, railing piecemeal against the latest dirty details of emerging scandals, war for oil, and the bad guy *du jour*. This ongoing harangue crowded out what might have been growing interest in our organization and its mission: culture change. But the temptation for liberals and progressives to conform to a *dominant critique*, rather than a radical or cultural critique, has set the tone ever since the defining moment of 9-11. That event, however meaningful, insidious and deserving of full exposure, seized public discourse and put the ecosystem second or third or fourth up against politics, social justice and economic issues.

The many new experts appearing on the alternative press scene were the newly enshrined author-bloggers. Some wrote passionately on oil and energy, admirably enough as "lay people." Their impetus was both the ongoing war for oil and the rising awareness of peak oil, as oil prices trended upward. Almost none of these writers had been big into traditional (pre 9-11) activism. I was frustrated by the lack of accuracy in writings on energy in particular. There was almost nothing to be found on collapse, except at a few websites such as CultureChange.org. Few of these prominent author-blogger writers understood the oil market, and almost all of them gave the technofix undue attention, as if solar panels were a major tool for revolution or for attaining Utopia. Despite this, I came to encounter and know several author-bloggers whose style influenced me somewhat – they were more "in your face" compared to our more careful prose of the 1990s. Just as importantly, I learned about various interrelated issues from some of the new writers, and I made new friends and colleagues. Their enthusiasm and knowledge, along with Culture Change's Internet presence, offset the loss of our magazine outreach.

One of the commonly ignored factors in the whole oil picture was (and remains) the huge subsidies for the industry and for driving cars. The subsidies weren't mentioned then and rarely mentioned today, except by Culture Change and on occasion in such online sources as The Daly News' columns of Brent Blackwelder. Forgetting about oil subsidies reflects and reinforces the public's lack of knowledge on the true costs of petroleum dependence. This causes frustration in my professional self, as if that matters.

Despite the fact that a fair understanding of peak oil makes clear that there is no comparable energy substitute, the technofix movement has expanded along with the overall rise in oil prices. By now I accept that the phony approach of techno-hope is at once deliberately misleading and psychologically imperative. The technofix energy sector, with its unproven prescription for the greener continuation of the consumer economy, offers "Hope" while being part of the wider tendency to promote painless-sounding reforms. Such "change" is mostly non-threatening to the profligate lifestyle of the corporate power structure that resists inconvenient conclusions suggesting fundamental change. This is not to say that renewable energy is generally hopeless. Certainly it is not if it is decentralized, modest, and for local applications that might enhance human society sustainably in an ecosystem. But what people really expect or hope for is an easy way out of ecocide and petrocollapse, should they have an inkling that affluence is unsustainable and unstable.

In 2004 I hooked up with the anti-plastics movement led by Captain Charles Moore. Fighting the plastic plague wasn't in vogue, which drew me in. Targeting plastics made entire sense to me as a petroleum industry analyst: a way to raise key, related issues all at once. I got caught up, with my eyes wide open, in municipal politics and advocacy related to banning or putting fees on plastic bags. Here I was pushing for a reform that meant a drop in the bucket of oil pollution globally. But I felt optimistic for greater change to flow from it. And as a sailor across oceans as a lad, living on the water, I could not bear the unchecked plastic plague on sea life.

"Go to San Francisco" - the Mothers, *We're Only In It For the Money*

2004 was a year that Culture Change received less than a tenth of our 1990s-era funding, and my lifestyle reflected it. As in 2003, in 2004 I availed myself of free food and shelter whenever possible. Family, friends, and activists put me up, which I did not find to be depressing or very constraining for my work. By 2005 I did accomplish long-term stints as a roommate in two good pads, first in Berkeley and then in San Francisco in 2006. Forgetting what I'd felt about dirty cities and "the belly of the beast" and "Babylon," I got my urban urge out. I was attracted to soaking up all I could of what the San Francisco Bay area offers. Hikes with friends in nearby fragments of natural ecosystems stand out in my mind as the most pleasurable things I did, essential for our sanity and peace.

I noticed that for the small Bay Area population of activists and visible artists, the pursuit of their creative urges took a back seat to the job of daily survival. I wasn't convinced this was entirely necessary. I saw that obtaining food and shelter were higher priorities, for young and old, than finding fellow musicians to experiment with, for example. This was a change from prior decades, probably unavoidable. The activists I was now meeting and observing took the time, as is their practice, for creative or radical projects by going to meetings and concentrating on activist tasks. But the movement I was looking for was on hold or quite tiny. Activists were primarily trying to survive economically and live well. No one can blame them. Some of them supported Culture Change. Protests were few and not huge, and never boisterous. I didn't know "everybody" on the scene, but I was lucky enough to get around well and meet many people. As a newcomer with some solid contacts in the Bay area, I was accepted warmly enough, but the general population wanted little to do with the likes of someone like me. Per capita, there were many more activists in Humboldt County.

The feeling of overall low-level activism and idealism I had in the Bay area tended to keep me writing and doing limited, focused tasks for Culture Change. This was a more isolating and individualistic way than in my "old days" of activism in Humboldt. Certainly the movement that I thought I'd signed up for in the late '80s was absent or dormant. The demise of the fabled radical, avant-garde Bay area culture did not shock me, but it saddened me.

It would not have been so if only the activists on hand could be more cohesive and daring. But they were boxed in and had little room economically to maneuver. For whatever reason — gentrification, corporate media consolidation, technology's onslaught at the expense of human interaction – the spirit of the 1960s and early '70s that was on display in San Francisco and Berkeley was gone. Now at UC Berkeley the prevailing idea of student political activity was to run for a campus government position to put on one's résumé. The cost of living in the Bay Area was by now far too dear, and the toughening economy had forced out — and is still forcing out — communities of low-income visionaries and misfits. So it wasn't surprising that visiting activists, artists and writers were essential to keeping the once radical scene somewhat vibrant.

Berkeley Babylon, as I called my next real hometown after Arcata, represented a place to be active and write from the belly of the beast. I was disgusted to learn of the planned David Brower Center Memorial Parking Garage that the environmental establishment was bent on building for itself. My letters to the *San Francisco Chronicle* and Berkeley's *Daily Planet,* my appearances against the project at public meetings, and writing in CultureChange.org were to no avail whatsoever. But my opposing the project did make visible to me and my few cohorts who exactly was putting development ahead of nature and ecological principle. I had respected unreservedly some prominent Bay area environmentalists, but they now gave me pause. And they resented my opposition to the big development with its huge amount of parking space.

Berkeley had its good points, a bit nicer for me than Oakland where I also lived during 2004-2005. Most of the time I lived a few blocks up hill from People's Park, near the Memorial Oak Grove threatened by the University's athletics dept. expansion. It was there that tree-sits and rallies braved police raids and my guitar playing "Protesting UCB." This is where I met Country Joe McDonald who appeared with his guitar and voice for the oak grove.

I continued to note the psychological state of friends and acquaintances living in Berkeley and Oakland. I kept noticing with a bit of sadness their priorities and material worries. This unbalanced me a bit, although I was treated as well as I could expect. They seemed to be clinging to their physical homes and possessions rather defensively, instead of enjoying the hipness or radicalness of their famous urban environment. The Black Panthers and other front-liners were gone, and in their place were frustrated but dedicated — albeit impotent — denizens of concrete and asphalt who perhaps felt they failed to join in "going back to the land." When people and even friends behave a bit tense and nervous, or downright crazy, the term Berserkly comes to mind with truth to it.

The lifestyle vibe I found was a different feel from days gone by when housing was more affordable and social movements were more potent and promising. Today, most of the people I know in the East Bay — few activists and artists can afford San Francisco — are caught up with paying the rent or mortgage, obtaining their food, using their appliances and cars, etc., in such a way that they have little rebellious or revolutionary zeal. Their personal struggles and trying to meet non-economic objectives (activism) make them somewhat uptight, although they are still functional and can offer hospitality. They may remain societal critics and activists, but they always have to crawl back into their separate, isolated little homes. Collective housing exists, but not so alive and well. It's not that jobs and career mean so much to them, nor are they trying to get rich. But they act as if they cannot live without or question seriously their connections to modern, city life. As politically correct people, they often appear radical, but they are almost as attached to their own brand of materialism as the blatant bourgeois, upper-middle classists who live similarly.

San Francisco is worse, having lost almost all of its population that lived for something greater than material comfort and wealth. Or, so it seemed to me, seeing affluence contrasted with the very poor (usually immigrants). Anti-war demonstrations still got a large crowd on occasion, but this was a once or twice a year activity for the average San Franciscan. And many of the demonstrators come from outside the City. The Dot Com Boom along with shady real estate development practices got rid of the great majority of the artists and activists from this side of the Bay. Yuppies are overwhelmingly the dominant life form here, and they live for their consuming and sophisticated comforts. The contingent of "Die Yuppie Scum" punks is 99% gone, having faded from the scene and gone over to Oakland or maybe Oregon — the far cheaper solution.

By 2005 I was planning Petrocollapse Conferences. The first one, Oct. 5 in Manhattan, was a success, and this paid for my "Amtrak Peak Oil Tour" (see Appendix), published in such places as Truthout.org. The next Petrocollapse Conference, in Washington, D.C. in May 2006, could not as shocking or attention-getting as the first one, but both events did connect a lot of people. It was my pleasure and honor to involve as speakers the authors Albert Bates, Jim Kunstler and Richard Heinberg, to name the best known friends I have in the peak oil corral. Richard, a fine violinist, played two concerts with me for peak oilers, which to me seemed the best use of our time and energy for raising awareness and potentially uniting the most people.

On January 28, 2006 I enjoyed a homecoming of sorts to L.A.: I headlined for a peak oil program at a large hall in the San Fernando Valley, at the Valley Cities Jewish Community Center in Sherman Oaks. With prior media saturation on KPFA radio where I did two shows, the hall was packed and standing-room-only. I recall giving a good ad lib talk, followed by local boys Ed Begley, Jr., the activist-actor, and then- Assemblyman Paul Koretz (now a Los Angeles City Councilmember).

"Peak Oil Realities & Solutions of the Looming Petroleum Shortage" was organized by Neighbors for Peace & Justice, a group that has carried on nonstop musical vigils on streets against the Iraq War. After my big show at the hall, I gave a few other smaller talks around town, busting out my guitar and voice at such venues as the historic South Central Community Farm. On this trip to my old stomping ground, where I saw several old friends, I enjoyed myself most when I played my song Peace Now at a boisterous Bush Step Down rally near in the middle of Hollywood, right below my old mansion in the. I met the jaw-dropping sexy actress Lucia Marano who was on fire for her anti-war speech. A critical mass bike ride followed, and it was a gas for me biking around in the middle of the streets of my familiar old Hollywood & Vine neighborhood. I was kindly put up at L.A. Ecovillage. A visitor came to me there, a beautiful stuntwoman in the film industry. I met her at the rally, and she had been to my talk. "So," I thought, "this is really living! Getting out there and meeting beautiful women who care about The Cause and who like my role." Enriching as this encounter was, like so many I have had, little came of it — except for my being able to say I have many, many friends, and more still. So, after all was said and done after my L.A. tour, what did I accomplish in a metro area of 13 million people? One mustn't fool oneself. A convention of Siamese cat owners would be larger and probably noisier. I didn't know it at the time that the public's interest in peak oil (and in Jan Lundberg), as small as it was, began to wane in 2006.

In spring of 2006 I spoke at two peak oil conferences and attended another, one in New York City and two in Washington, DC. Enjoyable and stimulating they all were — having dinner with *Overshoot* author William Catton was fantastic — but where were we getting? Anyway, I was barely making a living. Fortunately, for my activist fix, I was getting heavily into the campaign against the plastic plague. As our DC Petrocollapse Conference ended, one of the speakers, Albert Bates, took the documentary Our Synthetic Sea from me to Mexico where he made some headway. The anti-plastics movement thus got a rare international boost with his initiative. Just as important, because of the way the minds of Albert, myself and other activists work, it is this kind of networking that makes us think there is progress in small victories and greater outreach. It's not that we're fooling ourselves, but we do sometimes find we've signed up for a life that is all too real or even strange, when we look at worsening ecological trends and persistent human dysfunction.

After I attended the Earth First! Rendezvous in mid 2006 and went on a national tour of eco-villages, my next home was to be Oregon where I'd already deposited my possessions. However, I stopped in San Francisco to hang out with a fellow housesitter, Cal Simone. Cal and I were later both on the City's Peak Oil Preparedness Task Force. On this "visit" in 2006 I saw that I ought to begin organizing the third Petrocollapse Conference, to be held in San Francisco. There was initial interest in the Bay area, but it was starting to hit me that interest in peak oil and petrocollapse had just peaked. Peak oil and petrocollapse as major concerns were being shunted aside by fears about climate change, war, and the usual rat-race pressures. During the several weeks it took our volunteer steering committee to confirm as speaker Matt Simmons, the late petroleum industry investment banker, our ability to pull off a major conference was being pinched harder by waning general interest. This trend along with insufficient funding up front to do the job right meant the conference had to be indefinitely postponed. This probably did not go down well with a kind donor who subsidized the never-held San Francisco Petrocollapse Conference. But, timing is everything.

The concentration of my work shifted toward not only fighting plastics, but also publishing online more intensively, and trying to drum up speaking engagements and music gigs for my income. In 2007 I began to work on a science-and-politics project with one of the leaders of the Berkeley Free Speech Movement, Brad Cleaveland. Our adviser was Charles Moore, anti-plastics guru, with whom Brad had established the Berkeley Commune in 1968. Our report, designed for a high-level Planetary Emergency conference in Sicily, was never completed. We let Charlie down, which I attributed perhaps unfairly to Brad's advanced age and health.

On the personal front regarding a love life, I had a girlfriend for a several months in Berkeley in 2004-2005. We seemed to do alright together, and performed our music publicly as a duo. We played at San Francisco's Meridian Gallery for their opening of 1950s peace poster art. We played live on KPOO-FM, San Francisco, the oldest Black radio station west of the Mississippi. I was co-host for a couple years there on the noon-hour talk show Reality Sandwich (no relation to the website of the same name). I was initially quite excited about my girlfriend, but she was periodically of two minds about me, hot and cold. She had a split personality concerning my suitability. One day I was to her a poet and spiritual, but the next I could allegedly look like a bum and be lacking in the ability to fix a car (that latter was quite true). Her inconstancy or confusion dissipated my ardor in a staircase collapse of our romance, until I had no reason to see her again. I chalked it all up to the "Berserkly" factor.

The only other woman I dated in my four years in the Bay Area was a corporate health-care professional who had gotten rid of her car and her cable TV, a beautiful Black woman. However, we couldn't seem to get close, despite our visits and mutual interest in music making (she a cellist). She said she was in awe of me as an activist, and she liked my cooking and chivalrous treatment of her. But we failed to generate any heat or eventually keep up contact after her closest friend advised her against me (without meeting me): "Why do you want to go down that road?" This had nothing to do with my lacking money, as I was getting a paycheck at the time, for two grants had come in. But the average wage in the Bay Area is several times more than my best-ever month of compensation. Living inexpensively was and is an accomplishment in itself to me and to most of my friends. This does limit one's pool of possible girlfriends or wives. So the mere idea of an activist who has no well-paying job, and no car, soured my friend's friend, whose advice was apparently taken. Meanwhile, I had many female friends and male friends, which is the most important source of "wealth," companionship and pleasure. But, as an Earth First! campfire joke song goes in the title line, "If Hitler Had a Girlfriend Why Can't I?" Being picky as well being an activist, writer and musician are attributes that can be iffy when they contribute to being a self-contained guy with non-social solitary periods. The trend in activism is more solitary action, such as writing on one's personal computer, unless one is in a funded office workplace. And "activist, writer and musician" are strikes against you for a conventional woman in the U.S. economy when she's past her days of possible idealism.

Without a serious romance or finding a spot in the music scene, living in San Francisco had to have other attractions for me. Sometimes I felt stuck in that highly populated area because I had no other option and I was surviving. But living there was exciting in one important respect: in March of 2007 we activists worked with progressive City employees to pass a city ordinance to make San Francisco the first State in the U.S. to ban the use of plastic bags by large grocery stores. It was also the first ban or fee on plastics in the whole Western Hemisphere. I testified, wrote, sang, and raised & spent money for this cause.

To follow up nationally I visited the staff of the Speaker of the House in Washington, D.C. in 2008. But a national plastics ban or fee could get nowhere because they felt politically constrained, although they wanted to see it happen. They either had no guts or knew that Nancy Pelosi would never consider it. I'd hoped so, because her son Paul liked my anti-plastic work. This poor response told me that my effectiveness was limited, or that many years' work would get us only a bit further toward banning plastic and getting off petroleum. Perhaps my effectiveness might have peaked — for a time. It was if I had approached a politician with a request for a law to have young unwed mothers be provided with more counseling. That's an important notion, but plastics are giving those mothers' babies birth defects and contributing to adults' cancer, diabetes, and obesity. This thought doesn't enter the mind of an activist: "I'm fighting a lost cause." I will always hate plastics and the way they kill sea life and cause humans to get birth defects, cancer, diabetes and obesity, and I'll speak out even when I'm talking to mental walls. I must admit, though, that these plastic keys I'm typing on work fine for my purposes. On with the show — this book and the next meeting of the Sail Transport Network.

In 2006 - 2007 efforts were made to re-launch Sail Transport Network. We didn't clearly succeed, but we learned much as we built relationships. Three colleagues and friends came out of this: Albert Bates, Dmitry Orlov, and David Reid. Albert, besides being an author and speaker, runs the Ecovillage Training Center at The Farm, Tennessee. The project has charity connections in Latin America the nearest source of tropical products for North American demand, within reasonable sailing distance. Dmitry began a peak-oil writing career. One of his interests was and remains sailing. Dave was intrigued by Sail Transport Network, as were Albert and Dmitry, but Dave soon set up the first actual sail transport service, in Sept. 2008 in the Puget Sound (see Resources at the end of this book).

In early 2008 I made some major personal shifts. Open to living in another land in a traditional, indigenous culture, I traveled to Belize where Albert taught me permaculture. I thought I might remain there in the rainforest and on the coast to live in a society of greater cohesion and closer to nature. I soon found that it didn't seem readily doable, and I had family in the U.S. I wanted to be able to see more than once a year. So after a look-see I resolved to go back to San Francisco and keep at Culture Change. I returned by bus through Mexico. In Cancun I had an amazing experience in healing from an injury involving a hammock in Belize. To this day I still don't know what exactly Hector Reyes did, and maybe he does not either when it involves the ineffable and the cosmic. From Hector and his wife Maria Ros' super kind hospitality I went southwest to visit and enjoy Chiapas. I managed to see very up close some autonomous zones in rebellion. The Zapatistas and the Earth University near San Cristobal de las Casas were not only intriguing but made a lasting impression. The openness and hospitality of the people were more than I would have hoped for.

I kept moving, now on to Mexico City. There in the Federal District in the environmental agency's conference room I gave a public talk and mini-concert for a group of Mexican environmental activists. It was organized primarily by a friend and long-distance editor I finally got to meet: Miguel Valencia. He took me to Ivan Illich's former studio in Cuernavaca, now a thriving composting toilet business. Illich's spirit was in no way being dumped on.

Once back in the States I noticed that I was again in a land sprinkled liberally with homeless and deranged people on the streets. I had not seen any such down-and-out people in Belize or Mexico, despite the poverty I witnessed. On my way to San Francisco I stopped in Santa Barbara to see my mother for what proved to be the last time. I gave her Chiapas Indian goods and played her my latest songs.

That was late April. Upon my return to San Francisco I spoke at the International Ecocities Conference. Next I traveled to Washington, D.C. After some fruitless activism and a pointless fund-raising attempt there, I returned to San Francisco via Seattle and the San Juan Islands, where I wanted to relocate. But my wish to move to the Puget Sound was impeded by my finances and failing to drum up sufficient interest in bringing about a local project: an eco-music festival for the Pacific Northwest, one of my long-time goals.

Back to San Francisco and home, I faced the end of my Bay Area phase. I helped close down a 19-year "institution," Studio B, an activist/artist studio in an old warehouse where I had lived almost two years. My loft was eventually taken down, as the building was sold in a typical gentrification deal. I had one final activist event in town, The Big One — a teach-in convergence at Golden Gate Park, that I spent many hours and months helping to plan. Unfortunately the June afternoon weather was so cold with the sea breeze that we basically flopped. I played a recital to a very sparse audience, with stiff fingers, and afterward found that my workshop on fasting was a wasteland, as the Park was emptying early and quickly. The next day it was time to take the moving van north. With a friend's kind and necessary donation of cash to Culture Change, and another friend's help in renting a moving van, I left the Bay Area for good (I believe, but you never know!).

Chapter 12

2000s — The Adventure Gets Stranger

Commune at last

This period of my life was dominated by duty and patience. I would have preferred to have been able to live in a vibrant, secure ecological community, or at least enjoy the presence of family and friends in a home we would share. But I could only manage bare survival, able to help my daughters financially only a little. What sustained me was my work and hopes for being able to move my mother out her bogus hospice-institution to a better place with me. It was her only possible option, and what she wanted (without explicitly reminding me, such was her gentle way with me and with everyone).

I returned to Humboldt County and informally joined a commune. It is in a low-populated area with wonderful hiking trails above the seashore. Rather than a formal commune, it is called by the residents "an unintentional community." A kind, generous landowner likes to have people live there who appreciate nature and communal living, and it does function pretty well. I had borrowed a large tent from a former housemate of mine who was by now living happily at the commune. I enjoyed her and my other friends I already had living there, and made more friends there. The sauna with woodstove, the compost toilets, the fruit trees, solar-heated shower in an old redwood stump – I liked it all. I was beyond needing to own my own home or land, so this is what I wanted. There was no Internet or cell phone coverage, so one had to walk to the nearest village.

I knew how to get by on a low income thanks to my knowledge of the local Food Bank, etc. It was good to have the familiarity of the county and run into people I liked. But I had a predominantly sad feeling in Arcata, forced as I was to deal with memories from a more stable period of my life there with family around, when Arcata was less controlled by the local business elite.

Culture Change was becoming published online more

frequently, as part of my push for a stronger news-service that would, along with this book, keep our group and message in the public eye. Funding was starting to improve, so 2008 saw Culture Change become a bit more visible as we laid groundwork for attainment of projects and the wide acceptance of our message. The strategic purpose was to promote in a higher-profile fashion the ways of sustainable living, promote eco-activism, and debunk the technofix while clearing up misunderstandings about peak oil and petrocollapse. I realized the dream of making our online service daily. We kept up that frequency for several months, but ultimately had to revert to every-few-days in late 2009. This was due to finances and our reluctance to publish other organizations' material without their permission (although under the Copyright Act it is legal if done under the Fair Use clause for educational and nonprofit purposes).

"My mummy's dead" (John Lennon)

After an idyllic day at the commune on September 14, I went into cell-phone range and got a message from my mother's court-enforced Conservator that she (my mother) was "not doing well." I dreaded bad news, but having heard this before in the 7 years of her captivity in a hospice, I had reason to hope for the best. I phoned that night and talked at length with the Toltec Living Center's night staffer. He was very reassuring that she was sleeping comfortably. But when I called a few hours later in the morning when my mother would have been awake and available, I was asked, "Didn't the Conservator call you?" by the hospice home owner, who then said that my mother "passed at 4 A.M." I hung up on him without a word.

Either the night staffer was deliberately misleading me, being under orders to do so, so that I did not know my mother was dying, or she died suddenly within a few hours after I spoke to him. Something does not fit: either she was really ill prior to that evening, as the Conservator hinted, or she was not, and only announced to me in the early phone call as ill, so I could be prepared for her life ending (being taken). Months later I learned about the secret morphine factor in my mother's death (explained later in this section).

I viewed her death as the culmination and goal of sustained

elder abuse that began many years before. In recent years, direct and obvious causes of my mother's deterioration were from chronic lack of mobility, no physical therapy, and being deprived the ability to chew (her dentures were left at her last home, in Arcata in 2000, and never replaced). So I obtained an autopsy. I thus pushed on with her cause even though I had lost the race against time. She had held out until age 88.

Medical professionals know that someone in hospice who does not die in six months or much less time is transferred out and treated as anyone expected to live many years. It was obvious that Mesa Lundberg's being treated as if she were near death for so many years was a scam and part of major fraud. Part of this process was for her opponents to sell her home that she wanted to live in with me. My office was there by the time she became stuck at Toltec "Living" Center, perhaps hastening our opposition's almost frantic attempts to sell the house and deprive my mother of living with her anti-petroleum son. During this period, 2001-2004, the chance for her regaining her Lundberg Survey ownership was perhaps lost due to her lawyer Joe Bush's and Conservator Mary Lou Parks' deliberately dropping the multimillion-dollar ball.

My mother's being denied what she was entitled to — care befitting someone who was clearly not a hopeless near-death patient — and her being totally disposed and fleeced, on flimsy grounds, is to me a case of slow murder. What people did to her was no accident of some kind of valid difference of opinion, although that is how it was portrayed. Her and my losing the battle and the war had to do with who we were up against: well-connected, self-interested people playing loose with the facts. The late judge McLafferty, friend of attorney Joe Bush, pretended that home care is not a preferred option for care-giving, and that losing one's home against one's will is fine and dandy. For a Republican, his idea of "family values" was nonexistent in our case. But if more family support could have been brought to bear for our side, such as any of Mesa Lundberg's step-grandchildren or nieces and nephews appearing in court with a sense of purpose, we might have prevailed. I failed to put together a team effort. Mesa spent years raising their aunt and cousin Dana Lundberg, who loved her stepmother very much. But Dana might have been too ill (manic depression) to be able to handle a trip to court. Even worse was that my mother and I were unable to involve my busy daughters much in the case. On a practical material basis they might have done well for themselves to make sure their grandmother got to keep her valuable home (which would have gone to them). Their not staying in her home with me was pointed out by the Conservator as a justification to keep Mesa Lundberg from returning to her home. However, everyone knows that young adults need to be most free and learn on their own.

In having to fight almost alone, without back-up in the court room except one daughter on one occasion, I could not help but reflect on U.S. culture as especially lacking in family solidarity compared to traditional cultures.

Despite my many efforts to help my mother since she was forced into institutions in Santa Barbara in 2001, I clearly failed to obtain better care for her or spring her from the clutches of predatory professionals. She and I were opposed by a large number of opportunists and functionaries aligned with my sister, the Big Oil figure Trilby Lundberg. The autopsy showed more elder abuse than I suspected, and key details provided to law enforcement agencies were alarming: a smoking gun was documented, but I did not have a key portion of the report in my hands: A supplemental report went only to law enforcement agencies in Santa Barbara, but was described to me by the Chief Investigator of the Los Angeles County Coroner's Office, Craig Harvey. He told me while I was on Amtrak at the end of May, 2009, that my mother had elevated morphine in her system that aroused his strong suspicions. He clearly told me that her death was caused "at the hands of another," and he stated to me it was "murder or manslaughter." My train ride was made memorable in an awful way.

Isn't it remarkable that his opinion is about as interesting to Santa Barbara authorities as last month's bus schedule change?

Morphine is used in hospice cases when pain is terribly great and death is around the corner. But there was no medical condition for my mother justifying this exit drug. Nor, to my or my brother's knowledge, based on his visiting her days before she was killed, was my mother ill enough to be in danger of leaving us any time soon. I spoke with her two days before she died and she was happy and lucid enough to rejoice that I was living on a beautiful commune. At least that last voicing from her heart and mind was pleasant for my memories. I learned months later that at that time she was on accelerated morphine dosage for no apparent or

214

identifiable condition.

My mother's being alive was inconvenient for two financial reasons: as the rightful owner of Lundberg Survey (in the opinion of some, such as the managing director of McCutcheon, Brown and Enerson, John Morrisey), she was a threat to the person we believe swindled her. The other financial incentive for Mesa Lundberg's death sooner rather than later was the fact that she was only costing the hospice money: the business had cleverly obtained all her remaining money, $250,000, in exchange for her remaining at Toltec Living Center the rest of her life. This transaction was against her will and my wishes, but the judge was happy to approve it. The cost for her room and board only, plus medicating (but not the actual drugs), was $8,000 a month. What an attractive scam, I mean reputable business in such a place as $anta Barbara. When my mother was forced to fork over all her money, with no more forthcoming, there was no more incentive for the hospice-home to keep her alive. She was just taking up an eight-thousand-a-month bedroom. No wonder she was not allowed to live long after she lost all her money to the self-interested business. Mr. Harvey said to me, "The sooner she was gone, the more money they made." My attorney-friend John Shellabarger was disturbed over the conflict of interest, as was the late Dana Lundberg.

I obtained the autopsy not to discover murder or manslaughter (so it was shocking that I did) but to confirm for the record that her muscles were atrophied from unnecessarily sitting or lying down all the time. "Use it or lose it" is known universally, yet for $8,000 a month my mother basically read her books all day and was rarely assisted in the minimum walking she needed. Another way Toltec Living Center saved money was by feeding her the regular fare instead of using a blender to make foods she could get down. She had no upper teeth; indeed, the first thing Craig Harvey told me after the autopsy was "She could not chew food!" So my mother only ate toast dipped in coffee and other soft foods, for lack of a varied diet needing chewing (or blending in a food processor). This meant long-term malnourishment and a shortened life. But she could hardly complain when they had her involuntarily taking various drugs such as Remeron.

Two prominent professionals were named in the report, which suggested that (according to Harvey) with the murder or manslaughter, the persons might at least lose their licenses: Dr.

Michele Armet, and RN Charles Sciutto (owner of Toltec with his wife Joy). The revocation of a couple of licenses would be the kind of remedy or "solution" in the category of "limited hangout," as in political scandals and conspiracies where some less serious crimes in the whole scheme are dealt with. Such a tactic seemingly brings about justice, but the larger conspiracy remains in the shadows. [See the following section "Oil Money was Fatal for Mesa Vernell Lundberg"]

I'm "On the road again" (Willie Nelson, and Canned Heat)

Before I saw the main autopsy report I hit the road again in September 2008. With the aid of supporters of Culture Change I attended the annual meeting of the Association for the Study of Peak Oil and Gas — U.S.A. Chapter, in Sacramento. I had the sense that my views on the oil industry and the economy were being suppressed year-in, year-out. Only the late Matt Simmons represented my views, in part, as he galvanized the audience with his warning of a "run on the energy bank." He explained that it not only meant no gasoline for cars, but would result in a few days with a rapid loss of food supply for millions in the U.S. and beyond, as panic and chaos hits. This view was right out of the 1970s oil crises in terms of the market mechanisms on fuel storage shifting from the industry's normal flow to paralysis-inducing hoarding. His long-term view differed sharply from mine, as he and his petroleum-investment firm Simmons International anticipate and hope for a rebuilding of the oil industry after socioeconomic and physical infrastructure collapse. The firm was a significant sponsor of the ASPO-USA meetings. It is quite a loss to the peak oil movement that Matt Simmons suddenly died August 8, 2010 at the age of 67, just as he was embarking on something — like I did in 1988 — more enlightened than oil-related work: his Ocean Energy Institute. He had in his final days been quite active with interesting, sinister claims about the BP-Gulf oil spill, and he wanted the hole plugged by nuclear detonation. He was very kind to me in all the times we met, and I was amazed at his frankness before a mainly Pentagon audience in 2006: "Maybe the enemy is us."

From Sacramento I took the opportunity to travel directly to

Portland, Oregon. I considered it worth moving to, as I had a daughter living there and I could tap into the activist community for the Sail Transport Network. So I reluctantly gave up my communal life and California's coastal redwoods, realizing that there was no more reason to be nearer Santa Barbara where my mother was. Buying a cheap little sailboat, I settled in before the rain and snow hit. After my picture landed on the front page of Humboldt's daily newspaper (featuring the Sail Transport Network), the *Times-Standard*, I paid a visit to California with guitar in hand to honor a commitment to perform in Westhaven. I was well received, but not as if I were the energy-environmental Messiah or king of eco-rock they needed.

In Portland, more than the Bay Area, I sensed progress in a short time for Culture Change and the sail and pedal power activities. Bicycling in Portland is more popular than in any other U.S. city, despite few bike infrastructure improvements of late. Portland's progressive reputation, proudly called "weird" by many locals, is deserved — if small differences between U.S. cities are of major significance. I felt like I was seeing the same old patterns: The mayor spearheaded, for his first year in office a 12-lane Interstate Highway bridge across the Columbia River, and opposition was weak because of "green" aspects to the project. Thanks to economic reality, the mayor and other supporters have to reduce the grandiose aspects.

From time to time I become involved in "side projects," some of which I hatch. One recent one was a reaction to Haiti's devastating earthquake. The Fast For Haiti featured a simple formula: a relatively affluent person goes without food for a period of time, and donates to a Haiti relief charity the amount of money the person saved by not eating. The Fast For Haiti was well received here and there. Participants signed up and were listed on the Culture Change website. Two high schools in Michigan did the Fast, learning something about deprivation while helping others. In the midst of my 10 day fast I did an interview on Portland's community radio station, KBOO-FM. I had been on CBS Radio Network in August 2007 for the Climate Emergency Fast, bringing to the conversation with Dan Raviv such elements as petroleum dependence and plastics. When we did the show it was my 16th day on just water; I was to end up fasting 23 days. When I called him up to tell him about the Fast For Haiti he was quite negative as to

photo by Richard Register

Westhaven
Center for the Arts presents:
Singer-songwriter
Depaver Jan
Performs his eco-songs in a benefit concert for the

Admission: sliding scale, $1-100. Refreshments available. Jam session and discussion afterwards! Can you picture ocean-based renewable-energy passage and trade, with acoustic music? Come hear Ian's signature song Have a Global Warming Day (aired on NPR, sorry) and his other activist ditties such as Get Up and Change the World, Green is The Shelter and Against The Law as performed and recorded by The Depavers. Musician friends are apt to join him on stage! Web: **www.culturechange.org/depavers.html**

Sail Transport Network
Saturday Nov. 22, 7:30 PM
Westhaven
Center for the Arts
Reservations: 677-9493

Visiting Humboldt County, California, 2008. Attila Gyenis stepped up and accompanied on tambourine. Photo by Richard Register, 2005 the concept, because he thought so many organizations were working on the problem. I'm not sure why he sounded angry, but it crossed my mind that he may have gotten flack for letting an anti-corporate character such as myself get on the air with a message that was counter to buying cars, computers, or buying anything.

❧

This brings us to the present. In my work I have outdone myself in positioning myself to be exactly where I need to be, doing what I want to do. Although Portland is another over-paved city and has over a million people in the area, there are two advantages I found over the San Francisco Bay Area besides having 1/7th of the population: (1) the people are friendlier and more aware of the real nature of society, and (2) thanks to the urban growth boundary law at the state level, I can live on my boat and enjoy farms and wildlife areas in proximity, while traveling by river is a breeze most of the time. When I'm on my bicycle I'm aware I'm in the most bike-oriented, highest cyclist-per-capita city in the nation. Motorists anticipate and respect bicyclists more in Portland than most car-dominated cities.

As I write this, on another plastic table, our photo-journalist Becky "Wild Girl" Lerner is in the midst of a one-week diet of only wild, foraged foods. We are connecting this activity to sail transport, pedal power, and indigenous traditional ways, raising issues on our daily website entries about survival and connection to nature. Because of opportunities such as presenting this kind of journalism while attaining my preferred lifestyle, and meeting so many sincere people in Portland, I feel fortunate. I have enjoyed seeing my daughter and working with her as well. She put a lot of effort into the previous version of this book, and for this new version she supplied the cover art. (This autobiography replaced a massive mish-mosh of a book, so some of her work may have been for naught.) We both have a problem with the weather: days of rain without end, sometimes freezing temperatures (usually when the skies are clear), and dreary cityscapes. Then spring comes and transforms the whole place, giving hope again for cooperative community efforts as well as highs in personal creativity.

Since an autobiography is by necessity a personal book, I will offer my glimpse of a livable future that works for me:

For our present that we have to make the best of, we must abandon some dangerous habits such as irresponsible purchases and waste. Simultaneously, we can learn about our pre-existing conditions such as the violent history of dispossessing native peoples who had proven sustainability over millennia. This area of knowledge helps us regain community closeness and augment our useful skills. Before we are able to use them again as our great grandparents did, as part of our transition to a sustainable culture, we will most likely find ourselves having to get through the total collapse of the house-of-cards consumer economy that is based on fast-dwindling cheap oil. What comes after that phase, if we make it, is even more hotly disputed than the nature and speed of collapse. Ironically, some fans of *Ecotopia* who practice permaculture feel that we are all resigned to facing a violent end personally and of much life. But as I said in the beginning of this book, I say I am an optimist — not just for endless activism, but for seeing humanity correct its cultural direction and return to conscious symbiosis with nature. I must be right, because if I'm not, who will be around to say I wasn't?

Ted Rall attacked my vision as naïve in his 2010 book *Anti-American Manifesto*, a title that seems a poor concept. His advocating a violent revolution, out of desperation and sincere concern for people and environment, contributed to his dismissing what he saw as any peak-oil tinged dream for eventual peace and justice without a fight. Besides our disagreement on collapse and its outcome, I had to take him to task (e.g., on AlterNet.org) along with others promoting violence against humans. For one thing, the strategy of mass nonviolence is historically proven as ineffective.

I often think of the future's low-tech, post-industry ways of subsistence as beautiful, although challenging to adjust to. I am happy with the prospect of having no gasoline or electricity, although I recognize that clever people will rig up what they can if it is really called for. I have known the more relaxed, peaceful, convivial atmosphere of healthy nature, with bonfires, food from the land, clean water, and friendship. Money can feel superfluous. Only because it is available today do people use it and buy another car. But soon we will have to become self-sufficient in order to have basic tools and assure that our truly essential needs are met.

Bring it on.

Chapter 13

Family Members Killed By Oil Money and Elder Abuse

Message from a close friend:

"You may have been raised with lots more money than most Americans but your story is one that every American can feel. The loss of one's mother at the hands of unbridled greed resonates for all of us. We're all experiencing it with our Mother Earth and yet, the greed is so incredibly hard to curtail." – Camila Wren

Lundberg v. Lundberg, Santa Barbara: The Wrongful Death of an Oil Guru's Widow

14 September 2010, www.CultureChange.org

From 1972-1986 I worked in a family business serving the oil industry and government, known as Lundberg Survey. In 1988 I changed careers to join the environmental movement full time. After leaving the family business and moving to the other side of the U.S., terrible events in the family involving the courts took place despite my having left — not just leaving the oil analysis business but entering the nonprofit sector to stay. My mother, former chairman of the board, was, according to a new lawsuit, taken over by unscrupulous people who relieved her of a fortune and knowingly hastened her death.

On Sept. 13th 2010 I filed a Complaint in Superior Court of Santa Barbara, California, for the Wrongful Death of my mother, Mesa Vernell Lundberg. She died in a hospice facility on Sept. 15,

2008. She had resided there against her will for seven lonely years. My brother Darius Lundberg and I are the Plaintiffs. Defendants are mainly lawyers, two conservators, nurses, a medical doctor, a banker, and Trilby Lundberg of Lundberg Survey Incorporated.

Mesa Lundberg had become complete owner of Lundberg Survey after I left the firm in 1986. The firm's flagship publication, the *Lundberg Letter,* was known as "the bible of the oil industry, as it had accurately predicted the Second Oil Shock in 1979. Unfortunately, after her husband Dan Lundberg (founder of the firm and widely called "the Oil Guru") died in 1986, Mesa was to live the final quarter of her life in increasingly bad circumstances, except for a two-year respite in Arcata, California.

Some Culture Change readers already knew much of the above, and have followed the oil-industry connections of this publication's concerns and its founder. The court documents at the end of this introductory article contain much of the whole story plus new insights that make the case for wrongful death. Yet, despite the awful aspects of this sad and ugly saga, this case is an opportunity for anyone to learn from this family's experience with elder abuse and fraud. In fact, the implications of weakening community/family closeness were a factor in selecting the name Culture Change for the work of the organization I founded in 1988, then named Fossil Fuels Policy Action. In the Complaint filed on September 13, 2010 — the day after Mesa's birthday, unfortunately a Sunday so the courts were closed — the bigger picture is hinted at, in terms of social costs:

In addition to Plaintiffs' need for damages to be paid by the Defendants, both compensation and punitive, for abusing and shortening the life of their loving mother – depriving them of her companionship and ability to pass along an inheritance – the Plaintiffs hope that this complaint and the trial will help shine a light on the out-of-control and self-serving methods and conspiracies of fiends legalistically preying upon elderly and wealthy individuals who lack defenses against abuse and fraud. [Page 9, Paragraph 27 "Attachment 12"]

The greater costs must include the ecological on a global level: for the oil money that took down Mesa Lundberg is associated none other than with the lethal abuse of Mother Earth. It's obvious we must treat our mothers better, and come together to heal the Earth and each other. But not all of us see. Trilby Lundberg has publicly and repeatedly denied global warming, in service to her major oil company clients. As bad as Big Oil's money-influence is on the personal and local levels, such as in disasters at refineries and petroleum pipelines, it is the ongoing onslaught of the fossil fuels industries on the atmosphere and oceans that are the main threat to planetary health. It fits all too well that, individually, modern people are addicted to petroleum and suffer the consequences to their health and whole natural world. This is why this article is categorized in CultureChange.org's web site system under Petro-addiction and Health, rather than Latest News or Sail Transport Network.

Personal costs have been high within the Lundberg family, in addition to the total financial fleecing and loss of health suffered by Mesa Lundberg. For myself, I regret the long, on and off state of war that went on and on, costing me money but mainly costing me my time, which one can never get back. It's also oppressive to get sued for trying to make a living at one's only trade (in 1987); I had the express permission of the Chairwoman of the Board, to operate my own business, Lundberg Reports. But to have any basis to attack me in federal court, my opposition needed to claim (committing perjury) that I had taken proprietary information. The complete waste of time and funds in that case did nothing but wield costly weapons known as lawyers. I am fortunate that my post-oil industry years have been enriched by some worthwhile activism, priceless personal relationships, learning about peak oil and petrocollapse, and participating in creative and fun projects that protect the global climate, hopefully helping to bring on a sustainable future while we still have a chance.

Defendants Attachment
for Complaint form PLD-PI-001
Lundberg versus Lundberg

Trilby Lundberg
Mary Lou Parks, RN
Michelle Armet, MD [Michelle]
David Turpin, attorney-at-law
W. Joe Bush, attorney-at-law
John Parke, attorney-at-law
Margaret Barnes, attorney-at-law

Charles Sciutto, RN
Joy Sciutto
Marilyn Carliner [Carlander]
Debbie Hilton Ciambrone
Michael Markovitch, attorney-at-law

Attachment 12 Lundberg versus Lundberg

1. "Murder or manslaughter" is how the life of Mesa Vernell
Lundberg ("Mesa", mother of Plaintiffs) ended, according to a
statement by the Chief Investigator of the Los Angeles County
Coroner, Craig Harvey, to Plaintiff Jan Lundberg.
2. For almost a decade the Defendants knowingly failed to
conserve and protect Mesa's property and finances. Far worse, the
Defendants knowingly deprived her of a healthier, longer life by
preventing care and treatment befitting a non-terminally ill person.
Seven years of forced confinement in a hospice facility was uncalled
for when there were better alternatives in terms of appropriate
physical care and affordability. The facility, Toltec Living Center,
cost Mesa $8,000-plus per month for only room and board. No
physical or occupational therapy, or mobility such as walking were
available to Mesa during the seven years, except on rare occasion,
contributing to predictable ailments which she endured, with
resultant surgeries and deterioration of health. Yet Mesa hung on,
still able to walk just barely after recovering from preventable
setbacks, and was never terminally ill.
3. She consistently made clear her demands to leave Santa Barbara
and live in her own home (an idea approved by her home county
Court Investigator for Humboldt, northern California). In addition
to negligence and fraud against her, Mesa was subjected to years of
lying in her own urine each morning as the understaffed facility left
her in a caged bed, when she was capable of walking to the toilet
with her walker.
4. Finally, after she did not die after seven years, Mesa was placed
[on] a life-ending regime of morphine, unknown to Plaintiffs, on
September 10 and given increasing doses until she died on
September 15th. Mesa had no condition known to require
morphine, a well-known exit drug. To the knowledge of Plaintiffs
who were in close touch with her, she was not complaining of pain,

nor did she wish to die. The death certificate listed no cause of death indicating the need for morphine, such as painful cancer. The Chief Investigator of the Los Angeles Country Coroner told Plaintiff Jan Lundberg that "morphine did not seem to be indicated" and it was found at "higher levels than expected." Regarding the narcotic's administration he found the medical records to be "irregular" and "slapped together." He determined there was Suspected Elder Abuse, which he reported on Form 341 filed with law enforcement. On the form he stated Mesa's "death (was) occasioned by the actions of another." One reason for his suspicions in this case was that morphine's effect on a body is counter to any goal of enabling it to "thrive," while Mesa's death certificate's main cause of death listed "failure to thrive." On the same Form 341 the Chief Investigator identified culpable parties: Defendants Charles Sciutto and Michelle Armet. The Chief Investigator, Craig Harvey (over two decades on the job), also observed that Mesa's soonest death maximized the profit of Toltec, as the facility had seized (through most of the Defendants' actions) Mesa's last quarter million dollars for the right to reside at Toltec until she were to die.

5. Conveniently for the Defendants, she did not live long enough to use up much of that money, and on September 15, 2008 Toltec suddenly had an $8,000-a-month bedroom freed up. The conflict of interest for Toltec to keep Mesa alive is matched only by the conflict of interest in the possessive nature of the conservatorship that drained Mesa of all her health, property and happiness. (Trilby Lundberg was Mesa's first, and unwelcome, conservator.)

6. Plaintiffs had secured an autopsy of their mother Mesa in 2008 in order to show the years of consistent disuse of her muscles and inability to chew, conditions deliberately allowed to worsen by Defendants. Plaintiffs had on many occasions asked relevant Defendants to provide Mesa the therapy, mobility, and dental care she needed, and that food be provided for Mesa that she could chew (her dentures were missing for her entire stay at Toltec and her dental health was neglected). Plaintiffs were unprepared for Chief Harvey's news of "elevated morphine levels" and "death occasioned by the actions of another" (the definition of homicide, noted Chief Harvey to Jan Lundberg).

7. Despite her circumstances and the massive injustice to her, Mesa was always stoic and dignified, and did not believe in complaining

even in her own interest. She spoke quietly and slowly, whenever someone cared to pay attention to her. Behind her back some called her demented. For example, Trilby stated in a key pleading that "Mesa is too demented to decide her own residence." Mesa tried to enjoy life by reading mystery novels daily, listening to music, hoping for more visitors, talking on the phone, and she even babysat frequently the infants of the owners of the hospice business. At her request she was taken to shops, movies, and relatives' homes. Although Mesa coughed most days, her alleged pulmonary disease did not require Mesa to ever have oxygen administered, that the Plaintiffs know of. Mesa was not extremely healthy, but not in bad shape for a woman in her eighties who never got exercise or enough food (no special accommodation was made with the kitchen for her lack of teeth). Mesa had to witness many people dieing around her for years in the hospice facility, and their state when alive was what she was accused of being: incapable of intelligent conversation. Mesa's adult companionship at the hospice "home" was therefore next to nothing.

8. Only with the report on the autopsy did Plaintiffs learn their mother was being given morphine (large and frequent amounts, despite her being noted in records as "comfortable and sleeping" during her final hours and days at the end of the five days of constant morphine). Jan Lundberg spoke with his mother two days before she died, and she sounded lucid, happy, and wanting to see him and speak on the telephone again soon (as always). Darius Lundberg visited her a few days prior to her death, after Trilby Lundberg called him and said "Mesa is shutting down." He found this to be untrue when he immediately visited his mother and found her to be in her usual condition and steady, lucid frame of mind, without any mention or indication of pain or extra unhappiness. So he, like his brother Jan, was shocked at her death.

9. The death of Mesa on September 15, 2008 was from causes not limited to those on the death certificate, in two ways or phases:

10. In Phase Two, the more recent period, there are two causes of death apart from what is on the death certificate:

(A) The unusual amount of morphine was found in her system, when she had not been on the drug for any chronic condition, and she had not been "on hospice" to ease her pain to death. She did not want to die.

(B) Her physical condition was allowed to run down deliberately for years prior to death, as she was denied mobility and therapy, and she suffered from malnutrition due to having no upper teeth (and no special provisions were made for diet such as blended drinks with supplements).

11. How Phase One and Two were possible was largely through conservatorship that Mesa was forced into via fraud. Trilby Lundberg and her Lundberg Survey attorney Gary Faulkes were fully aware that Mesa Lundberg suffered the consequences of Trilby's perjury (that Trilby did not owe any money to Mesa as proposed conservatee, in 1995, and that Mesa could never recover).

12. Mesa resided at Toltec not just because persons named in this complaint were profiting off her wrongful residence at a hospice; the central idea was to make sure she did not get out alive in order to pursue her lost wealth and turn it against her philosophical enemy: major oil corporations (explained later in this Complaint's Attachment).

13. The Sciuttos had a fiduciary duty to maintain Mesa's health but they did not. The actions and omissions of the Sciuttos, Dr. Armet and their commander Mary Lou Parks, at the command of her friend Trilby Lundberg, were far beyond what is normally encountered as mere malpractice. The entire sequence of events over years reflected the modus operandi of a predatory group helping itself alone. Intimidation, lies and false promises of release were experienced and observed by Plaintiffs regarding their mother. She was incarcerated, in effect, at Toltec via fraudulent conservatorship, false statements, and obviously wrongful placement of a non-terminally ill person in a hospice facility for seven years. This was very profitable for some of the defendants, as approximately $825,000 can go around nicely. That figure only covered room and board, as the facility offered nothing but a place to die. Additional funds were from Medicare, which might not have been forthcoming if Mesa still owned a house and home. This might have spurred Defendants to dispose of the house and spend the proceeds on themselves, supposedly on behalf of Mesa. This complaint does not address Defendants' possible defrauding of the government and the taxpayers.

14. Mesa's house was liquidated and all proceeds, including over one million dollars cash that she had separately, went into the pockets of most Defendants.

15. For Phase One, the original and motivating crime that brought about Phase Two above was the swindle of corporate stock that Mesa owned. She lost it for a tiny portion of its market value, but it was due only to elder abuse by Trilby Lundberg and her attorneys. This loss of approximately $50 million was to the sole benefit of Defendant Trilby Lundberg, but Trilby may have had to pay other Defendants for their compliance in carrying out Phase Two above to keep Mesa in check and defenseless (especially with her do-nothing lawyer Joe Bush), and penniless, and finally gotten out of the way by her killing on September 15, 2008.

16. The Santa Barbara judge in the case, "Conservatorship of Mesa Lundberg," approved the arrangements devised by Defendants perhaps because he trusted their honesty and ability to conserve and protect Mesa's property, finances and health. The judge was lied to, misled, and he failed to take into account Mesa's practical needs for physical and financial health. Her clear wishes, regularly expressed, to live in her own home with far less expensive yet one-on-one professional care were ignored. Defendants expressed their feelings against the idea of Jan's living "for free" at Mesa's house, even through he had paid rent and had himself generated most of Mesa's wealth through his prior management of Lundberg Survey. Jan's operating the anti-Big Oil organization Culture Change out of Mesa's home, with her enthusiastic permission, was also something to be terminated in the eyes of the Defendants.

17. Mesa could have been more definite and aggressive to confront those opposing her, but it would have meant attacking her own daughter Trilby, which, like most parents, she could [not] bring herself to do strongly enough. Being unable to do so left Mesa vulnerable to allegations that she had insufficient mental capacity, although this was not confirmed or believed by her visitors who were not the Defendants or Does working for them. Also affecting her apparent mental condition, Mesa was forced to take drugs (such as the dangerous antidepressant Remeron) from October 2001 until she died, for the purpose of pacifying her and quell her demands for freedom. Mesa's family members and friends never knew her to be depressed, and her distaste for medical drugs was legendary. Despite the drugs Mesa was always able and willing to talk about anything, including complex matters, with wisdom and wry humor.

18. As stated above, Mesa was not demented as alleged in court, and she was not terminally ill. Through the Defendants' ignoring

Mesa's real situation and her rights, Mesa was elder-abused by Defendants and Does, and was a victim of fraud by Defendants. Unfortunately, a judge cannot get to know many of those greatly affected by his or her decisions, but if the judge in this case had taken the time to hear, know and understand Mesa, he might have realized she was not someone to be described and mistreated as she was. John Shellabarger, attorney-at-law in Santa Barbara, visited Mesa at Toltec and found her to be lucid and aware in terms of surroundings and the calendar. He informed Plaintiff Jan Lundberg in 2006 that his mother was suffering elder abuse.

19. Others who visited Mesa and did not find her to be demented or seriously ill were Barbara Shults, RN and Legal Nurse Consultant, and Mesa's relatives David Nathenson, Sonya Nathenson, and Yolanda Nathenson (Mesa's nephew and nieces), Dana Lundberg Sharp (stepdaughter), Dana's daughter Darla Sharp, and Erik Lundberg Scott (son of Guy Lundberg, stepson of Mesa). Erik saw her frequently over the years that Jan rode with him to Toltec to visit Mesa. Mesa's granddaughters Bronwyn Lundberg and Vernell Lundberg knew their grandmother was not demented, and it was with great joy that Mesa heard from them or saw them, or received news about them. Chief Harvey observed to Plaintiff Jan that "Mesa's brain must have been working when she wanted to go home."

20. Nurse Shults was initially shocked that Mesa was in an end stage facility, and believes that Toltec is not an appropriate facility for administering morphine, possibly lacking the license for such. Shults stated to Plaintiff Jan that there are other pain relievers to use – but they would not induce the apparently desired effect of respiratory failure, as morphine does. Morphine sedation reduces lung action, and serves to kill a person as in assisted suicide. Mesa Lundberg was not suicidal. She was a former lawyer who knew a money-grubbing game was being played around her for high stakes. She lamented her having any oil money, that it brought her great trouble and danger. She wanted to outlive the "attackers" (as she described her enemies) who were "bought off" (as she put it) so that she could see them hopefully live to experience their own conservatorship.

21. For Mesa or the Plaintiffs to have somehow forced those who were responsible to do the right thing by Mesa proved impossible, as it was most difficult without a huge war chest to counter

Defendants' relentless, unethical drive for profit at Mesa's expense. Mesa's plight was also determined by a flawed system: patients or victims of fraud are all too often placed and kept overly long in a facility where great profit is made not just by the facility, but by every self-interested professional (as in the Defendants) playing along and collecting a handsome fee. Letting a patient return home, despite savings of funds and better care and happiness for the patient, runs counter to the selfish needs of those wishing to profit; this happens with large hospitals as well as with small facilities involving a few people.

22. W. Joe Bush was Mesa's attorney (along with his partner John Parke) from 2001 on until her death. Bush (Defendant) refused to do anything for his client other than to take her occasional statement that she wanted to return to her own home in Humboldt County. Bush was a family friend of the judge, and repeatedly stated he wanted to move Mesa to his friend's new elder care facility (this did not occur). Bush was so disappointed that the judge had ordered a reduction in legal fees paid by Mesa that Bush cited this for his refusal to honor Mesa's request to appeal the judge's decision to sell her home and confine her to the hospice-home Toltec. Bush misinformed his client and Plaintiff Jan Lundberg about a possible jury trial on challenging the conservatorship: he said it was not possible. But through the Santa Barbara Court Investigator Jan and Mesa found in 2007 that he had misled and lied to us. Bush never challenged the conservatorship as his client wished as her annual right; only Jan did so, with no help whatsoever from Bush or Parke. Nor did they help Jan with his appeal of the judge's decision, even though his case was accepted as valid by the top firm Lasher and Lasher.

23. Xenia Lundberg, former business partner and sister-in-law to Defendant Trilby Lundberg, stated that Trilby confided, after her father Dan Lundberg died in 1986, "One down and one to go." – referring to Mesa. Trilby's prime motivation was to seize control of Lundberg Survey, which she did from a position of outsider, having been severed from the firm in 1985, taking it over and forcing all other family members out and becoming, illegitimately, the sole owner. Trilby swindled the family business from Mesa with the aid of elder abuse in a questionable transaction, based on a cash loan from Mesa to Trilby that gave Mesa 1/200th of the market value of the stock in Lundberg Survey. However, even the small payment was not consistently paid each month, and was never completed.

24. In the entire conservatorship and confinement of Mesa, Trilby has enjoyed the full cooperation of every professional and official involved with her mother's case, against Mesa's wishes and interests. Much money was to be made or safeguarded by Defendants all the way around. With Mesa's confinement and death their aims and improved pocketbooks were well realized. Mesa's visits were controlled by the conservator, against Mesa's and Plaintiff's wishes. Trilby Lundberg did not object to these rules, as she found them not applying to her anyway due to special treatment. The visitation rules were for number of consecutive hours (three) per day, 24-hour notice required, and restricting of content of discussion on where Mesa could live. Such rules prevented her from fulfilling her wish to attend the funeral of her brother-in-law Simon Nathenson in 2003, but Toltec took her to see the Getty Museum about the same time period, such was her sufficient health and state of mind. Trilby took Mesa for occasional long and exhausting trips. These rules were obtained deviously by Defendant Turpin when he submitted them to the judge after promising not to do so. The rules were contrived in part to justify the heavy drugging of Mesa to stop her from demanding to go home. She had gone on a hunger strike in October 2001, and got drugged thereafter and her visits by Plaintiffs discouraged and controlled.

25. Lundberg Survey has for decades been widely known as a service of and for the major oil corporations. So the money and wealth of Mesa Lundberg was from the oil industry, in two ways: (1) when her funds and assets were seized in conservatorship – launched against her by Trilby with the aid of perjury in 1995 – her money that was all from Big Oil was used against her (Mesa) to deprive her of her property, her freedom and fast-dwindling wealth. (2) The ongoing cash flow from Lundberg Survey at Trilby's disposal was of course Big Oil money as well, possible because Trilby owned and controlled the firm. Mesa attempted to gain back her stock by hiring the law firm McCutcheon, Brown and Enerson in 1999, as the firm believed she had a good case. Unfortunately, Mesa hired two Santa Barbara lawyers who failed to pursue her interests (Margaret Barnes and Joe Bush, Defendants), and they betrayed her when she was railroaded into eternal conservatorship and incarceration. The conservators Mary Lou Parks and Marilyn Carliner [Carlander] also failed in their fiduciary duty to pursue Mesa's claim to all of the Lundberg Survey stock, as the conservators and all the Defendants were loyal to Trilby Lundberg's each and every claim and desire against the interests of Mesa. Mesa clearly wanted the stock back in her name (not such a demented wish), and this may have been the reason that Trilby did not see or telephone or write to her mother for years prior to trapping her in Santa Barbara in 2001.

26. The role of Big Oil's money in the demise of Mesa's financial and physical health and earlier-than-necessary death is significant, given Mesa's political leanings and her well-known support of anti-oil activism. In the Culture Change magazine, Fall 2001, she is prominently quoted: "Shell Oil Company is why I do not walk well today." [in connection with pesticide exposure] Mesa Lundberg served as occasional editor of the magazine (previously known as the anti-oil pollution Auto-Free Times and the Paving Moratorium Update). The magazine's publisher, her son Jan Lundberg (Plaintiff), enjoyed Mesa's support on various levels for years. His activities against oil-industry expansion and ongoing pollution have been well documented, such as in the Washington Post, Associated Press, CNN-International, and elsewhere. Trilby and her major oil corporate masters did not want Jan Lundberg's and Mesa Lundberg's feelings on Big Oil to be (1) supported by one dollar of Mesa's estate or (2) result in Mesa's regaining control of Lundberg Survey. Jan Lundberg ran Lundberg Survey profitably prior to Trilby, but he left the firm voluntarily in 1986 for the sake of peace in the family.

27. In addition to Plaintiffs' need for damages to be paid by the Defendants, both compensation and punitive, for abusing and shortening the life of their loving mother – depriving them of her companionship and ability to pass along an inheritance – the Plaintiffs hope that this complaint and the trial will help shine a light on the out-of-control and self-serving methods and conspiracies of fiends legalistically preying upon elderly and wealthy individuals who lack defenses against abuse and fraud.

28. Defendants' roles in Lundberg versus Lundberg

29. The following persons in the Santa Barbara, California area were involved closely in Mesa Vernell Lundberg's estate, medical care, and legal proceedings. Their affiliations, jobs and roles concerning Mesa Vernell Lundberg are briefly described under their names. Most of them were mentioned above.

30. John Parke, attorney-at-law, partner of W. Joe Bush. Parke represented Mesa in court when Joe Bush was unavailable. When Parke appeared in Judge McLafferty's Santa Barbara Superior Court room, and did not argue for Mesa, he said upon the decision that Mesa would lose her house and be confined to Toltec Living Center against her will, "She will live ten more years and run out of money before that." This shows that he knew she was being mistreated or wronged with a faulty decision. He also knew that the impetus for arguing for such a decision was based on falsehoods, whether deliberate or not.

31. Charles Sciutto, RN, is the co-owner of Toltec Living Center ("Toltec"), a hospice-respite facility for wealthy elderly people. Mr. Sciutto and his wife Joy Sciutto formally accepted business from Mary Lou Parks to place Mesa Vernell Lundberg ("Mesa") at Toltec as a full time resident. Mr. Sciutto was fully aware that Mesa, whom he and Ms. Sciutto utilized on occasion as babysitter for their son, was not terminally ill for the seven years she was forced to remain at Toltec. Mr. and Ms. Sciutto were also fully aware that Mesa needed physical and occupational therapy, and simple mobility, instead of being confined to her bed in a cage or sitting alone all day.

32. Mr. and Mrs. Sciutto were also fully aware that Mesa was undernourished chronically as she lacked teeth. No effort was made to retrieve her dentures from Arcata where she wanted to be in her own home. Without teeth, Mesa needed smoothies and other food preparation and selection, but this never happened. Mr. and Mrs. Sciutto were also fully aware that lack of sufficient staff left Mesa in her bed each morning in a cage in her own urine, although going to the bathroom on her own was within her capabilities.

33. Joy Sciutto is the co-owner of Toltec Living Center, a hospice-respite facility for wealthy elderly people. Ms. Sciutto is business and domestic partner of Charles Sciutto. Ms. Sciutto and her husband were fully aware that Mesa did not want to remain at the facility around dying people year after year, and that Mesa would have benefited from a bit more care than that befitting a dying person, covered by the $8,000 plus monthly cost that Mesa paid for. On top of this sum, approximately $250,000 came to Mr. and Mrs. Sciutto for Mesa's perpetual care, in 2007, but she did not live to use much of the value of the sum. It could have been used for some physical and occupational therapy, or at least some staff assistance in the mornings to help Mesa walk to the bathroom, or for Mesa to go outside the facility and see some nature.

34. Michelle Armet, MD, was the principal medical doctor for Mesa. Dr. Armet was fully aware that Mesa responded well to physical and occupational therapy during the few occasions it was implemented, such as after Mesa's surgeries. Dr. Armet was also aware that the surgeries, for a broken hip and bowel obstruction, were caused substantially by lack of mobility and lack of therapy. However, Dr. Armet did not insist on or implement physical and occupational therapy for Mesa, even though Dr. Armet knew Mesa responded to it and was "doing well" in general, according to her statements to Jan Lundberg and Darius Lundberg. Dr. Armet was 100% compliant with the person paying her, Mary Lou Parks (Conservator), such that Mrs. Parks' refusal to allow Mesa to visit her home based on a claim of "frailty" were not refuted by Dr. Armet. Dr. Armet was fully aware that Mesa was being denied a re-evaluation of her neuro-psych condition, after a preliminary report in 2001 required follow up to measure Mesa's improved health.

35. Mary Lou Parks, RN, was Conservator of the Estate and Conservator of the Person of Mesa from 2001 until Mesa's death. Mrs. Parks was terminated in 2001 but was reinstated in a few weeks as her replacement, another RN, quit. Mesa simultaneously had a co-conservator, Mary Cardiff, Esq., an old friend, who insisted that Mesa return to her own home. Mrs. Parks initially agreed and promised that Mesa belonged and would be back in her own home in 2001, and begged Plaintiff Jan not to exercise the right to obtain county guardianship for his mother. After Parks' consultations with Trilby, Parks tried to quash Mesa's claim to the Lundberg Survey stock by reporting that Trilby was "not selling" Lundberg Survey. Mrs. Parks proceeded to follow all Trilby's wishes in opposing all Mesa's wishes and ignoring her best interests (e.g., one-on-one care, physical and occupational therapy, and saving money that was as Mrs. Parks acknowledged was "hemorrhaging). Mrs. Parks took undue initiatives that limited Mesa's freedom and health, and practiced a double standard, at the urgings of Trilby Lundberg. For example, Mesa wanted to return to her own home, in part for better care and to save money, but this was thwarted by forcing Mesa to take drugs she did not believe were necessary or safe (Remeron; Dr. Armet and the Sciuttos went along with this). Mesa was also denied liberal visiting by her children, but in practice Trilby alone was exempt with the full knowledge of Mrs. Parks, as Mesa was taken on long car trips by Trilby. Mrs. Parks was aware that in 2001 one of these trips resulted in Mesa's fainting but Trilby did not take Mesa to a hospital or call 911. Mrs. Parks first called the episode "suspicious" but that was before Mrs. Parks and Trilby became close friends. Mrs. Parks always behaved as if Trilby were her real client, and paid well to deprive Mesa of her rights and health. As the Humboldt County Court Investigator found, and reported to Plaintiff Jan, "Money talks."

36. Marilyn Carliner [Carlander], was acting co-conservator when Mesa died on September 15, 2008. Like Mrs. Parks, Ms. Carliner [Carlander] failed to inform Jan or Darius Lundberg of Mesa's true condition or that she had died. (The brothers only found out when Jan called Toltec to speak with his mother.) Ms. Carliner[Carlander] did not respond to repeated requests for Mesa's property to be seen and shared by Jan and Darius Lundberg, as Ms. Carliner [Carlander] only responded to the wishes of Trilby Lundberg.

37. Margaret Barnes is an attorney-at-law who represented Mesa in early 2001 but was replaced by Joe Bush. Mrs. Barnes proceeded to become lawyer for Mesa's estate. At no time did Mrs. Barnes take any action to protect Mesa's interests health-wise or financially. Apart from taking her handsome fees, Mrs. Barnes participated in the draining of Mesa's estate, knowing full well that home-care in a paid-for home, in a less expensive community (Arcata, Calif.), would conserve the estate. Mrs. Barnes also knew that Mesa's estate could afford physical and occupational therapy. However, Mrs. Barnes played along with her colleagues all profiting of Mesa's incarceration and poor treatment, as Mrs. Barnes referred to Mesa as "incapacitated." Mrs. Barnes knew full well that Mesa could carry on any conversation but was reluctant to confront her daughter. Mrs. Barnes also knew that Mesa was being deprived of her neuro-psych re-evaluation. Mrs. Barnes rubber-stamped each expenditure draining Mesa's estate that simultaneously deprived Mesa of proper care. Mrs. Barnes was also aware of Mesa's wishes to preserve her wealth and to care for her children's and grandchildren's financial welfare, such as retaining the family home for future generations, but did nothing.

38. W. Joe Bush is an attorney-at-law who represented Mesa from 2001 to her death in 2008. As far as can be known, he only represented Mesa in two things: conveying her clear and consistent wishes to the court to leave Santa Barbara and return to her own home where her son Jan Lundberg had care-givers in place; Mr. Bush never made a motion. He also seemed to represent her by offering to see that Jan Lundberg's loan to her for legal fees would be returned to him if he dropped the appeal he launched in 2003. As a friend of the Judge and Mrs. McLafferty, handling their trust matters, Mr. Bush never opposed the Judge's tendencies to deprive Mesa of her rights and to allow the rapid draining of her estate. Full legal fees were restricted by the Judge, but this gave Mr. Bush the excuse to do nothing for his client. He never challenged the conservatorship, an annual right. He completely failed to pursue her claim to owning the stock in Lundberg Survey that was taken from her by her daughter Trilby Lundberg. He gave all the stock-related materials to another attorney, Morris Getzels, over whom he (Bush) had no control and who never represented Mesa Lundberg.

39. Debby Hilton Ciambrone was Trustee of the Mesa V. Lundberg Family Trust, and was or is an employee of Bank of the West (previously SanWa Bank). Ms. Hilton (her maiden name) did nothing to ever save any of Mesa's funds being wasted on inappropriate end-stage care at extremely high costs. Ms. Hilton was fully aware of the ways Mesa was being defrauded, after meeting with Plaintiff Jan Lundberg, and that Mesa's real wealth was ownership of Lundberg Survey, but Ms. Hilton did nothing to alleviate or pursue these matters. Instead, she rubber-stamped each expenditure draining Mesa's estate that simultaneously deprived Mesa of proper care. Ms. Hilton was also aware of Mesa's wishes to preserve her wealth and to care for her children's and grandchildren's financial welfare, such as retaining the family home for future generations, but Hilton did nothing toward this.

40. David Turpin is an attorney-at-law for conservators. He was Mrs. Parks' lawyer and benefited from the substantial funds taken from Mesa for his own legal fees and for Mrs. Parks for her conservatorship fees. He was a friend of the late Judge McLafferty, judging from their conversation on a speaker phone in court when

Mr. Turpin was in the hospital with cancer. Mr. Turpin knowingly wasted Mesa's estate and saw her health deteriorate and fail to improve due to the wrongful facility Mesa was forced to dwell in. Mr. Turpin is a business partner with Mrs. Parks and worked with Mr. Faulkes to carry out Trilby Lundberg's wishes (such as to deprive Mesa of her rights and to oppose her in her wish to repay the loan Jan gave her to retain McCutcheon, Brown and Enersen). Mr. Turpin fully knew that McCutcheon, Brown and Enersen were of the opinion that Mesa had a good case for owning the stock in Lundberg Survey.

41. Michael Markovitch is an attorney-at-law who was preparing the Lundberg Family Trust when Dan Lundberg died. At Markovitch's first meeting with the family at Lundberg Survey after Dan Lundberg's death, Markovitch said it was clear that Jan Lundberg (Plaintiff) was to continue running Lundberg Survey. Yet Markovitch unaccountably and without honesty or clarity soon ceased working in Mesa's interest, coming to represent Trilby instead in her goals to take over Lundberg Survey. He knew Mesa was being elder abused and manipulated in her confusion and grief so soon after losing her husband, but instead he pretended to represent Mesa's interests, and facilitated along with Gary Faulkes (an attorney of Trilby and Lundberg Survey) and other Does the swindling of Lundberg Survey from Mesa (after Plaintiff Jan gave up his claims). Markovitch, Faulkes and Trilby produced a revised family trust instrument that did not include Mesa's rightful ownership of Lundberg Survey. Mesa was clearly ill from strokes during this time, but before that was stripped of her job at Lundberg Survey and lost her title of Chairman of the Board to Trilby. The only connections to Lundberg Survey in the Lundberg Family Trust instrument were large cash loans to Trilby which she was to pay back (and did not) that were used to buy the Lundberg Survey stock from Mesa at ridiculously low rates. Plaintiffs are informed and believe and thereon allege that Michael Markovitch may have continued to act on behalf of the Lundberg Family Trust up to the time of Mesa's death.

42. Trilby Lundberg is daughter of Mesa and sister of Jan and Darius Lundberg. Trilby is known as an elder abuser of her mother and of Dana Lundberg Sharp, whose untimely death in 2007 prompted Dana's niece to furnish a statement to the police in Santa Barbara. Trilby began her abuse and fraud of her mother after

Mesa's husband Dan Lundberg died in 1986, resulting in the swindle of Mesa Lundberg's ownership of all the stock in the family business, Lundberg Survey. Trilby was not content to sit on these ill-gotten gains, when in 1995 she perjured herself to force her mother into conservatorship. She did so again in 2001 when she trapped her mother in Santa Barbara County and deprived her of ever seeing her home again, to die penniless "by the actions of another," as reported by Chief Harvey of the Los Angeles County Coroner Department.

* * * * *

Note: the few words in brackets in the above Complaint Attachments signify clarification for Culture Change readers.

Further Reading:

"Questions for the Gasoline Guru-ess, Trilby Lundberg," Dec 12, 2006, Culture Change Letter #146: "Trilby Lundberg, guru of gasoline prices, has no idea how many miles her new Mercedes-Benz gets per gallon..." (Associated Press) MSNBC proclaimed, "Trilby Lundberg is 'Prophet of the Pumps'" (AP, by Jeff Wilson) on August 20, 2006. [*in this book*]
www.culturechange.org/cms/content/view/89/1/

Official Denial of Obvious Fraud, Abuse and Neglect

Date: November 20, 2009, via email
From: Jan Lundberg
To: Mary E. Barron [who did not answer, nor did her superior]
Deputy District Attorney
County of Santa Barbara

Dear Ms. Barron,

Your email to me of Oct. 20, 2009, below, asserts there is no
evidence of criminal abuse or neglect of my mother. To help
clarify matters, I must ask if your position hinges on semantics (the
word "kill"). You previously claimed that because there were
unanswered questions about unexplained elevated levels of
morphine in my mother, causing her death according to statements
to me by the L.A. County Coroner's office, this could not aid any
investigation. What you have left out is immense — the rest of
this unresolved case.

> (1) Did the completed SOC Form 341 state that my
> mother's life was ended "at the hands of another", or
> something to that effect? This phrase was given to me
> most clearly by the L.A. County Coroner's Chief
> Investigator, as being included in the completed form.

> (2) Did the same SOC Form 341 state that there are two
> culpable parties, Dr. Michele Armet and Charles Sciutto,
> RN, owner of Toltec Living Center? Their names and
> positions, with their blame, were specified to me by
> the L.A. County Coroner's Chief Investigator, as being in
> the completed form.

> (3) The suspected elder abuse reported by the Coroner's
> office seems to be an opportunity for you to ignore the
> crime or possibility of crime simply because of the word
> "suspected." If all your potential cases were ignored just
> because a crime is only "suspected" then you would have
> very few.

I have made additional points that are inescapable and just as serious, summarized again for you here:

(4) I had the autopsy done because elder abuse was already clear in a number of people's minds, including an officer of the court. The subsequent morphine issue was a surprise and a shock. When anyone looks at the larger case, and I repeat (for you to finally address), it cannot be denied that my mother was committed to seven years' hospice "care" without physical exercise or therapy and she was not in any way terminally ill — this without proper evaluation, as clear from the court record. Additionally, she was deliberately malnourished by not getting dental care; the Chief Investigator for the L.A. County Coroner confirmed to me that my mother had no upper teeth for chewing. In the absence of dentures and a diet of smoothies for necessary nutrition, we have plenty of evidence of abuse and fraud. With the absence of mobility and eating properly, slow homicide or murder seems obvious – or "suspected."

(5) Just because Judge McLafferty approved what my mother's foes requested (to deprive her of her clear wishes to live in her own home to save money and get far less expensive care that would be one-on-one), does not mean there's nothing to question about my mother's life and death. Is a judge never lied to? Is everyone favored in a courtroom honest, just because they are of the same affluent social circle and have their licenses? The L.A. County Coroner's Chief Investigator told me that it seemed clear that Dr. Armet and Mr. Sciutto could lose their licenses based on the Coroner office's findings. As anyone can tell after looking into this case, Armet and Sciutto are the tip of the iceberg. Have you heard any interest in a "limited hang out," whereby a couple of professionals take the heat in the matter of my mother's "murder or homicide" and "abuse" (words from the L.A. County Coroner's Chief Investigator)?

(6) My mother lived for seven years lying in her own urine

each morning in a caged bed simply because of the fraud that she was unable to do anything for herself. She is on record as having walked until 2008 not long before her demise, with less and less ability; everyone knows someone needs to use muscles to avoid atrophy. She was on a number of drugs against her will to control her vocal objections to incarceration (see court filings 2001–2002), one of which, Remeron, an anti-depressant, is known to cause suicide.

(7) Who benefits from a position that there was no elder abuse or fraud in this case? There are a number of people who profited from my mother's downfall and death. One thing that you have failed to acknowledge is that my mother's last quarter million was seized for the hospice home for her life long care, albeit approved by the judge, against my mother's wishes. As the Coroner agreed, the sooner she died, the more money the business made. A conflict of interest is clear here. Motive.

(8) If a patient or nursing home resident owns her home she cannot receive certain government medical payments. So with her house sold, against her will, more government money could flow to her handlers.

(9) My sister Trilby Lundberg master-minded and funded major decisions in this case, and all others' decisions conformed to Trilby Lundberg's every wish regarding our mother. Our niece Darla Sharp and I believe that Trilby's elder abuse of Dana Lundberg Sharp contributed to two heart attacks which killed Dana. But you have never shown any interest in that fact despite my calling it to your attention. The Santa Barbara police received Darla's letter to Trilby as evidence, and told me they were investigating, but then they supposedly did not. You, however, are able to investigate.

Others will take a much greater interest in this entire situation than you apparently have so far. There is a pattern throughout the whole nation, particularly in wealthy Santa Barbara, of elder abuse and fraud against helpless, moneyed people up against aggressors appearing as professionals and friends of the court. News reports have exposed how conservators have been an unregulated group reaping huge sums. My mother paid the ultimate price, starting with clear perjury that began the fraudulent conservatorship in 1995. I do understand that when siblings differ, there is opportunity for escalated conflict, although this does not excuse crimes of abuse and fraud.

My mother's story is not simple, I grant you. But by following the money, looking at the swindle of stock owned by my mother for the famous Lundberg Survey (ever more of a tool of major oil companies), makes it easy to see what's going on with this case dating from the late 1980s. You are one of a small number of people who know the facts but who deny what is in front of you. If you feel you do not know, what I have told you is in the court record, and witnesses are available. A far greater number have already seen this picture plain as day. There is still time for you to take action based on the truth, in the interest of the victim's family members and the public in need of protection from similar scams and crimes. You can at least give me the professional courtesy of recognizing my points above, (1) through (9) in a reply; even if one or more of these points are impossible to prove, or can be somehow refuted, the other points cannot be denied and are enough for responsible action by those holding the public trust. I await your soonest response.

Thank you in advance,

Jan Lundberg
fax and voice mail (215) 243–3144

On Oct 20, 2009, at 9:10 AM, Barron, Mary wrote:
Dear Mr. Lundberg,

I am responding to your e-mail sent yesterday. As part of my review of this matter, when I responded to you in July of this year, I had reviewed the "Soc 341" form. This form is a brief document which mandated reporters must complete when elder abuse is suspected. The key word there is suspected. Statements on the form are not proof of elder abuse. The form is merely a means to notify agencies such as law enforcement of suspected abuse. Contrary to what you have indicated previously, the form does not state that your mother was "killed at the hands of another." The contents of that form did not change my opinion reflected in my July 28, 2009 letter to you in which I indicated that there is no evidence of criminal abuse or neglect of Ms. Lundberg.

Best regards,

Mary E. Barron

MARY E. BARRON
Deputy District Attorney
County of Santa Barbara
1112 Santa Barbara Street
Santa Barbara, CA 93101
(805) 568-2433

Chapter 14

My personal relationship with the oil industry and my fight against Big Oily behavior

As a reluctant oil-industry loyalist in the distant past (1972–1988), producing my "objective" and "well-respected" surveys and analyses, I did not have to deal with climate-change concerns. Until Al Gore's 1988's U.S. Senate hearings, who did? The world's atmosphere and water seemed infinitely vast, though beset by smog and other "problems." Even though we now know so much about global warming from human activity, climate-change denialism is with us — probably until sea level rise drowns out denialists' voices. Denying climate change, it can be argued, is tantamount to something worse than Holocaust Denial. But I also have to be open-minded about the intentions of the deniers, for two long-time correspondents of Culture Change, very intelligent men, became anthropogenic climate-change deniers. So I must refrain from emotional despair and anger, thinking up a handy label for an enemy of all life. And I hate exaggerating or posing as some pure non-consumer, especially when I lived well off Exxon and Mobil *et al* for decades.

My last two clients for the oil industry were those two corporations before they merged. In 1988 I suddenly pulled the plug and did the unprecedented by turning my small firm into a nonprofit environmental group. Mobil was incredulous that I was turning down steady money. Over at Exxon my client and chief contact was owed money for work my firm had not completed, so I gave him some market reports off the shelf that satisfied the Lundberg Reports obligation to Exxon. Later as I formulated my environmental campaigns he sent me a letter whining that attacking oilmen was unfair, even though I was not attacking them as I carefully took on oil industry pollution.

These firms may have eventually been placated by my sister Trilby Lundberg's becoming a blatant climate-change denialist. Lundberg Survey is quoted frequently by the business press in the

U.S. Thus climate-change denialism is enabled by and for corporate America far more than some oily grants to the industry hacks named below.

Big Oil/Lundberg Survey Scare Tactics Against Climate Legislation

The foregoing personal background prepares the reader for the significance of the following news story published on CultureChange.org and the EnergyBulletin.net. For this report I combed through one of the only Lundberg Letters I had seen in over two decades — an ordeal, as I noted only similarities to our old "Bible of the oil industry" as it was formerly known. The font was the main resemblance. The nefarious purpose of this former gem of a family-business publishing house had become supportive of the worst plague in planetary history:

Lundberg Survey is regularly quoted across the U.S. on gasoline prices and related oil industry developments, even though the firm has dwindled from the 1970s and '80s when called "the Bible of the oil industry." It changed from an independent family business to a 100% tool for Big Oil, decrying "burdensome environmental regulations" while the corporation's head says global warming is "political hot air." So how can Lundberg Survey's study on climate legislation be accepted as credible?

The *Lundberg Letter* of July 8, 2009 is titled "Early Estimates, Under a 'Cap and Trade' Law: THE GASOLINE PRICE IMPACT OF CARBON PERMITS" (revised July 9, 2009). The summary on the firm's website and at the bottom of the gratis report says:

> If the American Clean Energy and Security Act or another "climate bill" becomes law, what would it do to the retail price of gasoline? This report finds that the price impact would be rather modest initially, maybe 30¢ gal. more than without the program. But under such a scheme the U.S. petroleum industry would wither [*sic*] as would the general economy. Barely a decade from now, U.S.-produced gasoline would have less than half the total gasoline pool.

In an editorial, the report tries to give credence to climate-change denial: "the trend is to cooling, not warming." This from the oft quoted source on oil information at CNN, Associated Press, and National Public Radio as well as countless local AP outlets. The report even suggests that if a cooling trend is discovered, "tax subsidies for coal and petroleum based energy would be required so global cooling would be prevented." The author is not aware, apparently, of the massive subsidies in place. To write these rabid sentiments shows that peak oil has not yet been examined objectively by Lundberg Survey.

Since I left the chief executive position of Lundberg Survey in 1986, all its publications and any news have been kept secret from me, understandable when I raised antitrust concerns and launched (along with my mother and brother) a legal effort to return the company to its rightful owner, Mesa Vernell Lundberg. So I have had to go by secondhand information on the former family business, until now, when I have obtained the new report on climate thanks to a web form.

The company always jealously guarded any studies, so maybe the climate-changing clients had the policy changed toward free distribution of this new propaganda.

Now we see an oil-industry financed attempt for my name — or the once highly respected firm built by my parents and me — to be used to fight climate change legislation. Unsurprisingly, given the nature of climate-change denialism and the imperative of oil pushers to boost profits, the new study contains many passages of unfounded, unprofessional nonsense.

The likes of Bjorn Lomborg and the Heritage Foundation are quoted to put fear into tinkering with the status quo of maximizing oil demand. Meanwhile, the specter of "developing nations" not paying for climate protection is trotted out as well. The *Lundberg Letter* in its heyday never stooped that low, nor would it have used George W. Bush as an authority on climate and economics, as this report does. Indeed, we attacked Reagan's policy of waging covert war on Central America — as an example of our independence and preferred politics.

Who was this new anti-climate report produced for, other than the oil industry and national business press? Well, news reports say far-right Republicans are targeting House Republicans who voted for the Waxman-Markey bill.

We at Culture Change have serious differences with weak, reformist climate legislation. It flies in the face of scientific findings making it clear that drastic cutbacks in emissions must be adopted now due to projected impacts of global temperature and sea level rise. In July 2009 we published an article on ocean acidification, a crisis irrefutably from, largely, fossil fuel burning. Need we add ongoing oil wars and traffic-death on our highways caused by car domination, to call for overall cutbacks in petroleum use?

From the Lundberg Survey Report

> GW is a bogeyman. Lore about it has been growing for at least 30 years, and to date no effort to expose it as such has gained enough traction to stop the stampede. The chances are good that one day, "global warming" will be dropped as a destructive fad of fiction, in favor of more practical threats to society. Unfortunately, so much running away from the bogeyman carries, if unintended, consequences to energy costs and supply, and would punish consumers for believing the myth.

At Culture Change we have many problems with that mindset, but also sympathy for anyone being a servant for polluting industries. We hope that more intelligent people can start to see through the "concern" the polluting elites and their henchmen have for the "common people" (consumers). Yes, consumers and more and more of them are critical to the growth scheme of capitalist economics. But to raise fears about disruptive change though a halfway reasonable reallocation of taxation is tantamount to a crime against humanity and all species. The corporate news media spew falsehoods from Trilby Lundberg and do not correct them, even when contacted and offered an alternative. One can ask legitimately if revenue from car advertising and its cousin oil advertising influences the newsroom.

If only the "U.S. petroleum industry would wither as would the general economy" were really to happen in a positive way, not just to save the climate. Because food is produced and distributed with dwindling petroleum throughout the modern world, the world's population is at risk from petrocollapse: shortage to cause complete crash and famine. If such a change away from petroleum could really be coming about from the current climate bill, in the delusional, fearful, lying minds defending the status quo, one can only imagine what a truly honest, effective climate bill would do to the hysterical mouthpieces. Since Culture Change does not put much stock into legislation when it is corrupted by compromise and lobbying, we anticipate that fundamental change will come from the people directly. It will likely be that they will be forced by a "global Katrina."

The climate-bill report from Lundberg Survey does not always read as if it were rigorously produced and edited. In places it seems slapped together as a gift to the corporation's main clients, the major oil companies. The report is still something I would recommend reading, as sections reflect some unusual insights and some valid background. Even though the best analysts at Lundberg Survey, in my opinion, were gotten rid of a long time ago, no doubt some of the databases have continued to be maintained adequately in order for the firm to stay alive. Then again, part of its *raison d'être* has been a funding mechanism for the oil industry to make sure Mesa Lundberg did not regain control so as to further support the vision of Culture Change as she did.

Study's Details

The new Lundberg Survey anti-climate study has for a cover graph a prominent "155.5"-cent per gallon gasoline price increase if a carbon permit is priced at $174 per metric ton, although lower price scenarios are shown too. However, the study admits that "carbon caps... are expected to attack coal use more than any other energy source."

The report goes on to list among its enumerated concerns at the top: "Our reasons: Price increases would hurt demand." Later in the report the claim is made that there has been "hobbled domestic capacity expansion." One must realize this study was written for the oil industry — its total spectrum including OPEC — in mind.

The claim that "about half [the population] wouldn't even pay one penny more [for gasoline], to reduce greenhouse gas emissions" is false, according to credible polls. But for Lundberg

Survey found a source that is, according to Wikipedia, a "self-described conservative think tank."

Another twisted "fact" in the *Lundberg Letter*, once known for its accuracy and credibility, is that "Refiners are warning that if greenhouse gas emissions are capped and a permit trading system is put into place, domestic capacity and associated jobs would flee overseas." This flies in the face of international programs through treaties that are designed to spread costs for carbon-emission reductions across the world, although the programs are not in place and may not work. Still, fomenting hysteria without careful research seems to be a new hallmark for the *Lundberg Letter*.

Ever defending the gasoline marketers, the study points out with some validity that "Upstream and downstream public relations would be damaged. (Any retail price hike fans the flames of vigilante blowhards, official and private, accusing anybody, from the smallest retailer to the biggest oil company, of 'gouging'.)" Whereas the Lundberg Survey of old, back in the Nixon Administration before Trilby Lundberg joined us at the business, helped the IRS roll back gouging — and proudly.

When *Lundberg Letter* states "[T]he number of deniers is growing. Cap and Trade pushers are therefore feeling a little more heat to hurry up and establish a new energy regime," we must face the possibility that Lundberg Survey is the most entrenched and respected climate-change denialist organization in U.S. corporate media and perhaps amidst the unwitting public as well.

"Refiners get 2% of the allowances [carbon permits] but must cover 44% of emissions," complained a National Petrochemical & Refiners Association spokesman interviewed for the Lundberg Survey study. This sounds delightful to Culture Change, since refineries are dispensing the most deadly products apart from greenhouse-gas emissions destroying our climate.

"[B]y 2020, domestically refined gasoline would represent just 49.10% of total U.S. gasoline supply. More than half of the pool would be handed over to its two competitors: foreign refiners and ethanol. The implications of this scenario for U.S. refiners are devastating." What the report forgot is that so much oil for the refineries is imported, therefore such gasoline from that oil is not really domestic! But the real reason there would be devastation for society (and the unmentioned ecosystem) is that there would still be too much gasoline made. In any case, since U.S. crude oil extraction peaked in 1970, more and more imports of oil and gasoline have been inevitable — but are not guaranteed.

The last section is an "Editorial," as if the preceding portion of the study was not. Phrases such as "control world climate" are used to distort science and well-intended, responsible policy. Bowing down to kiss the oil industry's behind, there are warnings shot through this study: e.g., "pressure [to pass a climate bill] (including from offshore) is building ominously."

"[C]ow-released methane is estimated to account for more greenhouse gas emissions than automobiles worldwide." We're sure Lundberg Survey is a pro-vegan company — Not. "Many leaders of the onslaught on development and consumption of fossil fuels have also embraced the concept that capitalism, the free market, is an enabler of this phenomenon that itself must be curbed, or even vanquished, to save the world." What has Trilby Lundberg been reading? The *Lundberg Letter* has now become pro-capitalism and pro-free market, which the founder, Dan Lundberg, would never allow, given his socialist and humanitarian philosophy.

The editorial distinguishes between "true believers" in "GW" and "hoaxsters" seeking to profit more sinfully than even the "power flaunting by moguls and tycoons of simple capitalism". The editorial is obviously paid for by oil industry funds that are subsidized by everyone else.

If Lundberg Survey really cared about the oil industry and the petroleum infrastructure, it would not advocate more and more consumption of gasoline. At over 130 billion gallons a year in the U.S., such unsustainable burning and spilling of this violent poison means the Earth is being drained of oil far too rapidly for any orderly scaled-down post-peak future for industrialism as we know it.

❧

Money talks; consumers listen:

> CNN (blog), November 22, 2010:
> **Gas prices up** – If news about airport hassles makes you want to drive, know that there's hassle in that option, too. Gas prices are about 23 cents higher than this time last year, clocking a national average of $2.87 per gallon for

self-serve unleaded gas, says publisher Trilby Lundberg of the Lundberg Survey.

CNN did a profile on Trilby Lundberg not long after AP's feature in 2006. As for the CNN story, I contacted the reporter by phone. I informed her that the article had some erroneous information I could correct about oil issues, and I offered myself as an independent analyst who was once CNN's favorite source on the subject of gasoline price and supply issues. Her response was, "No thanks, that was just a quick article." Hmmm....

Questions for the Gasoline Guru-ess, Trilby Lundberg

12 December 2006
Culture Change Letter #146

[Editor's note that appeared to Culture Change readers: I've been sitting on some questions on peak oil and climate change for my sister Trilby Lundberg the gasoline-price celebrity, as well as for the many reporters who cover her twice-monthly analyses. In the public interest, here are my questions and observations, after I've not heard back from her in several weeks. - JL]

MSNBC proclaimed, "Trilby Lundberg is 'Prophet of the Pumps'" (AP, by Jeff Wilson) on August 20, 2006.

After the wide syndication of the Associated Press feature on Trilby Lundberg and the firm I used to run, Lundberg Survey, there was very little reaction in websites or letters-to-the-editor. From within the family among environmentalist Lundbergs, and from some Culture Change readers, there was consternation about her comments. But I see an opportunity in stirring public debate on peak oil and climate change.

All too many news stories of relevance and significance pop up and are quickly overtaken by more news. But could it be that the newspapers and corporate websites were only too happy to print a pro-gas-guzzling feel-good story? After all, selling SUVs and lesser global warmers is the big revenue base for newspapers and most of the U.S. corporate media.

I thought it would serve the public and get Culture Change's message out if some follow-up could occur. Such as, has Lundberg Survey looked into peak oil? What is Trilby's thinking on peak oil and petrocollapse? Is it the Exxon view of perpetually rising plenty, or the stance of one of the more moderate oil companies? Does her climate-change denial have anything to do with a policy on peak oil? Perhaps more interviews with Trilby Lundberg will yield rounded journalistic inquiry as well as editorials.

Here are excerpts of the AP feature guaranteed to rankle not just most culturechange.org readers, but even the average reader of *Sierra* magazine (always replete with "green" car ads). Headlines varied, but usually contained fun phrases such as "Gas Guru" or "Princess of the Pumps":

"Trilby Lundberg, guru of gasoline prices, has no idea how many miles her new Mercedes-Benz gets per gallon..." [see photo section in this book] This is intended to convey her level of wealth, but some readers must have recoiled at unconsciousness regarding the besieged environment and the effects of U.S. oil/military policy around the world. No follow-up story appeared and challenged the all-too common uncaring attitude of gasoline extravagance until now; this reflects our not-so-conservationist times.

"'...the cost of crude oil isn't the only reason for the skyrocketing prices. Demand, taxes, weather and government regulations all figure into the complex equation...'", she said. [No factor is offered regarding war or destruction of either the environment or people's health.]

"[Trilby] condemns the 'overzealous meddling' of the Environmental Protection Agency and other federal agencies, and said government-mandated reformulation of unleaded gas and engine modifications aimed at curtailing emissions are more to blame for gas price increases than the worldwide Organization of Petroleum Exporting Countries."

Under my direction in the 1970s Lundberg Survey produced special reports for the EPA to help the agency phase the lead out of gasoline in the U.S. — was this "overzealous meddling?" Lundberg Survey, prior to Trilby's ascendance, published the "bible of the oil industry," the *Lundberg Letter*, and we never criticized environmental regulations — that was what the American Petroleum Institute (API) did. The API has always been, in addition to being statisticians and PR officials, rabid major-oil firm lobbyists that did not represent all oil-people's views or values.

"...she calls global warming a 'boogeyman' for political opportunism. Those who promote the theory are trying to create a power base and 'believe global warming is a reason to hike taxes and hike prices,' she said." It is as if Trilby is a consumer advocate for cheap gasoline, as are the Rev. Jesse Jackson and Hugo Chavez. However, those gentlemen are keenly aware of global warming.

"Lundberg balks at suggestions that she is a tool of the oil industry." [– good try, Jeff. You did successfully portray my sister's anti-environmentalism, even if the remarks embarrassed other Lundbergs.]

After the recent AP story came out, I reached the reporter, Jeff Wilson of the L.A. bureau, in hopes of interesting him in peak oil and other subjects "the other Lundberg" would discuss in a follow-up story. I was surprised when he told me he remembered me well at Lundberg Survey and that he knew about Culture Change. Since I was not in the story, it occurred to me that the previously personal-interview-shy Trilby needed a media boost and got the reporter to agree to eliminate certain topics such as me. Or, was AP just helping their affiliated newspapers sell more SUVs?

I tried to interest Jeff in a serious follow-up on oil issues, but he wasn't interested except to offer to mention me in an upcoming Los Angeles Auto Show story in November (as the guy who deliberately has no car). Disappointed in his lack of interest, I didn't have time to seek out more receptive reporters to generate a follow-up piece on peak oil and global warming. Hopefully, this response to the Gas Guru story may get a little traction if Culture Change readers send this to reporters, editors and AP offices.

Trilby Lundberg has emerged as one of the few media personalities willing to be openly anti-environment as well as denying the scientific reality of global warming. As a classical pianist, she could have a great time jamming with fellow classical pianist Condoleeza Rice, formerly of Chevron which used to be and may still be Lundberg Survey's top client. I suggest they have a go at Mason Williams' "Classical Gas," one of Trilby's favorites. According to a new study by NASA's Goddard Institute for Space Studies,

253

"Earth's temperature could be reaching its highest level in a million years, American scientists said yesterday... Comparison of the current global temperature with estimates of historical temperatures — based on a study of ocean sediment — showed the current temperature was now within 1C of the maximum temperature of the past million years." — September 26, 2006, *Guardian Unlimited*

Could the following carry more weight in the minds of too many media executives, reporters and Lundberg Survey?:

"I will be an active part of any leadership effort to prevent [global warming legislation] passing in the House." — Outgoing chairman of the House Energy and Commerce Committee, Rep. Joe Barton (R-TX), at an event hosted by the American Petroleum Institute, December 4, 2006.

This column's reply to the AP story comes when gasoline prices are not on one of their major, rapid upswings. Lundberg Survey reports national price averages twice a month, based on 7,000 stations that major oil companies want surveyed for competitive analysis and growth potential. National price trends are merely a bonus result of this purely market-oriented (non-academic) research, if the survey is conducted the way it was when we had hundreds of drivers wasting gasoline to pull into stations with clipboards. Until several years ago, Lundberg was the only data source.

It's a different "market feel" when consumers and Wall Street are disturbed by an oil or gasoline price spike that threatens to get out of control. Just because petroleum prices are a bit down now does not mean we are finished with high prices; they'll go right up due to the "fundamentals" (although the fundamentals are usually described as narrow market factors). In an essay on the Grist website on Sept. 22, 2006, I explain,

"As for when the oil crash will hit, it is possibly imminent considering geopolitical instability, extreme weather events, and the demand-driven 'industry fundamentals' of supply strain and high utilization of capacity. With falling production from key mega-oilfields, our days as oil guzzlers are numbered. It's not going to change because of some big find."

A counterbalancing interview with me might come about and inform those who were misled or appalled by the AP story. My erased history at Lundberg Survey is not anything approaching the gravity and urgency that most people feel about climate change and the coming crashing end of oil-guzzling. So here are a couple of questions a reporter might ask me, followed by my answers:

Q: Was peak oil ever discussed at Lundberg Survey prior to your leaving in 1986?

A: No; we too were lulled into believing the nation and the world were adept at discovering and extracting more and more oil, although I had always questioned the capacity of the Earth to give endless crude oil. I guess we also assumed technological advances would substitute for oil. I remember seeking out seminars on "synfuels" in the late 1970s. It was after leaving not just Lundberg Survey but upon leaving for-profit work in 1988 that I learned about peak oil, when I reviewed the book *Beyond Oil: The Threat to Food and Fuel in the Coming Decades*, for the journal *Population and Environment*.

Q: Was the family firm or the family itself rabid cheerleaders for oil and against the environmentalist cause?

A: No. Mesa Lundberg ran an organic ranch and took care of five kids while her husband worked two jobs, one of which was as the host of the very first television talk show, which ran for 7 years in Los Angeles. His programs were muckraking against pollution, monopolistic business lobbies, and other threats to public health and social justice. At the Lundberg Letter and on Nightly Business Report our message was against ethanol maximization as "agricultural strip mining" and we criticized Reaganism for its support of the Contras.

Q: Have you and Trilby always been at opposite ends of the political spectrum?

A: No, her humble car of the mid 1980s, prior to her being severed from Lundberg Survey until she returned, sported the bumper sticker "No Vietnam War in Central America." So, when I finally got to talk with her again about politics, at a mediation over our mother in 2001, and I told her I had participated in the famous anti-WTO protests in Seattle, I was surprised she made fun of it. We didn't get the chance to discuss what would happen to world trade once the cheap (subsidized) oil for transport is gone. At that point, we can all pursue something new. At one time all the Lundberg family was very close to nature, and we may return there along with the rest of the industrialized world as petrocollapse levels the playing field.

The Lundberg family saga got complicated when the members who had sailed to Europe had to move back to Los Angeles due to disagreement over the family business in 1969 — our downfall. To fast forward and make sense of the current "story" and Trilby, the AP story can use some more clarification:

"[Trilby Lundberg] worked closely with her father before his death." The opposite is closer to the truth. "I'm self-made or lucky," she said. An interesting question might be, "how did she take over Lundberg Survey without being self-made, or just 'lucky?'" The AP story went on, "Lundberg took over the market research firm in 1986 after the death of her father, Dan Lundberg." There was no mention of the two CEOs between "Oil Guru" Dan Lundberg and Trilby, namely Jan Lundberg and Dan's widow and our mother Mesa Vernell Lundberg. (I decided to leave under a settlement with our mother, the next Chairman.)

The "lucky" aspect of Trilby's career is tied to a corporate take-over, assisted by her former OPECer then-husband. This was at a time when the rightful owner (Mesa) had suffered a stroke, and when the previous CEO and co-owner, me, had left quietly for peace in the family and was delighted to "escape L.A." to go live in Virginia. This was my lucky development, as I soon abandoned working for oil companies, government and utilities in favor of fighting for the environment. *USA Today* had the headline about my activities in 1988, "Lundberg Lines Up With Nature." Without Trilby's ambitious drive, I might still be in southern California and answering to Chevron. After twenty years, and Chevron's admission of the reality of peak oil, now we can and should indeed all get together, as petroleum experts and as a society of oil addicts, putting differences and the past behind, to discuss and prepare for petrocollapse, climate change and culture change.

* * * * *

Further Reading and Links:

Lundberg Survey:
www.lundbergsurvey.com

"(How can we already be) looking at the end of the age of oil and abundant energy" - by Jan Lundberg:
gristmill.grist.org

"Popular Lundberg fuel price survey is a real gas," by Jeff Wilson of Associated Press, August 21, 2006
seattlepi.nwsource.com

Beyond Oil: The Threat to Food and Fuel in the Coming Decades, excerpt of Jan Lundberg's review in Population and Environment:
www.dieoff.com/page20.htm

"Earth's temperature is dangerously high, NASA scientists warn" – Sept. 26, 2006, *Guardian Unlimited*
www.guardian.co.uk

Essays on family cohesion and the Lundberg family saga in the cultural context of urban sprawl and materialism (Mesa Lundberg's legal case was lost on appeal, so the last link relates to non-current information):
culturechange.org/e-letter-13cont.html
culturechange.org/issue19/familycohesion.htm
culturechange.org/MVLundberg_page.html

Oil Money Was Not Only Fatal for Mesa Lundberg, It Squelched Peak Oil Awareness

Although the matter of my mother's death may appear to be off the topic of petrocollapse and culture change, there are two relevant implications that I will reveal in my family's tragedy. To do so I'll first fill in a bit more history on what became of the most trusted name in energy information.

My mother Mesa Vernell Lundberg inherited Lundberg Survey after her husband Dan Lundberg died in 1986. When I gave up my claims and exited the firm soon after, she became chairwoman of the board of directors and sole stockholder. I could live with that. But she was deprived of what she earned.

After I left the West Coast to live near D.C., my mother was in bed for months in 1988, suffering from the loss of not only her husband but her job at the family business. I had learned she lost her corporate titles and was retired. She was put out to pasture and was powerless. She could not even send me a *Lundberg Letter* or bring about any communication between me and Trilby.

Trilby's biggest career move as an entrepreneuse who took someone else's work was to go *ex parte* at Superior Court in Van Nuys to place our mother into conservatorship of the person and of the estate.

My mother was upset, and hoped that if only I would leave town, all might be peaceful again and Trilby would back off. I told my mother, "If you ask her on the phone to drop the conservatorship, and she agrees, I'll leave." It was sad to watch my mother be refused. When my brother and I saw Trilby's pleadings the next day in court, we were shocked to see that Trilby claimed to own Lundberg Survey outright. We also saw that Trilby claimed not to be "a debtor to proposed conservatee." This was false; perjury. A bogus report by an MD we had never heard of gave credence to the supposed need for conservatorship. Darius was described as someone who would not work and who was costing his mother money.

Our poor legal representation — we later got a judgment against our lawyer in a State Bar dispute — helped assure Mesa Lundberg was caught up in the wheels of the conservatorship scam. Professional conservators and a court–appointed lawyer were assigned, costing enormous amounts of money. These players had absolutely no interest in undoing the fraudulent conservatorship, the elder abuse, and the right our mother had to complete ownership of the family business. The conservators were professionals, but of an unregulated profession. Frumeh Labow and Jeff Kestenbaum took full advantage. My mother's court-appointed lawyer was Jack Rameson. All they did was collect huge court–approved fees and see their client get screwed by her "attackers" (as she called them). An agreement was struck for Darius to move out of the house. He complied, but he also got my mother out of the house where she lived in hiding with a nursing couple from the Philippines. The conservator informally blamed me for this development even though I was 3,000 miles away at the time.

In 1996 the personal aspect of conservatorship was lifted (but not fiscal or estate conservatorship), and Darius returned to the family home. My mother still had not had any serious rehabilitation from strokes, and was withdrawn in bed with the television always on. A stroke victim is typically unmotivated and often unable to remember how to do things easily done before the stroke.

Trilby ceased to visit, and I began to search for a lawyer who could handle not only elder abuse but financial fraud. I felt terribly that my daughters and other family members were being robbed of their inheritance. By 1997 a lawyer named Gary Brown had brought about "discovery" (a legal term) that showed how my mother was defrauded, and I was able to see the revised family trust that did not mention Lundberg Survey. The sweetheart deal or swindle was this: my mother forked over $75,000 cash to Trilby as a loan, which Trilby then used to buy the entire stock for approximately $250,000 at the rate of about $1,000 a month. The value was about 1/20th of the market value, which we had demonstrated to Superior Court to no avail. But we had the goods now for a separate court action. However, when Brown reported back to the court on the stock transaction — after he went silent for several weeks — he said there was nothing to report of any suspicious nature. He requested a small fee, got it, and he resumed being incommunicado. My brother and I suspected he had been paid off. We had already had that impression with other professionals whose fees were probably augmented on the side considerably. The pattern of professionals supporting Trilby's wishes was to become even more obvious years later, and remains in effect to this day.

In 1997 my older daughter and I moved my mother up to Arcata to live with us. A daily routine of professional health care was put into place that had immediate results. My mother, sans TV, had therapy of various kinds, caregivers for walking, bathing, and outings to doctors and the dentist. My mother became an active part of the household, helping to cook, edit the *Auto-Free Times* magazine I was publishing, and she could walk around alone somewhat. Although in her 70s and written off in Los Angeles, she showed she could heal as well as anyone and rejoin family life fully. She also began to face more and more that her daughter, who never called or visited, had taken all the family fortune. My mother wanted the stock back in her name.

I mortgaged my house to raise the retainer, for my mother's law firm was a most prestigious one for stock matters: McCutcheon, Brown and Enerson. The firm anticipated helping the newly rescued Lundberg Survey to be transformed via a merger and public offering on Wall Street, to an entity worth many more times than the approximately $30 million that the company was worth when I left it in 1986.

Unfortunately, my brother and I developed a strange rift as I was moving away from Arcata. Without consulting me he moved our mother to Santa Barbara in early 2000, when I was living on my boat in the Puget Sound. I returned to Arcata and moved into her house (I had sold mine), preparing for her return. But Trilby Lundberg re-entered our mother's life and again went *ex–parte* to a Santa Barbara judge to force personal conservatorship once again. The medical/legal community became a trap for my mother, who never got to see her home again. I lost patience after my mother broke her hip in 2001, and my legal motions to extricate her from Santa Barbara were denied. She went from facility to facility, at huge cost, against her will, but never getting the care she needed and deserved.

My mother was incarcerated, in effect, into the hospice-respite home, Toltec Living Center, in October of 2001. The first time I visited it was for a few hours, and I returned to the family home in Arcata. Weeks later I learned that after I left my mother she went on a hunger strike, demanding to go home. This I learned from a court filing later that was filed against her and me. I was surprised at her gutsiness, but I was dismayed that it was used as a means of silencing her. The court filing created visiting restrictions and a gag order on discussions I could have with my mother on her moving back to her own home. The court document disclosed that my mother was put on anti-depressants to "calm her down," as of the day I visited. I was painted as "riling her up," although this was the first I'd heard about any such characterization of our calm visit.

Trilby Lundberg's wishes were being followed to the letter. Trilby claimed her mother was too "demented" to decide on her residence. This went unquestioned by the judge, J. William McLafferty, even though she was never evaluated after a 2001 finding that she had mild dementia. It was from being isolated and bed-ridden for the prior year. Every single court decision, except for when I bought some time, went in my sister's favor. Every court-approved professional sided with Trilby. In the next court challenge, where I revealed that my mother's own lawyer was accused by the Conservator of riling up his own client, I made a clear cost-benefit case for my mother to receive one-on-one care in her own home. This would improve her health and save her thousands of dollars per month. I was opposed with mud slinging, as I had a Registered Nurse in my mother's guesthouse who was alleged to be my girlfriend in Trilby's declaration, and I was described as believing in fasting and thus endangering my mother. The judge ordered that the Humboldt County Court Investigator check out the home in Arcata and my live-in care plan.

The Investigator found unequivocally for my mother's clear wishes to be back in her own home. My care plan was deemed excellent. However, the report included that there had previously been some mildew that I was advised to clear up, which I did to the Investigator's satisfaction. You may ask what Mesa's lawyer was doing for her. The only thing W. Joe Bush ever did was on two occasions get her clear statement signed that she wanted to live in her own home. He also tried to get her transferred to his friend's new nursing home, unsuccessfully. Bush is a friend of the judge's wife, doing her estate work.

The judge, William McLafferty, ignored the official recommendation from Humboldt and ordered my mother's house sold in order to pay for the hospice-respite "home" (at $8,000 a month for just room and board for the dying). When I asked him why, he said "mildew and the declarations." He cut me off and started joking about his using the phrase "forthwith" to describe his order to sell the house. My mother was devastated, prompting my older daughter present to burst into tears. My mother's lawyer's partner told me "She'll live another ten years and be out of money before that."

So I appealed the case. Her law firm refused to help, due to the McLafferty's previous order to limit fees. My appeal was first handled by Lasher & Lasher, the top appellate firm in the state. They quit as soon as my second installment of $6,000 was a little slow in coming. So I filed *in pro per*, with the help of another lawyer. My filing was complete, and my story laid out with the whole history revealed. Courtroom observers told me as I left after making my verbal argument, "You won your case." However, the

judges eventually said my case was "dead on arrival" —
suspiciously repeating the phrase used by my opposition (who was
fighting my mother and me with her money that I'd made for her
at Lundberg Survey).

I found that even before the decision came down, the day before
the verbal argument in court, the house had been sold without this
being disclosed to the court. I called the court's attention to this,
but it was ignored. So, my mother and I were defeated. The
appellate court's district location was Ventura, the hometown of
Trilby Lundberg. No one ever explained clearly how my case was
flawed, except that a Superior Court judge is allowed to make any
decision he wants, especially in conservatorship cases. My claim
that he disregarded evidence, and that my mother had
Constitutional rights, fell on deaf ears. An appeal normally has to
find a procedural flaw or some other major error, for the appeal to
win. But Lasher & Lasher thought it was a good case. It is
possible they damaged my case in their withdrawal. A lawyer is
not allowed to quit over lack of funding, so the firm filed a false
statement about my being a bad client. I would have enjoyed the
luxury of taking them before the State Bar, had I the time.

My mother thus lived the next five years in an institution where
she was neglected, not fed properly, and got no exercise or therapy.
The visitation rules were never lifted, although her daughter
violated them any time she took our mother to Ventura. My then-
lawyer John Shellabarger advised me that my mother was
undergoing elder abuse. She never complained or made demands
or any fuss, consistent with her character of a lifetime. She was
also under the influence of various drugs, including the dangerous
antidepressant Remeron. She spoke softly and slowly, but was not
demented. Her life became centered around reading novels and
listening to CDs I gave her. Visits from family and friends were
not frequent. My visits a few times a year from northern California
were not easy for me financially, coming to Santa Barbara which is
car oriented and expensive.

My mother finally died on September 15, 2008. Her life was
clearly shortened by lack of care and abuse, so I had an autopsy
done. It showed she could not have been chewing any food, and I
believe her muscle tone would have revealed neglect too. I was
shocked along with my brother to learn from the L.A. County
Coroner that our mother was killed "at the hands of another" via

morphine — when she had no reason to be on the drug, according to forensic and medical record evidence — under "suspected elder abuse." The "culpable" parties were named as Dr. Michele Armet and Charles Sciutto, RN and owner of Toltec Living Center, respectively. These two were under the control of the Conservator Mary Lou Parks, RN, who proved to be a friend of Trilby. Parks had retired, but told the court she would keep just one client: Mesa Lundberg. A co-conservator, Mary Carlander, entered the picture and I had to assume she was part of the set up to separate my mother from her money and most of her family. Indeed, even before my mother's death Carlander did not return calls or emails to me, and she was responsible for my mother's disappeared personal items upon the freeing up of the $8,000 a month bed.

The Damning Autopsy

Mesa Lundberg was killed, and it was oil money that did it, with direct links to major oil company interests. How exactly did this occur? In two ways: Her own money, income from Lundberg Survey in the service of the major oil companies, was used against her. More directly was the use of ongoing oil-company funding by her daughter to attack and restrict Mesa Lundberg and deny her rights and property.

My mother said many times, no doubt as a "demented" person would, that her problem was money. She knew she was targeted for it by her "attackers." She also said "The judge was bought off." I have no evidence of this, and neither did my mother who was a retired attorney and avid reader of mysteries until she died.

The money my mother was saddled with was not her rightful ownership of Lundberg Survey, but what she had salted away from the firm before her husband died, and what she had coming to her in life insurance after his death. As the person in charge of clients and government contracts before I took over all aspects of the business, I made my mother a small fortune apart from the value of the stock.

My mother spent the last quarter of her 88 years directly under elder abuse (financial and indirect only from 1997-1999). She ultimately was murdered, in the unofficial interpretation of the Chief Investigator of the Los Angeles County Coroner's office. He used the words "murder" and "homicide" in a telephone conversation with me, based on a report "not for public disclosure" that he sent only to law enforcement. At this writing I have not been able to obtain it via the Freedom of Information Act, but he sent me a letter acknowledging this report's existence as an attachment to the autopsy report. He also confirmed the form's contents in a visit I made to his office.

My mother was clearly too dangerous to be left alive. Perhaps it's not that she was the threat, but the victim in a scenario whereby I was a threat as long as she was alive. As her close son, who works against the oil industry and might be in a position of influence over Lundberg Survey if it could be wrested back into Mesa Lundberg's possession, she and I had to be separated and neutralized once and for all.

A second reason for my mother's sped up demise is her having been fleeced for her last quarter million dollars by the hospice-respite homeowners: For the right to live on the premises for the rest of her life, she parted with all her money. This was against her wishes, but her lawyer did not fight it, and the judge could see no possible conflict of interest among the fine professionals regularly profiting before his bench.

Judge McLafferty died on January 15, 2009. An obituary contained in the headline "Respected." Those whose rights were trampled and families disintegrated did not agree. The Santa Barbara *Independent*, which had never reported on Mesa Lundberg's plight, reported in the obituary "McLafferty also presided over the probate and conservatorship calendar, a prickly case load involving the mental competence of senior citizens and the disposition of their wealth by those assigned to care for them. Last year, there were a spate of controversies surrounding conservatorship cases, and McLafferty became the subject of criticism from a group claiming that the court was appointing conservators when it needn't and shouldn't." Having served the insurance industry before deciding cases on the elderly, he did not seem to know that in-home care is superior when available. A recall attempt failed, but had I known of it I could have assisted.

My mother would surely have loved to outlive him in order to see him forever gone and lessen her hell. He was a monster in the eyes of much of my family. A Republican who must have known he was acting against my activities against the oil industry and my mother's support of same, McLafferty certainly didn't live up to the conservative "family values" label when he all but destroyed Mesa Lundberg. He never knew her or was aware that her intellectual capacity was above his. She appreciated such writings as Culture Change essays until her death, while McLafferty probably would have tripped over the first paragraph of anything I published. His absence does not necessarily reduce the scandalous conspiracies against the elderly in Santa Barbara, for McLafferty was just a tool whether he knew it or not. The only question is how close he was to the perpetrators.

History was altered when Trilby Lundberg took Lundberg Survey and got her mother out of the way

What does this tragic story have to do with petrocollapse and culture change? Mesa Lundberg's treatment and killing could not have happened in a culture in which oil money and media manipulation don't rule the roost. Firstly: When greed and material security are top values and common in society, not to be questioned, and protected by the laws of property, there will be abuses to play the system. Secondly, the materialistic culture's influence on a child is stronger than parental influence, in many cases. Thirdly, the oil industry and being a corporate CEO carry weight with judges and other authorities, such that this can be used for selfish ends. As time has gone on, the news media — owned by fewer and fewer huge conglomerates — have become less and less interested in the dark side of Lundberg Survey (whether about its climate-change denialism or the "High Octane Family Feud" that the *Washington Post* saw fit to report on in 1987).

In terms of petrocollapse, one could say no single individual could affect peak oil or the fate of the oil industry and our petroleum-dependent society. That would be true. But if Mesa Lundberg could have prevailed in regaining her stock, Lundberg Survey would have regained its integrity. If the company had been independent beyond its 1970s-mid '80s heyday, the nation could possibly have been steered in a significantly different, positive direction. After all, the *Lundberg Letter* was the "bible of the oil industry" in the public's mind, and our capital was in our acknowledge credibility. The dollars didn't matter. We could not be bought.

That was squandered or cashed in the day Trilby and her OPECer husband took over. His role was in the background, as he dominated in personality. They divorced a few years later. It seems reasonable to me that the most trusted, popular energy newsletter/data source in the nation, the *Lundberg Letter*, could have instead proceeded to promote conservation, alternative energy, non-militaristic energy policy, and awareness about peak oil — while somehow maintaining the major oil company client base. If not, with our name and reputation, we could have served more intensively other sectors that already followed us. After all, we had already accurately predicted the Second Oil Shock in 1979, and we knew better than anyone how the oil supply and price are impacted by geopolitical or other events.

For Mesa Lundberg to suffer and die the way she did, with the complicity of powerful figures and corporate entities, helped bring on and guarantee the worst possible outcome for U.S. petroleum dependence. Now the nation is in a huge recession that can have no recovery of growth stemming from cheap, abundant oil based on high net energy. We as a nation shot our wad on cheap thrills: the benefits of oil. In so doing the nation's vaunted social values of family and community have been shredded. (See prior chapter for correspondence between me and the deputy District Attorney of Santa Barbara.)

There may be culprits, but I don't take their deeds against me and my family completely personally. For,

> "*Society prepares the crime and the guilty person is only the instrument.*" (Adolphe Quetelet, 1835, a Belgian statistician)

Part 2

Mainly the Message

This section of my autobiography consists of essays and reports, some already published on wwww.CultureChange.org, that are more about me than objective discussions about issues of energy and society.

Chapter 15

Radical Truth Means Liberation Can Feel Strange

The line of work I've been in since 1988, when I cut myself off from the corporate teat, has been in comparison "interesting" — a term that while ironic enough doesn't capture the essence or magnitude of my post-oil industry world. The unanticipated rewards have been of a different texture and color than the material results I had previously pursued. The different road traveled sets one apart. Activists and artists know this. For example, when you may ask someone "How's biz?" this is a simple question for someone selling shoes or performing massages. Success is quantifiable, as the person has been busy being a good worker and accumulating money. However, an activist, especially one who doesn't enjoy a well-paid day job, has a hard time answering the question.

For me to be asked "How's biz?" requires me to admit failure — in saving the world from fossil fuels, for example. So my success is in failing to the worst degree per amount of effort. After all, if some of the more visionary activists for fundamental change had been successful by now, perhaps the question "How's biz?" would hardly ever be asked. But in the market economy, activism in the U.S. has become more results-oriented and money-dependent, so the program-rich reformist environmental group, for example, can say "Business is great! We have a bigger budget and reached more people than ever!" But all the groups have to admit that the dire news on climate change feeds our fire perversely by making our message more urgent. When we're glad for more bad news, we need to check into an activist burnout therapy program, or retire.

We hope for cutting edge activism that has to persevere even if it means running on fumes. Upholding that tradition, the following three thought progressions comprise my current critique in a nutshell. With personal background they introduce my perspective of the oil industry's direct affect on me and my family. The first section, on money, is a personal application to a hard-learned principle:

Money or No Money, It's a Weird Life!

Take it from someone who has been in both worlds, of privilege and simple living. There is no lasting satisfaction or attainment of enlightenment when one is "blessed" by material wealth, even if one is in good health. It seems to work this way: as many of us sense disturbance and dissatisfaction on the physical, social and spiritual levels, we concentrate on getting more wealth so as to insulate ourselves and "buy freedom." Another approach to righting this disturbance and dissatisfaction can be the attempt to attain wellbeing through perfecting our health or physical discipline — highly structured physical yoga, for example. Similarly, deep yearnings or agitation from desiring a better way of living — somewhere else, with someone else — can become a fixation with destructive outcomes if a positive change is not made ethically and for the "soul."

The *Bhagavad-Gita* provides guidance: "Be not affected by success or failure. This equipoise is called Yoga."

In L.A. in the 1970s though the mid '80s I had an enviable life: expensive car, fine home, club memberships, beautiful wife (twice), wonderful daughter (twice), professional pride and some prestige, travel, good health, friends, a solid family (so it seemed) — not necessarily in that order. Perhaps that sequencing off the top of my head reflects a prioritization that I figured readers could relate to. Some things not on the list were on the back burner, way back: music and activism.

These past "advantages" in life, what hundreds of millions of people would have called luxurious and fulfilling, were built on sand. I was living the compromise of big-city conditions that weren't very healthful. It went without saying that one always locked the doors, even in daytime. Society's problems were never solved; rather, they were replaced or added to. After the tumultuous 1960s, spectacles such as Watergate seemed to suggest major political changes following the shake up of culture; this wasn't the case. Environmental protection seemed new and on the way toward complete resolution. The Indochina war was ending, or over, so it was time to worry about one's self: the Me Generation. I did a good job of it, and thought I didn't think I was letting go of my values or my social conscience.

269

I realized that something was wrong with my life as I muddled through it, wanting more of this or that. A good social life did not cut it. And I would catch colds or the flu a too often for a health nut. My fasts would blow them away, but without a change in lifestyle, and despite organic food, in six months I'd come down with something again. (I eventually gave up fasting for several years.) I was dissatisfied with my appetites and perceived needs. Was I getting enough sex? Didn't the world owe me a Mercedes? And why did our oil analysis firm lag in not having an office in Washington, D.C.? This was normal, ambitious stuff. I eventually came to understand that it was indicative of not being close enough to nature and not having a village-culture to make me feel grounded and secure. But as a young man in L.A. I wasn't yet "sold" on my better ideals enough to actually take action and make changes. So I felt trapped and wanted my one life to be about adventure.

I stumbled upon a distraction as I sought peace and pleasure in pursuing Japanese culture. I didn't particularly want to go to Japan, knowing no one but a few energy industry types as acquaintances. I simply loved the music, the food, the philosophies, the massages, the furniture, and the escape these offered from my commuting/corporate existence. Nothing wrong in learning about another culture, but I should have looked harder at why I had this need for daily release and monetary expenditure (sushi and shiatsu aren't cheap). My circumstances were a bit unusual, keeping me in L.A. and limiting my travel to the U.S. pretty much. What bound me was being in a family business where I was being groomed for the top. When I was getting near the top and when I got there, before everything changed in 1986, I did feel more at ease, with purpose. But the feeling was mostly from appreciating fatherhood.

So what's weird about any of this? "$uccess" in "$ociety" had appeal for me, but as a substitute for what I really wanted and needed. As recounted in Part One, my dream as I finished high school was to be far from L.A., back to my previous lifestyle of sailing to other countries, living in pleasant foreign cities, speaking other languages, or just grooving on a commune with fellow hipsters close to the land — even in California. I gave up my academic career at U.C. campuses for the family business, which I had to admit taught me more disciplines faster than any academic environment could.

But I felt empty and frustrated. My lowest point was after being abused by the (formerly) Immigration and Naturalization "Service" when I tried to keep my girlfriend in the U.S. by marrying her in 1975. I had some kind of nervous breakdown, and around that time I happened to have been heavy into Zen Buddhism. This did not help me and even confused me. I was only 23, but I thought I was a total adult and man of the world. I was actually scared, but I never knew if it was just about an iffy marriage or reality in general. My normally whiz–bang work performance started to suffer as if I were impotent. Instead of really solving my problems by changing my life, I managed to stabilize and get back to living a safe, not so thrilling routine. I didn't do it for the money; I just needed moorings.

From birth up through my mid thirties, I had never a monetary worry. The road ahead always looked promising on various levels — as long as I didn't notice the increasing weirdness of a society in crisis get to me. What you don't know doesn't hurt you, to an extent, so it may have helped that I didn't know much about living on the edge without money and without the family support that I thought would exist forever. For being stripped of advantages opens up the window wide to see the world as it really is. Fortunately, in learning to understand the weirdness, the wisdom and insight, and gaining new, close friendships, this results in a more grounded understanding of reality through cultural and ecological awareness.

Just as one learns more outside school or after one's schooling, I was to find that my biggest, richest education was outside and after the family business and the privileged life I gave up upon abandoning my spot in L.A.'s Establishment. It has been this post-oil-industry, post–affluence education that I've passed on to others through hundreds of Culture Change essays and reports I've authored. It could only happen through being reborn in 1988 as an adventurer, an idealist, and big-ego'd nonprofit organizer.

One of the many unanticipated changes in my post-affluent personality or attitude regarding money is that for me, a small amount of it can seem like a lot. I do stretch it, sometimes quite well. Simple living can be another term for being broke and having to struggle, but not in all ways. In the dance of non-materialist living one must keep one ear listening for the sudden change in tempo or entire song, and be ready to deal with the demands of the world of money. Either come up with a large amount fast, or step aside and perhaps suffer.

Before learned to be content with small amounts of money I came to appreciate what much of the growing homeless population seems to have learned. They were folk who, I observed, were by and large too gentle or honest for conforming to the dog-eat-dog world of competition. No doubt many are disturbed and sometimes violent. But it's very worthwhile to speak with homeless people frequently. I learned after I left the for–profit world that a good many homeless people really have "The System's number" — they know how economic stratification and the laws of property really run the show, with corruption and brutality all too often. They know inequality is built in though sanctifying greed and "$uccess." I was quite impressed with those who enjoyed being houseless rather than homeless, as they lived with little money but with some key social acceptance. Many enjoyed love, friendship, free time, pursuit of music, and more. These folks' enviable (to me) lifestyles were possible mostly through giving themselves to a cause and their community: helping other poor people or defending healthy nature as in ancient redwood forests.

That's a big part of my post-corporate, post-marriages education. I actually had to go do it to learn it: be broke and much more free. I hated the "four-walled prison" of a house. This was not just because of the unreal conveniences of being able to waste unlimited water and electric power, being cut off from the elements, living like a master in a petty castle. My unhappy condition emanated from the surrounding "community," or so I felt. I was caught in the U.S. "box lifestyle" enough to throw it aside. In its full form it centers around leaving the house day after day by getting into a car (through a garage ideally) to get to a job — something fairly meaningless in terms of directly meeting basic needs for food, shelter, heat and clothing. To me the houses seemed more and more like little bastions of isolation for consuming, where neighbors didn't know each other. The big, crowded, noisy roads set our sense of place, with little nature or interaction with others outside one's home. Friends can visit, or be visited, but in the present modern culture they're more of a break in the routine, no matter if we treasure them.

I did have three kinds of help in achieving my goal of living on little money and on my wits. First, with the elder abuse of my mother and the legal mess that demanded my attention, I was choosing to work on the family crisis instead of my own material or financial state.

Second, in terms of "outside help": with the message of our nonprofit group being too radical to join the thin gravy train of Wall Street foundation money for safe "activism," we walked away from the easier money.

Adding to those two kinds of help, the hits Fossil Fuels Policy Action took with the take-over attempts by close colleagues, in 1992, 1994, and 1997, were instructive. These co-workers went from trusted friends to sudden opponents of my leadership, with no holds barred. They didn't mind deliberately fouling up operations and relationships with funders. My diplomatic and easy demeanor, and being a dreamer, had given the impression that I was a push-over. I must have appeared that I couldn't be devastatingly decisive in defending what I'd founded. These disturbed individuals' take-over attempts during involvement in a cause, and having hip, "alternative values," brought on shocking (to me) corporate-suites shenanigans. My friends-turned-instant-opponents, when they thought they could prevail, exemplified the very culture we were supposed to be changing. More than money it was power they sought.

Eventually, these three factors in sapping the potential for my progress in my work served as fine examples of why the present culture has to change fundamentally — hence Culture Change, to succeed our land–use/energy/transportation focus.

I wasn't always poor in my post-corporate life; indeed in the years since leaving L.A. in 1986 I came to own another house and another sailboat (to replace the fancier house and $100,000 boat I gave up in 1987 when I started looking for a new career). I managed to show one of my daughters India in 1996 (with her money that I had made for my mother who gave it to my daughter). She blossomed into a terrifically popular tree-sitter and lock-down civil-disobedience artist when she wasn't belting out eco-tunes. Our lives had richness in the way of wonderful friends, experiences in nature, making our own music and performing it, and becoming celebrated activists.

But all was not well for the whole family, as we were to learn in a few years. And it was only money to blame.

273

I had started to notice things that I hadn't in my previous life when I was sucking the corporate and government teat. I had to become more observant and responsive to my changing situation. My growing awareness was sometimes surprising, as my old notions were upset and I had to let them go. For example, on more than one occasion when a sizable grant came in, I noticed I felt no different or any better than prior to receiving the grant. Part of what I felt was the obligation to put my abilities to work once again on the financial plane, usually to put out another edition of the *Auto-Free Times*. Spending money, not saving it, was the only way to get things done and move ahead; it was always a risk or a dream: one more push for a triumph and to make a difference. After years of being the only peak-oil group, fighting car culture, something had to give: one way was in *the mind*. So after a while the efforts seemed questionable, or the seeds we were planting were not sprouting in great enough number or vigorously enough.

I was somewhat horrified to realize after a few years of nonprofit work that I had not left the dominant culture behind. My routine was still all about office work, money, paperwork, computers, deadlines, using up resources, interpersonal relations involving hierarchy (although, less), and stress. It would have been more tolerable if the goal of getting society off fossil fuels was getting closer. Or if more volunteers showed up and make it more fun. Instead, it was a moderately paced merry-go-round of a small staff's struggling to afford to publish and publicize our work, sifting through the often unappreciated initiatives of others that could distract us. This was before email. What changed with email was the quickened pace, and the quantity of material which went up exponentially — if one was inclined to look at so much.

With climate change seen as accelerating, and peak oil coming on, one might wonder — naïvely, as an activist should — "Are we arriving at the point we anticipated, with our way clear to make changes individually and as a society?" No. Instead, even with the financial meltdown and this post-peak Great Recession (as I write this in late 2010), we are just as hooked on petroleum and money. We can state that little is changing so far. A few bright spots to demonstrate sustainable living, such as the spread of permaculture, the fledgling Sail Transport Network, a respectable bike culture, etc., give us hope and keep us at this vital work. But even these pursuits in opposition to the dominant paradigm require money.

Just try sustaining any project on no money; it has gotten next to impossible to do it on a volunteer basis since the more leisurely, more affluent 1970s. Since that decade per-capita real income has steadily declined and working hours have risen steadily for the average worker.

When one gets a "healthy sum of money," even to put it to a great, selfless use, there is no exit from Western Civilization. One can leave these United Paved Precincts of America, but there's nowhere to run to and hide in a globalized, climate-fucked, nuclear-threatened world.

This is spoken by someone not worrying about his next meal, although sometimes I have actually had to deal with that. Whether I'm in that mode or am able to make a relatively grand gesture involving money and property, I can't forget that the commercial culture still runs things — into the ground. The separateness and alienation of people in this culture is manifested everywhere they walk (or, worse, drive). As alarming as their damage to the ecosphere is, it is their sheep-like trance of consuming, in slavery to a fatally flawed system that promises results only in terms of money, that makes one want to give up or leave (but to where?).

In a world dominated by the rich and their money, massive armaments, and manipulation of the media — while the natural world is systematically removed and disintegrates — it is only harder to live well and stay alive when one has little wealth. Nothing new in that observation, although many are still in that proverbial river in Egypt (denial).

Instead of risking radical change, the mainstream person's only remedy seems to be striving for more dollars in the pocket or bank. One's financial advantage does not change the state of pained existence on a finite world surrounded by a culture valuing materialism and fixed on unending expansion — as my own experience makes clear, I hope.

From William Catton's 1995 paper "The Problem of Denial":

> [T]he classic assertion by Paul Sears [in 1964] [is] that ecology "if taken seriously as an instrument for the long-run welfare of mankind, would ... endanger the assumptions and practices accepted by modern societies..." Ecological understanding of nature's limits and man's place in nature contradicts deeply entrenched cultural

expectations of endless material progress. Garrett Hardin (1985) contended three decades later, ecology "demands that our current political, social, economic, and moral order be stood on its head." (Catton authored the 1980 book *Overshoot: The Ecological Basis of Revolutionary Change*)

I'm not able to totally capture and portray the weirdness of daily living, rich or poor, that pervades these United Paved Precincts of America. If I did it as starkly as it deserves, it might not be "accessible" to the public. Artists and novelists can succeed at it for their devoted fans. On an emotional level, which is often a healthier way to communicate than the constant rational analysis in an irrational, ecocidal culture, one could scream poetically or paint a picture of incomprehensible chaos. This never reaches the multitudes. Music, however, is an outlet for expression that even when wild, crazy and weird finds occasional mass acceptance — providing the corporate record and radio outlets don't completely prevent people from tasting the non-conventional. Art of whatever kind, as a personal expression and for getting active in one's own interests (including the Earth's), is a solid antidote for the pressures of money and modern stress.

I asked my friend Albert Bates, author of such books as *Post-Petroleum Survival Guide and Cookbook*, how he can manage to find peace when he knows so very much about the deterioration of Earth's climate. He answered that he takes a break to do something artistic with his hands. This physical, right-brain activity is essential for all of us, as it also was back in the comparatively innocent days up through the 1970s when the world seemed larger and less fragile.

What would you rather have if you were in a jam and all alone: a huge pile of cash or ten people that love you? Which would be the weird? Which would reflect your true, subconscious dreams? In the end will you be glad of your art and adventure, or about having paid all your bills on time for every imaginable comfort?

The Curse of the Petroleum Blessing

The advancement of humanity has become an illusion based on technical achievements and expansion — both of population and encroachment into all habitats. What about progress of the neglected spiritual aspect of our living? As long as people buy the myths of civilization's progress and humans' permanent hierarchy in evolution, the proliferation of dazzling technical developments blinds us to honoring and enjoying the Earth in the here and now.

Modern society has patted itself on the back for finding solutions to technical problems, but often these developments only saved some labor in order to build up a surplus for the elite's growing wealth. What have been called problems have often been natural limits on control and expansion. What society has not done is openly admit that the quest for "solutions" and control have backfired and destroyed much of the natural world. So a self-kick in the ass is far more appropriate than a pat on the back.

The ingenuity of science has been exaggerated with religious fervor, while the true basis for "progress" has been cheap non-renewable energy and abundant, high-energy materials. The clever exploitation of "resources" has raged while the Earth's material and biological basis has steadily dwindled and degraded. Modern humanity has maximized exploitation while using technology to undermine the survival of not just countless life forms but most life forms. For species-extinction and the rising suffering of our own species to go on unchecked, mainly through the elite's system of socioeconomic control, people surely have failed to use their innate intelligence and wisdom.

The wonders of petroleum in its many forms and uses have mesmerized most people into believing our species and the dominant culture are successful beyond words. I am writing this on an ingenious and dazzling laptop computer whose material content is petroleum-plastic and a large measure of other toxics such as heavy metals. The electric power grid and radiation waves for communication are also "essential" to my habit and the many gadgets used by millions of people (before dumping the used-up junk into the landfill or the ocean, as recycling is problematical). The constant "improvement" of technology and the prospect of recycling and other "green" practices continue to blind us to what we are doing to ourselves and the ecosystem.

As hopeless as all this sounds so far, there are ways of living that are far better for health and happiness. These ways happen to offer a way out of our ecocidal predicament. But as long as big money is made on maintaining the status quo, the alternative to extinction is pushed aside. Those who love freedom and have respect for all life forms have always rejected the bogus arguments of domination and "progress" while striving to live independently in a true community context. But we have to admit those new smart phones are dazzlers. "I think I need one too!"

My Petrochemical Plastic Misadventures

Each year the world creates 205 million additional tons of plastic, and U.S. consumers throw away a billion plastic bags. A bag typically differs molecularly ever so slightly from its source, usually natural gas (a form of petroleum). The plastic plague is turning out to be a global mistake on the order of nuclear waste, as it is for the most part here "forever." Attacking this figurative mountain, I have helped cities ban or place fees on shopping bags given out at supermarkets, with mixed success. But the trend is hopeful. The seemingly pointless gesture of going after one kind of plastic does allow one to raise publicly the related issues of petroleum and our materialist culture. Inspired by my friend Captain Charles Moore, who discovered the North Pacific Gyre's Garbage Patch, I took steps to get plastic out of my life and out of the environment as well. From about 2004 – 2007 I sometimes felt like I took Mr. Robinson's advice in the film The Graduate: "Plastics!"

The most insidious petroleum blessing of all, and perhaps of the whole modern techno-realm, is probably the plastic plague. Some people don't mind plastic at all, and wouldn't do without it. They consistently tear extra plastic bags off the grocery store spools for their bananas and onions, oblivious to the petroleum consumed. Sometimes I get the nerve to point out to a shopper that those kinds of foods have non-toxic wrappers already installed by nature.

Best to stay mindlessly addicted to plastics, unless one enjoys what awareness brings: a worsening nightmare from which there is no escape! Maybe I feel better from being a self–appointed crusader against poison wastes, as I share daily with others my discoveries and regrets. Being rational about plastics is, paradoxically, to be irrational about our present society — as I cling to the hope of starting a trend. And there's always safety in numbers. Until then, I've been called "obsessed" and insensitive to food workers' forced duties.

Although awareness is rising, folks have a long way to go to arrive at my level of rational irrationality. Perfectly intelligent and educated food retailers usually have no idea they are selling endocrine disrupters in the form of plastics, for example with packaging. As the checker is about to tilt my food or drink container for scanning, I take the opportunity to tell them what the seal is made of inside bottle and jar caps: bisphenol-A, a wonder-plastic that also lines food cans and appears in lots of other products. I am listened to politely, mostly for reasons of "customer relations." About one in a hundred checkers want more information. What about their ethics and pride in knowing what one is selling? Are birth defects, obesity, diabetes and cancer from such plastics just part of our interesting, modern world that needs to be milked by consumers for maximum self-gratification?

Ironically, avoiding plastic poisons can be hazardous. Once I was taking a swig from a big glass bottle of water. The cap was partially of bisphenol-A, so I was pouring the water into my mouth without touching the top of the bottle to my lips. I almost chipped a tooth because the bottle was big and heavy. If I had done what most people do, allowing the bottle to partially rest on my puckered lips, sucking the endocrine disruptor-plastic residue, I would have been safer. Or if I were swigging from a plastic bottle, *no problema.*

In a more serious mishap, I was in a recently remodeled bathroom whose materials were almost all plastic. Months after the completion of the remodeling, the plastic off-gassing was still bad smelling. So I propped a window open with a mop stick. All was well as I sat on the library throne until the window came crashing down onto my occipital bone, as the mop stick slowly slipped and give way. I got a good lump on my head but no broken skin. The frame of the window had hit me instead of the glass, but it turns out it was imitation plastic glass for the windowpane. The restroom's cheap construction may not last like a good wooden and metal bathroom will, but the plastic pollution materials may last many centuries, probably in a landfill. We are such a clever, modern culture! Besides inhaling the poisons in such a bathroom, what about the plastic piping carrying very hot water that would likely pick up toxins to go into our skin? I can do without hot water most of the time, but one can't resist the handy fossil-fueled hot water for a shower. I tried to see if I could save energy by taking cold baths instead of hot or warm ones. That was a one-time experiment!

They say life is hazardous, but we prefer it to the alternative of not living. Is avoiding plastic too inconvenient or even hazardous to do something other than go with the flow? Is washing our hair without the plasticized hot water going to leave unsightly soap residue on our bodies and hair, and is a cold shower in winter anything that will ever happen voluntarily?

I think about plastic a lot, I admit. It did not start, as one might assume, when I saw the mind-blowing documentary Our Synthetic Sea. Back in the early 1970s I "invented" a disease: plastic transfer syndrome, which I brought up when I saw anyone sucking or chewing a plastic pen — if you can taste the chemicals they have to be bad for you. I also was removing the thin portion of any cheese next to the plastic wrapping. Decades later I discovered that I was right on the money all along with imagining plastic transfer syndrome. Even before that, I wrote a song for my daughter we sang and recorded, Green Is the Shelter, with the line "Plastic disaster is creeping on me..." (1996)

Now that I live on a sailboat that's not a traditional wooden design, and is instead made of fiberglass, plywood and sporting Dacron sails, I am more and more disturbed by plastic around me and what I see happening to the river and the sea. This doesn't stop me from doing whatever I have to for repairs and maintenance, involving more plastic and any petroleum-fueled transport for any parts I obtain.

I lost a large vinyl mattress/cushion in a sudden windstorm, and I hope someone salvaged it as it made its way down river. The guilt I have for doing that to the environment is immense. But I reflected, what if I had used it for its maximum "life," or what if someone found it and did the same? In the end there'd still be a mini-disaster just from the thing's having been manufactured.

I stay at a dock these days that has plastic/synthetic-wood composition, with wooden logs and Styrofoam floats underneath for buoyancy. My prior marina was much more Styrofoam dependent, and I always saw bits of the plastic floating. It soaks up the ambient water's pollutants and then is eaten by creatures. The poisons go up the food chain. My next dock will be the sea floor, perhaps, as I drop anchor — connected to a polyester rope. Hemp ropes may have to await both legalization and petrocollapse.

My history is soaked in petroleum, the industry for which supported my global adventures as a sailor on the high seas as I was growing up. I continued on this path until quitting my oil-industry analysis career in 1988. Along the way, I generated my share of plastic waste, and saw my family poisoned by pesticides of petroleum while living on our ketch in the Caribbean Sea.

Back to the present, here I am tapping plastic keys while complaining about plastic. One solution: let's call the whole thing off. If enough of us reject plastic and everything that goes with it, we'll feel better and lead others to a more liberated if less convenient lifestyle. As long as petroleum is plentiful and there's a consumer economy, little will change socioeconomically. So join me in bringing down this toxic system of exploitation of the Earth, by boycotting petroleum — plastic, as one manifestation. This will simultaneously keep your trading as local as possible. After all, you probably don't have a petroleum refinery nearby. If you do, despite the growing appeal of localness, see what you can do to shut it down — imagine enough demand-destruction causing the petroleum industry and our plastic culture to implode. As John Lennon would have come to sing, "Imagine there's no plastic."

Here's to wooden toys, natural rubber, hemp sails and rope, and bicycles made largely of bamboo!

Chapter 16

Discovering Human Closeness: Outside the U.S.

26 May 2010

Thanks to a Bolivian merchant's error of inserting an extra digit in a
bankcard charge, delaying my departure back to the Northern Hemisphere,
my history was changed. In the three extra days in the country, where I
needed to rest up after an altitude related illness, I reached a surprising
level of involvement in the community where I happen to have gotten
stuck. This was my journal entry:

The word "culture" does not suffice when experiencing the eye-opening revelations of days lived amongst aware people. I am
fortunate to be doing this now in Bolivia. The differences between
modern and traditional peoples are far deeper than facile analysis
or sociological comparisons. To understand fully is to feel and live
the alternative, the "real reality."

After one month in this richly endowed, mostly indigenous
country, I feel fortunate to reach quantum leaps of insight after a
requisite time for initiation and becoming familiar. What a
difference a few more days makes.

Having sailed to dozens of countries as a boy, I have always
known that my own peculiarly insular and often arrogant country,
the U.S., lacks the social cohesion of places that are more
community based and closer to nature.

Perhaps, as author Chellis Glendinning observes, U.S.Anians
are a sick people, increasingly unhealthy for reasons of toxicity,
radiation, and fast paced modern living. This trend helps explain
the high incidence of stress and social posing that seems to
dominate in the U.S.

For example, a "bruja" or sorceress in Bolivia, in her supportive
circle, is able to be totally down to Earth, kind, and passionate.
Loved or revered by the average person, not seen as really
different. In the U.S. one who gravitates toward similar interests
is separated by choice from the mainstream and can appear as a nut
case (deservedly or not). Our Bolivian bruja has practical wisdom,
such as her observation that "in the North life is about work, work,

work and the South it's fiesta, fiesta, fiesta." This is probably in her book, *Yo, Bruja.*

How well is one able to enjoy the amount of friendship, family ties, work, money, art, recreation, etc. that is available? Sustainability and absence of militarism count too. The U.S. citizen, particularly one who is able to pay his or her bills, has much pride on all these counts, regardless of objective reality. This is partly because of lack of knowledge about the rest of the world (usually depicted as more dangerous and deprived). Overwork and poor health in the U.S. have been on the rise for decades, coinciding with top-dog overcompensation and greed. Meanwhile, what the U.S. public is told about poverty neglects to include the likelihood that being poorer materially may be connected to having more social intimacy and time for family — generally, outside the U.S.

Bolivia is "the poorest nation in South America," but the country is enviable in many ways. The people strike me as just as dignified and proud as any people I have seen in other parts of the world. Could it be in part due to that no Wal-Marts or McDonalds are in Bolivia, resulting in a crucial advantage over, say, the more economically devastated, less educated, strife-torn Mexico (the land of my birth)?

Granted, Bolivia is not one, big egalitarian love-in. Indeed, the legacy of colonialism and hierarchy from the European (partial) conquest for half a millennium endures, although President Evo Morales (an Aymara) represents a departure as he provides inspiration for 100% native pride.

A visitor here can develop a sense of being more alive when the structures of the far more materialist and imperialist culture of the U.S. are far away. For many back in my home country, the trade-offs are not worth it: contracting an intestinal infection (de rigueur) or risking a deadly Amazonian fever becomes the be-all, end-all of comparative existence. If we add the northerner's cherished greater order to traffic, better sidewalks, predictable bathroom plumbing, and more, the list starts to go on forever.

But here the fresher, local food, the greater informality of movement and scheduling, more expression of physical affection, constant safety for a woman or child walking alone on a road at night — these are readily apparent in any country that does not, like the U.S., have such rigid control between people and within the individual. How can these values be readily perceived?

In general, says the bruja, who is originally from Spain, only a tiny segment of the population of the world thinks much. Instead, they accept the story told to them by society, the government, and surrounding fellow citizens. So that, when people of greater awareness can meet and get together in mutual support, a dividing line is clear between the two segments of people. Yet, she is not able to speak as a U.S. citizen might, with the usual pressures and challenges of our less happy society. The Bolivian functions and feels to be more a part of a community, which colors his or her perspective.

In my present location, this small, intentional community/eco hotel/publishing house of aware people, surrounded by the outside world of destructive forces such as commercialization, capitalist exploitation and unhealthful influences, more love and teaching are shared constantly. Within such communities the personal transformation is undertaken without waiting for social change or a general awakening. Bonds — both between individuals and for the group — are created, proliferated and strengthened. Such realities of lifestyle and perception are more powerful for the spirit of unity and personal growth than any changes in political developments or cultural adjustments (e.g., more internet, a Black man in the White House, etc.).

How could I be so lucky to fall into such a scene as this, what with the blinders I had on to a greater extent than I had realized? My discovery started with a sense in March that I should go to Bolivia to attend the World Peoples Conference on Climate Change and the Rights of Mother Earth in April. Staying beyond its conclusion was crucial, if only to not waste a major jet trip. Perhaps a twist of the Fates then made all the difference.

I fell ill with one week and a half left to my stay in South America. I had already decided to refrain from maximum travel (e.g., to explore Peru and the whole west coast to investigate Sail Transport Network potential). It made more sense to enjoy a restful stay in the beautiful Bolivian countryside in order to work on my manuscripts, giving my body a break from the rigors of an active, not very tranquil routine.

Fortunately, when I was hit by the combination of high altitude, a month of sometimes questionable fried foods, rough car & bus rides amidst traffic with uncontrolled exhaust systems, combined with a unique climate, I had landed in a favorable location for support. Fasting, organic food and massage are normal in this compound. With artistic gardens and natural-building structures, the price per night of seven dollars U.S. was quite the incentive to stay. The business aspect of the community is the eco-hotel Planeta Luz. The season is not a busy one, allowing my hostel-dorm option to be enjoyed with no other guests. Nevertheless, becoming violently ill with unfamiliar symptoms in unfamiliar surroundings, among people I didn't really know, caused unlimited stress while I wondered where all my strength had gone. How could I manage to leave or travel?

I would have been gone today (May 16th) if not for the merchant error with my card. Both the U.S. and Bolivian banks involved were supposedly unable to reverse immediately the obvious mistake. But after my revelations today, it turns out to be most fortunate that my failed attempts to make bureaucracy work in my favor meant that I had to remain where I was. I was too ill to stand in lines and catch planes, but I needed to descend thousands of feet if only to escape the sleep apnea from the "mal de altitud."

Stuck I was, feeling like the character in "Hotel California" (big in Bolivia today): "You can check out any time you like, but you can never leave." Then I met the bruja Inka Lecumberri and her fellow shaman Luis Espinoza Chamalu, founder of the community. She was available for a healing session, so I grabbed the opportunity for possible relief and salvation. Using for divination an egg dropped into a glass of water to observe the tendrils of egg white representing my issues and problems, and laying her hands upon me, she delivered wise analysis and advice. To unblock my pathways she used knuckles on areas such as my sternum and legs that had me howling, screaming and laughing. The entire grounds and adjacent village heard it, but it was nothing new. I was soon spending a long time by myself on the same spot, lying on the ground, hands on Mother Earth, meditating in such a way to welcome other voices that Inka said I needed to allow into my life more frequently.

By then I realized I had to simply accept my longer stay, grateful for a bit more time to gird myself for three airplane rides including the 6 ½ hour flight to Miami. I was not instantly cured from my session with Inka, as I have seen happen in my own prior cases in Nepal and Mexico with traditional, unfathomable healers. But Inka made me realize that I had somehow blocked my awareness that I am in a personal transformation. Getting closer to the energy of Mother Earth (Pachamama) was a major part of Inka's message to me, and I immediately knew that this is worth remembering more than my usual daily fixation on trying to be a more effective, successful activist and writer.

It was the next day — today — that I again perchance was exposed and immersed into the community that I had just begun to be part of. I had gotten to know most of the staff and volunteers, young people from around South America who were attracted to the open, radical philosophy of the founder of this 20-year community.

Human relations that I have been witnessing here are devoid, apparently, of the game-playing jockeying for quick gratification that I have observed even among the best grassroots activists in the U.S. that I have known for decades. I include Earth First!ers, who in their semi-tribal non-organization have effectively saved ancient trees and made successful calls for protection of mountains threatened by coal mining, for example. When surrounded by "Babylon" (modern culture and society) it is impossible to be as one would like to be in harmony with others and with the land, no matter what the well-intended aspirations of a fine individual may be.

Here the lack of both hierarchy and self-motivated behavior, as well as the slower paced acceptance of daily life and of the entire world, is obvious — although it is only the natural way of living that is being pursued. It is seemingly without ego or private gain. Rather it is the group and the land that come first, with an easy grace for one's usual responsibilities and interactions.

It must not be the first time that a guest becomes welcome to join this partially self-sufficient community. It touches my heart. I would be by far the oldest person here, an unproven worker, and my Spanish leaves a lot to be desired. My being too weak to play my songs for them on my guitar may have helped, or maybe the songs would have made me even more desirable. I don't seem able to exhaust my new friends' goodwill, as I ask for help walking the paths or for another cup of lemon tea.

This feels better than scoring a pile of great DVDs or going on a glorious hike back in Oregon. Do my new friends have a real idea of how different I am, with my more intense upbringing geared toward accomplishment, goals, and ego? I sense that they feel I am more than a fellow traveler who claims to work for Mother Earth.

The patience and helpfulness in all ways that I am receiving is refreshing and relaxing. This experience carries more weight than being able to set down sooner on U.S. soil and being able to shop at Whole Foods or an organic food co-op. For now I've traded that and the U.S. soundtrack of street noise, sirens and televisions in for my current exotic sound-background of Bolivian music, choruses of feral dogs, and unfamiliar bird and frog sounds. Pigs being slaughtered nearby sound like children screaming, disturbing this vegetarian community. In the U.S. one might never hear such a thing because factory farms are away from villages and towns.

Changing my flight ticket again today meant being on the atrocious roads and viewing the apparent chaos of street vending and zero discernible traffic discipline. But it was definitely worth it because of my company: my new friends. Still, since my health collapsed I have longed to see my old friends and family back in the U.S. But it is with expanding perspective that I have to wonder where I ought to want to live.

Endnote:

Mother Earth (or Pachamama) is not some separate entity like a god in the sky. The Earth is right here and is where we all come from. The more we worship, revere, love or respect the Earth, and consider it a feminine being that gave birth to us, the better off we and the Earth are.

The more we give to Pachamama, the more we get. The more we can offer other people, the more support we get in return. When we diminish ourselves by remaining incapable of caring for others and ourselves, because we use up the best part of our time working for our own or others' aggrandizement, we will receive less from others when we need them.

The gift economy is about one's ability to help others more than requiring the help of others (especially distant corporations), indicating self-reliance. The reward or payment received only rises when the individual lets go of selfish concerns and instead benefits the whole group.

There is less and less social cohesion in industrial society. People don't have much time between jobs or school, but when they can consume alone they do so, using computers, iPods, cell phones and televisions. It is a fascist, institutional lifestyle dressed up as gee-whiz progress and status-oriented consuming.

Corporate control has tightened in recent years, part of a longer trend. This is clear from the inability of activists to get as much press regarding environmental and health issues as they used to, and in the ability of Trilby Lundberg to go uncriticized as a global-warming denialist quoted in the corporate press.

Sonoran observation
- on a bus northwest to Tijuana

I spent most of April 2008 up and down Mexico, and this is one of the essays hand-written in a notebook.

Beyond the usual thoughts and feelings that dominate in my daily life, such as those about food, bus tickets, beautiful Mexican women, etc., insightful observations come to me that I sometimes commit to paper. My good and bad luck as well as keen interest in the future have enabled me — with my self-preservation discipline — a bit of heightened awareness. If it's useless in the coming industrial collapse, call it a hobby.

As I view the beautiful countryside north of Hermosillo and marvel at the steady if not eternal overall dryness that somehow permits so much life, a tranquility and peacefulness descend on me. Others around me, and those who have been here, seem to share it.

If I took much notice of the rarely appearing rude soldier or even more rare bitter fellow passenger, I would miss the intense pastels of this land, and my calm and open state of mind would not form in the first place. Then again, I belong here because I was born in this country, and I thus have an incentive to understand it.

I regret the commitments of modernity that speed me along and deprive me of meeting wise old locals who might share secrets of the land. What experiences await the horseback rider beyond those intriguing rocky mountains?

Writing these passages or paying attention to a Hollywood

movie on this bus can make me miss a garbage bag flapping on a barbed wire fence. Who would want to go in past there anyway? I surely would, to reach the protective shadows of a wild canyon and seek out a spring.

To the south, time spent on a Guaymas beach presented me with two beings I never had had the pleasure to meet. As I waded into the turquoise water, marking the rocks beneath me to avoid, one "rock" shot ahead of me as it skirted the bottom: a ray skated away to avoid being stepped on and perhaps stinging me. The last time I saw a ray was in Tenacatita Bay, hundreds of miles to the south almost to Manzanillo — a manta ray bigger than a skiff, and a lot more graceful besides. The image stays in my mind forty years later.

Back on the Guaymas beach: a rather big lizard, almost as big as an iguana (or a species of iguana), performed push ups on a rock before my close presence sent it scurrying into a hole in the rocks. How did the reptile get any fresh water in that dry area? It is wise enough to do so, but a city human without the petroleum support-system would die of thirst here. Another wise native of this desert, a huge hare, also drinks enough water somehow.

We humans can slice open a cactus and build a shelter, and more. But, thanks to a relatively recent divergence from loving nature, that we can call Western Civilization, we stand naked next to our technology, imagining it doesn't fail and that it can self-perpetuate to convenience us forever.

So we are vulnerable to self-destruction: both of the collapse variety that cuts off supplies, and to the consequences of opening ourselves to dangerous swings in weather from the climate change we have wrought. The bus powers along and disturbs the harmony and air of the desert and the planet.

Chapter 17

Now What?
Lessons and (Hopefully) Wisdom

Lessons Learned by Culture Change After 20 Years
[press release September 2008]

When Jan Lundberg was asked in 2008 what he had learned about energy and environmental activism in the 20 years since founding Culture Change, he listed these lessons and principles:

> • As an approach to dealing with pollution, professional environmentalists heavily favor the technological fix and regulatory compromise over conservation. This is to the detriment of us all including other species.
> • Ecosystem health has been taken for granted, as if accumulation of toxic chemicals and greenhouse gases are something to slow down a little. This is the attitude of many of the funded, professional environmentalists, although many of them know better, while government and industry interests are even guiltier.
> • Entropy — the second law of thermodynamics that says waste and disorder are an automatic result of transforming matter with energy — is ignored or swept under the rug in order to compromise away the urgent need to stop pollution.
> • The economy, as it steadily globalized in recent decades, has been beyond criticism even though fundamental change to protect the environment is required. Similarly, drastic changes to global trade will come with dwindling oil supplies, but trade and oil are similarly swept under the rug or dealt with superficially.

• Renewable energy is not awaiting us as our salvation. Not all energy is equal to other forms of energy, which Lundberg suspected during his oil industry days. The two ways this is true are (1) gain from the extraction process, and (2) only petroleum supplies the many fuels, chemicals and materials we take for granted as essential in "unlimited" quantity.

• Transportation policy in the U.S. and at state levels is not about efficiency or safety but rather how to maximize cars, trucks and asphalt. This contributes to war over oil.

• Population growth is generally not to be discussed in government or in environmentalists' campaigns. Besides, the reasoning goes, it is Third World countries that are overpopulated and not the U.S. The average U.S. consumer uses many more times the resources than the typical consumer or villager elsewhere.

"The average person is not aware of these workings and imperatives," Lundberg said. "Many people believe to this day that industrial processes and emissions are regulated safely and that products from corporations must be safe if sold. This is one factor in the failure of the population to rise up and take action, such as depriving corporate offenders of our hard-earned dollars."

The biggest sneak attack on our ecosystem and public health has been the growth of plastics. "This is like a giant toxic oil spill that keeps on growing, mostly ending up in the ailing oceans."

Since 2001, Jan's work has gone beyond energy, land use, protecting ancient forests, and peace activism. "We began to focus on the bigger picture: what are society's values when the best farmland is paved over, and the family structure is weakened by materialism, elder abuse and isolation?" Hence, Culture Change became the goal and the name. Nonetheless, Jan's work has continued with a main focus on energy in part because "peak oil" has finally become well known. His essay published on CultureChange.org in summer 2008, "The Fastest Way to Put the Brakes on Global Heating" targets what he sees as dangerous ignorance surrounding oil issues among "activists and commentators who often misuse the news media and mislead

291

grassroots activists to further an increasingly discredited world view in service to the unraveling dominant culture. Meanwhile, we are wasting precious time as we needlessly resist a low-energy-consumption lifestyle that will allow a sustainable culture ahead."

A strange feeling as a way of life
Making sense of our predicament, shaping our future

Culture Change Letter #169 - October 14, 2007

Is everything alright? It should be, but it increasingly feels like it's not — even though we may have enough to eat and have a comfortable roof over our heads. We can go buy anything we imagine we need. Besides more war and a corporate-lackey government, what's wrong with our lives in what's supposed to be a democracy?

Many social philosophers have explored this question. Some answers have emerged. But they usually don't offer a realistic, current analysis of what's happening to the economy and infrastructure of "developed, rich" countries. Nor do they flesh out well the likely scenarios of a world without abundant exosomatic energy as we've come to expect with electricity, transport and petroleum-grown/distributed food.

If the world has become an ugly place because of civilization, few people dare oppose something so monumental as what's assumed to be the totality of exalted, wondrous human history. Civilization. Is it forever? Do we have any control over our lives or the future?

The isolation of daily existence that lacks village/tribal culture takes a constant toll, but it's not closely analyzed, quantified or publicized. For that could interfere with profits and getting people to keep going to work. And nothing is allowed to interfere with mass education's purpose of conformity and brainwashing.

We are instead told, through Big Brother's messages (government and corporate media), that everything is normal and part of amazing progress. Like the combatant told to get back on the battlefield to kill and die, when the psychiatric analysis conveniently denies shell-shock and battle fatigue, the worker or consumer must carry on and smile away the day. So we soldier on as regimented and industrial units aware of some things wrong, but not able to pinpoint the real trouble perhaps. Distractions can soothe while digging our graves.

Some of us are more aware or concerned about today's threatening state of the world than others, but we have trouble admitting that we've been significantly dehumanized. In today's cultural expectations for the elite and celebrities, everyone else is inconsequential and allowed to aspire to hyper consumerism as the goal of "life."

Young modern people often cope with the conditions of alienation by having someone else address it: they seek refuge and solace in musical groups' lyrics and the artist's image of freedom and honest expression. Idolatry of musicians (usually poets) is relatively recent, only decades old, for the masses of Western peoples. For the very few individuals, authors serve as moral and artistic leaders. Tom Robbins, Edward Abbey and Daniel Quinn are among the few who have serious cults about them, in a loose and positive sense. James Howard Kunstler and Richard Heinberg sit atop a most practical new genre, petrocollapse, gaining them conscious adherents.

Outside one's world of favorite music and books, or, in the more common case, television or video games, there is a constant assault on the sensibilities of our animal and spiritual selves. Besides the hard pavement and lack of nature (a lawn does not quite qualify) stained with toxic oil, with exhaust hovering about, the refuges of the supermarket or even the health food store are hardly fulfilling or truly welcoming. They are experiences of packaging, plastic touching food, and the roar of fossil-fueled machines for cooling and freezing. Same with many restaurants, except upscale ones that most of us cannot afford: they are noisy experiences, where the music played — usually techno and of no lyrical importance — barely disguises the machines' hum.

The amount of food and products shipped from afar is astounding. The abundance and affluence represented by a single Whole Foods Market is such that one should wonder how it can keep going in terms of shipping and quantities. How much the customer questions this petroleum-fired frenzy to satiate with a fleeting cornucopia is not known, but is not significant if we judge by action. The average person does not lift a finger to produce food locally in any way, even if it can lower one's cost, improve health, reduce global warming, cut petroleum consumption, and offer social opportunities.

The workers in these markets, restaurants and other retail stores are mere units for production with no say over business practices or, almost as rarely, over environmental policy. Wages are not enough to survive on without combining households with other people. The minimum wage, poor-benefit slavery is not quite questioned; proof is that unions are weak and grassroots organizing such as wildcat strikes are exceedingly rare.

One reason for the lack of resistance to stultifying and dead-end conditions is poor health and low mental energy via pharmaceutical drugs. Half the people are on some antidepressant or mood-altering drug, and a good many more are on painkillers, antibiotics, tranquilizers, sleeping pills, cold medicine, and more. As discussed in Culture Change Letter #45, Dec. 2, 2003 ("Brain control of the masses via pollutants"), the constant exposure to toxic chemicals serves as mind control: Carbon monoxide, lead, and fluoride are only a few. Hormones in food, pesticides residues and estrogenic plastics are influencing not just health but the future of families and the collective state of mind. Younger and younger menstruations, and birth defects of boys feminized by chemicals in plastics, are more and more common and swept under the rug. The human race becomes weaker and less wild day by day. The domestication of the human is our downfall, but is championed by the capitalist and bureaucrat. There are even those who enslave themselves through their mental attitude, to emulate their masters, as Steven Biko and Bob Marley reminded us.

As all these problems keep going unaddressed and allowed to worsen, it is no wonder that our very existence is under threat without a fight against climate disruption. Is it so very hard for people to imagine living in different ways — some just minor changes anyone can do — that we must jump off "the ecological cliff like motorized lemmings" (to quote our featured cartoonist Andy Singer, from his cover art of an *Auto-Free Times* magazine)?

Perception from on high is disturbing

Climbing to the top of my nearest hill in San Francisco, my purpose is not to enjoy the view but to experience a bit of fresh air and nature. Some birds dwell in these urban islands of trees, bushes and soil. So few people are there, but they are happy, relaxed and friendly (unless deranged and out to rob). I find the view of San Francisco Bay and the megalopolis most disturbing, seeing in all directions the industrial activity and oil-fueled trade of questionable imported products. Massive port facilities dwarf the human scale of sustainable import/export. A very small number of sailboats for pleasure can't quite offer a vision of renewable-energy travel and exchange. Passenger planes take off, military jets show off their ear-splitting capabilities, all against the backdrop of polluted air that is warming in general thanks to commercial activity and the mindless consumption by the individual. The hills are full of roads and energy-wasting houses. It's not like this everywhere; the hills around Kyoto are pitch black at night, for they consist of forest, trails and small, outdoor temples.

Seven million people surround me in this metastasized, metropolitan area. Those among them who really care whether Barry Bonds used steroids to hit baseballs, or what pregnant celebrity has checked into a drug rehab facility, are not likely to be trying to live lightly on the planet. Normal citizens under the spell of mass media want to consume, and be given answers and easy fixes. Such citizens, I suspect, would argue about the color-coordination of the shoes and handbag of the person in front of them in the line, like sheep, to the slaughterhouse. For they are already there in line, as they want to know badly what's on cable TV and what's in the freezer to eat. They may get what they want tonight, and again, and again, but it will come to an abrupt end, and will people pick up a shovel to plant food or pick up the gun to take others' food? That depends on the area affected, the culture (urban U.S. or otherwise), and population size.

Why should I be disturbed by what I see now, when all is basically calm? Or feel uneasy as I putter about in the safety of my comfortable home? Is not San Francisco and the surrounding area a great city, with many wonderful people and activities to appreciate? What about the noble struggles of valiant, compromised hard-working people, or the dysfunctional and disabled folk who are really kind? The social injustice that is still pervasive, in our vaunted age of scientific and technological prowess, is outrageous and occupies many of the best hearts and minds in the world that live in our very midst. Much of what ails people, it is thought, is that they do not have enough cheap, affordable energy or material things that are supposed to both satisfy and uplift. More public funds for health care, through an end to costly, imperialist wars, would be the ticket to a healthy society, in the eyes of more and more.

Except, that altruistic aspiration is becoming clouded with the uncertainty and fright growing around our awakening to climate change. In the buzzing Bay Area and every other large and small city, we are behaving as if there is no threat to the climate and thus our future survival as a species. Just looking around at the unceasing traffic, it is clear that basic, radical but easy solutions are being kept on the shelf or buried. Tiny changes, usually just initiatives that don't threaten the current life style (e.g., different engines), are called "green." Green this and green that. But the big "greening" will be the rediscovery of community and working with others as if our survival depends on our collaboration as equals. Our bosses and political leaders have been as useful in the needed transition as — to borrow an expression from my late father — tits on a bull.

As I pointed out in a CBS Radio Network interview aired Sept. 21, 2007, with Dan Raviv, we have caused and are witnessing such rapid changes in climate that the planet is approaching a state not seen in 55 million years. So I did add to general paranoia, but I did not do it gratuitously. For I was explaining why I had gone, at that point, 16 days without any nourishment whatsoever in the Climate Emergency Fast. I also mentioned solutions such as car-free living and slashing petroleum use now, rather than waiting for the renewable energy technofix. I had to bring up two more scary situations we cannot just wipe away with an ideal election outcome: we have arrived at peak oil, and we all have plastics in our bodies.

I have written 168 columns and reports before this one on culturechange.org, exploring our dominant culture's weaknesses and fatal flaws, and identifying examples of destructive policies and individuals. The bad guys are not really the problem, and the good guys will not save us. We have to be our own leaders. We can do two things to help our own cause as individuals, as members of our true community just ahead, and as a species. I believe those two things are

(1) to appreciate how dependent modern society is on a broken system of exploitation of both nature and our fellow human beings, and face that we are thus facing imminent collapse. It is economic/financial, related to energy. It is also related to both our bodily and ecological health that has been compromised, as outlined in the beginning of this essay. Climate chaos has been assured and it is widely known, but most people sit on their hands as the executioner prepares to swing the axe. Do I have to spell out that we ought to stop sitting on our hands, and disarm the executioner by ceasing our own fossil-fueled self-destruction?

(2) In the absence of a movement over the past few decades to deal with these issues most meaningfully, when smaller collective actions would have still made a major difference, we must resign ourselves to (A) seeing "nature bat last" and knock us out of the ball park. That's a train wreck we can no longer stop, although we can slow it down a tad and allow for some survivors. The other runaway train is (B) the collapsing economy. Smoke and mirrors are keeping it alive, such as with "free trade agreements" such as CAFTA, the Central American Free Trade Agreement. Like other such schemes, it will open more areas to exploitation and ramping up of exports and petroleum usage — even if for a short while as oil dwindles quickly. With these two main train wrecks (A and B) disposing of society as we know it, our hopes must be in retaining and reviving models of sustainability. CultureChange.org has dwelled on them, and has described tools of sustainability as well;

they are not really "doom and gloom" unless we allow it and we abhor change.

When we finally find ourselves unable to keep up the treadmill of high-energy economic activity such as employment and shopping, chaos will quickly ensue. We will then become painfully aware of the reality of overpopulation. We will yearn for some productive land and clean water, but there hasn't been enough to go around for some time here and in most parts of our human-heavy world. To "get by" comfortably or exuberantly — expanding the economy and population — we tapped the Earth's store of fossil energy, to the tune of anywhere from six to ten Earths' equivalent of sustainable photosynthetic energy and nonrenewable resources.

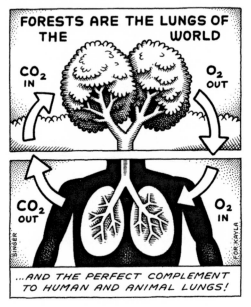

FORESTS ARE THE LUNGS OF THE WORLD

CO_2 IN

O_2 OUT

CO_2 OUT

O_2 IN

...AND THE PERFECT COMPLEMENT TO HUMAN AND ANIMAL LUNGS!

I am in just one part of the industrialized world, in a large, sophisticated city filled with thrill seekers concerned more with consuming than changing their consciousness and saving the world. But I remain hopeful of a return to the raising of mass awareness as happened in the 1960s. One might say the awakening was not complete, and change was thwarted by secret government programs and the ongoing lure of technological gold. People went back to sleep. But we still have music that can change the world, and we have power we are letting lie dormant for now. San Francisco is the Western Hemisphere's leader in banning petroleum plastic bags, and the city has banned its own use of plastic water bottles. Maybe this is rather significant for our common future.

The global peak in oil extraction has been recognized by the City and County of San Francisco, and the crisis is being explored for mitigation in part through education of the citizenry. I am honored to have been appointed by the Board of Supervisors on Oct. 4th, 2007 to be a member of the new Peak Oil Preparedness Task Force. On it I can only try to share my knowledge and my enthusiasm for meaningful social change through both policy and individual life-style transformation. The goal in my heart and mind is to help point the way to a "new" culture of frugal, local energy use and climate-saving daily living for our precious Earth and all its species. Be assured the technofix is not going to get a free pass on my watch, nor, I suspect, from my esteemed fellow task force members.

With some luck, solidarity, hard work and widespread openness in these increasingly "interesting times," maybe my "strange feeling" will no longer be "a way of life," but will give way to a more fulfilled sense of purpose buoyed by tangible results on the bioregional level.

* * * * *

Andy Singer's website: andysinger.com

City Repair Project's co-founder is architect Mark Lakeman. This group has managed to get Portland, Oregon city code to allow any intersection to be converted into a neighborhood community center. See drawing next page, by Andy Singer. City Repair website: cityrepair.org

William R. Catton, author of *Overshoot: The Ecological Basis of Revolutionary Change*, Foreword by Stewart Udall

"Overextension: our American way of life is not sustainable" by Chris Clugston, in Culture Change: culturechange.org/cms

"Fasting for the climate and self: The Climate Emergency Fast continues" by Jan Lundberg, Culture Change Letter #166, Sept. 12, 2007 culturechange.org/cms

Village Building Convergence (City Repair Project

Anywhere, UPPA (United Paved Precincts of America)

Andy "Convivial" Singer shows us the way again!

New Decisions, Given 6°C Warming

Does the Earth's biosphere have a chance? Since nature has been thrown out of balance, probably around the time Rachel Carson's *Silent Spring* was published in 1962, we cannot count on the principle threats backing off while the economic juggernaut rolls on. China's coal production could peak as soon a 2015. It is unacceptable to trust in such an eventuality, or even in total petrocollapse, as reason to put off the cultural revolution of conscious lifestyle change.

Never mind the United Nations' climate efforts or the environmental movement; it comes down to individual choice: if you have a certain length of time to live, does this not change your plans and your present routine?

With some of us, no. I have one good friend very dissatisfied with his unhappy situation, but he stays within artificial bounds because he feels beaten down by his family and by society. Although he does have serious problems, as so many of us do, he doesn't seem to take simple steps to break out of his self-imposed confines. I have another friend with a terminal illness, and he believes he'll be dead within a year. I have suggested he change his course of treatment by going on a fast, arguing he has nothing to lose and much to gain. But he will not consider it, as if he might lose some of the time remaining to his life (even though it is increasingly miserable).

Then there are others who change course radically because a new approach is justified as feasible. The risk is in giving up what you have. Why do some make that effort while most do not? Most do not until they are finally pushed or knocked in a new direction.

My decision for a new direction is that if humanity is indeed running out of time to have a livable world, as species go extinct and we lose the favorable climate our species has known for many thousands of years (or even hundreds of thousands of years), I must now try something different. I will follow where my heart tells me to go. In general, I have lived my life this way since leaving the family-business nest at age 34. This may be cast as insane according to the business-as-usual way of getting by. But as people increasingly face that there is no future in continuing the

301

conveniently polluting lifestyle — supporting more global warming and an inequitable economic system — they will join me in what I'm doing, most likely with their own unique version.

Several years ago I gave up on the present system of corporations' offering jobs and other crumbs from the major sources of employment and sustenance: the global economic pie and the elite's gluttony. For that only allowed for an impotent governmental or civil–society sector trying to improve ecological health and stopping the recurring wars. Working within the system has not worked out well, although one can say the system would be worse if activists and reformers had not done their best. However, it wasn't good enough. For there is a new assessment from climate scientists: we are heading toward the worse case scenario of 6°c warming — resulting in an unlivable planet except for remnants of humans and nature as we know it.

There are some equally passionate advocates for nature's survival that I believe have been driven insane by the challenge and lack of progress toward global responsibility. They have fallen prey to embracing violence, i.e., wishing to kill people to stop the destruction of the environment. They are so few that they may not even exist except in their fantasies. The so-called violent eco-terrorists that have been identified by the government have not hurt any humans or animals, as they only target property and facilities. But the insane minority advocating the killing of government and corporate officials or their servants are beating a drum they call militant resistance (beyond civil disobedience). They don't realize they are mimicking the system they abhor, offering no improvement in tactics or ethics as the end justifies the means. I went into the details of this fallacious argument in an essay titled "Greeting the Fall of the Empire: a Message of Peace" dated January 3, 2011 on CultureChange.org.

For myself, not deluded that there is a mass movement to abandon the car or to begin depaving the cities to create urban gardens, I am not Gandhi with his following. Nor do I see another Gandhi to follow. So I will do what I most believe in: tell what I know in the most artful and sincere way I know: my songs. The music is from dreams, or at least the initial ideas. Often the words are too. Poems or song lyrics put to music may be the most soul-bearing form of expression, which is why it can reach so many people on a deep level.

So my decision in light of our slipping climate is to give myself over to promoting my message through music and books. This book makes much of songs and their possible role. When I tour the nation and the world to get my message out and sell the book, I will do as I have done for two decades: bring my guitar and sing out to the people. Initially I will follow my old formula of doing one song before speaking. Eventually I will just let the lyrics of songs be my way of speaking. My hundreds of songs have touched on the same ideas as my essays and my book, referring the end of cheap energy, the need to honor nature and live in harmony with her, and take action to come together for community living without corporate domination.

To make a contribution one must have confidence in whatever one's talent of project is. For my songs, this means believing they have positive attributes and are enjoyable, at least to me. Whatever we do in a deliberate fashion for meaning, we must believe in it if we are to help others. We may then break through and reach someone, or reach a few — even millions.

When my book is at a point where I can concentrate on another project, that will be to do more recording of songs and go back out on the road (or rails, or sailing lanes). All the while, Culture Change will continue, but without my spending hours a day formatting and editing on the computer. A replacement "poster" is being groomed already!

Al Gore's recent book *Our Choice* "reflects the experience of someone who knows that it is lawmakers and business leaders who can implement the 'laws and policies we really need, including getting a global climate treaty.'" – *Newsweek*, The Evolution Of An Eco-Prophet *Al Gore's views on climate change are advancing as rapidly as the phenomenon itself.* Sharon Begley, *Newsweek* Oct. 31, 2009.

This is a dangerous view, because it denies the power the grassroots has to implement the change needed (unplugging the global warming lifestyle). For anyone who really has concern over the climate to trust government and corporations — the corporate state — to deal with the threat of climate disaster, there is either a dissonance or corruption.

Source information: www.independent.co.uk/environment/climate–change/world–on–course–for–catastrophic–6deg–rise–reveal–scientists–1822396.html

World on Course for Catastrophic 6° C Rise, Reveal Scientists

Fast-rising carbon emissions mean that worst-case predictions for climate change are coming true
By Steve Connor and Michael McCarthy
18 November 2009

The world is now firmly on course for the worst-case scenario in terms of climate change, with average global temperatures rising by up to 6°C by the end of the century, leading scientists said yesterday. Such a rise — which would be much higher nearer the poles — would have cataclysmic and irreversible consequences for the Earth, making large parts of the planet uninhabitable...
www.news.bbc.co.uk/2/hi/science/nature/8364926.stm

Earth 'Heading for 6°C' of Warming

By Richard Black
Environment correspondent, BBC News website

Average global temperatures are on course to rise by up to 6°C without urgent action to curb CO_2 emissions... Emissions rose by 29% between 2000 and 2008, says the Global Carbon Project. All of that growth came in developing countries, but a quarter of it came through production of goods for consumption in industrialised nations...
www.guardian.co.uk/uk/2002/jul/07/research.waste

Chapter 18

Activism's Transformation

Why Do We Destroy Our World in Our Descent into Chaos?

As we struggle on various levels today to reverse ecological damage, we sometimes forget to ask why we must have the problem in the first place. As one reader named Gary wrote to us on Nov. 12, 2008,

> Why do industrialists pollute the world they themselves live in? Why are capitalists so greedy? Why does man seem so hell-bent on his own destruction?
>
> The day before, I was incorporating that basic question into what might be a new theory. I was alternating in my mind between despair over the way we destroy nature, and worrying about my own needs and desires being met. It seemed to be one mindset or the other — not integrated, I realized.

My notion of a new theory came as I wondered — trying to relax while feeling some confusion — "How we can let the world be destroyed?" (By "we" I mean modern people.) At the same time this sad question weighed upon me, I was just as aware of my own desires and goals — adventure, accomplishment, romance, and having my creature comforts and conveniences. I aspire to enjoy life and I worry about my own problems so much that I successfully put out of my mind, most of the time, the unpleasant realities of our besieged modern world. So I put all these facts together and I pinpointed this:

People allow the Earth to be destroyed and even aid in it because one's own orgasm is more important than the cosmic orgasm. We've become separated from feeling the life force and knowing we are all one with everything. The modern world has minimized the ecstasy of living in the moment, so it is increasingly rare and devalued. We instead strive to better our own conditions, and not the community's (and the ecosystem's). We need pleasure in order to cope with oppression. The system of domination drives people to seek personal relief, allowing general deterioration. At least with collapse and die-off we will get back to tribes and nature, and understand that the personal orgasm (or pleasure, or comfort, or material gain) is not the point of existence — but this culture has told us that it is! That's our fatal flaw. So to deal with this we now have to be enemies of the dominant culture and its lethal socioeconomic system.

The artist Jane Evershed read the draft of this essay and pointed out, "The suppression of the sexual/sensual self is at the heart of our being out of touch with nature. We have butchered the sexual/sensual in the same way that nature has been butchered." This goes a long way to explain why we have exalted individualized orgasm — and, by extension or substitution, our personal wants on Earth — instead of seeing our experience and needs as part of the whole. The beautiful Earth provides, and all that is required is that we participate in the dance of life instead of sitting back trying to use remote control to gratify ourselves with high-entropy material surplus.

We can synthesize the me-first concept further to say that the dilemma we are faced with is our being saddled with short-term-goal thinking. So how do we lengthen the goal to give ourselves a fighting chance at long-term survival? Maybe once infected with short-term, selfish values there is no cure.

Fasting does get rid of physical and some psychological addictions, so it's worth a try for cultural addictions too. On the macro level we can go on a fast from fossil fuels and most technology, and see what that does. To do so today all alone can almost be suicidal, so, advanced behavior for the greater good must be exalted and supported. Do not be afraid of starting now, if only for the valuable education and friendships to be gained right off the bat.

Peak-oil activist approach for the coming change in culture

This column was first published in the Peak Oil Review by the Association for the Study of Peak Oil and Gas - USA chapter, and picked up by the Energy Bulletin, January 19, 2009.

Culture Change Letter #229

Peak oil is something to heed more today than ever, no matter where crude oil and gasoline prices go or what they may do to oil consumption. Peak-oil awareness has risen greatly in recent years, but this has not resulted in wide understanding of energy in our fast changing world of mounting crises and distractions. Even among those knowledgeable about peak oil there is confusion about energy and oil, based on old assumptions. Kinds of peak-oil awareness can be based on levels of knowledge or worldviews — some of which are seen as obsolete in the last several months: "Peak money" has passed, both from the private sector and government spending. Oil costs were a major factor leading up to the economy's meltdown marked by peak money.

The unpleasant truth of US society's waste and excess has been widely known since the 1960s, when the "Sixties Movement" meant lifestyle change more than mere politicking. Awareness of stifling consumerism and materialism spurred a rejection of "plastic society" as articulated by popular avant-garde artists. This era of awareness peaked around 1970. Energy and environment were not hot topics compared to the US war on the Indochinese. But some of us made note of the fact that the bombers and naval ships were all running on lots of oil. This was not considered a "news" item, when other issues and passions raged.

The consciousness of the late 1960s was inseparable from protesting and the quest for one's liberation. This tradition has endured to the present, when one can still meet young back-to-the-landers who cherish the Earth. They know oil and other materials are not something to waste or spew into the environment, and they feel painfully the equity issues in a world of greed. In a conscious fashion such non-consumers assure that polluters don't get many of their dollars, and this impulse is a form of relocalization.

It makes no difference if such aware folk know about peak oil. For those in this group who have learned about peak oil, it has not changed their philosophy, ethics or lifestyle. What does change from such folks' peak-oil awareness is, in many cases, the intensity of focus on the timing of inevitable collapse of the industrial economy. It also sends people to develop manual skills including fluency with alternative energy.

The peak-oil movement is diverse, thus reflecting the population. So most peak oilists have no background in "living simply" or growing food. Even less common is the peak oilist who was an activist for social change. While peak oilists are often activists in the sense that they spread the word on oil, and may take up gardening or survivalism, activists are not the majority of peak-oil-aware folk. Nor are they usually hands-on food producers involved in the greater community. This is why Transition Town and Post Carbon affiliates, plus ASPO and its chapters, are important for peak-oil outreach to citizens, politicians and others.

When peak oilists lack an activist orientation or background, they are more likely to be stuck in conventional "plastic society" and to wish to retain their machines (suburban "toys" and commonplace gadgets). Not only does lifestyle change elude them, as they lack appreciation for the need for activist tactics for radical change, they may be unable to grasp the full meaning of peak oil. Then there are those who fully understand while cynically taking steps to benefit personally or squelch debate.

When peak oilists are inveterate energy users fond of the American Dream, and don't recognize the full implications and opportunities posed by the peaking of global oil extraction, such folk face the future with total consternation. They lament the loss of energy-intensive affluence, and want to see the continuation of all the (including alleged) benefits of industrial society. They thus see technological solutions as ideal, and perhaps chant, "Maybe the net energy will get higher and government spending can be brought to bear!" This flies in the face of basic peak-oil reality when products' energy embeddedness of petroleum and the liquid-fuels issues are considered. And in keeping with the fact that the nation's infrastructure is based on petroleum, lead-time to scale up is utterly lacking.

The average consumer is not willingly letting go of the artificial world wrought by technological society and the growth paradigm. Thus, as the economic collapse that we're starting to see is ushering in the Post-Industrial Age along with localism and eventually tribalism, the fear of change and the wish for a continuation of the status quo prevent us from using remaining abundant energy to manage an intelligent transition. Politics as well seem to dictate that the automotive industries and the military-industrial complex — besides the more unpopular

Goliaths of oil and banking — carry on much as before, regardless of cost. But we must all face the fact that the U.S. and its global reach relies on fast dwindling fuel in addition to exponential cash based on hyper consumption.

There are additional reasons for peak oilists to assume the global corporate economy will keep chugging along. Apart from "progress" as a recent historical concept enjoying blind acceptance, wide understanding of the dynamics of price and supply is rare. Matt Simmons is one of the few voices in or out of the oil industry who gets the fact that panic buying and hoarding are more significant for society's overall stability than how much crude oil may be forthcoming from estimated reserves. The bell-shaped curve of Hubbert's oil extraction's rise and fall is not going to end up symmetrical.

We are all in a new historic phase, looking at a depression caused in great part by extremely high oil prices in recent years. (In addition to the nominal price, subsidies were and are causing us to pay far more, indirectly, than the known price.) Now that overall collapse and extreme social unrest are probably upon us — as indicated by ominous hints such as the recent Wal-Mart stampede that killed a worker and the arrival of 40,000 people at a farm in Colorado to pick crop gleanings — we can either view the world from an activist's heart-felt and intellectual discipline, or as worried, passive victims, or even as opportunistic aggressors.

We must distinguish between policy-reform activism and grassroots activism that fights for much greater social justice and against basic harm to the ecosystem. Grassroots activists may not all desire the deepest, fundamental social change, but in opposing bureaucratic or political obstacles to peace and environmental health, an awakening takes place that does away with one's innocence regarding the ability of the status quo to change. Beautifully simple, common-sense goals are sought by grassroots activism that resist being subverted by compromise — although dreams are run over and often left behind when money calls.

A revolution in lifestyle change is overdue for modern humans. It is a challenge even for a grassroots activist to relate to, especially when peak oil is not known or understood. To recognize the need to meet the future in a proactive fashion — to slash energy use now — is to seize the opportunity to lessen the shock of losing the "cheap" energy and products that have filled and distorted our lives.

To live with as little petroleum and other non-renewable resources as possible right now is to embrace a new world of localized economics and a lower-tech set of practices and processes formerly termed Appropriate Technology. But if we instead hope for as little change as possible in the near future, we will probably bring on the worst consequences of recent decades' energy gluttony. If we take seriously the possibility of a phase of massive disorder and depopulation from petrocollapse and climate extinction, we are better able to choose available options for survival and implement them while we can.

Jan Lundberg was an oil-industry analyst who ran Lundberg Survey in the 1980s. Since then, in addition to becoming an environmental advocate he became a generalist. In 1988 he formed the nonprofit Fossil Fuels Policy Action, now Culture Change, the longest running peak oil group. Reach him via email at jan "at" culturechange.org or tel./fax (215) 243-3144. Website: www.culturechange.org

(Note by ASPO-USA editor: Commentaries do not necessarily represent ASPO-USA's positions; they are personal statements and observations by informed commentators. In fact, we sometimes disagree with significant points, as here, but let them run.)

This disclaimer is normal for ASPO-USA except for the second specially added sentence for this occasion. When asked why the sentence had to appear, the response was that there were stylistic objections; specific disagreements couldn't be identified. Regardless, the appearance of this article in ASPO-USA's Peak Oil Review is meaningful for the target audience: those in legislatures, particularly, who need to look at resource limits perhaps for the first time. This time, with this column, related ideas possibly more disturbing were presented for a conventional audience.

ASPO-USA's website is aspo-usa.com. The weekly Peak Oil Review and mid week updates on world events are extremely informative.

Energy Bulletin's website is energybulletin.net. The wealth of stories there daily on energy and peak oil, and related topics, is extraordinary.

Chapter 19

Songs for the Eco-Liberation Movement from a Depaver

This first song doesn't have a name, because when I asked my mother if she thought it could be "America," after I played and sang the song to her over the telephone, she didn't like the idea. I had written the tune from a dream. I had woken up on the dunes near the open Pacific, in summer 2003, relishing the peace and my independence, even though I had no home other than wherever I happened to be at the moment. I had my bicycle and guitar, and they worked fine.

> I walk the Earth in search of land
> To feed myself by my own hand
> The ocean waves are crashing near
> And add to misty atmosphere
>
> America a name for this
> Since whiter skins enslaved the place
> Some feel the need to change their ways
> But not alone to face the day
>
> For beauty we come naturally
> To love the Earth so joyfully
> We do whatever pleases us
> In solidarity we trust
>
> So many people living here
> To use the oil but now they fear
> The heavy handed ruling class
> Is hoarding wealth and kicks your ass
>
> Accept the deal right off the shelf
> But I have the right to defend myself
> We'll meet upon the streets and fields
> And if the blood spills may we heal

Song: **Mother Earth First**

> *This song, a favorite of my younger daughter Bronwyn, was performed at her graduation at Virginia Commonwealth University in May, 2008. But it was a guerilla operation: The large crowd of mainly parents were waiting an interminable amount of time for the graduates to appear and get on stage and into the special seats in the huge gymnasium. But another ceremony nearby was running late, involving some double major students, so we had to wait in the gym. Every half hour or so an official would get on the stage and advise us to be patient. I noticed that the mic at the podium was live, and being wasted. So I just walked up and picked it up, and sang a song a cappella. My ex-wife was mortified that I did this, and asked me why I did. Could it have been I'm a guerilla activist?*

> *This short song is a bit longer than it would appear from the mere five lines below; there is a guitar solo at the end that sounds good with tambourine.*

You are here on Mother Earth
Take your place behind Earth First!
My head is achin' from deforestation
Don't let it last too long
I hope we can live

> *The song was from a dream wherein The Doors were going from one room into another through a door, fittingly enough. I wrote it in 1992 and it remained a cappella for a few years until I was shown it had a rock 'n roll soul.*

Song: **408**

This four o eight This four o eight
This four o eight I'm gonna take a late
Train to the countryside
Then I'm jumpin' off
When it's goin' slow enough
To walk down to the riverside

Nature is our home Won'tcha come along
I got a little place where people can be safe
From Spotsylvania shopping malls
We'll gather our own food
And sleep out on the land
Just the way the Indians do

Gonna leave this town Gotta leave this place
There's something going down
That's gonna be too hard
For millions of us to survive
They opened up the gates
And everybody came
To live here in this concrete cage

We're cut off from the land It's all been fenced or paved
The corporations say "just keep on buyin' junk"
To make us think that we are free
They're tearin' up the Earth
But we should do the same
Take pavement up and plant some trees

This four o eight

408 is on the Depavers' album Have a Global Warming Day. It has hand drumming only, a mistake as the song sounds great with a rock drum set. I sang the last verse's first three lines to Angela Davis at a large gathering in Arcata in 2000.

Song: "**Party On Fossil Fools**"

My daughter Bronwyn suggested presenting the lyrics of what I would believe to be my "most important song." However, I have no idea which one it might be. This one I wrote on a hike in Arcata in 2002, is unique for its not coming from one of my dreams, but has been popular at my performances. The first line is a Pixies-like exhortation shouted between one down stroke each on the guitar of

313

chords E and C. Then begins medium-tempo rock featuring
typical chord progressions, in the key of G:

> Party on!

> Party on fossil fools
> Party on fossil fools
> It ain't cool but I think I love 'em too
> I'm another fossil dude

> Global warming coming on
> Babble on Babylon
> We're so hot we can shop and shop and shop
> Missiles ships and tanks and bombs

> I've got my stash
> Car house and cash
> I've won the game
> My neighbors are the same
> What's their name by the way

> Police control on the street
> Cops are keepin' steady beat
> In the trees they will show you what they mean
> Let's pretend that they are sweet

> Pickin' berries by the stream
> Many years ago we dreamed
> What a place out here is like
> When the car gave way to bikes
> Population had to peak

The lyrics are straightforward, but someone outside Humboldt
County or outside any timber zone would not know that the fourth
verse refers to tree sitting by forest activists. I was thinking of the
Freshwater redwoods, where a woman named Wren remained up
in an ancient tree for 10 months. She later became my assistant for
a time, and is a great friend. The police rarely climbed the trees
themselves, but they worked with the loggers and timber bosses
hand in hand to try to smash the protests. A hired tree climber

named Eric was infamous for terrorizing tree-sitters, usually by cutting away branches, lines, and confiscating equipment. One protester, Yarrow, lost her support high up in a tree and free fell for many yards when a loop on her person caught a short stub of a former branch, breaking her fall just in time before she would have smashed to the ground and died.

The introductory "Party on!" is spoken or yelled after the chords E and C when I pause, to give a Pixies punk group feel. The song is in G. The tempo is about the pace of a march, and the beat is 4/4. In one of the guitar solos I sometimes call out "This is the Pink Floyd chord" (E minor). My songs tend to have a lot of chords and changes, whereas the average pop song would not have both E and E minor, for example. This song is one of my unrecorded tunes, at this writing, but it can be recorded easily, ideally with a drum set, bass guitar, and overdubbing of my solos if necessary. When I perform this song I sometimes flub one of the solos, which serves me right because it's a rip off from Steve Miller Band's "Goin' to Mexico." Fortunately in my song's debut at Humboldt State University, where I performed for a rally observing the second anniversary of the 9-11 attacks, I executed the song well.

"Party On Fossil Fools" is not from a dream, and so is more about the lyrics than the music for its own sake (as is the case for all my other songs). My dream songs that have lyrics have an element of strangeness to the opening lines, oftentimes. An example is my song "Have a Global Warming Day." When I write music from a dream that had no lyrics in the dream, I invariably put in lyrics as my aid to remembering the music. There is much to remember besides the melody, such as the harmony (chords), rhythm and tempo.

Despite my greater interest in pure music, or my placing music on at least the same level of importance as lyrics, I have put so much thought and feeling into my lyrics that they stand as a body of work much like the totality of my essays or this book. Sometimes my lyrics make statements much more strongly and simply than in mere prose, causing me to refrain publishing the lyrics and avoid performing the song among strangers. In recent years I have loosened up and let them out, what with the more extreme politics and intensifying crises facing us all today.

Song: **Freedom calls**

> Freedom calls
> Freedom calls
> Hear the voices reaching you
> Some from heart to heart
> In Africa the cash crop is a scam
> Like border factories 'cross the Rio Grande
>
> We're told we're lucky to have
> Chances to make rich The Man
> When we give up power we are damned slammed
>
> Freedom from lying scum
> That's our reward for
> Working so hard we're dumb
>
> Peace may come
> Peace may come
> When we are all one
> Can you feel the people's needs
> Bleeding in the sun
>
> The Earth's soil is exploited to the point
> Where deserts have replaced the forests moist
>
> We're told the market can give
> Everything needed to live
>
> Corporations fabrications enrich
> Greedy beasts
> Fear unleashed
> We'll keep on going
> Until our growing's ceased
>
> Freedom calls
> Freedom calls
> Join our hands and take a stand
> For a world for all

Song: **Singing the Earth into Harmony**

I had on November 20, 2007 one of the greatest and most hopeful experiences of my life. It was one of the most intense and meaningful musical dreams I ever had. In the dream, a woman was singing with a message that all the world's people needed to sing at once in order to heal the planet. She was so convincing and the idea so sound that I started to more than picture it and feel it happening. I awoke with joy, sure that this could work. The power of it was stronger than a feeling of love for a lover at hand. As I woke up further I switched from my right-brain to left-brain state, and I knew I had a new song to work with. Yet I could feel my sensation of hope dissipate. I still believed the singer in the dream was right, however. It became simply an idea and interesting story, and a song for me. But I wonder, did I tap into something real, just waiting to be tried? I circulated a quickie recording of the song, rock style, to friends and relatives, but did not get much interest. They just did not feel what I had felt from that dream. It's as if I received a cosmic gift from the heart of the Earth, expressing a truth very few modern people can relate to.

Her voice was most reassuring now
With warmth and harmony
I had a dream and a woman sang
The sound was sweet and complete
I think it meant that humankind
Can help the Earth to heal

It takes one voice of all the people
Singing the Earth into harmony
Can you hear and feel
Guns will be laid down on the ground
After we learn
As forests burn

There may not be a grocery store
With neon lights in your eyes
We're going back to Nature's Way
Before the ice all melts

Chapter 20

Fasting for Health and Social Change

The Nature of a Fast on the River is Part Subversion

I hadn't thought of fasting as a way to fight the system, but I've seen the light. Taking your time to heal is subversive. It is a time for reflection and for not being "productive." Fasting, therefore, is not what employers and capitalists want workers to do. Nor is it what the school authorities want young people to do. Instead, pills, nostrums and stimulants are promoted, and when these eventually allow health to deteriorate there's always surgery, radiation, amputation, etc.

Instead of taking the program and being a consumer who has confused the buying of medical treatment with actual healing, I fast and I watch my diet. Sometimes I have to go "out of commission," because one can't really work or drive when the body's dealing with deep healing. Taking it easy by the river and watching the life in and around it, as I've just done for a week, is quite worthwhile. Who's life is it, anyway?

One could do this and heal on one's vacation, but rather than taking that opportunity to restore health the average consumer figures "this is my time to enjoy myself (and possibly be decadent)." Besides, modern freedom has been reduced mostly to the right to have a job and shop. Enjoying food, especially the processed kind to cater to jaded taste buds, is more important than anything to a good many people just trying to get by.

Such are the thoughts that can come from taking a real rest. The fast, when it's water only, gives the body a chance to heal because the immense work of digesting is suspended. So the body cleans itself out, while raising immunity thanks to the quick reduction in toxins.

Anyone in modern society exposed to industrialized food, car exhaust, stifling artificial buildings, petrochemical-pharmaceutical drugs, and rat-race stress has toxins piling up. With immunity thus taken down, it's natural that one falls prey to colds and worse.

The suffering people go through, told that being able to pay for medical insurance ensures health, is tragic and part of modern medicine's scam. I don't dispute the wonderful knowledge that medical science possesses. But when it dominates blindly we are worse than shortchanged.

On the River of Cottonwood Spores

Since I went on my 3 1/2 day fast in April [2009] for the Climate Emergency that was called when Congress went back into session, I moved my floating home, a humble sailboat. Now I'm in a more natural surrounding that is far more peaceful and entertaining. I've traded in mallard ducks at a more industrial marina for bald eagles, ospreys, herons, and other critters.

My short fast in April had the benefit of fixing my knees. Up until then they were giving me more and more trouble, despite my daily practice of hanging from a branch or bar to stretch my back. As I struggled on the pavements I wondered if this was just my aging or the cumulative effects of hard, unnatural surfaces. I received massage, Rolfing, and I applied stinging nettles to my knees. These helped a little, but temporarily. So I'm delighted to say that the feeling I'd had that my legs were falling apart disappeared completely because of that short fast. (At this interjection, nine months later, my knees are still great.) I would have fasted longer but there was a crisis with my boat that caused me to vacate for some days. Having been raised to allow a fast to complete its cycle, I am always reluctant to break it prematurely.

This time I went for 5 1/2 days, terminating it two days ago (mid July). If it were not for my confusion about the Oregon Country Fair schedule of events and my need to attend to more boat issues, I would have gone on longer, perhaps 20 days. (My record is 23 days in 2007). I feel now more energetic than before the fast, and find that the slight allergy symptoms that were irritating me are gone.

I am so moved by the peaceful river's flow, despite its obvious hidden pollution and sediment. There's almost no development where I am, and so it is almost always quiet here. The Urban Growth Boundary law of Oregon has saved this area for farms and wildlife. I have seen eagles, ospreys, herons, water rodents, bats, and more.

Very little trash floats by, amazingly. I now see a plastic bottle, he second I've seen in two months. Of course, almost all modern)oats are like complex plastic containers.

The motor boaters are unfortunately out in force each afternoon, :specially weekends. They are to sailboats and kayaks what cars are o bicycles. The motorboats cause unpleasant and even destructive vakes as the global warming machines churn the waters without egard to the lives of river creatures. Last summer when gasoline ;ot to $4 a gallon the river was a lot quieter.

Since we clearly have the same global energy situation and 'rightening climate trends now as we did last summer, it's safe to ay that people have not learned much. Or they just don't care. They will simply have to have their petroleum taken away from hem by larger events out of their control. What's silly about the party on, fossil fools" mindset is that it could be tomorrow that a 'ersian Gulf geopolitical meltdown can immediately seize up the oil narket, throwing the flow of supplies into paralysis (with kyrocketing prices, panic buying and hoarding as everyone peculates). Then we find out the unpleasant truth that alternative ìuels aren't ready on a big enough scale, are mainly for electricity)nly, and are an anemic answer for the way of life modern people lepend on.

The river has much to teach. Why does the flow and current 'ary? Why does the color change subtly every few hours? How :an sail transport work without favorable winds and we may not 1ave motor fuel? I can almost see the ancient canoes that hugged he banks for thousands of years.

The former native population got a lot of fish and other food out)f the river, otherwise known as work in our culture. Now the most uccessful fisherman I see of all the players on this river is the)sprey who is batting 1.000. Who all is eating who? What about ne, what can I eat out of the river safely? I was told that the carp ire a bad idea, too contaminated. The salmon and steelhead are a)etter bet as they're just passing through. The crawfish on the)ottom can be caged at the surface waters and fed vegetables to)urify them.

Whitey is a domestic looking goose who paddles up and down he river. Since he (or she) doesn't seem to have a mate, that would)e the goose for us to cook in order to be a bit compassionate. Nhitey likes the boysenberries I feed him, but his wild brethren don't. I try to talk to all the geese, but I usually sound like a duck. I don't know what a wild goose would taste like. And aren't they all contaminated on the river anyway?

The wild Canadian Aleutian geese are quite common. Their heads and necks are more slender than domestic geese. I was surprised to see mixed families: a semi-domestic-looking goose and his or her mate looking more wild. They have offspring that look mostly wild. The wild geese are fond of feasting on the floating cottonwood spores that sometimes make the river look like a garlanded mythical river. For weeks there's often a snow fall of millions of spores flitting around. I've not breathed too many yet.

Watching the birds and the river, seeing or hearing a big fish jump every few minutes, is a new way of spending the majority of one's day. I'm still tied to this blasted computer, but I'm out in the open and don't miss much. Being able to look up often and gaze into the distance at nature is definitely not what the average urban worker is able to do. It should be a crime to ask someone to work in a cubicle or factory for many hours at a time day after day. Do we have the power of choice, or not?

What should be so radical or outrageous about people demanding to be out in nature daily and taking the time to heal in nature, fasting and taking a break from industrialism?

Health Care in America

Treatments are pursued with dollars, with trust in technology and experts, just as society pursues a cure for the fossil-fueled economy with technological treatments and dollars. Each has failed and will continue to fail.

To buy some health is like trying to buy some spirituality by going to church while not changing one's way of life to really honor "Creation." The shallow dabbling into health, spirituality and ecological remediation through technofix exercises are all part of the consumer culture's superficial "solutions" that don't get to the root. If we do not detoxify our bodies, we can eventually get seriously ill and die before our time.

By the same token, if society does not stop generating toxic-wastes, it will self-destruct. Maybe no one will survive.

That a person or society allows exposure to toxicity as a matter of course is an indication of severe lack of judgment from the get go. There is little likelihood or opportunity for voluntarily detoxifying oneself or the ecosystem in the modernized world. Trying to argue for it may be a total waste of time with people who fear change and would rather make wishes instead of taking action.

Just as a sick person or someone of mediocre health believes a slight change in diet is a big deal eliminating red meat, for example — most people believe that changes on this level (including more recycling or minor reductions in carbon emissions) is quite significant and part of a major shift. The trouble with being satisfied with these kinds of changes is the timing: too little and too late. These changes may indicate a positive trend, but a point has already been reached where radical detoxification or culture change are required immediately. The other problem with the approach of limiting ourselves to minor changes or reforms is that the present ecocidal, unjust system is not treated as requiring immediate replacement.

Medical Insurance Does Not Equal Health or Healing

The "Check Your Neck" campaign is one of many that prompt Dr. Kramer [Barnett S.] Kramer, the associate director for disease prevention at the National Institutes of Health] to compare mass cancer screening to a lottery. "In exchange for those few who win the lottery," he said, "there are many, many others who have to pay the price in human costs." – *New York Times,* July 24, 2009, "Forty Years' War In Push for Cancer Screening, Limited Benefits"

To buy some health is like trying to buy some spirituality by going to church while not changing one's way of life to really honor "Creation." The shallow dabbling into health, spirituality and ecological remediation through technofix exercises are all part of the consumer culture's superficial "solutions" that don't get to the root.

If money can't buy love, why could it buy health?

Health Care in a Phantom Democracy

In 2002 I wrote The Health Care Tribe, but not in response to high health care costs. Rather, my concern was that people need to take care of one another: family, friends, and neighbors. Sounds a little odd for the U.S., does it not?

Low cost health care, or rather medical care as it really is constituted, is not a benefit if healing is not the purpose. "Getting better" perhaps — through treatments purchased — is what's hoped for, even for the rich. In their case, life is sometimes extended through great expense, but is it worth living hooked up to machines? Democracy has come to mean the poor too are on multiple legal drugs, with side effects requiring still more drugs.

More and more middle aged people in this nation look and feel like they are older: out of shape, and sometimes in the grip of chronic illness. The ultimate direction is early death. Health is a puzzlement to most people, just as buying a large house may or may not present structural or other flaws: surprises can happen, so we throw money at it and hope for the best. Too bad it doesn't work with the body. What does work, for the petrochemical pharmaceutical makers, is an increasingly addicted generation of sufferers.

Before we can solve this worsening scam, though a tribal community approach, one must take personal responsibility to care for one's body. Garbage in, garbage out. Get the garbage out through detoxifying.

Injecting self-care and community-care into the current "health care debate" requires redefining the power of the individual and the concept of community. If a maximum of community is desirable, tribal bonding (i.e., organized mutual aid) ought to be considered ideal, because less community through employment or other servitude results in a sham of community.

As innovative and effective as the Health Care Tribe concept may be, it cannot compete with big bucks from the capitalist medical/insurance establishment. Although we can reach many people with the health care tribe concept, and a few of them might implement it, we are almost entirely shut out of the national public discussions — not just on health but on everything. This is how our "democracy" works. It is not an accident or a flaw; it is deliberate.

When money and powerful interests dominate, there is no democracy. If you agree with the accuracy of that assessment, you must entertain the possibility that there has never been democracy under the U.S. system.

323

Yet we repeatedly try to participate in the phantom democracy, for we have little other recourse that would not be in some way embarrassingly pointless or suicidal. Our futile efforts at exercising real democracy are as sad as someone trying to elicit love from a heartless family member who has power enough to never relent.

On many fronts — climate protection, safeguarding public health from radiation poisoning, and the lack of health care — society shows it is dominated by the merciless, selfish bosses and puppet masters. How many more fronts need to be opened up before people see the hopelessness of the increasingly warped U.S. system and begin to establish the next society on the community level? It would greatly harken back to older, proven ways and principles.

The formation of tribes will happen, but it's well nigh impossible to make them work within the present order's chaotic but rigid deterioration. Nevertheless, the best preparation one can make for future survival is not "the dream solar power installation" or even "a great piece of land" but rather the creation of a tribe that can make it through societal collapse. The Health Care Tribe is a start, because our physical health is necessary for anything else we want to be possible.

A similar approach is the Time Bank (www.timebanks.org), "an exchange of services [e.g., elder care] on an hour for hour basis, free from taxation." Mission: "Strengthening communities through reciprocity."

҈

Source notes:
> *New York Times*, July 24, 2009, "Forty Years' War In Push for Cancer Screening, Limited Benefits"

Fasting for Healing and Inner Peace

Introduction

Healing through nature has been essential to sustainable cultures everywhere for untold millennia. However, today's dominant materialist culture has, mainly in the U.S., all but turned health care into a dubious and corrupt industry. So, addressing root causes — as fasting does with its detoxification and complete rest — is ignored or attacked as dangerous, typically by those interests who see fasting as unprofitable. (This certainly does not mean that all people who oppose fasting are insincere.)

Meanwhile, the raging debate on medical insurance and health-care costs rarely includes discussion on cheaper, more preventive and natural approaches to health and disease. This essay invites discussion of car-dependence and plastics-pollution as major factors in declining public (and ecological) health, but those issues have been dealt with in recent Culture Change Letters.

Especially in super-capitalistic USA, recent generations have grown up with commercials for pain relief instead of the elders' indigenous knowledge of local healing herbs, for example. The conventional approach to health in the U.S. has increasingly been to just attack symptoms. It's very clear why this is so when we see General Electric — a major, criminal polluter — in the "health care" field (it makes medical equipment), profiting off diseases it may have contributed to.

Health has been sacrificed for profit even in the classroom: Public schools were targets of beef and dairy industry efforts in the "innocent 1950s" to get children brainwashed to eat more of their products. The "Four Food Groups," two of which were meat and dairy, was simply propaganda, and was replaced in the late 1980s by the U.S. Dept. of Agriculture's Food Pyramid, whereby the base is grains, beans and vegetables, with little meat or dairy. Not addressed was the fact that higher up the food chain more toxins are present. Also, almost all the animals are given hormones, antibiotics and pesticides, fed "downed" animals, are poorly treated. Many times the amount of water and fossil fuels are utilized to make the same amount of animal- rather than vegetable-protein. However, vegetable diets in the U.S., especially, do not escape genetically modified organisms (GMOs) or the increased petroleum pesticides GMO crops require.

It is legal in most of the world for industry to constantly foist untested chemicals and radiation upon people and the environment, with certain but often-improvable long-term ill effects. We are expected or forced to accept tainted food/water/air, and especially in the USA to keep driving, stay at the computer, pop pills and drink coffee to keep going — anything but stop and challenge or change the status quo. The present socioeconomic system probably cannot be fixed, so it's up to us to take charge of our health and everything we see affecting us. To do so, we may, as individuals, have to rock our own worlds if we go on a fast, thus telling family members or authoritarians to back off and mind their own business.

What Is Fasting, and What's the Fuss?

Fasting (i.e., water only) for health is a human and animal process that needs no scientist, although the extent of knowledge from western medical science is wondrous and can help a patient. Once a fast is directly experienced, however, one can see how superfluous medical doctors can appear.

Doctors realize this themselves when faced with natural healing methods, and they see that their income would plummet from fasting. So it is no surprise that fear of fasting is instilled by for-profit medical professionals, academia, media, and their corporate support base. In contrast, there are at least several countries — especially where health care is socialized — that utilize fasting openly and do not consign it to the closet of ignorance.

It is well known that any animal overfed does not live as long as an animal fed significantly less. Up to a point, the less an animal is fed, the longer it lives. People in modern society are increasingly obese, sometimes due to psychological disorders or gland dysfunction. The overweight consumer is no surprise since security has been defined often as having a stockpile of frozen, canned and dehydrated foods that are processed for jaded tastes. People may overeat due to conditioning and for lack of freedom to really go out and enjoy an active life. Most of us are wage slaves, or may have such material deprivation, that taking the time to fast or take a vacation for health is as unthinkable as moving to the countryside to live in beauty and ease. That's a lost dream for the downtrodden and the unimaginative.

Fasting works. The Bible is full of references to it, and there is a good reason our first meal of the day is called breakfast: the body needs to have little or no food in it during sleep. Going right to sleep on a full stomach causes discomfort or disturbed sleep. Fasting equals real rest.

Apart from a spiritual minority's need for vision-questing and meditation, fasting in today's more secular world is just for physical health. It is almost always a good thing at any time if one is free to do it and does it right. But fasting barely addresses diseases' root causes such as a stressful lifestyle in a polluted environment. Fasting is not very compatible with pursuits of the modern world that demand our relentless speed, multi-tasking, and unthinking slavery. Taking some medical drug (usually made from fossil fuels) as a quick fix, or even getting sicker by neglecting our bodies and our mounting toxicity, are preferred by those who can't conceive of an alternative to the daily onslaught of stress, pollution and second-rate eating habits.

The Nitty Gritty of Water Fasting

In a fast, patience is the key to lasting as long as an effective fast requires. Patience is necessary for correct management of the fast and for the critical post-fast period. Impatience causes premature termination of a fast, which can precipitate an adverse reaction as well as bring the fast's healing process to a virtual stop. Sometimes one wishes to fast patiently but is too active mentally about one's projects and problems. If one is fasting while attempting to accomplish tasks of the materialist world, this is only to the detriment of the fast. Fasting requires much resting horizontally and getting enough sleep. Insomnia does not help a fast, so this is when a fasting coach or supervisor, or spouse or lover, can make all the difference by providing encouragement and such favors as a massage to facilitate sleep.

There is a simple cycle to a full fast. On Day One, eating is abruptly ended and bed rest may be necessary. One can, if not suffering from a miserable cold or flu, function normally doing a day or two of fasting without missing work or school.

Some fasters or would-be fasters believe religiously in first undergoing a mechanical colonic cleanse, although I have never seen anyone fail to have a good fast just because they skipped having a colonic cleanse.

After missing a few meals, whatever pain(s) the body has disappears almost entirely, in most cases. Hunger can be slightly bothersome during the first day or two of a fast. Then changes in the body and emotional or spiritual state start to become more

327

obvious. Instead of the pain of whatever symptoms, such as sore throat or toothache, the body mainly experiences an acceleration of toxic elimination, and hunger generally abates. The mind, however, may be more attached to the thought of food than the body is.

During the pre-fasting symptoms — the evidence of illness that may prompt us to fast — the discharge of mucus is an unpleasant inconvenience and irritation. Those symptoms may continue until the fast is nearly finished. The urge to stop the symptoms, whether one is fasting or not, is understandable. However, even people's cherished natural treatments, e.g., echinacea, vitamin C and homeopathic medicine, are temporary measures that do not offer a long-term solution, nor do they always work. Fasting always takes effect and means complete rest, and is more of a long-term solution. But it is not "the solution" because it does not by itself permanently change, for example, the habitual intake of artery-cloggers known as cheeseburgers, nor the intake of carbon monoxide and other toxins from sitting in cars.

Non-Fasters' Denial and Self-Imposed Misery

Life-style change is the real cure, which medical doctors generally agree with more and more nowadays. Unfortunately, the fact that life-style change is the real factor in preventing heart attacks — and not the heart bypass operations that may not fix all the vulnerable areas — is not disclosed to hapless patients, according to David Cundiff, MD, author of *The Right Medicine*. His long experience tells him that the $40-50,000 heart-bypass cost is a waste, but the cost outlay and the doctor's orders do ignite a scared patient's dietary change, cessation of smoking cigarettes, and the adoption of more exercise.

I have known many people, including family members, who have suffered allergies or respiratory ailments for many years. Instead of trying a fast or attempting a mucusless diet, they may rely on medicines and accept a lack of top physical performance in order to cope. Their misery, however, continues and stifles their capabilities and denies them their best mood. Worse, the toxification has not been addressed and it only increases. If simple ailments are allowed to remain because they are not addressed through improved diet, elimination of pollution and better rest and exercise, and intense detoxification through fasting does not ensue, the body may take on a serious disease. One could say the body's purpose in so doing is to really get the person's attention, just as nerves signal the brain that a hand on a hot stove is a bad idea.

With cancer, the body's notification — to our distracted, stressed-out minds — of something seriously wrong, may be, by definition, too late. But faced with choosing between radiation and chemotherapy, which frequently kill the patient, I would fast and improve my environment instead of "destroying the village in order to save it." The fear of ignoring authority and one's peer group and missing some meals prompts people to choose super-expensive anti-life treatments. It should be remembered that the word antibiotic means anti-life. There are more and more doctors who advocate a natural-healing approach to diseases such as cancer. And, there are cases where chemotherapy and radiation do work. Perhaps a post-medical-treatment fast would restore some of the body's immunity and rid the body of certain residues.

One may live with a chronic disease, but life may be shortened, or a fatal disease can come along. At that point, a fast may still be possible to turn around one's health, but one may find the freedom to fast no longer exists. Certainly in the case of Terri Schiavo, who was famously disconnected from her feeding tubes, the "fast" was terminal, non-healing, and arguably a blessing. In fact, some people at the end of their long lives choose a dignified, painless ending through fasting, as was the choice of well-known activists Helen and Scott Nearing.

There are times when fasting will not work to rejuvenate and restore, and fasting would be inadvisable — but the alternative can be worse: in addition to radiation or chemotherapy, surgery and mishaps kill patients; even a non-critical hospital stay can kill because of medical or bureaucratic mistakes and the germ-ridden environments of hospitals. The food at hospitals is notoriously poor, although many would argue it is wholesome, just like a corporate cafeteria or a prison offers the best organic, fresh, local ingredients — not!

The resistance to fasting is largely psychological, or is often based on misinformation and fear. Rather than miss even two meals, the chronically mucus-congested person may stubbornly refuse to try a short fast of 24 hours. One of my family members, addicted to nose drops to relieve sinusitis for years, tried just a day and a half fast and got unprecedented relief. However, that experiment was never repeated or expanded, despite the clear success, and she went back to nose drops chronically — even though on the container the directions say not to use the drug longer than a few days consecutively.

Food addiction is real. It is a joke-phrase, when we all need food, but some people cannot bear the idea of missing a meal no matter how miserable they are because they do not give their bodies a complete rest through fasting.

People — doctors and non-doctors alike — have varied and endless arguments against fasting. Some say it is dangerous for a person to fast if one is too underweight or has a certain kind of blood condition. A chiropractor priding herself on holistic healing once assured me, when I told her about a successful fast I recently had had, that "fasting causes brain damage." Any brain damage I might have ever had, however, must have predated the fast — when I think of how foolish I had been to go to her in the first place, as she eventually inflicted an injury on me by punching down on my chest to "adjust" a rib!

Arguments for Fasting

The thin person can and should fast, particularly if weight-gain has been difficult even when eating has been adequate. In my experience, fasting rebuilds the body and one attains a clean slate, making weight-gain finally possible beyond replacing the pounds lost in the fast.

In today's toxic world, when PCBs and DDT are in breast milk, and all Americans have one or more forms of plastic or plastic additives in their urine, one would think that detoxification is vital. However, fasting is so unknown and ignored that I know of no before/after studies that have measured how much less a body's petrochemical contamination is after a thorough fast. One therefore must base progress or improved safety "by feel," and how much more immunity to disease, such as colds, may be clearly obtained by fasting. Fortunately, benefits such as immunity are substantial and noticeable.

Other benefits of fasting include improving erectile function. Generally, one does not feel like engaging in sex during a fast, but it is possible and pleasurable. The big point here is the future reward that helps make the fast worthwhile, if improved erections are desired. (Or take some Viagra and keep treating your body like a machine.) Another noticeable benefit from a fast is the improved retaining of one's urine longer and more comfortably.

During a fast, just sleeping is a sheer pleasure. This particular feeling cannot be achieved by any other means, such as drugs or alcohol or sex. It's fortuitous I'm on a little fast right now as I write; because I had forgotten the special sweetness of sleeping that can happen in a fast. Sometimes this pleasurable feeling is only upon waking up in the morning. The feeling can be absent or fleeting if one is not ready to eat. If the fast has done all its detoxification — through all one's cells, it seems — then the ecstasy of awakening is long lasting and strong, causing one to bound out of bed in joy. Some of us take longer to reach certain points in the fast, and a full-cycle fast can take longer depending on age, toxicity and weight.

During the fast and one's slowed pace, a peaceful though somewhat melancholy vibe usually takes over. Worries fall away and one relaxes while the mind lets go. Thoughts don't stop; one does daydream, but stress is less. This feeling is meditative and deep, and may be hard to achieve or impossible to imagine without the fast. One's usual eating state — while having the typical, modern, chronically high toxin level — seems to block the mind and spirit from becoming one with nature and the universe. Being on a short fast as I write this, I marvel at the more peaceful feeling I am enjoying. Slowing down our often frantic and usually busy day is vital for health and reflection. We evolved in a calmer, natural state, with a slower pace, than today's industrial and technological lifestyle. Primitive people worked less than people of cultures of the Agricultural and Industrial Revolutions.

Many people want to be more spiritual and have a spiritual experience, in addition to being healthy. But many such people refuse to try the fasting route. Their interest in meditation and spirituality translates mainly to sitting, while their whole body is still distracted by the work of digestion (even between meals, the body is not cleansed of food and waste for long). They read, go on quests at retreats, and sing the praises of calming the mind to "tune into" the universe without workaday distractions. This is sincere but lacking in the most ready experience of total mind & body meditation: fasting with just water. Communion with nature and one's own soul are easy and constant with fasting, lasting for days, but this sure-fire meditation is rejected or avoided simply because of one's culture and our mind's conditioned rules of habitual eating.

People are much more likely to take various mind-altering drugs for some instant Nirvana or cheap high than to try a fast. If they do later fast, the drug residues just have to come out, making the elimination phase of the fast that much longer.

People preach about meditation and spirituality, but for various reasons have never tried a fast except perhaps to go on a juice diet for a few days. Jesus reportedly fasted 40 days, but he was less unusual in his time and place than such a faster in the U.S. and many countries today. I know he must have gotten a lot out of his fast, an idea that anti-fasters of the Christian sects would also swear by as an article of faith — even though they never fast, as if Western medicine and the god of science take precedence over Jesus' ways and teachings.

Some Downsides of the Fast

In my lifetime of fasting and witnessing others fast, I have never seen an adverse reaction to fasting; I have only seen mistakes upon eating before one is ready, or eating too much too soon, or eating too richly. The main consequences of those common pitfalls are (1) usually a sudden dissipation of the finished fast's nirvana–like pleasure of feeling alive, and (2) the immediate loss of the renewed taste buds' newfound thrill after the fast. Self-control is difficult, so a knowledgeable companion or caregiver is very helpful.

One friend, who took it upon herself to fast 26 days, after I described my experiences, endured a significant hair loss after the fast had ended several days before, but it all grew back. I do not know exactly how the fast was conducted or what constituted the resumption of eating. This event was worrisome to the woman, because she was unprepared for it. It was rare enough that I had never heard of it. She was glad she fasted anyway, as she had spent years handling chemicals as a painter and she wanted to detoxify.

Early symptoms of poor health or low immunity, such as a runny nose, are messages from the body to our conscious minds that there is an imbalance with our bodies, and that there needs to be rest and our intake altered. During the fast, elimination of mucus can start to increase or decrease, but the consistency of the mucus gets more concentrated. The smell and taste of the discharge, and the odor of the breath and urine, get stronger. The strongest elimination is that of vomiting, after which one feels much better.

Drinking water throughout is important, although may not be as pleasant as when we have just eaten a large salty meal. The middle portion of the fast is characterized by heavy elimination, and vomiting can be nightly two or three nights in a row. The mind and facial expression of the faster in this period are sometimes sad, bored, and possibly impatient. Nevertheless, healing is proceeding regardless and rapidly during this phase, and the fast should not be broken at this point. When the body has eliminated most of its toxins, the original "dis-ease" is gone, and pain-relief is usually complete, but the fast continues its final cleansing of the body's toxins. Hunger may start to return slightly, and the tendency is for one to want to terminate the fast to shake off the boredom, enjoy normality once again, and taste those fabulous foods one has missed.

However, a white/yellow-coated tongue and listless behavior indicate that the fast should not be broken at such a time, despite the excellent detoxification that has been taking place. Letting the fast continue is important for maximum healing, as is complete rest. No vitamins or herbal teas should be taken to interrupt the fast (activating the digestive system and distracting the heart from sending the maximum amount of healing-blood to the rest of the body).

Walking in the garden is fine, but stress such as business calls is counter-indicated. The body can take some stress if there is no purpose to the walk other than to shake off some boredom and to behold the wonder of nature. Nature, and life itself, by the middle of the fast, have taken over the mind and spirit, and one's full contemplation of nature and indoor surroundings is inescapable. Time has slowed down in the fast, which may be a consequence of the meditative state achieved by the complete rest and the desire to see the end of the fast. The memory of foods becomes almost overpowering. Paradoxically, the yearning for food and to indulge in taste sensations at this stage are an indication the fast is not complete. One needs to return to the novel or to quietly talk with a friend or family member. Great rewards come when detoxification is complete and the body and spirit feel better than ever.

An alternative to the fast that seems to detoxify is the Master Cleanse: a drink one makes of water, lemon juice, grade B maple syrup, and cayenne. A "salt water flush" is done once a day. The Master Cleanse calls for certain preparations and quantities of the ingredients. Judging from the white tongue during the Master Cleanse that clears up after several days, and the need to rest most of the time, the Master Cleanse may be just right for many of us. It appears to be a way to keep up a semblance of a normal schedule, because calories are available to deal with some work or schooling. Somehow, though, the water-only fast would be much preferable for its simplicity, purity and faster results — and perhaps for the meditative benefit. The ingredients of the Master Cleanse comprise a strange diet, one must admit. It may be harder to refuse substantial food when one is on a very restrictive diet and the body is in an eating/digestion mode. But if people are opposed to fasting, or cannot obtain the privacy and support they deserve, they should perhaps try the Master Cleanse.

Triumphing Over Sickness and Narrow Habits

The end of the fast clearly approaches when mood improves, symptoms disappear, energy returns, and hunger may reappear or intensify. However, the full return of energy, as in the capability to run, and the joy of feeling alive, along with clear, beautiful eyes, for example, are the real indicators that the fast is complete — one has forgotten about the fixation on food. A bowel movement may be the best indication a fast is over. When calm and euphoria coexist in a clean, happy body and mind, and one desires — with freedom rather than obsession or conditioning — to resume nourishment and end the fast, it is a good time to eat.

It is particularly critical not to break a fast with "heavy food" such as refined or processed or heavily cooked foods. Combinations are a bad idea, so a fast is to be safely broken with one small item of raw, organic food. I have found that cooked brown rice or miso soup also work well, even though they are not raw. Over the next few meals, one has only one food at a time. If one broke a fast on one large raw carrot, one can, by day three of eating (after a fast of ten or fifteen days, for example), eat two large carrots for a meal. No salad dressing! One can switch immediately, upon breaking the fast on one food, to another food for the subsequent meals. Meals should be spaced apart by at least two to four hours, and eating should only occur when hunger is present.

After a few days, simple combinations are fine and quantities are increased. Generally, one cannot eat a pizza and wash it down with beer until the fast has had its full rebuilding time afterward: the same amount of time as the fast. So, a six-day fast must have another six days of eating very carefully, and one guards against overeating and unwise combinations. Fortunately, one does not have any desire for alcohol or other drugs (including refined sugar) after a fast if the period after breaking the fast is carefully handled.

I eventually fasted voluntarily as a child and was not forced. I have been around people fasting and have assisted them, but I don't pressure them to fast. Fasting is an individual decision and must only be undertaken when conditions are conducive and the opportunity is there.

When one has to drive a car or meet a deadline, for example, it is not a good idea to fast because rest is imperative. For a full-cycle fast with no arbitrary end point, one needs to block out time such as one's entire winter or spring vacation, or longer. Good books and someone to help pamper are good ideas. It is also vital to accept a slowing down of one's world and the unpleasantness of toxin-elimination. Right after one of my fasts in Los Angeles, where I would lapse right back into habits that created the discomforts that prompted me to fast, I was struck by the notion that driving a car is a violation of the spirit. I did not know what that meant exactly, but I could feel it.

I have been amazed at how much good a one-day fast (24 hours) has occasionally done me. On a New Year's Day in 1997 perhaps, a family bike ride — all of us fasting — made it memorable for the beauty of the beach we rode to. I later noted that my hay fever did not return that season ahead.

My father fasted 40 days with just Perrier water, upon contracting myasthenia gravis in 1974. It seemed just a bad flu at first. Aristotle Onassis caught the same disease at the same time in the same place, and the most expensive medical help in the world could not save him. My father was written off as dying by doctors and friends who paid their last respects. When his test results started turning around in the middle of the fast, the doctors dismissed it all as a fluke. Fasting is very unprofitable for doctors whose bread and butter are just drugs and surgery. Dan Lundberg, my father, got rid of his asthma permanently during that 40 day fast. His recovery from myasthenia gravis was rapid, and he lived twelve more years to age 73.

Western medical history has been full of deadly treatments by doctors who eventually went on, after many victims, to less harmful or different treatments. Bloodletting was long common centuries ago, along with many cockamamie methods. Circumcision was a cure for masturbation that supposedly caused blindness or distraction from going to church or the factory. Nowadays, tonsils are not removed; when I was a child my brothers and sisters were different for keeping my tonsils. X-rays were touted as miraculous and harmful, but over the years the "sage dosage" has been diminishing and diminishing, so that there is no harmless level at all according to scientists. The point here is that the harmful things doctors do are still with us, although practices and fads change.

My own fasts started with the very short ones that sufficed when I was a small child, whereby a cold or flue was dispensed with completely. When I got into my teens, the three-day fast did not do the trick, and several days became necessary. At age 20 I did a twelve day fast: on the twelfth day before breaking the fast, I ran on the beach faster and further than I ever had before. I also experienced euphoria of enjoying smells, thoughts, and familiar Beatles songs whose humor had sometimes eluded me before.

I have had other fasts that benefited me regarding some of the unpleasant effects of aging (I'm 52 [when I wrote this]). And one fast of nine days last September completely alleviated a nerve injury to my collarbone area that an overzealous masseuse caused. I have accomplished such feats as eliminating my hay fever long-term, stopped completely the toothache pain that Ibuprofen was powerless to help, and at age 20 I erased acne scars. As I have increased my happiness and peace of mind after a fast, it has occurred to me that mental illness can be said to be a disease of the head. The brain, or the mind, is a piece of meat like the stomach or liver. If the body is unhealthy, the mind cannot be healthy. Healing needs to take place in the mind and cannot be accomplished fully if the body is toxic or overstressed.

It is commonly believed that modern society has increased longevity, whereas the quality of life slips. However, has life really been extended when the statistics rely on averages and distortions? Lessened infant mortality can make it look like adults stopped dying typically at 45 and instead live many years longer. At the other end of the spectrum, people are kept alive beyond their capacity to live normally (e.g., the Schiavo case) that boosts "life expectancy." Medical science helps, but most people do not benefit, and the public health and real life expectancy must be slipping, as evidenced by rising cancer rates.

I have never had a vaccination. I never got any of the diseases that shots can prevent, but plenty of people have gotten the disease directly from the shot. The materials in vaccines have included poisons that the body must process out if possible. With high immunity, diseases are successfully fought off. If a disease comes, it means that detoxifying and immunity raising are urgent.

Caveats Include the Influenced Mind

While society says it is alright for young people to eat junk food, sit in front of the TV for hours a day, drive cars, and use questionable and legal medications, young people are somehow not supposed to learn about fasting. One of my classroom experiences was in Hollywood High, in my senior year in 1970, when the health teacher told us to do a report on any topic on health. The teacher came to me after the assignment was given and said the principal forbade my reporting on fasting. But one student heard me talking about it and went on what turned out to be a twelve-day fast on her own accord. She transformed herself from an overweight, pimply girl into a beautiful, happy, young adolescent. The teacher was not interested, or, was more interested in keeping her job.

Fasting can be used as a weapon when its mention is designed to instill fear or paint a person as out of the mainstream or a kook. Ex–spouses contesting custody of a child sometimes have resorted to accusations of fasting. And in a conservatorship trial, I was accused by my sister, who seized control of the family oil information business, as believing in fasting when she was persuading Santa Barbara Superior Court Judge J. William McLafferty to deny our mother — railroaded into conservatorship

ind over time dispossessed of all he wealth I had made for her —
he right to live in her own home.

Instead, Mesa Lundberg languishes, healthy enough but lonely
ind neglected, in a costly nursing home. She is there against her
vill where warehousing the dying, and not healing, is the for-profit
ibjective. There was more to the case, such as the accusation that
.ome mild mildew in Mesa's nice home in moist Humboldt County,
California, was by implication dangerous mold. Obviously, clean
ind healthful conditions — and not just good diet — are vital for
good health. But as to fasting, Mesa had made clear to the judge
hat fasting was not an issue for anyone to worry about, and he
ippeared satisfied. Interestingly, Mesa's "anti-fasting" daughter is
·xpert at fasting, from the earliest age onward.

My family knew Herbert Shelton, the well-known fasting
iractitioner and owner of clinics and healing resorts. He wrote
nany books on fasting and digestion. My father started the family
in fasting when he met a former patient of Shelton's who helped
:ure, via fasting, my older brother and sister of deadly childhood
lysentery in Mexico. For a lifestyle change, the family later went
iff to live by a pristine river, in a big tent in Kern County,
California.

One should not advise fasting unless a competent and qualified
ielper is on hand to assist, as one needs guidance and support. It
:an't be overstated that one's stress must be minimized during and
ust after the fast. (I have had heart-rate unpleasantness from
rying to do too many things in succession right after a 15 day fast,
:ausing me to have to suddenly lie down and stop my activity for a
ialf an hour.)

I once fasted in jail for three days because I didn't like the idea of
he food there, and I had the opportunity to lie around and read. I
vas there because of a false arrest in a Critical Mass bicycling
irotest, in 1996 during the ongoing deforestation of ancient
·edwoods in Humboldt County, California. Subconsciously I must
iave wanted to see the inside of a cell. The downside was that the
vater in jail was foul, the fluorescent lights never went off, and the
emperature was too cool for comfortable fasting. Guards made
ure one did not get under the blanket during daylight hours even
o keep warm — no explanation. They did not know or care I was
in an apparent hunger strike.

Recent observation on the human body's durability without food has been from hunger strikes ending in death. In Ireland, rebels fasted over 50 days before succumbing to starvation. Irreversible damage to the prisoners' health no doubt preceded the day of death. The person's age and size has everything to do with how long one can fast, so it is important not to assume a young, thin person can go many days. A truly healthy person needs a truly short fast.

Anyone intending to fast or who has started a fast may face interference from a well-intentioned person during a fast if the person is concerned that "starvation" is taking place, or if symptoms (elimination of toxins and listlessness) are misconstrued as a threat to health rather than evidence of a healing crisis. Privacy and calm, therefore, are advisable. There are medical doctors who advocate and can assist in fasting, although they are rare. It is not for me to advocate the disregarding of medical advice, nor to give medical advice or practice medicine. For in the words of Richard Milhous Nixon during Watergate, "That would be wrong, that's for sure."

Happy fasting, happy eating, long and beautiful life — through being closer to nature. This treatise has been about healing oneself and about inner peace, but I also believe there is potential for healing the world and bringing about more peace if many more people will come to fast.

— *San Francisco, California*

* * * * *

Herbert Shelton's books can be bought at
www.nelsonsbooks.com/index37.html
One can also find one or two of them, along with booklet "Food Combining Made Easy" (the science of digestion) in health food stores.
www.thenazareneway.com/diet/fasting.htm
www.hps-online.com/fasting.htm
curezone.com practices "educating instead of medicating" and is forum-based for public interchange of ideas and experience, including fasting.
From a fasting clinic:
www.healthpromoting.com/Fasting/fasting.htm

Appendices

I
Our Post-Peak Oil Future
A Comparison of Two Scenarios Following the Global Peak in Oil
Production produced by Bay Localize, Oakland, California, and
Culture Change
Original at www.baylocalize.org/files/Our_Post-
Peak_Oil_Future.pdf

II
World Oil Reduction for the Gulf Resolution
(What to do about the BP gusher in the Gulf of Mexico, and
subsequent disasters)
WORG at www.WorldOilReduction.org

III
My Amtrak Peak Oil Tour
November 28, 2005
Culture Change Letter #115
Original at
www.culturechange.org/cms/index.php?option=com_content&tas
k=view&id=32&Itemid=2

IV
Cars and car ads slammed in pro-car corporate newspaper
Two letters published in the *San Francisco Examiner* from Jan
Lundberg

Jan Lundberg

Our Post-Peak Oil Future

A Comparison of Two Scenarios Following the Global Peak in Oil Production

Modern society is tied to petroleum more than any source of energy and materials. Peak global extraction of oil means ever diminishing supplies – with no alternative source or combination of sources capable of replacing oil at anywhere near the same net-energy balance, flow rate, or volume.

Hubbert's Peak
Bell-shaped Curve

In the 1950s the well known U.S. geologist M. King Hubbert noted that oil discoveries graphed over time tended to follow a bell-shaped curve. He supposed that the rate of oil production would follow a similar curve, now known as the "Hubbert Curve" (see figure above). Despite widespread criticism at the time,

Hubbert successfully predicted that the continental United States would peak in oil production in the early 1970s – a daunting reality that has made the U.S. economy increasingly reliant on oil imports to meet growing domestic demand.

Despite growing agreement that Hubbert's general theory is sound, considerable debate remains as to how the inevitable decline in oil supplies will play out, and what the implications will be for society at large. In this appendix, we've outlined two contrasting theories: (1.) author John Michael Greer's "Catabolic Collapse" theory, which predicts that energy descent will follow a stair-step pattern of overall decline, punctuated by brief periods of economic recovery; and (2.) oil analyst Jan Lundberg's "petrocollapse" theory, which postulates a steep, cliff-like drop-off in oil production, with dramatic consequences for our economy.

Catabolic Collapse: Stair-step Decline
Excerpted from Frank Kaminski's review of John Michael Greer's The Long Descent

In his book, *The Long Descent*, John Michael Greer foresees a period of glacial deindustrialization driven by a process that he refers to as "catabolic collapse." Greer begins with a bit of background on peak oil, the Club of Rome's *The Limits to Growth* study, some lessons from past societal collapses and the difference between problems (which are solvable) and predicaments (which aren't). He makes a strong case for peak oil being a predicament rather than a problem.

Drawing on the theory of catabolic collapse, Greer outlines in detail how our predicament is likely to play out during the decades and centuries ahead. His theory shows how civilizations headed for collapse tend to decline in a gradual, downward stair-step of repeated crises and recoveries. They don't undergo the sudden, catastrophic free fall envisioned by diehard peak oil doomers.

How will our own society's catabolic collapse proceed? Greer sees us on the verge of a couple of decades of economic contraction, chronic energy shortages, declining public health, political turmoil and vanishing knowledge and cultural heritage. This crisis period, he predicts, will be followed by a respite of perhaps 25 years or so, during which industrial civilization's newfound relief from the lavish energy demands of universal motoring and electrification,

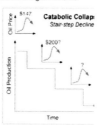

Catabolic Collap...
Stair-step Decline

climate-controlled buildings, modern medicine and other present-day amenities will buy it a little breathing room. But this respite will, in turn, be followed by another round of crises that will rid our civilization of further layers of social complexity, and so on.

Eventually, the developed world will assume an agrarian lifestyle built around local communities and sustainable resources. But this change will happen so slowly that no one alive today will be around to witness the end result. Thus, Greer maintains, our energies should be focused not on surviving the end of industrial civilization, but on making it through the imminent crisis period that will be but one brief interval within that larger context.

To this end, Greer lays out some strategies and technologies for weathering the coming decades of crisis. The appropriate response to the challenges we face, Greer believes, is not to set up survivalist enclaves or lifeboat communities, but to reshape our existing cities, towns and rural neighborhoods in order to better meet those challenges.

On an individual level, everyone needs to sharply curtail energy usage and find low-tech ways of doing things, in order to prepare for the inevitable shortages. We also need to position ourselves into occupational niches that meet actual human needs, since these are the jobs that are likely to stay in demand. In the face of declining public health, each person should learn to take charge of his or her own health. Lastly, we must help foster local community networking, which will be essential in preserving basic services like public safety and sanitation when the federal government proves ineffectual.

Petrocollapse: A Steep Drop-off in Oil
by Jan Lundberg, CultureChange.org

We face an imminent and abrupt oil-free future with dramatically lower per capita energy use. Most literate people have heard of peak oil, but many have been led to assume there will be a slow, down-slope of extracted supply past the peak. This is theoretical, based on estimates of reserves remaining in the ground, accurate or not.

What must be appreciated are the market-supply dynamics and oil industry functions such as refinery constraints. These inflexibilities will trigger not just sudden, crippling shortages but the inability of the oil industry to maintain a flow of products at a sustained, long-term level – a scenario which I call "petrocollapse."

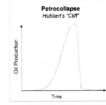

Petrocollapse
Hubbert's "Cliff"

Oil Production

Time

In 1979 my firm Lundberg Survey accurately predicted that a 9% shortfall would lead to skyrocketing prices, panic buying, and hoarding – what oil investment banker Matthew Simmons calls a "run on the energy bank." When the next global supply crisis occurs without the oil industry's or government's ability to come to the rescue, the socioeconomic effects will be rapid and devastating. In days, grocery stores and community gardens will be stripped clean, and car commuters will not be able to get to jobs. Businesses will shut, in part due to their reliance on "just in time delivery." There will be no floor to the crash until local food supplies can meet what the remaining population size has become.

The oil industry's only model is growth. The only large-scale economic model known is for growth, made possible in the past from petroleum supplies in ever-increasing abundance. These sources are collapsing in oil-producing countries, and demand will never be met by tar sands, heavy oils, or biofuels. As oil supply plummets, the industry will be unable to adapt. It cannot just ratchet down its refining output to follow a smooth depletion curve. Refineries must utilize their capacity at high levels to produce a balance of products (gasoline, distillates, fuel oils). This need will remain even as lower-producing wells are capped and already rusting facilities require ever-growing investments and retrofits.

The quick slackening of business and employment along with worldwide demand-destruction for oil are features of petrocollapse. We are in an early phase, with a sudden, massive supply-crunch inevitable. The hoped-for "recovery" without cheap energy and other resources for a growing population cannot happen. It is just a matter of time for the next Oil Shock and great demand-destruction for oil and other key consumer products. This will transform the modern lifestyle to post-industrial, local living.

Bay Localize – September 2009

World Oil Reduction for the Gulf Resolution

It is time for the environmentally aware and all who love the Earth to unite in order to save it. We must make immediate cuts in petroleum if we are to counteract and mitigate the quantity of oil and methane that has spewed from the catastrophic gusher in the Gulf of Mexico. We must also begin to live as if resources in a fragile, finite world have limits. Insatiable energy demand is unsustainable in the face of increasingly difficult-to-access supplies. In the absence of responsible leadership, the following Resolution looks to the American people and their local representatives to take action and guide a nation in understanding that the actions of each and every one of us ultimately affect all life on Earth.

Whereas the Gulf of Mexico accident involving British Petroleum's Deepwater Horizon oil rig and well on April 20, 2010 is the biggest oil release in history, spewing unprecedented pollution into the environment, harming sea creatures and clean-up workers, and threatening the livelihood and health of millions of people;

Whereas the entire petroleum industry and consumption of its products are an ongoing "spill" into the global environment — approximately 85 million barrels of oil a day – the vast gusher in

the Gulf adds a spike of additional greenhouse gas emissions from oil-burning and methane into our already stressed atmosphere;
Whereas the damage caused by the BP catastrophe will be long lasting and not fully remedied by clean up, the citizenry must take steps to counteract the damage by reducing oil consumption for Earth's ecosystem;
Whereas people can reduce oil consumption and production in a variety of ways immediately, such behavior can make this oil reduction in an amount equivalent to or even exceeding the quantity assaulting the Gulf of Mexico and global environment. Means of reduction include car-pooling, bicycling, public transit, banning many disposable plastics, and ceasing purchase of foreign foods shipped long distances via oil. Closing oilrigs and refineries of the renegade corporation BP might be another rapid way to cut global pollution as well;
Whereas a "clean energy future" as a sole approach to cutting petroleum use cannot be immediate, nor on a scale relative to cheap oil, this can serve to keep putting off curtailment of fossil fuels; many people avoid slashing energy use now in hopes of sustainable energy. Renewable energy investment, while advisable, cannot be fast enough to ameliorate releases of petroleum from accidents and ongoing petroleum production.

Therefore, be it resolved:
This [city of ___ / state of ___ / national gov't of ___ / community of ___] will commence to reduce its petroleum consumption in order to help bring about the global reduction of petroleum extraction and refining. In so doing we do our part to meet a planetary goal of counteracting the petroleum gusher in the Gulf of Mexico caused by BP and lax U.S. oversight. We hereby authorize a [committee / task force / Commission] to explore how to most quickly and thoroughly advance this Resolution. The appointed body, subject to periodic re-selection by the electorate, will hasten to gather research and recommend steps to implement measures that this [government / community] may approve, to be followed with the force of law.

Drafted by Jan Lundberg, independent oil industry analyst, Culture
Change, July 10, 2010

My Amtrak Peak Oil Tour

November 28, 2005
Culture Change Letter #115

After a going away party, on September 6 I took a train from
Emeryville, California bound for Washington, D.C. That was my
base for five conferences, mostly in the Eastern U.S., where I had
been hired to speak on peak oil and petrocollapse. Here's some of
what I said, and what I learned during my odyssey:

Meeting interesting people, making new friends, and seeing
wonderful places is a good life. Travel is second nature to me,
having visited dozens of countries mostly by sailboat back when
environmental consciousness was not even in its infancy. (Today
it's in its infancy, which explains how the fortunes of car
manufacturers are allowed to be treated as a bigger news story
than the crashing of ecosystems.)

Encountering so many Americans and making conversation in
the dining car while the landscape rolls by allows one to take a
reading on the national mood. It was clear to me that there is
almost no support for the Iraq War, no matter what walk of life I
ran into. The most support I found for the soldiers was that the
stateside loved ones had a sense of quiet pride clouded by fear for
the soldiers' safety. A rising number of citizens seems to grasp the
foolhardiness of killing for oil far away as we consume our way to
our uncertain greenhouse future.

Train travelers are a bit more aware of the absurdity of car
domination, and generally would be more likely to be anti-Bush.
But hardly anyone is embracing much of a lifestyle change. Few
people in the U.S. seem to understand their own culture. After my
ten weeks of travel around the country, I reaffirm that this lack of
understanding and inaction includes my hometown of Berkeley,
California: environmental awareness and leftism and are only a bit
more common here than in the rest of the nation.

Such insights might be as worthwhile as the other aspects of my
ten-week trip. On many an occasion I enhanced my own enjoyment
by getting a rise out of people when I answered their question
"where do you live?" by responding, "I live on Amtrak." It is
tolerable to criss-cross the continent on Amtrak if one brings along

alternatives to the corporate food and water on the train. I also brought along a good, fat book, *Crossing the Rubicon*, by Michael Ruppert.

I had been pent up in Arcata, in redwood country, for years trying to assist my mother who was dispossessed of Lundberg Survey, the petroleum information firm. She was subsequently denied her freedom to live in her own home thanks to elder abuse and fraud. Now, after my presence there was unnecessary and the legal case was lost ("Money talks," opined the Humboldt County Court Investigator), I could finally live my fantasy of taking my message out on the road (or rails) with my guitar.

On this tour I exhibited and distributed the award–winning film "Our Synthetic Sea," about the shocking amount of plastics pollution in the Pacific Ocean. I play up the fact that plastics — while being dangerous, non-biodegradable toxic petroleum — represent a great opportunity to educate people about both needless consumption and the bigger picture of peak oil. The 22-minute film has an impact that can even distract from basic issues at peak oil conferences, but I figure it's vital to wake people up regarding any and all petroleum issues. Thanks mostly to the efforts of researcher Captain Charles Moore who stars in the film, you will soon see the first municipality in North America pass an ordinance for a fee on plastic bags at supermarket checkout counters.

In my previous focus of fighting road-construction and publishing the *Auto-Free Times*, our repeating facts such as *one million animals slaughtered on U.S. roads daily* did not change many people's behavior — even among animal-rights activists. So it is with idealistic hope that the plastic plague and petrocollapse are able to hit home today, even though during and after our Alliance for a Paving Moratorium's decade of activism the disastrous and corrupt land-use and transportation patterns continued as if the Earth is limitless.

After a stay in DC highlighted by meeting Congressman Roscoe "Peak Oil" Bartlett and his staff, my first speech was Sept. 18 in Philadelphia at the "Beyond Oil" conference. It turned out that I was really there to give two short talks on different panels, and I found myself in a mix of voices that did not all understand peak oil, let alone petrocollapse. One speaker, associated with the Nigerian movement to remember the executed activist Ken Saro-

Wiwa, spoke on two panels and claimed that Iraqi oil is so plentiful on the market that the world's supply is not an issue. Uninformed viewpoints can get attention at peak oil conferences if the organizers are rather open to getting social-justice activists represented. It is easy for activists including some environmental leaders to imagine they fully understand oil and that oil is mainly just another issue threatening poor people.

Another panelist, a green economist, bemoaned the possibility of post-peak oil prices going down enough so as to revive demand and thus warm the globe further. Hazel Henderson's famous quote, "Economics is a form of brain damage," applies more than ever today. Listen up economists: peak oil and geology are not subject to later revision based on theory of demand and supply!

There in Philadelphia, as in all my talks and interviews, I pointed out that my former firm predicted the Second Oil Shock in 1979 based on our data revealing a 9% shortfall of gasoline for March of that year. Most significantly, the 1970s oil crises were in a context of rising global oil extraction and a much smaller population of humans and cars. Our present contrasting circumstances prompt one to ponder what the imminent gap between supply and demand will do to a world economy based only on growth. And, no matter the hype or promise of alternative energies and materials, they are not ready and cannot be gotten ready *on a meaningful scale* in time to avoid petrocollapse.

Even Amtrak, the most energy-efficient and least polluting mode of motorized transport in the U.S., with a huge existing system, cannot be easily expanded rapidly. Its tracks are already limited by freight-train priority. There is little possibility of renewable-energy powered engines in the near future.

Leaving behind new friends, Quakers and other kind folks whom I tried to enthuse with the good tidings of post-collapse sustainable culture, I rode the rails to Cincinnati, the nearest stop to Yellow Springs, Ohio where the Second U.S. Conference on Peak Oil and Community Solutions Conference was being held Sept. 23-25. Partly because of the longer time for the whole event, speeches could allow for full presentation of ideas. The star of the conference, who provided three presentations, was author Richard Heinberg. His PowerPoint presentation on peak oil is always first–rate, and his violin playing is excellent too — we performed Have a

Global Warming Day and other ditties I wrote, with scant rehearsal.

I was happy with my speech, even if I had to really reach to give the audience of 350 some good news: advocating activism to bring about local-based economies, I brought up the pepperspray torture trial having ended in the favor of the protesters in the redwoods (Culture Change Letter #94). One of my readers from New Zealand had approached me the night before and said, "We don't have an energy crisis, we have a culture crisis." So I trotted this out for the audience in giving my good news/bad news analysis of petrocollapse and what may ensue as *a revival of community for a sustainable culture.*

My analysis was largely confirmed by the new film shown at this conference, called "The Power of Community: How Cuba Survived Peak Oil." This excellent documentary, filmed by Greg Greene ("The End of Suburbia"), was produced by the Yellow Springs conference organizers (Community Service, Inc.) and was kindly lent to us for the Petrocollapse Conference in New York. The film was recently shown at ASPO-USA (Association for the Study of Peak Oil and Gas) in Denver last month, by Megan Quinn of Yellow Springs.

I next traveled to Colorado's western slope where the High County Citizen Alliance has its annual Sustainable Communities Symposium in the Gunnison Valley. The scenic highlight is the village of Crested Butte at 9,000 feet. Unlike some at the Yellow Springs peak oil conference who believe they can survive petrocollapse by doing small farming as a community *near large population centers,* Gunnison Valley residents really question surviving a suddenly energy-poor world where economics as we know it has gone out the window. Instead of a big population center nearby, offering the prospect of many migrating, hungry former consumers, Gunnison Valley has extreme cold along with more extreme cold every winter. Numerous people pointed out to me that the Indians never tried to live year round in the high country. Wherever one is when petrocollapse hits, every place will have its strengths and drawbacks: climate, remoteness, population size, citizens' awareness and knowledge, energy sources, etc.

The highlight of visiting Colorado was hearing my co-speaker Wes Jackson of The Land Institute. A legendary and visionary agriculturalist who understands energy inputs and the need to do things very differently from today's conventions, he paid me the ultimate compliment after my ad-lib talk: "I could take my next hour speaking by just saying Amen, Amen." He proceeded to blow everybody's mind with his amazing lecture.

The hospitality and charm of the locals in Gunnison Valley, as with Philadelphia and Yellow Springs, was endearing to me and made me consider carefully such places as to viability for living through petrocollapse. In the case of such places as Philly, the SF Bay area and New York, they are to be appreciated prior to their energy/resources termination — in other words, enjoy them before people start yelling "Sal si puedes!" (Get out if you can.)

While there I missed Congressman Bartlett's peak oil conference in Frederick, Maryland, where I had to decline speaking due to other commitments. The Sept. 26th event had Matthew Simmons, whom I hope to meet and debate future economic growth. His belief that collapse could be imminent with a 50% probability is akin to mine, but he also speaks of bridging the energy gap to accommodate growth.

I rode Amtrak to New York's Penn Station and was met by my new friends and fellow organizers for our Petrocollapse Conference. The Peak Oil Meet-up group, affiliated with Post Carbon Institute, had been thinking of holding its own conference but kindly jumped in to make the Culture Change-sponsored Oct. 5th day-long event a success. (You be the judge by listening to the talks; link is at bottom.) The group there is putting on another peak oil conference this spring. As New York City, with its 25 million people in the metro area, is unsustainable, the few who are aware of peak oil and are getting together with kindred scared spirits are pursuing practical survival strategies. Some are acquiring skills useful in rural and wild areas, some are buying gold to weather economic collapse, and some hope to set sail for lower populated areas beyond the United Paved Precincts of America (the USA).

The Petrocollapse Conference was a wonderful experience, a first for us all: a few hundred people from all sectors of society attending in a supportive, civil manner. It was fun to play music afterwards and see speakers such as Jim Kunstler chatting with Jason "Plan B" Meggs at the bar. The mainstream media were well aware of our conference, but our best exposure turned out to be the alternative press such as Free Speech Radio. One piece of coverage turned out to be a hatchet job stemming from a speaker who was privately criticized for not addressing petrocollapse. The incident brought to light that the impotence of the reformist/technofix approach makes its proponents angry at those who point out that the emperor has no clothes; i.e., that petrosociety has no future. And discussing die-off honestly as a reality of our biological and energy predicament can elicit ad–hominem attacks by any journalist overcome by emotional bias.

I enjoyed the Big Apple with more friends landing from afar, soaking in the museums, thinking it could be our last time there together. Such a notion — that the pearl of Western Civilization could become a hell-hole where urban remnant gangs roast rats over furniture fires — makes a mainstream believer in civilization red with rage or doubled over in incredulous laughter.

On to D.C. again and Virginia. I walked the halls of Congressional offices with John Darnell of Congressman Bartlett's office as we distributed The Oil Age Poster and the book *The End of Fossil Energy and The Last Chance for Sustainability* (John G. Howe, author). Roscoe Bartlett asked me if I perceived rising interest in peak oil by the general public, and I replied that I did. He shared with me that a shipping magnate had expressed to him the idea that greatly increased oil prices spell "disaster."

Showdown Over "The Hydrogen Highway"

Amtrakking back to the West Coast I took a more southerly route, as I had one more appearance: Santa Barbara. The Institute of Reverential Ecology, The Community Environmental Council, and the Santa Barbara Permaculture Network presented a "Community Design and Energy Forum" on Nov. 19.

Almost 37 years ago the president of Union Oil Company frantically called my father in Greece to ask for public relations advice on the infamous 1969 oil spill off Santa Barbara. Today, after the players have changed but the problems of oil remain and are much more advanced, some of us are struggling to turn the situation around armed with much more information and experience. The approach is going to have to involve radical conservation, as I told the Nov. 19 forum.

This was clearly grasped by one speaker, the recent director of the Community Environmental Council, Bob Ferris. He admitted that peak oil means needing to personally relocate so as to survive socioeconomic collapse. Essentially, the day-long event was a show down between well-paid technofixers touting the "Hydrogen Highway" and the anti-car, mostly poorly funded activists. The low-tech solution for post peak oil survival was probably best portrayed by the Cuba film that I presented during lunch.

The Milken Institute's senior fellow Woody Clark, who works with Jeremy Rifkin for a "Hydrogen Economy," was a major draw, but he was delayed on Highway 101 by an overturned oil tanker truck. This ironic demonstration of our wonderful transportation system should have settled any argument, as the county is divided over whether to allow more lane-widening or build a rail system to supplement Amtrak. In the opinion of my mother Mesa Lundberg, let out for an afternoon from the "hospice/respite facility" and in good health, her son argued his position "very well." A local nonprofit group, For the Future, best deflated the technofixers' fantasy by pointing out that their "new paradigm" of newer cars was really the old paradigm and would solve nothing. The Milken consultant Clark said he disagreed with me, presumably about the impact of peak oil and our future low-energy culture, but he did not specify.

Thanks to Robert Hirsch's latest report in *World Oil*, I was able to inform the Santa Barbara audience that the Hubbert bell curve on peak oil extraction appears to have a sharp, unseen crest. As Culture Change has been saying all along, post-peak extraction will be a steeper decline than most people assume. Hirsch confirmed this by tracking available country-data on past peak-oil experience, and postulated that the world's upcoming experience could reflect nations' and regions' histories.

Although I was in town to give my talk on "Energy and Community Design in a Catastrophic Future," and I was billed as "a former oil industry insider and Peak Oil theorist," my main accomplishment might have been presenting a few days later at the Community Environmental Council the film "Our Synthetic Sea." Although it is about plastic pollution in the middle of the Pacific Ocean and a main source, mega-urban runoff, let's look to Santa Barbara to give Berkeley, San Francisco and Arcata a run for their money at being the first North American municipality to put a fee on plastic bags distributed at supermarkets.

One tragic note was the sight of my friend's 40' ketch ruined on the beach in Santa Barbara. A treacherous anchorage dashed his hopes for continuing what might have been a solo voyage around the world. When I was hatching the Sail Transport Network (STN) in the Puget Sound in 2000 he was the first yachtsman I approached. STN was a bit before its time, but maybe only by a factor of weeks now, if this winter's global petroleum demand rocks the oil market and the corporate economy.

End of a Low-Petroleum-Consumption Odyssey

Lugging too much luggage on and off many a train and subway resulted in a rotator cuff injury, but I was blessed to discover osteopuncture and acupuncture. These treatments are good for healing more than just my shoulder. But I must caution the would-be touring troubadour relying on donations that health care can eat up much of the savings obtained from buying used clothing and friends buying you a beer.

Overall, the learning and the adventure via poor old Amtrak are far better than sitting in one's pseudo–community anywhere in The United Paved Precincts of America — no matter how many DVDs, CDs, selection of herbal teas, drums, and whatever else surrounds us in a four-walled box we may call home. That's just the perspective of a single man with a mission. But no matter what our differences and struggles are today, our real home and community await us in the near future, and I hope to meet you there or on the way.

* * * * *

Resources:
For a grasp of what wind energy can really contribute, listen to Michael Kane's speech at the Petrocollapse Conference at www.culturechange.org/petrocollapse/#audio

Listen to the Petrocollapse Conference's introduction by Jenna Orkin and Jan Lundberg's opening address, at www.culturechange.org/petrocollapse/#audio

Robert Hirsch's "Shaping the peak of world oil production" from World Oil, Oct. 2005

Get The Oil Age Poster at www.oilposter.org

"Our Synthetic Sea" DVD available from algalita.org/videos.html (Mention you learned about it from Culture Change)

Mesa Vernell Lundberg, prisoner of oil, and the eviction of Culture Change from her home (Culture Change Letter #13): www.culturechange.org/e-letter-13cont.html

For assurance that you cannot be tortured in the U.S. for protesting, read this syndicated Culture Change Letter: www.culturechange.org/e-letter-pspraytorture.html

[Note: the above two cases involving grandmother and granddaughter are significant human rights cases, one pursued *in pro per*, and one pursued by celebrated lawyers. It's no wonder the latter case is the one that won.]

Second U.S. Conference on Peak Oil and Community Solutions Conference: www.communitysolution.org/p2conf1.html
Richard Heinberg's Museletter: museletter.com/

Santa Barbara's Community Environmental Council website: www.communityenvironmentalcouncil.org/

Santa Barbara Permaculture Network and Southern California Permaculture Guild:
www.sbpermaculture.org/resources.html

The Institute of Reverential Ecology:
www.reverentialecology.org/

High Country Citizens Alliance: www.hccaonline.org/

The Land Institute: www.landinstitute.org/

Beyond Oil Philadelphia conference website: phillybeyondoil.org/

Cars and car ads slammed in pro-car corporate newspaper

There was some bad press against the regular Critical Mass Bike Ride at the end of March, 2007 in San Francisco. A woman's carload of kids and hubby were supposedly terrorized (in reality a reaction against her road-rage against cyclists daring to take up the intersection). The *San Francisco Chronicle*'s coverage was fairly careful and printed lots of views, but the daily tabloid *The Examiner* ran a nasty editorial against bicyclists. So I wrote the following that they printed without one change. This is the first time I've ever gotten a letter printed that actually criticized or even mentioned the same media outlet's car-ad revenue and its influence on coverage and editorial!

The Examiner
April 10, 2007

Cars to blame

Your editorial on Critical Mass and headline ("Welcome to a city nightmare," April 7) was objectionable and divisive. The real nightmare in San Francisco is not a few occasionally rowdy bicyclists in a monthly parade of thousands of peaceful non-global-warmers, but rather car dominance making streets deadly, filthy and noisy every day.

Pro-car corporate news media can incite middle-of-the-road motorists' fears for the sake of sensationalizing a nonexistent or infinitesimal terror. Your *Wheels* section shows your real priorities and reveals which industries are calling the editorial tune, when there are no two- or three-wheeled pedal machines in your whole *Wheels* section.

The *Examiner* can take seriously climate change and global peaking of petroleum extraction by recognizing the need to green The City via maximum energy curtailment and fostering closer community. Bike culture enhances both of those, and lessens war-for-oil pressures as well, while cars and the overpaved landscape just continue the nightmare and the waste.

Jan Lundberg
Director, Culture Change
Arcata

I wrote to my friends, "But what does the newspaper do the next day? On the front page there's a picture of a new red sports car with the big headline, "Cool Product Expo Celebrates the Cutting Edge". — Makes you wonder about the efficacy of one's reactive media work! So send me a pat on the back quick, and remind me of how we're planting seeds, etc.!"

One activist wrote to me about my letter, "I am amazed they printed it... love ya, bill" – *Bill Le Bon, cross-the-country roller blader raising awareness on global warming, 1990, and former co-editor of the Auto-Free Times magazine (predecessor of Culture Change).*

Another Letter published by the *San Francisco Examiner* on cars and oil, May 2008:

Dear editor,

Music reviewer Nancy Dunham's "Love Psychedelico's CD looks cool, sounds even cooler" (May 9) harmed more than her own review of a new band. When she says the album is "perfect for... cruisin' round town with the top down" she glorifies a car culture that will be banished to the trash can of history.

Isn't driving cars passé at a time of $124-a-barrel oil, and when global heating is threatening the survival of billions of people and countless species? Unnecessary car dependence is also tragic, as seen in the story of the Pittsburg, California May 7 killing of a five-year-old by a mother driving over her tricycling daughter.

It is time to see the connections between our life-style and the low value we inadvertently put on life, whether human or of the whole natural world. Don't like the war on Iraq? Boycott petroleum to the extent you can.

Jan Lundberg
member, City of San Francisco Peak Oil Preparedness
Task Force
Publisher, Culturechange.org
1045 17th Street
San Francisco, California 94107
(415) — ——

Photographs

The yacht Passat, 50-foot steel ketch that sailed the Lundbergs from Los Angeles to Greece, 1965-1969. Note the ladders welded to the mast, and the exhaust pipe doubling as the mizzenmast – both were designs of Dan Lundberg. Photo 2010 by Brian of My Flotsam.

Mesa Vernell Lundberg's home, 2002: 1375 Grant Avenue, Arcata, Humboldt, Calif.
The hermaphrodite was restored by amateur Dan Lundberg.
From left, Vernell Zephyr Lundberg, Jan Lundberg, Bronwyn Lundberg.
This old-growth redwood house was called "ramshackle" by Mesa's conservator Mary
Lou Parks who had never seen it. It was sold to pay for Mesa's high cost
incarceration, against her will, in a hospice where she was killed.

Dan and Mesa Lundberg in kitchen of their Hollywood Hills Home,
circa 1973. The adjacent dining room had a massive table and chairs, including
"thrones," from Hearst Castle.

Jan at 17, L.A.'s San Fernando Valley, in the back yard of his sister Dana's house, North Hollywood

Athens, Greece, 1977. Jan Lundberg sitting with first
wife and high-school friend Xenia

Bronwyn Lundberg (holding camera) next to me on the good sloop Adventure,
May 2009, Willamette River

Jan near Alexandria, Virginia, August 2010, by Shirin Wertime

Jan in his redwood forest home, February 2004, above Arcata, Humboldt.

Jan Lundberg towing *Auto-Free Times* magazines on with Danny Franks' bike cart, Arcata, Humboldt, California, 2000.

Dan and Jan Lundberg in guess where, spring 1967, in search of a boarding school.

The Depavers, Bayside Grange, Humboldt, California, Oct. 1998, a benefit for
Measure F, historic ballot measure that prohibits corporate chain stores in Arcata.
From left, Ayr on mandolin, Depaver Jan, and (knee only) Tofu, drums. Not pictured:
Rick O'Keefe, bass, and April Richards, percussion, both on stage.

The Depavers rock People's Park on its 38th anniversary festival, Berkeley. Ayr on mandolin. Jan was greeted as he stepped down the stage by Country Joe McDonald. Photo: Terri Compost, Peoples Park historian, a plaintiff with my daughter Vernell in the civil rights case against police torture via pepperspray.

Jan Lundberg at U.S. Conference on Peak Oil and Community Solutions, 2005, Ohio

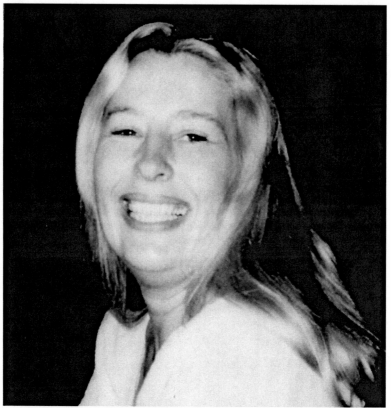

Dana Lundberg, a.k.a. Chula, *circa* mid 1970s in the Lundbergs' Hollywood Hills living room. Brilliant, kind and funny were prominent traits. Of frail health in her sixties, Dana had two heart attacks. They occurred immediately after stressful visits with her sister Trilby Lundberg. Dana's second heart attack killed her, as reported to the Santa Barbara, Calif. Police.

Kathleen McCarthy (Guy's first wife), Darius Lundberg, Guy Lundberg in Porto Santo Stefano, Italy,1967, in the Passat's dugout canoe we brought from Central America.

Wedding at Canoga Park: Dan, his former secretary Roberta (sister to his wife Mesa) and her groom Si Nathenson

Jan and Mesa Lundberg, 2001, Santa Barbara. Kept in bed by the greedy handlers, instead of assisted to regain walking, it was if she was a hopeless case. This photo was on the front page of the daily newspaper.

Mesa visited by nieces and nephew (children of Roberta & Si Nathanson), Toltec "Living" Center. From right, Jamie Roberta Mann, on lap of mother Yolanda Bandholtz, Mesa, David Nathenson; top, Sonya Brite, her husband Chris Brite.

Mesa Lundberg posing in Conservator's "gift" to family members, 2001. She
stood out at the hospice-respite "home" where she was fraudulently incarcerated
Toltec Living (dying) Center, as inconveniently alert and functional, although drugged
against her will.

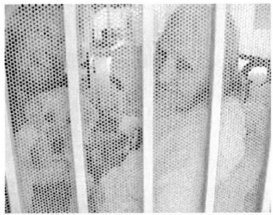

A more realistic picture of the same captive, at Toltec, photographed by her
nephew David Nathenson, 2003, with his dog Penny. The bars separated the inmate
and the terminally ill patients from the peaceful street. My attorney John
Shellabarger visited her and found her lucid, and advised me in 2006 that she was a
victim of elder abuse (which we knew).

Jan Lundberg

Part II—FRI., JUNE 8, 1962 — *Los Angeles Times* ★

SHE'S A LAWYER NOW—Mrs. Mesa Lundberg, mother of five, was among the more than 300 admitted to practice of law. With her is son, Darius, 5.

371

Darius Jaime Lundberg, named in part after Jaime "Jim" Hinton

Dan on the set of the first talk show in television history, The Dan Lundberg Show, Hollywood, California. Airing Sunday nights for seven years, each program was a discussion of a researched issue featuring expert guests, on politics, public health, ecology, etc. The sponsor was in effect the owner of the network, Mr. Copley of KCOP. Dan was seriously discouraged from using the "unknown word" ecology. During many of these years Dan was also anchorman for the KCBS News for Los Angeles. Most of his time during the week was spent working with the downstream sector of the oil industry in his own niche.

Dan Lundberg – there wasn't anybody remotely like him

Dan Lundberg in back yard of his Hollywood Hills home, 1970s. Off in the darkness: Universal Studios, which had ravaged its natural, hilly location with endless paving.

Dan Lundberg, Avalon Harbor, Catalina Island, *circa* 1983.

Vernell Zephyr Lundberg and father Jan holding Bear the Bagel Eating Beagle and
her family, Arcata, *circa* 1994.

Erik Lundberg Scott, Royce Sharp, Darla Sharp in Avalon Harbor, Catalina Island, *circa* 1971

Darius Lundberg, Mesa Lundberg, caregiver Kris Halstrom, Jan, at Daybreak Café, Arcata, 1999. Painting above was part of anti-war exhibition by Rising Ground, Belgian Earth First!er.

Trilby Lundberg in her Mercedes, 2006, of which Associate Press said she had no idea what fuel mileage it got. See section of this book "Questions for the Gasoline Guru-ess". A Los Angeles Times reporter told me in Sept. 2010 that the conflict between my sister and me was ideological. True, but I have good friends who are conservative and have fancy cars. AP Images.

Trilby Lundberg flanked by OPECers, *circa* 1981

Epilogue

I have realized only now after writing my autobiography that it is a moral tale. This is not what I intended, but if that's what is for some readers, this is acceptable to me. As a neo-traditionalist I had thought my message in this book had to do only with the better functioning of culture, maximizing reverence of nature, and passing along knowledge of oil and energy.

Morality is seldom discussed these days in political critiques, peak oil forums, or climate science blogs. Frying the planet for the most part stems from materialism, as seen in greedy capitalism and laissez-faire consumerism. But still this is seldom spoken of as a moral issue. Why is the moral aspect of our global crisis apparently put aside?

Organized religions speak of morality, but do not concern themselves with sustainability. This would appear odd, but it points to their origins prior to an historic awakening: we cannot endlessly expand economically and take and take.

What is the moral tale of *Songs of Petroleum*? Is it that family loyalty must be restored everywhere it has weakened, or that one must fight to do unto others before they do it to you? Ought we work for Mother Earth instead of corporate polluters, and if so, right now? Or some day when it's too late?

Is the moral tale of this book that an ethical or self-respecting person must carry out his or her best instincts and never take the easy way out? These are questions for the individual to answer, hopefully made easier by reading this book. As for me, solidarity and love are where I ended up after my unusually interesting and sometimes challenging childhood and young adulthood. I was fortunate, but had to work at it. I still have to work at it. I recommend solidarity and love as the only way to find peace of mind and survive the coming increasingly "interesting times." - JL

Resources

A few post-collapse and sustainability groups & websites:

Albert Bates
Director of the Ecovillage Training Center, at
The Farm
Summertown, Tennessee
www.thefarm.org
His blog: thegreatchange.com

Bay Localize
San Francisco Bay area nonprofit group
BayLocalize.org

Community Solutions
Makers of the documentary "The Power of Community: How Cuba Survived Peak Oil"
Yellow Springs, Ohio
www.communitysolution.org

Diana Leafe Christian
A living resource on Ecovillages (US and abroad)
www.dianaleafechristian.org

Ecocity Builders
Founder, Richard "The Depaving King" Register
www.ecocitybuilders.org

Portland, Oregon projects
City Repair/Village Building Convergence
www.vbc.cityrepair.org

Post Carbon Institute
www.PostCarbon.org and www.EnergyBulletin.net

Club Orlov
www.ClubOrlov.com

Sail Transport Network
www.SailTransportNetwork.com

Sail Transport Company, Puget Sound:
www.SailTransportCompany.com

Songs
Online recordings, such as Mother Earth First (lyrics in this book's
Songs section) and Have A Global Warming Day (heard on
National Public Radio and seen on CNN-International, with
Japanese translation), can be found and heard at
www.culturechange.org/go.html?225

Have A Global Warming Day, Depavers album 1998

Best of Redwood Dreams, Depaver Jan, 2007, from 1993-2002

YouTube videos of Depaver Jan's performances

Hootenanny: A Songbook Of Radical Campfire Songs, available at
AK Press - www.akpress.org
and Earth First! Journal – www.earthfirstjournal.org

Book Recommendations

Ishmael, by Daniel Quinn, 1992

Overshoot: The Ecological Basis of Revolutionary Change, by William Catton, 1980

Beyond Oil: The Threat to Food and Fuel in the Coming Decades, by Gever, Kauffman, *et al.,* 1986.

The Post–Petroleum Survival Guide and Cookbook, by Albert Bates, 2006

Plan C: Community Survival Strategies for Peak Oil and Climate Change, by Pat Murphy, 2008

The Party's Over, by Richard Heinberg, 2003

Eating Oil, by Maurice Green, 1975

People of The Earth, by Brian Fagan, 1989

Ecotopia, by Ernest Callenbach, 1975

The Geography of Nowhere, by James Howard Kunstler

Reinventing Collapse - The Soviet Example and American Prospects, by Dmitry Orlov, 2008 (first edition)

Blood on the tracks: The Life and Times of S. Brian Willson, by himself, PM Press in May 2011

A Green History of the World: The Environment and the Collapse of Great Civilizations, by Clive Ponting, 1993

Acknowledgments

What has sustained me to be able to finally put my work into book form is the support from friends and family. They are:

- Personal friends who knew me before my days of oil-industry association and my activism, especially the Wertime family;

- The inspiring friends I made along the way by virtue of meeting them on the common ground of sustainability and liberated living, especially Mike, Camila, Dick, Albert, Phil, Kevin, John, Charlie, Jim, David, Wren, Jeff, Juniper, Ayr, Lia, Barbara, Attila, Janet, Lumby, Jen, Richard, Michael, Roger, Daniel, Monica, Jim, Larry, Peter, Raul, Jenna, Ethan, Miguel, Robert, Tim B, Raines, Paul, Greg, and Ben, and others I fear I neglected to mention. A blanket thank-you (not a blankety-blank you) also goes to many friends whom I know so far only in cyberspace or on the telephone;

- My friend known as The Universe. I'll explain: I have had the feeling many, many times that I have enjoyed a kind of fortuitous, unaccountable luck that has enabled me to keep going somehow, in good health, even in the face of having no money on more than one occasion. It is this "surfing my cosmic wave," and not wiping out, that has something to do with my ability to get through thousands of days and nights without the privileges and advantages I once knew from merely the accident of birth.

- My family has been struck down and warped over the years, but among the living I have been encouraged and sustained by love from Bronwyn, Vernell, Darius, Erik, Darla, Royce, Ralegh and David, without mentioning more family members whom I love but didn't seem very interested in my work. My first wife Xenia helped me many times from the other side of the world long after our marriage ended. My parents, Dan and Mesa Lundberg, are like the co-creators of this book, for it could not have happened without their incredible and exemplary devotion and vision. My sister Dana gave me as much encouragement as anyone, and more, to do what I wanted and needed to do. I wish I had been able to do more for her in the last several years of her life.

- The art for the front and back covers of this book is by my daughter Bronwyn Lundberg. Nice to have such an artist in the family and who happens to relate to Dad's work.

Index

Note: e-book users can use Find or Search for any words or names.

260671BV00001B/1/P

9 780615 343730